If I can stop one heart from breaking
I shall not live in vain
If I can ease one life the aching
Or cool one pain
Or help one fainting robin
Unto his nest again
I shall not live in vain

EMILY DICKINSON

FELDHEIM PUBLISHERS Jerusalem / New York

MIRIAM ADAHAN

It's all a
GIFT
(though it may not
seem like it at first glance)

The royalties from this book will be distributed among impoverished families in Eretz Yisrael.

The examples contained in this book are all true. Unless both first and last names are given, the names have been changed to protect the privacy of those involved. Any similarity to people with these names is purely coincidental.

Library of Congress Cataloging-in-Publication Data

Adahan, Miriam.
    It's all a gift / by Miriam Adahan.
       p.   cm.
    ISBN 0-87306-609-X
    1. Conduct of life. I. Title.
BF637.C5A33 1992
158--dc20   92-13105

FELDHEIM PUBLISHERS
200 Airport Executive Park
Nanuet, NY 10954

POB 35002
Jerusalem, Israel

10 9 8 7 6

Printed in Israel

*This book is dedicated to my EMETT family
which is spread throughout the world,
and whose devotion to the principles of the Torah
are a constant source of inspiration
and joy to me.*

Acknowledgments

First and foremost, I want to thank Irene Klass of *The Jewish Press*, who published my first article in 1978. I never expected her to print it. But she did and she even called me to tell me to write more, saying that readers were responding positively. Her support gave me the confidence to write another article, and then another, until the articles became a book and one book led to another. Her encouragement, and the enthusiasm of readers who cared enough to let me know how much my work helped them, gave me the impetus and courage to continue writing, despite a great lack of self-confidence.

Mrs. Klass demonstrated the power of positive feedback, the power of one person's love for another. Her kindness encouraged me to actualize a potential I didn't even know existed. Without such love, our essence remains hidden, even to ourselves.

Many others have been influential and helpful. More than anything, I thank my husband, Carmeli, and my wonderful children, Dalya, Yosef, Moshe and Eliahu, who have been my greatest gifts.

I thank Rabbi Zelig Pliskin, author of *Love Your Neighbor*, *Gateway to Happiness*, and many other helpful books, for his support and guidance; Rebbetzin Tzippora Heller of Neve Yerushalayim, who is an ongoing source of inspiration; and the staff at Feldheim Publishers, for their positive response and patience with a writer who is constantly rewriting what they thought was final copy!

I thank Bracha Steinberg of Feldheim Publishers, whose superb editing greatly improved the quality of this book.

I thank my EMETT family of friends, whose love and encouragement helped to heal many wounds.

I am profoundly grateful to Hashem, for having given me the circumstances which enabled me to write this book.

בע"ה

Today, our general society is crisis laden and prone to inner despair, though outwardly it pretends to optimistic competitiveness. The miraculous Torah revival within segments of our people worldwide, but especially in Eretz Yisrael, has not granted us immunity from inner tension and anguish — in reflection of R. Yehudah HaLevi's teaching that "Israel is the heart of the nations." By extension, then, the Torah community is the heart of Israel. And the *teshuvah* movement now is our great hope, after two centuries of growing assimilation.

In crucial corners of the Jewish world, the Torah-people are winning the war, but seem not yet to be winning the peace. Conflict, poverty, suffering, the unfinished inner battle between our own two inclinations, and family disharmony continue to wound us deeply.

There are so many, within the holiest segment of our people, who cry out for help. When you get to that point, *chalilah*, of suffering that paralyzes, remember that the essence of our *bechirah* is not to surrender to despair or *ye'ush*. The essence of *bechirah* is that one can overcome despair.

Once again, Miriam Adahan has authored a work of healing, for which so many are waiting. *It's All a Gift* is suffused with the fundamental principle that the test of suffering — though we cannot fathom its meaning when it strikes us — is nevertheless a vehicle for liberation from all that paralyzes our souls and bodies; that we can learn its educational and ennobling handwriting, until we say with Yeshayahu: "*Odecha Hashem ki anafta bi* — I thank you, Hashem, that You have been angry with me" — until we say with Iyov: "*Hen yikteleni lo ayachel* — though He slay me, to Him do I hope."

This book offers us hundreds of illustrations on how to translate suffering into the illumination of life's Divine meaning. Would that *It's All a Gift* finds its way into all the homes and lives which yearn for the power of its message.

Rabbi Nachman Bulman
Kiryat Nachliel, Migdal HaEmek
Israel

בע"ה

The Creator gives us many gifts throughout our lives. Some of the gifts are easy to recognize and others are disguised. The awareness that life's difficulties contain an inherent blessing will transform your life. Painful situations might still be painful, but these will now be perceived as growing pains.

Fortunate is the reader who internalizes the basic message of It's All a Gift. For some, this will, at first, seem impossible. But as you repeat the message over and over again, it will become your reality. This perspective will enhance all areas of your life.

Rabbi Zelig Pliskin
Torah-based Cognitive Counselor

Contents

It's all a
GIFT

*(though it may not
seem like it at first glance)*

Introduction

A life in quest of truth is a life of struggle in which peace and easily won comforts have no part.
— RABBI MENACHEM MENDEL OF KOTSK

As I write this introduction, the Jewish People stand before the Day of Judgment, 5742. What will be our fate as a People? What is in store for me individually? We are blind. We know nothing. All we can do is pray that we will be able to make God King, no matter what happens to us this coming year.

Why this word "make"? God is already King. Who are we to "make" Him anything? And yet the word is significant because it expresses our essential spiritual *avodah*; it is up to us to make the effort to remember that God *is* King, that He determines what will happen to us. We forget this simple, basic truth because we also have a desire to be God-like, to run our own affairs and determine our fate. Our opposition to His will creates anger and despair. It is only by putting forth the effort to see Him as King that we will be able to accept His will with love and live with joy despite the hardships and losses which we all experience.

Near the end of the book of *Shemoth* (33:13-20), Moshe Rabbenu has a poignant exchange with God that goes like this:

> Moshe: "And now, if I have found grace in Your sight, let me know, I pray You, Your ways, that I may know You, to the end that I may find grace in Your sight."
>
> God: "My presence will go [with you] and I will give you rest..."
>
> Moshe: "Show me, I pray You, Your glory."
>
> God: "I will cause all my goodness to pass before you and I will proclaim the name of God before you...[But] you cannot see My Face, for man shall not see Me and live."

Is this not the plea of each of us — to understand the ways of God, to feel His presence with us at all times? We can't see God directly. We have to put forth the effort to intuit His presence in everything that happens to us, to *know* with heartfelt certainty that He is here, especially in the midst of darkness.

A True Story: Escape from Iran

When I moved to Eretz Yisrael, in 1981, we lived for a while in an absorption center. There, I became friendly with a young widow with four children who had come from Iran a year and a half before. Although she lived in a tiny, one-room apartment and worked as a clerk in the local post office, she had a regal dignity which hinted at a refined background. As our eleven-year-old daughters became best friends, the story of her previous life emerged.

In Iran, they had been very wealthy, with servants, fancy cars and expensive vacations abroad. Then came the overthrow of the Shah and the reign of terror against the Jews. One day, a gang of thugs entered her husband's rug store and shot him to death. They defaced the walls with his blood, proclaiming him an agent of the Shah.

Informed of the awful tragedy, the grief-stricken widow knew that she had to leave Iran immediately to save herself and her children. Desperately trying to stay in control, she contacted a man who was known to be helping Jews escape over the treacherous mountains into Turkey. Since unauthorized travel was forbidden and the sale of any household items might arouse suspicion, she had to leave most of her wealth behind. She could not tell anyone of her plans, not even her own children. She could not pack suitcases, as neighbors might see and report her to the police.

Trembling, trying not to let her terror show, she took whatever little cash and jewelry she had on hand and, telling the children that they were going shopping, left her home, never to return. In the darkness of night, they met their guide at the edge of Teheran. Handing over most of her money, the harrowing nightmare began for this brave widow and her four children, the youngest a girl of three.

For the first few days, they spent eighteen hours at a time on camels. The pain they suffered was so excruciating that they often felt they would collapse. The mother sustained permanent damage to her back. But each time they complained, their guide yelled that he would shoot them if they said another word. They had no choice but to go on. At one point, the mother was robbed of all her remaining money and jewelry by bandits who preyed on fleeing Iranian Jews.

By day, the sun scorched them. By night, they froze. As the mountains got steeper, they switched to riding donkeys. Often, the precipices were so narrow that one wrong move meant certain death and the donkey and its rider would plunge into the abyss below. Once, in their rush to cross a freezing stream, they all lost their shoes in the mucky water. Then, when they reached the other side, they had to walk barefoot on prickly cactus plants and sharp stones. Wincing in pain, they tried not to cry out as the thorns and pebbles cut into their flesh. Almost stupefied with pain and fatigue, the mother and her oldest son took turns carrying the youngest child.

At another point, they had to make their way across a flimsy bridge made of ropes and wooden slats which stretched between two mountain peaks and spanned a deep ravine. The ropes looked as though they could barely hold their own weight, let alone a group of terrified Jewish refugees. Looking down into the abyss below, the mother froze in utter terror, crying out that she could not possibly go on. Again, their guide took out his gun and threatened her and her children with death if they did not move. Taking her three year old by the hand, she forced herself to grab the ropes, fueled by anger toward the Iranian guide who urged them on so gruffly.

After two-and-a-half weeks of this continuous torture, the small group of Jewish refugees arrived at the Turkish border. There, the guide, who had always been so harsh, suddenly embraced each child warmly and said, "Before I leave you, I want to tell you that I, too, am Jewish. I'm sorry I had to be so tough. But if I had been nice to you, you wouldn't have made it. I had to scare you into moving, or you would not have been able to go on." With tears in his eyes he said, "I'm proud of each and every one of you. You are all true *gibborim* [heroes]." With that, he turned and left to go back in the direction of Iran.

Like this heroic family, we, too, are on a journey which is often treacherous and filled with pain. One thing we can know for sure: when we get to the World of Truth, we will see that our Guide always loved us, and that all the difficulties we went through in this world were necessary in order to reveal the greatness and the Godliness in us and in others.

In order to reach this level of God-consciousness, we must internalize a positive attitude toward affliction. This attitude is best illustrated by another story.

"My Neshamah Begged for This"

The following story has been attributed to Rabbi Nachman of Breslav.

> Once there was a rich man who died. When he reached Heaven, he stood in line with the many people entering Gan Eden. But when his turn came, an angel told him firmly to go sit on a bench near the door.
>
> The rich man yelled at him, "But I'm a rich man. I gave a lot of *tzedakah* when I was alive. So I deserve to go in right away!"
>
> The angel replied, "Be quiet and do as you were told."
>
> After hours, he banged on the door, demanding to be told why he wasn't being allowed in.
>
> The angel answered and said, "There's a debate going on as to whether you're to be allowed in or not."
>
> "But I gave a lot of *tzedakah*," cried the rich man.
>
> "True," said the angel, "you did give *tzedakah*, but you did so because it made you feel important and superior. You were extremely arrogant. Sometimes when people came asking for money, you slammed the door in their faces or threw a coin on the ground. You often yelled at your servants and didn't pay them fair wages. You never thanked God for your money. You never even thought about where your money came from. God wasn't part of your life at all. That's why there is a debate now as to whether or not you'll be allowed into Gan Eden. So go sit down and be patient."
>
> After a few more hours, the angel came out and said, "We couldn't decide where to send you. So we decided that you have to go back down to earth and learn humility. Remember, treat all people kindly. Make God part of your life! Be humble."
>
> "Oy," cried the rich man, "that's impossible. If I have to go back down, at least make me poor, then I'll be sure to be humble!"
>
> "Oh, no," said the angel. "You have to go back and be rich and

humble at the same time! That's your particular test."

"I can't," cried the rich man. "Please, please make me poor. Please, I beg you. Let me be poor. If I'm poor, I'll feel dependent on God and I'll really be humble!"

"Okay," said the angel finally in exasperation, "but remember, your *neshamah* begged for this!"

Gratefully the rich man thanked him, saying, "Don't worry, I promise to remember that my *neshamah* begged to be poor so that I could learn humility."

Soon he was reborn to very impoverished parents. But from the time he was small, he was bitter and ashamed of being poor. He spent his whole life eaten up with envy at those who had more. He forgot to form a connection to God. He completely forgot that his *neshamah* had begged for this test so that he could perfect himself.

The moral of this story is that we must always remember what we're here for, especially in times of pain and disappointment. It is then that we need most to remember, My *neshamah* begged for this "gift" so that I can come closer to God and perfect my *middoth*.

The Torah Attitude toward Affliction

At first, the words "it's a gift," or "my *neshamah* begged for this" may be said insincerely. However, if you keep repeating these phrases, you'll find that they immediately orient you to a spiritual way of thinking. They remind you that painful events are not unfair, absurd and meaningless, though they may seem so on the surface.

The inner meaning can be revealed only by putting our spiritual tools into practice. When we resist God's will, painful situations are always more painful. But when we accept the situation as offering us gifts of understanding and growth, we no longer feel so angry or bitter.

> Behold, I set before you this day a blessing and a curse...
> — DEVARIM 11:26

The same situation can feel to us like a blessing or a curse. The difference is in our attitude.

The goal of this book is to teach you how to use painful events positively, so that you grow in love, understanding and appreciation of God, others and yourself. Remember, the phrase "it's a gift" is not some strange "Adahanism." This idea can be found throughout Torah and *Tehillim* (e.g., *Bereshith Rabbah*, 51:3; *Devarim* 8:3; *Tehillim* 136, 145)

A word of warning: Please do not tell people that their loss is a gift when they are in the midst of expressing grief over it. Be sympathetic and share in their sorrow. Depending on the extent of the loss and the level of spiritual awareness of the person, you might try at some later time to ask, "Please tell me how you have grown in understanding and sensitivity from having gone through this. I really want to hear what you have learned."

When you try to explain this idea to some people, they may say, "This gift idea is utter nonsense!" This response, too, is a gift, for it gives you the opportunity to bear disapproval with love in your heart and not to feel threatened by disagreement or even ridicule.

It may take many years to see certain painful situations as gifts. When I told Rebbetzin Ruchoma Shain the title of this book, she smiled her wise, loving smile and said, "Ah, yes, now that I am almost eighty, I can look back on my life and see that everything I went through really was a gift." So, be patient with yourself as you work to integrate this attitude.

A few months ago, a friend whose first child was born with severe cerebral palsy, called to tell me that she had given birth to a healthy daughter. "I just wanted to tell you," she said, "that from the moment I felt those first contractions, I told myself that whatever happens, I will see it as a gift. I kept telling myself 'See it all as a gift,' as we drove to the hospital, got stuck in a traffic jam and got to the hospital with only ten minutes to spare. Having learned this phrase from EMETT classes and having practiced it for the last four years is what kept me calm and made me feel that I would have the strength to cope with whatever God would give me."

I hope that many readers will, like this friend, integrate this concept so that they too will face life's difficulties with strength, love and joy.

I hope that after describing my own struggle to extricate myself from my particular darkness, others will be inspired to believe that they, too, can overcome the barriers which make them feel isolated, inadequate and unlovable. Iran, like *Mitzrayim*, is a metaphor for the forces of separateness, hatred and bitterness. Those who have been in there can very effectively show others the way out.

> I am the Lord your God, who brought you out of the land of Egypt to be your God... — BEMIDBAR 13:41

It is God who brings us out of enslavement. But He wants us to put forth the effort first. That starts with our attitude.

PART I

Attitudes

1 | The Gift of Seeing Everything as a Gift

Who is rich? He who is happy with his portion.
— AVOTH 4:1

This *mishnah* does not say, "A rich person is one who accepts his portion with stoic resignation," but rather, he who is happy, truly happy with what God gives him. In being happy with what we have, we are expressing true love for God. The problem is, how do we get to that level?

Some people seem to be born with sunny, optimistic natures. But for those of us to whom *kvetch*ing and criticizing come more naturally, developing a positive attitude is difficult mental work, as hard as changing any other deeply ingrained bad habit.

Why should this be so difficult? After all, life would be so much easier if we stopped complaining and automatically said to ourselves, "Thank You, God, for these painful events. I welcome these challenges as opportunities to develop inner strengths and wisdom!" What's so hard about that?

Well, if you've been thinking that you really are an unlovable, incompetent failure for your whole life or that you have no choice but to be hot-tempered or depressed, then adopting a positive attitude feels phony and frightening. Firstly, because when you give up a bad habit, you may feel as though you are lying to yourself. Secondly, if you can change an attitude at the flick of a brain wave, then you are left with the unsettling truth that you can create *any* reality. That is an awesome responsibility, one you may not want to accept, because it means that you alone are responsible for your happiness and that your happiness is, in essence, independent of other people and external circumstances!

Thirdly, some people fear self-transformation because they think, If I change, who will I be? Will I lose my identity? They do not realize that spiritual transformation simply brings out a person's hidden potential, making him more of what he is capable of becoming.

When you first heard about how Rabbi Akiva had a peaceful smile on his face and uttered the *Shema* while his body was being lacerated with hot iron combs by his Roman torturers, you probably dismissed this as a level which only a Rabbi Akiva could reach. When his Roman executioner asked him if he was a sorcerer who could overcome the pain he was suffering, Rabbi Akiva replied, "I am no sorcerer, but I rejoice at the opportunity now given me to love my God with all my life."

Rabbi Akiva must have experienced physical pain. But he was so focused on the mitzvah that he experienced true joy at the same time (*Midrash Eleh Ezkerah*).

May God keep us from such tests! However, He does test each of us in our own way, with the "hot combs" of poverty, mental or physical handicaps, and numerous losses and disappointments. Each of us, in our own way, can learn to find meaning in, if not actually rejoice in, stressful events only if we constantly practice throughout each and every day, the discipline of seeing every difficult person or experience as a gift, as an opportunity to grow in our attachment to God and the values of Torah. It is all a matter of where we focus our attention.

Rabbi Moshe Feinstein *z.t.l.* once underwent a difficult medical procedure without anesthesia. When he did not cry out, his doctor asked him how this was possible. Rav Moshe replied that he was able to bear the pain because he was totally focused on how much more sensitive he now would be to the pain others might suffer who had to go through similar experiences. In other words, he concentrated on what he was getting in terms of his own expanded awareness, and not what he was feeling.

We cannot escape physical and emotional suffering. But we can "rejoice at the opportunities" which God gives us to serve Him.

In the *Ashrei* prayer the word *kol* (all) appears seventeen times to remind us that our spiritual *avodah* is to practice seeing *everything* as a gift, to truly *experience* that whatever He does is necessary, wise and good. It is not an easy attitude to adopt.

We don't have much of a choice. Either we focus on the gifts, such as the revelations about man and God and the sensitivity and understanding which challenging situations bring us, or we become bitter and deadened to the Godliness in ourselves and in the world.

The words are often forced, not sincere, at first

In the beginning, you may feel hypocritical saying "it's a gift," "it's a challenge," or "my *neshamah* begged for this." Grief-stricken and angry, how can you believe that this car accident, this broken engagement, this horrible illness is a gift? How will it help to lie to yourself? Yet, you will find the following:

1. The first time you say the words, the phrase may seem like a lie. However, you are programming your brain with new information, like a parent teaching a small child to say the *Shema*. What does the child know of God, let alone His oneness? Nevertheless, the parent teaches the child the prayer because he hopes that one day he will say it with some degree of understanding. It may take time for you, too, to say the words with understanding and sincerity, but the effort will be rewarded.

2. The phrase "it's a gift" is the Torah's attitude toward life. Life itself is a gift. Saying the words lets God know that you want to reach the level of being able to see this truth, even if you cannot do so at the present time. You are making God King, accepting that he knows better than you what you need.

> ◊ EXAMPLE: "My husband had just purchased a new car a few days earlier when I asked him if I could use it to go three blocks to the grocery store. I promised to be very careful. Well, as God would have it, I was waiting at a traffic light when a woman lost control of her car and crashed into ours. I thought to myself, Oy, how am I going to tell my husband? He'll be furious even though it wasn't my fault. When I got home, I said to my husband, 'Here's another situation in which we have to make God's will our will.' When I showed him the big dent in the car, he was unusually calm and said, 'You're right. It's God's will. Well, it's good that we've been practicing this attitude on the little things so that it can help us with this now.''

3. The reward for saying the words is that you will eventually see the event as a gift. You will get your answers — within minutes or hours or years. But the answers will come.

4. This phrase will eventually transform your life. You will see the world entirely differently. You will have less anger and grief. You will be more at peace with life's unavoidable losses.

5. These words are not meant to eliminate pain, just to help you bear it.

6. You can't tell others what the gift is for them, nor can they tell you what the gift is for you. You must discover this on your own. The answers you get are in tune with what you need to hear. They come from your own inner Godly essence. Another person's reasons for the same problem may not comfort you. That's why you have to say the words over and over and struggle on your own to receive answers.

Become a pearl maker: ask "what's the gift?"

> The Kotzker Rebbe *z.t.l.* once asked, "Where does God dwell?" A wise man answered, "The whole world is filled with His glory." Whereupon the Rebbe replied, "I know that, too. But the truth is that God dwells wherever man permits Him to enter."
>
> — AND NOTHING BUT THE TRUTH, p. 17

Throughout the day, we have the opportunity to make God part of our lives. It is our choice. The best way to learn how to do this is to keep asking "what's the gift?" whenever we are in a painful situation.

> ◊ EXAMPLE: "I went to a wedding and all I could think of was how fat I looked and how my weight is spoiling everything for me. Then I thought, What's the gift? In a flash it occurred to me that my excess body weight is just like *shlepp*ing around 200 pounds of excess condemnations. At that moment, I thought that perhaps if I work on dropping my condemnations of myself and others, that perhaps my physical weight will drop also. The idea delighted me so much that I made the effort to enjoy myself instead of stewing in self-contempt, which was my old habit."

> ◊ EXAMPLE: "It was just after candlelighting when we had a blackout. Then the plumbing overflowed. All I could think of was how

could I possibly spend the next twenty-five hours with this mess, without hot water or hot food? Then the words hit me: 'see it as a gift.' What gift? Where? How? But as the words penetrated, I thought of all the adversity that Jews have survived, in conditions which were undescribable. This was only a minor discomfort in comparison. I would manage and I would teach my children to bear discomfort with good will and to focus on solutions. After this is over, we'll all be a lot more grateful for things we take for granted.''

What an incredible challenge it is to bring Godliness into every minute aspect of our lives!

◊ EXAMPLE: "The principal of my son's *yeshivah* called again to complain about my son's behavior. I thought, My *neshamah* begged for this? No way! Yet the words calmed me down and reminded me of the gift in having two extremely active children who challenge me to the limits of my endurance. I was so arrogant before I had children! I thought it was enough to be loving. I thought any mother with wild kids was lazy, stupid or uncaring. Now I know that despite all my love and all my effort, there's just so much one can do to mold a child's personality. It's very humbling."

◊ EXAMPLE: "Last night I was so angry with myself for losing my keys. Then this morning, my son told me that he had lost a library book. I'm sure that if I hadn't lost my keys, I would have been furious and yelled at him for being irresponsible and untrustworthy. It was only the loss of my own keys that reminded me not to judge him harshly. My lost keys reminded me to be humble and give the benefit of the doubt. That's a gift I often forget."

◊ EXAMPLE: "We are on an extremely limited budget, so I tend to get hysterical over every wasted penny. Yesterday, I put my oven on 'broil', and when smoke came out I remembered that I'd put a pot in there to soak the night before. My favorite forty-dollar pot was ruined. I was about to have a fit when I remembered a phrase from my EMETT meeting a few nights before: 'money is a triviality in comparison to my mental health.' I would never have seen this as a triviality before EMETT. As soon as I thought, Hey, the pot really is a triviality, I calmed down. It was the first time I had used that phrase and I was surprised that it worked! It was a gift for me to see that EMETT works after all my skepticism and doubts.''

From a personal, ego point of view, we want only to be comfortable and to maximize our physical pleasure in this world. When anything disturbs our comfort, we tend to get angry, thinking, It's not fair. I don't deserve this! We may even become paranoid, thinking, God's doing this on purpose just to punish me. He must not love me! Yes, we should examine our deeds and decide how to improve, but condemnations block insight and change.

However, from a *neshamah* perspective, we seek opportunities to break through barriers which keep us from experiencing holiness in this world. And that is best done by facing adversity with courage, faith and dignity.

> ◊ EXAMPLE: "When my wife yelled at me for something, I thought to myself, God, I'm going to let my ego get smashed! It's just my ego, not anything really important. If I pass over my feelings and don't retaliate or bear a grudge, perhaps You'll forgive my sins (*Yoma* 23a). I'm going to lock my lips and let this pass and focus on the reward. Looking for gifts is a great diversionary tactic when you're in pain!''

Seeing problems from a *neshamah* point of view takes training, since it is not the usual way of looking at things. If you are just starting this training, take small losses and disappointments first, and then work up to the major ones. Otherwise, you are apt to feel that this is a silly and ineffective mind trip.

If we never made mistakes, how would we learn humility? If we never experienced pain, how would we develop sensitivity to others? If we never lost control, how would we learn to forgive others?

When I was going through a very difficult time, it occurred to me that an oyster makes beautiful pearls only after foreign matter gets under its shell. It uses the irritation to create a jewel. So I thought to myself, I'm having trouble coping right now, but pearls will come out of this. The pearls were my ever-growing closeness to God and Torah and my ever-growing understanding of people.

Seeing things as a gift or a challenge does not always take away the pain we feel about our losses. But it does make them more bearable because they no longer seem absurd, unfair or meaningless.

Improved interpersonal relationships

The Rock, His work is perfect. — DEVARIM 32:4

When you adopt the attitude that every irritation is an opportunity to make another spiritual pearl, your life changes dramatically, especially your interpersonal relationships.

◊ EXAMPLE: "I hired a young woman to run my clothing store in the mornings. Two days after she started working, I called the store to see how things were. No one answered. I was furious. From an ego point of view, I should have phoned her home and blasted her right then and there. But from a *neshamah* point of view, I realized that the situation was a gift because it gave me the opportunity to give the benefit of the doubt and not take vengeance. Maybe something happened to her on the way to work or perhaps she is irresponsible and untrustworthy. If that's the case, I can simply find someone else. As soon as I saw the situation as a gift, my anger subsided."

◊ EXAMPLE: "My oldest was teasing her younger brother to the point of fury, so I told the younger one, 'When your sister calls you a name, say, "Thank you for giving me the chance to get a reward from God by not hurting you back."'' That stopped her cold! It may take years for them to really understand this concept, but by starting out when they're young, I'm sure it will become part of their way of thinking, especially since they see me saying this to those who hurt my feelings. Like, when I'm driving the car and someone cuts in front of me or gives me a nasty look, I say to the person in the other car, who of course can't hear me, 'Thank you for giving me the opportunity to work on my *middoth*.' It delights the kids to hear me talking like this."

◊ EXAMPLE: "I was furious when I was awakened at 4:30 A.M. by my husband making noise in the kitchen. I get very hysterical when I don't get my sleep. Angrily, I thought to myself, Okay *neshamah*, tell me, how is this a gift? Right away I realized that my *neshamah* begged for this chance to practice self-discipline and act in a Torah manner even if I'm in distress. So I forgave him instead of screaming. Instantly, I had a sense of self-respect because I saw myself handling a stressful event in a constructive manner instead of getting violent."

◊ EXAMPLE: "My very sensitive child shatters at the merest hint of disapproval. At first I couldn't stand having a child so similar to myself. I tried to toughen her up and made light of her fears and pushed her away when she was clingy. It took me a long time to realize that there is no way we can change our nature. I simply had to be more sensitive and supportive. The gift she gave me is that by becoming more accepting of her, I've become more accepting of myself."

◊ EXAMPLE: "When my son spilled glue all over the kitchen table, I was about to throttle him. Then the words 'see it as a gift' came into my mind. I stood there fuming, not wanting to hear the words. But I couldn't escape them. It was true. It was an opportunity to practice self-discipline, to show my son the meaning of a triviality. I said, 'We don't emotionalize trivialities. We just find solutions.' Then we cleaned it up without all the emotional drama which comes from my tendency to catastrophize. I was able to respond calmly and bring God into my kitchen at that moment. What I used to think of as intolerable, unbearable and catastrophic became tolerable. For a high-strung, easily angered person like myself, that was a major *tikkun*!"

◊ EXAMPLE: "When a neighbor came over to borrow my husband's ladder, I was upset thinking, Last week, when we needed their drill, they told us they don't lend out their tools! So let them go someplace else for a ladder. Then I thought, Wait! This is an opportunity to avoid taking vengeance or bearing a grudge, just like it says in *Vayikra* 19:18. After giving him the ladder, I called the children together and told them how exciting it was for me to perform this mitzvah and to do what God wants instead of giving into my desire for revenge!"

◊ EXAMPLE: "I came home and found my wife on the phone and the kitchen a mess. I was furious. She can leave dishes and dirty diapers around for days. It drives me up the wall. I tried to figure out how my *neshamah* could have begged to be married to someone so messy and disorganized! I struggled to find the gift. Then it hit me: this is an opportunity to work on accepting people. I'm very critical, so having a wife like this gives me the chance to do real *tikkun* because I am totally helpless to force her to change. I have the choice to either clean it up myself or to ignore the mess. At that moment, I learned the greatest gift of all: that

I can create happiness in an instant, any time I want, simply by changing my attitude toward my environment!"

We can all cater to our lowest impulses, becoming enraged and angrily shooting off our mouths whenever we feel like it. The way we can keep our tongue off the "trigger" is to focus on the long-range goal (i.e., spiritual growth) instead of going for quick ego relief.

The greater the loss, the greater the mental effort required to see things in a gift perspective. So, strengthen your "spiritual muscles" slowly by starting with small things, such as delays, social snubs, stains, children's squabbles, loss of sleep, bad moods, nonthreatening minor illnesses and disappointments, etc.

◊ EXAMPLE: "It was one of those late Friday night Shabbos meals and my two youngest children said they were too tired to eat. The two middle ones were fighting over who was going to bring the soda. I was about to pass out from fatigue and was hoping for a nervous breakdown. Suddenly, I started saying, albeit insincerely at first, 'Oh, what a gift that you guys are giving me such a hard time. You're giving me the opportunity to perfect my *middoth*.' Well, it was amazing! I calmed down and felt more in control. I said, 'Let's not make catastrophes out of trivialities. Let's solutionize.' I moved into my control mode from my nervous breakdown mode, put the two smaller ones to sleep and gave strict orders to the others to 'lock lips unless you're singing *zemiroth*.' What a victory! My husband looked at me with new respect in his eyes."

Your day is filled with such small and large annoyances and losses. You can take charge of your life when you realize that you always have a choice of responses: you can stew in bitterness and anger, or you can use the event to grow spiritually.

The choice: to feed your godly or ungodly side

To fulfill the Torah it is not necessary to fear Heaven greatly but to possess the virtue of gratitude... This virtue alone will lead to the fulfillment of the whole Torah. — LEV ELIYAHU, p. 88

When we don't get what we want, we tend to lose our sense of attachment to God. But when we take the attitude of "it's a gift," we make God our partner. Instead of seeing Him as the enemy who is victimizing us unfairly, we feel He is with us. This gives us strength to go on. Seeing events as gifts can be done anywhere, at any time.

> ◊ EXAMPLE: "I have a degenerative eye disease and am going blind. One of the things I do to make me happy, especially when my grandchildren come over, is to play what I call The Marble Game. I take two cups and I fill one with marbles. Then each time either I or the children transfer a marble into the empty cup, we say something we're thankful to God for. I'm determined to keep my spirits up!"

Obviously, you won't always say these words sincerely at first. Your initial response to a major loss is likely to be "I hate this! I don't want it! This is unfair and cruel!" But if you keep saying "it's a gift" over and over, you will eventually see most situations in a positive light. Your life will change drastically as you begin to integrate the realization that no event is absurd or meaningless. Eventually you do see that everything God does helps you to grow in understanding and insight despite the heartbreak you may be experiencing, and how much more assertive and constructive you are in responding to difficult situations.

The wisdom which you acquire from painful events may not seem worth it at first. You may think, I don't care about depth and sensitivity! It's not worth it! I'd rather be healthy, wealthy and comfortable! I'd rather have my loved one back! Yet, in the struggle not to let painful situations crush you, this realization eventually brings a measure of relief.

> ◊ EXAMPLE: "For three years I've been hearing my EMETT leader talk about seeing things as a gift. And for three years, I've thought to myself that it's ridiculous. Then, just before candlelighting last Shabbos, a neighbor banged on my front door, and when I opened it, yelled at me that he was taking my husband to court because of a minor dispute they had had. Well, there was nothing I could do at that moment. I didn't want the incident to spoil my Shabbos, and the only thing I could think of was to tell him that we'd discuss it after Shabbos. I sat down and said to myself, It's a gift. If this is what God wants, then I will it to be like this. It's a test to see if we can respond in a Torah manner. I was amazed that the words put me at peace the whole Shabbos. Each time I started to

get anxious, I reminded myself that whatever God willed, we would will it, too. And things did work out in the end."

◊ EXAMPLE: "When my wallet was stolen, it felt like a catastrophe at first — a ten on the scale of zero to ten. I not only felt victimized by the thief, I felt that God was punishing me unfairly. It took me a few minutes to calm down and say, 'What's the gift? What's the Torah attitude?' And it came to me to be grateful that I hadn't been physically hurt and also to see the loss as a *kapparah*, as wiping away some Heavenly debt which I would have had to pay sooner or later. The more I kept thinking of the gift, the more functional and focused I became. Even when it came to the hassle of canceling my credit cards and getting some documents replaced, I kept saying it to calm myself down."

◊ EXAMPLE: "I finally got my baby to sleep around 2 A.M. At 2:20, my two year old woke me up. I thought I would die. Instead I said, 'This is a gift. God is showing me what incredible inner strength I have. I can manage! I will manage.' Just saying the words, even insincerely at first, made me realize they were true."

Spiritual weightlifting

A musician will practice eight or ten hours a day to keep in shape. Similarly, you must practice "seeing the gift" throughout the day to strengthen yourself spiritually and to begin thinking this way automatically.

◊ EXAMPLE: "My husband is a very introverted type who either falls asleep when guests are over or else doesn't talk to them. I always hated when he did this until I started seeing it as a gift. The gift for me is that this trait gives me a chance to work on acceptance and love. I used to burn with envy at women who had more sociable husbands. Now I tell myself that if I can overcome my jealous tendencies and accept God's will concerning the husband He gave me, then I'll be able to strengthen myself spiritually so that I can handle life's bigger disappointments."

◊ EXAMPLE: "I was stuck in a traffic jam on the way to a very important business meeting. I found myself thinking, Nothing ever works out for me! Immediately it was replaced with 'it's a gift,' and I realized that this is an opportunity to practice recognizing that God, not I, is running the world, and that if I miss my appointment, it is God's will and it will somehow be for the best. It was an opportunity for me to practice *emunah* instead of stewing about my rotten luck."

◊ EXAMPLE: "My kids woke me up at 5:30 A.M. and the baby had been up most of the night. By 9 A.M., all I could think of was how miserable my life was and that I couldn't possibly make it through another long, boring, stifling day. Then I asked myself, Okay, what's the gift in being depressed? I remembered a *rav* who said that depression is often rooted in laziness, in not wanting to think holy thoughts or take positive actions. So instead of wallowing in self-pity and getting hostile, which is my usual response, I pulled myself together and made plans to get out of the house so I'd feel better."

From the time we are children, we expect others to make us happy. As adults, we find that we are responsible for overcoming our own negative moods and impulses.

◊ EXAMPLE: "I am married to a man who suffers from depression. I was at my wits end until a friend told me, 'See him as a gift. He's going to force you to get disciplined.' At first, I thought, She's crazy! But I started saying the words anyway. In time, I realized that she was right. I had blamed my husband for ruining my life, but when I started taking responsibility for my own moods, I saw that I didn't have to stay in a victim role. I got out of the house more, got a job, and developed strengths I never knew I had. It's difficult, but I've grown tremendously from this."

Mental handicaps are very painful, whether they are our own or others'. But if we focus on how to use these defects for our spiritual growth, we become grateful instead of angry.

◊ EXAMPLE: "I have a very critical boss who makes life unpleasant for me. I used to stew in silent hostility the entire day until I began saying, 'She's a gift.' Since I can't change jobs, I use this as an opportunity to remind myself that my value comes from God, not people. For someone like me, who was always so easily crushed by people's opinions, I feel like a winner on the spiritual plane, even if she thinks I'm a loser. It's painful to face her day after day. In fact, I feel like my ego is being pulverized. But if that's what God wants me to deal with right now, then I can use criticism to strengthen my sense of my inherent Godly value."

We often want to see ordinary events as unbearable, overwhelming and threatening because then we feel we have an excuse not to practice self-control. Then we can think, "See, it's no use trying to control myself. I just can't. So I might as well just go ahead and scream, binge, slam doors, walk out, etc. At least then I'll feel better!" When we see that these childish tactics don't work, then we start developing our spiritual muscles.

Facing bigger issues

By practicing thinking "it's a gift" on the trivial events, we build up our "spiritual muscles."

◊ EXAMPLE: "I was so glad that I'd been saying 'it's a gift' for years so that when I lost a baby to crib death, I could keep saying the words over and over to keep myself sane. In the midst of my profound grief, I kept saying, 'Oh...so this is what death is all about.' There was no way I could have known how excruciatingly painful it is to lose someone you love except to go through this. Since then, when I meet people who have lost a loved one, I feel a bond and an understanding which could not have existed there before. There is no other way to gain this understanding. Because of what I'm going through, I have a lot of compassion for others who are grieving, because I'm always grieving on some level."

◊ EXAMPLE: "I have a brain-damaged teenager. It used to drive me crazy when he would stand around like a *golem* doing nothing, or I'd see how untidy and uncoordinated he was. He wouldn't wash a dish or brush his teeth without pressure. When I'd finally push him to do something, he'd get frustrated quickly and stop, and I'd get so bitter. Just being in the same room with him used to be very painful. Then a friend asked me how this child is a gift. I looked at her like she was crazy! But after a few minutes I had to admit that he alone could teach me to love unconditionally. You see, I'm from a family of *talmidei chachamim*. Brilliance was everything to me. If a person wasn't brilliant, he was nothing. I began to see my son as a *tikkun* for my intellectual snobbery and arrogance. Having him certainly has humbled me and made me much more understanding of other mothers with problematic children. I had rejected a child who deserved love as much as any normal child. Once I became more compassionate, he was less hostile. He's even been going to an occupational therapist, who is of some help.''

◊ EXAMPLE: "I have an extremely painful and often debilitating physical illness. Sometimes I have to be hospitalized for weeks and must leave my children with neighbors. It's very difficult for me to see what this is doing to my marriage and my children. I must focus on why my *neshamah* and their *neshamahs* begged for this or I sink into terrible gloom. I hope that my children learn to be self-sufficient and help each other, and that they will learn to pray with real *kavanah*, because there is no one to turn to except God. I say, 'It's a gift,' even if it seems stupid at the time because the words are like a safety net. I can cry, but also feel that God is with me and He will give me the strength to bear this pain.''

Suffering is a harsh teacher. We don't always want the information which painful events have to teach us, but there is no other way to gain true insight into ourselves and compassion for others.

Don't just feel the pain, do something!

Often, the gift is that we give a gift to others because of what we have experienced.

◊ EXAMPLE: "I had a terrible experience in the hospital with one of the nurses who was crude, crass and cruel. I was stewing in fury until I started saying 'it's a gift.' What I came up with was that I was going to elevate this experience by doing everything possible to see that she either changed her approach or was removed from her job.''

◊ EXAMPLE: "My daughter had a very strict teacher who would often criticize girls in front of the entire class. She crushed my daughter's spirit with the critical comments she made on her papers. At first, I thought the gift was that my daughter would toughen up and learn to be more forgiving of disturbed people. But then she started having asthma attacks, which she had never had before. Then I knew that passivity was the wrong course. I asked the principal to please sit in on the classes and teach this teacher to give more praise, especially to the weaker girls, like mine. After a few weeks, her asthma attacks stopped."

We can be paralyzed by anger. Or we can fight to improve whatever can be improved.

When life gives you rocks, build bridges, not walls

Events don't cease to be painful just because we say "it's a gift." We can know intellectually that a certain loss is God's will, but that doesn't always keep us from wanting things to be different or from experiencing pain over the loss. What this phrase can do is to keep us from feeling victimized and from being immersed in anger or bitterness.

> ◊ EXAMPLE: "I'm going through a very traumatic divorce from a very abusive man. I was also abused as a child, so I've never felt loved. When I look back on my life, it looks like one disaster after another. On the other hand, I can look at the wealth of information which I have gained. As a therapist, I know that I could not possibly give my clients the gift of real compassion if I hadn't been through almost everything they are going through. My doctorate in psychology would be meaningless without my real Ph.D. in overcoming hard knocks. And I don't think I would have become an Observant Jew if I hadn't experienced so much rejection and pain in my life."

When a woman, whom I'll call Sharon, came to see me, her hands trembled as she spoke of the suffering she had undergone since her husband had lost all their savings a year ago. What with the terrible anxiety about law suits, unscrupulous lawyers and the humiliation of having to take *tzedakah*, she thought death was the only path to relief. Tranquilizers and antidepressants weren't helping. She was surprised when I asked her to tell me what the gifts were in this situation.

"How can I get in touch with those answers?" she asked. I told her, "By role playing. I'll play you, and you'll be your *neshamah*." So I, playing Sharon, asked her, "*Neshamah*, why did we have to lose all our money? Why do my children have to see a mother who is gloomy and about to have a breakdown? Why?"

And Sharon, playing her *neshamah*, thought of the following answers:

"So that you could learn to be more independent. All your life, your parents or your husband gave you whatever you wanted. Now it's time for you to take responsibility for your family's welfare.

"So that you could learn humility. You always thought you could control your life. Now you see that it's in God's hands.

"By turning to your family for help, you've brought together various relatives who haven't been on speaking terms for years. You've made peace between them.

"You have certain talents which you've never developed because you haven't had to work. You've been so sheltered that you still feel like a child. Now you're forced to get out into the world and use your talents as a teacher.

"You and your husband have become much closer as a result of this. You've learned to care for and be supportive of each other as equals.

"Your children will learn to be more independent.

"You will now learn how to be joyful even if you don't get all that you want. When your children see this, it will teach them that being happy isn't a function of being rich, but of serving God. You are showing them that they can be happy anywhere at any time, just by focusing on the mitzvoth you do."

When Sharon finished, she gave me a big smile and a sigh of relief. She had never before considered the gift in this situation. Once she did, her life changed. She called me the next day to say that that morning she had gotten up and said *Modeh Ani* with true, heartfelt joy at the opportunity to practice being happy even if she didn't have her heart's desires fulfilled.

Recently at a wedding, I sat next to a woman I'll call Esther. When she told me that she had no children after ten years of marriage, I felt so sad for her. Then I asked her, "And what is the gift of having no children?"

After a moment, she answered the following:

"I can't tell you how elevated I feel, how close to God, because if I lose touch with Him for one minute, I cannot bear to go on.

"When I go to *Olam Ha-ba*, no one will ask me how many children I have, only what were my *mitzvoth*. Hashem has given me this *nisayon*. I didn't ask for it, and I pray that it will soon come to an end, but in the meantime, I've tried to get whatever good I could out of it.

"I had very difficult parents. They were very nervous, very critical and overbearing. I'm sure I would have been the same with my children if I had had one after another like most of my friends. I see how little communication there is, how they take their children for granted and don't even appreciate what a miracle it is to have them. I have so much awareness now that if I were to have a child, I would see him as a true miracle. I wouldn't allow myself to take him for granted or fall into lax communication habits with him because I see how precious every life is.

"I also appreciate my husband very much. We have such a deep relationship. I see many women who are critical of their husbands or vice versa. They don't appreciate each other because all they think of is what they can get. They always want more. I've learned how a crisis can bring a husband and wife closer.

"I've become so much less judgmental. I appreciate every person for doing as well as he's doing. I know how it is to go out and smile at people. No one sees that on the inside, I'm crying with grief. So I assume that others are in grief, too, and I give them the benefit of the doubt.

"I've been through so many medical procedures. Now I know that I can't put my faith in doctors. It's all up to Hashem. I have to put myself in His hands.

"Each month, when I see that I am not pregnant, I tell Hashem, 'What do You want? More tears? I'll give you more tears. You want more prayer? I'll give You more prayer. You want the *kiddush Hashem* to be even greater? Okay, I accept Your will with all of my heart and with all of my love.'"

Esther concluded, "If you believe in Hashem, you thank Him for everything — the good and the bad. Then the pain is there, but it doesn't overwhelm you."

Sharon and Esther had never defined their private gifts before to anyone, but when I asked them to tell me how they'd grown, they did not hesitate to do so. We all have a *neshamah*, a part of God Himself, which is a wellspring of wisdom within us. We can tune into it at any time. All we have to do is want the information.

Figuring out the gift

If you're having trouble figuring out what the gift is, it is helpful to imagine yourself talking to your *neshamah*, which has clarity of vision about why you need to go through various trials and tribulations. It is especially helpful to find someone to play you, or your ego, while you take the role of your own *neshamah*. Start with: "This situation is an opportunity to...

A. Perfect *middoth*. E.g., practice *bitachon* and *emunah*, cheerfulness, compassion, courage, forgiveness, love, patience, silence, truthfulness, perseverence, etc.

B. Take needed action. E.g., pray, study Torah, go to a doctor, talk to a *rav*, exercise, confront assertively, share feelings, empathize, walk away with compassion, apologize or take a risk instead of exploding angrily, withdrawing in icy silence, *kvetch*ing, criticizing or wallowing in self-pity.

C. Strengthen attachment to spiritual values.

> ◊ EXAMPLE: "Losing a child is the most horrible, painful thing imaginable. If I had my choice, of course, I'd rather have my child back and not have the sensitivity and awareness I got from this tragedy. And yet, when I talk to someone who has suffered a similar tragedy, I understand their pain, which helps us both. Being in so much pain helps me remember that this world is not all there is to life. It reminds me not to get too attached to physical reality, but only to use events to strengthen myself spiritually and to be patient until I get to the World of Truth and find out what all this has meant."

Remember, no one can decide what the gift is for you. That's for you to figure out.

The gift of tikkun and kapparah

> "Rabbi Yehoshua ben Levi said, 'One who is happy in the afflictions that come to him brings salvation to the world.'"
> — TA'ANITH 8A

> "Rabbi Yitzchak said, 'No *berachah* is found except which is hidden from the eye.'"
> — TA'ANITH 8B

◊ EXAMPLE: "I had a small growth on my tongue which had to be removed surgically. I walked into the dental surgeon's office quite happily. When he asked why, I told him, 'I'm happy about any pain I might possibly have to go through if it will be a *kapparah* for any *lashon ha-ra* I have spoken.' And even afterwards, when the anesthetic wore off and I was in considerable pain, the fact that I was truly welcoming the pain was, I am sure, a factor in my being able to be in a good mood despite it."

◊ EXAMPLE: "I was on my way to a wedding in a taxi when my two year old threw up all over me. I had to ask the driver to turn around and go back home. On my way back, I thought, The gift here is that by remaining calm and seeing the gift, I'm preparing myself for life's bigger pains. With kids, you get lots of practice!"

The gift in stressful events has to do with your *tikkun* in life. For example, if you tend to be a depressed and dependent approval-seeker, you can use critical people to remind you not to be influenced by others' opinions. If you're resentful and *kvetchy*, you can use disappointments to remind you to be grateful and forgiving. If you are anxiety-ridden and unconfident, those moments of insecurity are opportunities to build confidence by taking risks, asserting your rights or saying *Tehillim*.

Remember, the more difficult it is to do something, the greater the spiritual reward!

So, mentally thank those nasty people and bless those painful events. They are meant to bring you closer to an awareness of the essential goodness of existence and to see God in a positive light.

Don't be put off by the fact that you feel foolish or insincere when you say "it's a gift," or "my *neshamah* begged for this." Say them anyway, and you will eventually experience the Godly spark within every event. You, too, can become an expert "pearl maker."

2| The Gift of Suffering: Revelations about the Nature of Man and God

Shir Ha-shirim shows how all earthly feelings...
are only to help us understand the only thing that
really exists, that is the love of God.
—BOOK OF OUR HERITAGE, p. 310

This is an extraordinary statement. How can nothing exist except the love of God? Don't I exist? Don't trees and animals exist? Don't my other emotions, such as anger, grief or fear exist? What Rabbi Kitov *z.t.l.* is saying is that ultimately, nothing has permanence except the love we have for each other and for God. Love is the only lasting reality. Love is the only thing which makes us truly alive and which gives life meaning.

The degree to which we can accept God's will with love determines the degree of joy in our lives. If we understand that we are here to develop this capacity, then we can eventually learn to see every life experience as capable of bringing us to a deeper level of love. Suffering is meant to teach us about love, because love is the only thing which makes our losses bearable and allows us to face pain with dignity.

Revealing the spiritual

...the Lord will scatter you among the peoples...but from thence [from that place of darkness and anguish] you will seek the Lord your God and you will find Him if you search after Him with all your heart and with all your soul...In your distress...you

will return...and hearken to His voice, for a merciful God is the
Lord thy God... — DEVARIM 4:27-29

All of our Patriarchs and Matriarchs suffered deeply. They endured war, famine, imprisonment, childlessness, trickery and exile.
They didn't always have *nachath* from their children, nor were their
most fervent desires satisfied immediately. Why? Because pain intensified their yearning for closeness with God and revealed their
inner greatness.

No man in the world is free from pain. — YALKUT SHIMONI

If a person lives forty consecutive days without experiencing
troubles, he has used up his entire reward in the World to Come.
—ARACHIN 16b.

The Hebrew word for world (*olam*) comes from the word for
hidden. What is hidden, of course, is the true innermost Godliness in
ourselves and in the world. And what impels us to reveal this inner
truth, to strip away the barriers which hide the Godliness in ourselves
and in the world? Often, it is pain and disappointment which create
a yearning for more than the satisfactions which the physical world
can provide.

Suffering has the power to bring into actuality that which is
dormant in ourselves. But in order for our potential for revelation of
Godliness to be realized, we must practice certain spiritual disciplines, such as compassion, forgiveness, giving the benefit of the
doubt and having faith in the midst of pain.

When things are going well, we tend to fall asleep spiritually, for
we don't feel any strong need for God. But when we are in pain, we
see that the people and pleasures of this world cannot provide
enduring satisfaction, only temporary escape. The resulting emptiness can cause us to sink into despair, or it can make us want to attach
ourselves to something greater. Disappointment and loss teach us
that we will never be truly happy as long as we seek only to satisfy
our personal, materialistic desires. True joy comes when we attach
ourselves to a goal which is greater than ourselves, which pulls us
up and elevates us beyond our self-absorption and misery.

...what is needed is an *extreme effort* to retain contact with one's
awareness of the Creator: an effort against nature, almost

> against gravity. Let go for an instant and it slips away from you.
> — MALBIM ON MISHLEI 4:13

For ordinary people, who might not experience how spiritually deficient we are when everything is going our way, pain is often the only thing that forces us to make that extreme effort, to try to understand and to cry out in anguish, "Why did this happen to me? What do You want of me? What do I have to do to stop suffering?" It is always from the depths that this cry is made. The cry is the first step to an expansion of consciousness.

> From the depths I called upon the Lord; He answered me with expansiveness. — TEHILLIM 118:5

The Vilna Gaon, in his commentary on *Mishlei* 3:34, states that if, in the midst of suffering, we strive to retain a sense of hope and love, we are rewarded with *chen* or grace, which is the ability to radiate Godliness from within ourselves.

We acquire *chen* by trusting that whatever God gives us, even the most painful event, is good, right and necessary for us. The challenge is to retain this trust when He seems most hidden and when we are most distraught. It is this effort to bring His presence into our lives during times of suffering that brings about a profound, intimate sense of closeness to Him. And it is this sense of His closeness that makes the pain bearable. Thus,

> God joins His name to a human being in the world only if that person has suffered. — MIDRASH RABBAH, VAYIGASH

Gratefulness and love of God are natural responses when we get what we want. But the natural response to frustration is to get angry. Whenever then *Bnei Yisrael* were frustrated, they complained. They even protested angrily to God, "You took us out of Egypt because You hate us" (*Devarim* 9:28).

When we reject the painful events which God gives us, it is as if we are rejecting God. It is the essence of faith to realize that, "There is no place devoid of Him" (*Tikkunei Zohar* 57:91b). Nothing God does is meaningless or unfair, except that we are so limited by our finite intelligence that events often appear that way.

People who have never suffered major losses are sometimes terribly arrogant, shallow, insensitive and lacking in compassion. So it must be that those who suffer many losses are meant to develop the opposite traits: humility, depth, sensitivity and compassion. When we suffer a loss, our task is to strengthen our ties to God. Otherwise, suffering makes us cruel, bitter or emotionally frozen.

Making pain meaningful: gathering revelations

Just as one must recite a blessing for the good, we must also recite a blessing for misfortune. — BERACHOTH 9:5

One of the greatest joys a person can experience is the joy of accomplishment. We see this even in very small children, whose excitement at discovering something new or mastering a skill brings so much joy to them and to those around them. The greatest accomplishment we adults can experience is the sense of transcending the physical, emotional, mental or spiritual limitations of yesterday and arriving at a new level of understanding or mastery today.

Spiritually, our ultimate goal is to achieve a level of God consciousness in which we see everything as a gift, when we can say with heartfelt sincerity, "The Rock; His work is perfect" (*Devarim* 32:4). When we do so, we can understand how Rabbi Akiva could say, "Suffering is precious to me" (*Sanhedrin* 101a). But getting to this level is like climbing a sheer cliff, often requiring years of struggle to go beyond our limited, subjective view.

What pushes us to keep climbing? Often it is the desire to find a meaning for our inner turmoil and anguish. The worst pain a human being can suffer is to feel that his pain is meaningless. Finding meaning for our losses does not necessarily eliminate the heartbreak and grief. But it becomes easier to bear the loss if we feel that it has brought us closer to spiritual truths that were not discernible before. If we got everything we ever asked for, we would have no interest in striving for these truths!

Every stressful event, even the most minor, has the potential to reveal Godliness to us. The following questions will help you become aware of these truths:

1. How has my relationship with God been strengthened because of this loss?

It only takes a fast day to remind us of our complete physical dependency on God, as the source of our physical sustenance. Every loss strips away the illusion that we are autonomous and independent and makes us realize how dependent we are on God for our emotional and spiritual sustenance as well.

> ◊ EXAMPLE: "In January 1991, when the air raid sirens sounded for the first time in Israel at the start of the Gulf War, and we went into our sealed rooms and donned gas masks, I believe that what was in my heart was also in the hearts of most people: a feeling of total dependency on God. It was so clear that only He could keep us from harm. We felt totally in His hands as we uttered our *Tehillim* fervently."

In everyday life, we rarely experience such an intense awareness of our dependency on God. But any threatening situation can bring us to this realization. Or, the opposite can happen. The Gulf War also triggered a huge increase in addictive behavior — spousal abuse and child battering. Events are merely catalysts to push us in whatever direction we choose to go.

> ...He afflicts you to prove you, to know what was in your heart, whether you would keep His commandments or not.
> — DEVARIM 8:2

> Of the Rock that begot you, you were unmindful and did forget God who brought you forth from the womb.
> — DEVARIM 32:18

This can be compared to a small child playing happily in the sandbox, oblivious to anything other than pursuing his own pleasure, when suddenly there is a crashing clap of thunder. Immediately, he runs to clutch his mother. As they rush home in the pelting rain, he clings ever more tightly to her with each thunderclap. We are like that child. When we feel endangered or in pain, we search for some source of comfort. When nothing in this physical world brings satisfaction, we either sink into despair or we turn to God.

We wouldn't search for God unless we felt something important was missing in our lives. Longing and deprivation intensify the desire for closeness. But how are we to forge a relationship with a God who cannot be seen, heard or felt through our tactile senses? How do we experience God as real, and not merely an awesome silence or a cruel

Being who hurts us for no good reason? To internalize God as a positive reality, we have to experience turning to Him and getting real relief, comfort and joy.

> Return to Me and I shall return to you... — MALACHI 3:7

Pain reminds us of the need to reconnect to what is eternal, and to be less dependent on people and things to make us happy. The more internalized our sense of Godliness, the less angry and depressed we will be about external events. But we have to make the first move to connect to God. The result of this effort is a sense of His presence as a reality in our lives.

> ◊ EXAMPLE: "Despite my doctor's reassurance that my cancer is in remission, I must struggle constantly to retain a positive attitude. Every minor ache or pain anywhere in my body, whether it is real or imagined, makes me think that the cancer has recurred. I have no choice but to have God constantly on my mind, and to realize that this world is not all there is. Otherwise I'm paralyzed by fear."

2. What has been revealed about communication with God?

People who never picked up a book of *Tehillim* before in their lives often do so when they are sitting outside an operating room or are faced with a major crisis. Prayer is communication with God. When things are going well, we often pray mechanically. Prayer may even be experienced as a burdensome obligation. But when a painful event hits, we see the truth: that prayer *is* meaningful, that communication with God is possible and comforting.

We are told that our Matriarchs, Sarah, Rivka and Rachel, were barren for so many years because God wanted their prayers, the kind of prayers which only someone in an intense state of longing can offer. When Rachel realized that she could not rely on Ya'akov's prayer, she proceeded to pray on her own behalf. When she gave birth, she credited God alone for having given her a child (*Bereshith* 30:22-23).

The strength of a relationship is determined by the one who wants it least. You can love a person, but if that person wants nothing to do with you, then there is no relationship. Similarly, God loves us. He wants a 100 percent relationship with us. But we are often busy with other things. When we cry out to Him, we have the beginning of a relationship.

Rabbi Zelig Pliskin quotes Rabbi Moshe of Kobrin, "When a person suffers, he shouldn't say that things are *bad*. Rather, he should say that the situation is *bitter*. The Almighty does nothing bad. Just as medicine, although it might be bitter, is beneficial, so too events are always beneficial even if they are bitter" (*Gateway to Happiness*, p. 235).

◊ EXAMPLE: "After trying everything to achieve some degree of emotional closeness with my husband, I finally realized that he simply cannot connect to me or anyone else. He is often angry and refuses to see anyone for counseling. I decided to stay with him even though I was suffering and I spent many years crying, feeling totally alone, unwanted and unloved. But eventually my loneliness forced me to turn to God, since I had no one else. I said to Him, 'If this is the person You wanted me to marry, it must be what I needed. If I, a person who has always craved emotional contact so desperately, cannot get it from the person who means the most to me, it must be because You wanted me to develop my potential to experience Your closeness.'"

◊ EXAMPLE: "After eleven years of marriage with no children, I finally got pregnant and then had a stillborn baby. I felt like I had died with her. I was like a forest that had been totally destroyed by fire. Nothing was left of me. Months of grief, emptiness and despair followed. Finally, just to get myself out of bed in the morning, I started talking to God. I said, 'My mind cannot fathom Your wisdom. If You, who gives babies year after year to women on my street, cannot spare one little soul for me, You must have a reason. I put myself in Your hands. You take over, because I have nothing to live for. You will have to teach me how to go on.' After months of deadness, my conversations had an effect. I began to feel hope growing within me, like the little shoots of green that arise from the ashes after a forest fire. If I let go of my trust in God's wisdom for one second, I plunge into despair again. I have faced death. I know that when I die, everything will be taken away from me. Even if I do have children some day, I will have to leave them. So what do I have? With children or without, all a person ultimately has is his mitzvoth. So that is what I focus on. Love of God is often born of desperation and grief."

It takes many years of struggling with pain to reach this level.

> ◊ EXAMPLE: "My beautiful twelve year old was in a car accident and became brain-damaged as a result. How many tears I shed, how many sleepless nights I've had, how much anguish and sorrow it has taken to get me to the point where I can look at her and see a *tzelem Elokim,* and not just a damaged body. How much anguish I have borne to be able to have compassion for those who stare at me when I take her outdoors. How much I have gone through to be able to say to God, "Okay, if this is what You wanted, then I will learn to make Your will my will. Like a flower that pushes its way through a crack in the concrete, I'm determined to live with joy despite what has happened, because this is what You want.' Sometimes I break down with grief, but I've learned that this attitude is what maintains my sanity."

It is natural to ignore God when things are going smoothly and to think that it is through our own efforts that we are successful. Our natural tendency is to forget the Source of our abundance and to complain about what we lack. It takes extreme effort to constantly remember Who sustains us, because the awareness slips away time after time.

It is said that a piece of land which receives only sunlight becomes a desert. A person who never feels the longing for God which is born of pain is a desert of a human being. We need depth, and that depth is created only when we confront loss constructively.

On the other hand, pain can have a deadening, destructive effect as well. For example, within a year following the death of a child, 70 percent of the affected parents divorce (*Time,* January 23, 1989). Tragedy highlights the weaknesses as well as the strengths in a relationship.

The same is true about our relationship with God. God wants us to experience a connection for *our* good, so that He will be a reality in our lives and not simply some abstract, intellectual concept.

We have all experienced how, in a crisis, we see clearly who our real friends are. The friends who come through for us, who are not afraid to give to us, are the ones we treasure. God tests us to find out if we abandon Him when the going gets rough.

3. What inner strengths have been revealed as a result of this?

In times of stress, we see who we really are. In pain, we see our deficiencies, but also our strengths. It is easy to think we are civilized and spiritual, until we are faced with a loss, rejection or disappointment. Then we find out if we have real strength of character or not.

> ◊ EXAMPLE: "Having cancer in my thirties and with nine children has been the most horrendous experience a person can ever imagine. After all the chemotherapy and operations, my doctors do not give me long to live. And yet, the gift? I've learned that I have oceans of strength...oceans."

Those who have been through wars and other crises admit that they saw their own and others' true character during the most stressful times. Who reached out to help? Who ran away? Who shared? Who hoarded? Who stood up to evil? Who had faith?

In a recent radio program on Kol Yisrael (June, 1991), a Moscow Jew who was being interviewed said, "When the KGB was after us, we knew whom to trust because the teachers who risked their lives to teach Hebrew and Judaism had to be extremely courageous. Conditions were such that only highly devoted, special people were willing to take the risks. Now that anyone can teach, we don't know whom to trust in terms of their Yiddishkeit because their motivations are no longer so clear. Before, people taught for the pure love of Torah. Now, there may be political or monetary considerations. We don't know who's out for money and who is really knowledgeable and cares" [paraphrased].

We cannot wear masks of piety or love in a crisis. The truth is revealed, whether we like it or not. In a crisis or when faced with an ongoing disappointment, we find out who we really are.

> ◊ EXAMPLE: "My wife suffers from manic-depressive cycles and an obsessive-compulsive disorder. For years, I was very angry and bitter about having married someone so difficult. But I learned that when God closes one door, He opens another. The door He opened was that I developed a level of compassion and acceptance I never had before. As a teacher, I find myself much more compassionate toward my students with emotional disturbances than I was before."

> ◊ EXAMPLE: "I was rejected for a job I wanted very badly. I ranted and raved angrily about the unfairness of it until I realized that

this incident showed me how lacking I was in my ability to accept God's will with love. I saw that all my spirituality was nothing unless I could trust that God does what is best for me, even if I don't recognize it at the time.''

The true test of a person is not how he acts when he is around saints, but how he acts when he is around people who are imperfect; not how he acts when he gets what he wants, but how he responds when his desires are not fulfilled. What would Ya'akov have been without Esav and Lavan? What would Yosef have been if he'd never been in a pit or been imprisoned? What would the many courageous Russian refuseniks have been like without the KGB? We all have our "Esavs and Lavans" who seek to crush us. We all have our "pit experiences," when we feel like we are immersed in a dark, cold cell from which there is no escape. But that is where we are humbled. When we have nothing else to comfort us, that is when we reach out for God.

When Chedva Silverfarb *z.l.*, a young mother of three small children, was diagnosed as having cancer, she decided to devote whatever time was left to her to speaking out against the sin of *lashon ha-ra*. She had never spoken in public before and had thought of herself as an ordinary housewife, until her mission brought her before huge audiences throughout Israel. This mission did not lessen her anguish at having to leave her young children motherless, but the knowledge that her tearful pleas were influencing thousands of people to be more careful about the sin of *ona'ath devarim* (hurting people with words) gave her great joy during those difficult days.

◊ EXAMPLE: "I was brought up in a large house with servants and a swimming pool. Now I am Observant, living in a tiny apartment with seven kids and barely have enough money to feed us all. I never knew I had the ability to cope with such poverty. I would have remained a pampered princess, completely unaware of my strengths, if circumstances had not forced me to develop them.''

◊ EXAMPLE: "Before I lost a child, I was very judgmental of people who didn't function at top capacity. Then when I saw how hard it was for me to function, how I would smile on the outside while my insides were being torn apart, that's when I realized that I have no right to judge anyone. I lost my arrogant, judgmental attitude. I realized that I have no idea what anyone else is dealing with behind the mask they put on for the world. Now I give everyone the benefit of the doubt."

Fill in the blanks: "The following painful events made me aware of strengths which I didn't know I had."

A. Event: _____
   Strength: _____
B. Event: _____
   Strength: _____
C. Event: _____
   Strength: _____

Like a blind person whose hearing becomes more acute, painful events can create heightened spiritual sensitivity or spiritual numbness as manifest in chronic bitterness and anger. Every stressful event brings us some gift. Our task is to focus intently on the gift, not the grief.

4. What truths have been revealed about the ultimate source of our worth, security and pleasure?

As children, we were graded, marked, monitored and judged by adults and peers throughout most of our waking hours. We looked to others for our sense of value, safety and for happiness. We treasured the good marks, the words of praise and the looks of approval as if these determined our value. To the same extent, we were devastated when we were snubbed, left out, criticized, ridiculed or rejected. Furthermore, we looked to the physical world — spending money, indulging in physical pleasures — to make us happy. Thus, throughout our entire childhood, we were externally defined.

Only through great pain can we liberate ourselves from this dependency on external sources of approval and happiness and see the truth: that our worth and our source of joy is rooted in God, not man. Pain either propels us into addictive escapes or makes us aware of this truth.

◊ EXAMPLE: "I finally realized that I can sincerely thank God for giving me very critical parents and then a very critical husband. For years, criticism crushed me to the point of suicidal depression. Finally I began to create my own independent sense of self-esteem. I realized that my sense of self-worth must be rooted in my Godly essence, not in other people's opinions. People can put me down, but they cannot take away this essence. This realization enabled me to stop giving people the power to determine my worth."

In order to form a mature attachment to God, our belief in the power of people and money to satisfy our desire for a sense of value and approval must be broken. This "smashing of the idols" is a painful process. We cry out angrily to people, "Feed me! Make me feel happy, loved and important." It takes many painful events to force the realization upon us that people and things cannot give us our ultimate worth or security.

In experiencing the emptiness and impermanence of the material world, the spiritual world may become more attractive.

The week after the American Stock Exchange suffered its worse-plunge in almost forty years, the October 30, 1987 edition of the *Jewish Press* stated, "The Sinai Heritage Center...reported a tremendous increase in attendance at the classes in Torah and *hashkafah*. Whereas usually [there are] fifteen or twenty students, this night brought in over 100 Wall Streeters who were seeking information on a stock whose value can only rise. Rabbi Chaim Herman, director of the Belz Center which is geared to the needs of the Wall Street clientele, expressed the hope that more and more people will turn to Torah as the source of true wealth, the kind that can never suffer a decline."

No doubt, there were many who found other ways of dealing with their pain, such as trying to drown their sorrow in alcohol. However, others found that reconnecting to the Eternal one was the only way to really soothe the feelings of vulnerability and helplessness which arise when we see how quickly the things we are attached to can be destroyed.

> ◊ EXAMPLE: "I am a widow with only one daughter, who is unmarried. She is very cold to me and bitter about her life. I used to eat myself up with jealousy when other women spoke about their grandchildren, for I may never have any. To get my mind off my sorrow, I do volunteer work and attend *shiurim* instead of depending on her to make me feel happy and fulfilled."

5. What has been revealed about people and life and what have

I accomplished because of this?

When we suffer, we tend to become disillusioned with the world. Then we discover that, "The world stands on three things: Torah, prayer and acts of lovingkindness" (*Avoth* 1:2), and they are precisely what sustain us and enable us to go on living when we are heartbroken.

◊ EXAMPLE: "After my daughter died, I was in such grief that I could barely function. The only thing that brought me any comfort was studying Torah and doing *chesed* for those less fortunate than myself. During that time, I discovered that only by giving to others and lifting their spirits was my suffering lessened."

◊ EXAMPLE: "Desperation over my unhappy marriage drove me to do volunteer work in a hospital. I may have to go through life without ever experiencing the love of my spouse, which is very tragic, but I can still be a loving person."

Loss is the catalyst that gets us moving.

◊ EXAMPLE: "I had never even known a handicapped person when I gave birth to a deaf child. I was bitter and angry at first. But I eventually learned sign language, organized an afternoon art program for handicapped children and started a newsletter for parents of these children. I never would have done any of this if I had not had a special child."

◊ EXAMPLE: "When I lost my job, I was terribly depressed. I just wanted to die. Then finally I picked myself up out of the depths of despair and entered a *kollel*. I had no idea I could be so happy learning Torah. I had a learning disability as a child and had written myself off as incapable of learning. But I love doing it now."

If we got everything we wanted, there would be no impetus for us to grow, to struggle for meaning, to develop our inner resources, or to seek connection with God.

6. What do I appreciate now that I didn't appreciate before my loss?

If we never experienced deprivation, we would never appreciate what we have. How we appreciate Shabbath after a busy week! How we appreciate health after a stay in the hospital! How we appreciate a loving word after a disappointment. No one appreciates light like one who has been immersed in darkness. The darkness is a prerequisite for yearning and appreciating light.

In pain our bonds with God are either strengthened or weakened.

> ◊ EXAMPLE: "I'd always been a very independent person. Then I broke my leg and had to rely on family and neighbors to help with my children and do the cooking and cleaning. I had never had more than a superficial relationship with certain neighbors, but when I saw how much they were willing to help, I came to appreciate them. Now I look at them differently."

> ◊ EXAMPLE: "Though I didn't let others know, I was a very envious person, always unhappy because others had what I wanted. Then I found out I had cancer. Suddenly, life became very precious. I started focusing on the little things in life which I could appreciate, like flowers and music. My friendships took on an intensity they never had before. I never felt that what I had was so precious until I was faced with losing it."

7. What truth has been revealed about unconditional love?

A seventh truth is discovered in pain — that we tend to love in a selfish manner, with strings attached. We keep score: "How much am I getting? That's how much I'll give!" The ability to love unconditionally can only be developed if we don't get what we want.

A husband can profess to love to his wife, but if he is stingy and runs away whenever she needs his help, his love will seem phony.

When things are going well, a child tends to feel, God loves me. We too say, "God was looking after me, so I managed to come away from the accident with only minor bruises." Or, "God has blessed me with success in business and a healthy child." Few people say, "God has blessed me with illness" (or, poverty or a handicapped child). It's easy to view God as loving us when we get what we want. But the real test is how we act when we don't get it.

An "inferior" form of love is based on getting something. By choosing to love even if we aren't loved in return or don't get what we want, our love is pure and we serve Hashem *leshem Shamayim*.

Most people tend to feel more loving toward God when their desires are met. Every loss is a potential threat to their ability to love God, because children grow up thinking that love means getting what they want. When they suffer a loss, they feel betrayed and alone. Likewise, people love those who satisfy their needs and try to live up to their expectations. But what if they don't? Are they no longer deserving of love and respect? Is joy possible only if one is healthy and financially secure?

◊ EXAMPLE: "I must admit that I lost respect for my husband when I realized that he was not the brilliant *talmid chacham* that I initially thought he was. I felt bitter and betrayed by God. It took me years to love him as he is, with all his good qualities, and give up my belief that I could only love someone who was perfect. If he had been brilliant, my love would have been conditional. This way, I've learned to love just for the sake of loving."

◊ EXAMPLE: "Before I had children, I was sure I'd be the perfect mother and have perfect children. Well, my oldest is quite bossy and defiant. She has clearly shown me how limited parents are in their ability to mold a child's personality, which is very humbling. She has also forced me to develop patience and self-discipline. If I lose control or am hostile toward her, she gets even more defiant. The only thing that gets her in back in control is for me to set firm limits with love in my heart. She's so sensitive that she knows the instant I feel hateful. I can be loving only if I think of how much she forces me to work on my *middoth*. It's often very difficult and painful to deal with her, but at least I'm more compassionate toward other mothers with less than perfect children now."

◊ EXAMPLE: "When years went by and I didn't have children, I made a bargain with God: 'I'll really love You if You give me a child.' It didn't work. I had to learn to accept His will with total love no matter what happened to me."

8. What has been revealed about the nature of suffering? When we suffer a loss, we see how untrue our childhood beliefs about suffering have been. For example, how untrue it is to think that:

A. Bad things happen only to bad people. Therefore, if someone suffers, he must be bad. If I suffer, it means I'm bad and don't deserve love or respect.

B. If God can do this to me, He's uncaring and cruel.

C. If God loved me, He would give me what I want.

D. I cannot be happy unless I get what I want. Anger is strength! It is the best way to achieve my desires.

E. I'll love God only if He gives me what I want.

Each time we are in pain, we have the opportunity to erase these erroneous beliefs from our mental computer and enter truths:

A. Everyone lives with pain. We all deserve love, respect and compassion because we were created in His image. To love others is a way of showing love to God.

B. Everything God does is rooted in goodness, only it may not be apparent because we are so limited by our physical bodies and our inability to see beyond our physical time-space framework.

C. God satisfies the needs of all. Strength is forged in the face of adversity. There's no other way to achieve a nobility of character or an understanding of human nature.

D. True happiness is wanting what we get, not getting what we want. Anger is not strength nor does it provide protection. Love is what heals and protects.

E. Unconditional love of God is created in pain.

9. What inner deficiences have been revealed?

Pain is sometimes the only thing which makes us see how we are harming ourselves with our destructive thoughts or actions. For example, those who have physical addictions often admit, "I didn't stop smoking until I had a heart attack" or "I was terribly overweight until I became diabetic."

Similarly, people have emotional addictions to being angry, depressed or guilt ridden. When God brings us various stressful events, the resulting emotional pain is often the catalyst which forces us to change. Those who experience no pain over their bad habits don't change them.

> Consider in your heart that as a man rebukes his son, so the
> Lord your God rebukes you. And you shall keep the
> commandments of God, to walk in His ways and to fear Him....
> — DEVARIM 8:5-6

◊ EXAMPLE: "When I was growing up, my parents fought a lot in front of us and my mother was often depressed. I promised myself that when I married, I would be different. But I acted the same way when I had children. Then one day I realized that if I really love my children then I have to love them enough to control myself and not let them be poisoned by my own moods. So now when I'm upset, I force myself to 'wear the mask' of peace and cheerfulness. I don't argue with my husband in front of the children. I thought I was doing this just for my children, but I know that I've benefited the most from controlling my harmful impulses."

10. What sensitivities have been revealed?

We are in this world in order to develop our capacity to relate lovingly to others. But we cannot really understand others unless we are able to put ourselves in their shoes, and that can be done if we have been through similar experiences. Many doctors admit that they had no real appreciation for the suffering of their patients until they, themselves, became sick. Many parents tell their children, "You can't understand how we feel until you are parents!" And how true it is that when these children become parents, they say, "Ah...so this is what it was like for my parents — sleepless nights, endless worries, the sense of failure when the children are uncooperative, etc."

"Ah... so this is what it's like" is a phrase we repeat often throughout our lives. Each new bit of understanding helps us be more compassionate toward others who are in the same pain. "Ah...so this is what it's like to be old, lonely, unemployed, rejected, impoverished, seriously ill, grieving over the loss of a loved one, etc." True, the sensitivity we may acquire often seems to pale in the face of such enormous loss. Yet we must trust that "my *neshamah* begged for this," that we needed to acquire this awareness in order to better understand the people around us and to yearn for closeness with God.

◊ EXAMPLE: "When my husband died suddenly of a heart attack, I realized how little I had understood my widowed friends who said they felt so helpless and alone. When my widowed friends came to me during *shiva*, I apologized to them for having thought I could understand what they were going through. I couldn't even begin to imagine their pain until I'd been through it myself."

Each person's particular losses enable him to form special bonds of closeness with others who have suffered similar losses.

◊ EXAMPLE: "One of the gifts which our severely handicapped child has given me is the friendships I've made from having helped or been helped by other parents who sat with us night and day in the hospital while waiting to hear how their children were. These friendships have a depth which ordinary relationships do not. I would never want to go through such agony again, but I almost miss the intensity and closeness of the relationships I formed with these parents who are now widely scattered around the country."

◊ EXAMPLE: "When a close friend had a miscarriage, I felt I was very sympathetic. Then, a week later, I had my first miscarriage. Immediately I realized that I hadn't really grasped what she was going through. Afterwards when we met, I related to her on a level which was impossible before. There was a feeling of closeness and understanding which had not existed previously."

Each loss sensitizes us to others who have had the same losses. Only someone who has lost a loved one, been robbed, had a malignant illness or a mentally disturbed family member can fully understand the anguish of dealing with such problems. Our pain allows us to connect on a more profound level. And it is these deep connections which enable us to experience love. We find out who we really are only in relationship to others (which is why so many people run away from closeness!).

The proliferation of support groups for widows, cancer patients, parents of handicapped children, relatives of the mentally ill, and numerous other painful situations is one indication of the need for people with similar problems to relate to each other as only they can relate. These people forge deep bonds of love with their caring support of each other.

If we had no pain, we would never be able to relate to others on anything but the most superficial level. Without pain, we would be incapable of really connecting to others. If we got everything we wanted, we would not want anything to be different. We would be happy with who we are and would cease to grow.

11. How has the revelation of my strengths strengthened others?

The previous Gerrer Rebbe, who lost ten children in the Holocaust, said, "I lost ten and went on with my life. Those who lose one should see me and know that they too can go on."

The Klausenberger Rebbe, who lost twelve children in the Holocaust, built the Laniado Hospital in Kiryat Sanz. The hospital is devoted to *chesed*. At the dedication he said, "I, who have experienced so much destruction, want only to build."

◊ EXAMPLE: "I used to suffer from suicidal depressions. Only someone like myself can know what tremendous effort it took to come back from the edge of death to where I am now. I had to change all my negative mental habits in order to focus on the positive in life, in myself and in people, instead of always focusing on the negative. I force myself to say *Modeh Ani* with a real appreciation for the gift of life. When I wash my hands before saying a *berachah*, I remind myself to wash away the negativity which continually builds up in my heart and mind. I know what it means to have to fight for my mental health. Without a constant feeling of God's presence in my life, I'd feel lost and despairing again. Someone with a naturally sunny nature and a loving family can't know what it is to have to struggle like this. When I talk to other depressed mothers, I tell them that I've had to struggle for my mental health inch by painful inch, while everyone around me tried to crush me. So they know I'm not just mouthing cliches. If I managed to free myself, that gives hope to others, too."

◊ EXAMPLE: "As soon as I was told that I had given birth to a brain-damaged baby who was not expected to live, the hospital social worker put us in touch with a couple who had gone through the same trauma three months earlier. My husband and I agreed that, although friends and family members tried to be understanding, only this couple could really console us. Seeing that they had somehow lived through it and were getting on with their lives gave us hope that we would too. Not only this, but they felt that they were strengthened by having been in a position to help us. Once the man told us, 'The loss of our baby doesn't seem so futile when you see that we were at least able to help someone else.' So I hope our loss will help someone else some day."

12. How has this event revealed the importance of humility?

Humility means recognizing the limitations of our ability to control life and people.

And He afflicted you, and suffered you hunger and fed you with manna...that He might make you know that not by bread alone does a man live, but rather from an utterance of God...
— DEVARIM 8:2-3

When things are going well, we feel in control of our lives. We may even feel that it's because we are so righteous that these good things are happening to us. But when a loss occurs, we are faced with the truth: we're not running the show, God is. Control over our lives is an illusion. Success is up to God, not us. We can only put forth the effort. The result is not in our hands. We cannot possibly think of ourselves as so self-important or powerful when we suffer a loss.

> ◊ EXAMPLE: "I go out on one *shidduch* date after another, but no one seems even close to being what I want. When I start getting frantic, I remind myself that success in this area is up to God. All I can do is put forth the greatest effort."

> ◊ EXAMPLE: "I put a lot of time and money into planning for the special opening of my store. There was a blizzard opening night and no one came. Business has been very slow. It has taught me to humbly accept that the success of my efforts is not in my hands. I have to trust totally that whatever God wants for me is for my good."

> ◊ EXAMPLE: "From the time I was little, I was intelligent and successful. I felt I was in control of my life and my feelings. I could always fix whatever went wrong. I looked down on emotional types and people with problems as being inferior and stupid. Then my daughter was paralyzed in a car accident. Here was something I couldn't fix and felt pain I couldn't suppress. Now, when I meet others who have suffered losses, I no longer feel superior. I feel a bond. In fact, I wanted to apologize to the people who I looked down on before, because I realized that my so-called sympathy was superficial. It took this accident to make me human."

13. How has this event revealed the process of *kapparah* and *tikkun* in this world?

We all come into this world with spiritual handicaps. Our awareness of our imperfections is the catalyst which spurs us toward perfection. In striving to overcome our defects, we experience the joy which comes from accomplishing something difficult. There is nothing more difficult than fixing ourselves. This work of self transformation is called *tikkun*.

Another way of looking at painful events is to consider the pain as a means of paying off a debt to God for the sins we have committed.

◊ EXAMPLE: "Whenever I get hurt, I tell my kids, 'Let this pain be a *kapparah* for all the hurtful things I've done to others.' I see how quickly my children have used the same idea when they get a bruise. They're learning to welcome God's will instead of fighting it."

The concept of punishment can be devastating if used wrongly:

◊ EXAMPLE: "After my baby died, one woman told me it was a punishment. How awful that made me feel! It wasn't enough that I was in so much grief? She had to make me feel like I had murdered my baby because of some sin I didn't even know I committed?"

Punishment should not be thought of in the same way you viewed it as a child. Then, punishment was something others did to you in the heat of anger and which you probably felt you did not deserve, even if you had done something wrong. You also probably hated the people doing the punishing. If you think in these terms now, you'll only feel angry at God.

The purpose of punishment is to cause you to do *teshuvah*, to return to God by changing your life and becoming a better person so that you will ultimately be happier. If this is how you think, then it is the right concept for you to focus on.

◊ EXAMPLE: "When my children are disrespectful, I realize that I really deserve this because I was so defiant and obnoxious as a child. I accept the pain gratefully because only now can I understand the grief I caused my parents and be truly sorry for it. I've asked their forgiveness, which has helped our relationship greatly."

◊ EXAMPLE: "When my children were little, I explained to them that God gives each person a certain amount of suffering, kind of like a mountain. Whenever they would suffer some pain, I'd say, 'Mazal Tov! You just made the mountain smaller! Now you have less to go through later on.' That attitude has helped both me and them many times."

However, if you have low self-esteem and the thought of punishment makes you feel like you are bad and undeserving of love or respect from God or man, then it is not be the best attitude for you to adopt in this particular situation. In general, people with low self-esteem feel more miserable if they think in terms of pain as punishment. Most people do not want to think they suffered a tragedy because of some *averah* they did or because they were straying from God. People want to know why. No one wants to hear that a child died to bring the parent closer to God. That is not enough to ease a broken heart. Therefore, they should focus on the other gifts in the above list. Arrogant people, on the other hand, are often humbled by the thought of being punished.

14. How has this experience revealed my ability to have *emunah* and *bitachon*?

There are many gifts which we can only learn the hard way:

A. That the only way to stay sane in the midst of pain is to constantly have God in mind.

B. That there is no other true power other than the power of God — not money, doctors, medicine, television, food, influence, etc.

C. That we're all on a "spiritual respirator" — our existence is dependent on Him.

D. That the only true pleasure is knowing Him, studying His Torah and performing His will.

E. That self-discipline is necessary for mental health, especially disciplining our mouths to say something only if it will help people see the good and the God in life and people.

F. That if Hashem sends us pain, it's an alarm clock. It means that He could not get His message across in any other way. Fear and despair are sometimes the only ways to get us moving, to get us to do *teshuvah*, to recognize Him as King.

G. That we shouldn't get overly attached to the pleasures or the pains of this physical existence, or hope that things and people can bring us lasting fulfillment. This world is merely the testing grounds where we have the opportunity to perfect our *middoth*. When all else fails us, then we find that what gives us a sense of purpose and allows us to live a Godly life anywhere, at any time, is "Torah, *avodah* (prayer) and acts of lovingkindness" (*Avoth* 1:2).

How else would we come to these truths if not for the painful events which strip us of our illusions? Thus, pain always provide the opportunity for increased wisdom.

◊ EXAMPLE: "I have had my share of tragedies. There are times when I feel so terribly alone and disillusioned with life and people. That's when I turn to my little Book of Insights, which I've been keeping for many years. In that book, I've jotted down the revelations which I've gained from all that has happened to me. Everything has enriched me in some way and helped me understand myself and mankind."

From your limited point of view, you might think, I don't care if I develop sensitivity or insights! I don't want to suffer abuse, rejection, old age, loneliness and illness so that I can relate to others in the same boat! These insights aren't worth the pain I'll have to go through to get them. I'd rather not know!

Yet these revelations are worth the pain, because they bring us closer to what we really want: greater God-consciousness.

3 | The Gift of Acting and Thinking "As If"

*A person should always occupy himself with Torah
and mitzvoth even if not for their own sake (shelo
lishmah), because out of doing them from an
ulterior motive, one can come to do them for their
own sake (lishmah).*

— PESACHIM 50b

One of the major obstacles to growth is that we tend to feel awkward,
phony and unnatural when we attempt to make a change in our
habitual way of thinking, speaking or acting. For example, if you
haven't exercised for years, moving your muscles in an unfamiliar
way simply won't feel honest or natural for the first few weeks.

The same is true spiritually. Does a three year old understand
why he wears a *kippah* or *tzitzith*? Does he understand the real
meaning of *Shema Yisrael*? Does he really believe that God is with
him at this very moment, and that He sees all that happens? Of course
not. Yet we train our children to pray and perform other mitzvoth so
that they will be connected to the truth even though they cannot fully
understand or appreciate what they are doing. We hope that, eventually, the truth will sink in.

In the same way, if you want to be on a spiritual path, you must
overcome your initial objection to what may seem awkward or even
dishonest. For example, you might think, How can I pretend to
believe that I love my neighbor as myself (*Vayikra* 19:18) when the
truth is that I can't stand him?

◊ EXAMPLE: "When I first became Observant, I loved everything
except the '*Baruch Hashem* mentality' of Orthodox Jews. I

53

couldn't understand why people would pretend to be grateful when I knew that they were suffering from serious problems, especially those who were poverty-stricken or sick. But as I began to say what I felt was a lie, I realized that the words were like a magnet, pulling me upward toward a spiritual truth that I hadn't seen or felt before. Saying the words, even sarcastically, eventually made me become genuinely grateful. I realized that the ability to serve God, even while suffering, is the most incredible gift of all."

When we don't feel like being cheerful, moderate, patient or compassionate (see the forty-eight ways to acquire Torah, *Avoth* 6:6), we sometimes have to make these insincere gestures anyway. It's not because we are phony or dishonest, but because:

Outer movements awaken inner ones. — THE PATH OF THE JUST, p. 91

The first time you rode a bike, went to a new school, used a computer, entertained guests, worked at a new job, diapered a baby, drove a car or tried anything else new, you didn't feel confident. But if you persisted, habit soon became nature.

The mind is shaped by actions. — SEFER HA-CHINUCH, precept 16

The first time a young doctor performs an operation or goes out on the wards, he doesn't feel confident. But he knows that by acting as if he does, the feeling of confidence will become real. Confidence comes not from waiting to feel confident, but by taking risks and acting despite one's fears.

So too, when you apply spiritual principles to your life, such as giving the benefit of the doubt or being happy with your portion (*Avoth* 1:6, 4:1), you might not feel natural or genuine. But if you want to grow spiritually, you must persevere nevertheless.

◊ EXAMPLE: "Ten years ago, I was an emotional wreck. I felt like a total failure, was very depressed and couldn't get along with anyone. I screamed at my kids and hit a lot. Often I felt numb and hateful toward them. No therapist was able to get me out of this mess. Then I joined an EMETT group, which teaches people how to reprogram their minds to emphasize the positive. At the time, I was so negative that I secretly thought that I would attend this class only to show that EMETT was nonsense and that I was hopeless. When my EMETT leader told me to repeat certain phrases which are meant to build self-confidence and *emunah* (see the EMETT example sheet, Appendix A), I told her, 'I can't say this! It's a bunch of lies! I feel bad enough as it is without having to feel like a liar! How can lying make me healthy?' Nevertheless, I persisted in saying what seemed to me like silly phrases, and little by little, I began to emerge from the awful pit into which I had sunk."

Among sick folk, some long and yearn for things unfit for food, such as earth and charcoal, and have an aversion to wholesome foods... Similarly, human beings whose souls are sick and love evil dispositions and hate the way that is good and are too indolent to walk therein ...find it [good] exceedingly irksome because of their illness. — RAMBAM, HILCHOTH DEOTH 2:1

Sick souls fight the duties of the heart, though they may be super-strict about everything else! The degree of their illness is determined by the degree to which they crave "earth and charcoal," i.e., hatred, bitterness and envy.

At first, those who want to overcome this illness must force themselves to act as if these truths are real to them. They must trust that what seem like lies are not lies, but actually sublime truths that cannot be comprehended because their mental programming causes them to think that falsehood is truth. This barrier can only be overcome slowly, by struggling to "...be holy" (*Vayikra* 20:7), i.e., by thinking and acting in a Torah manner even if these thoughts or acts seem phony, dishonest and meaningless at the time. By doing so, they express the yearning to connect to Godly truth. That yearning is all God needs to respond in kind.

The Lord is close to all who call upon Him, to all who call upon Him sincerely. — TEHILLIM 145:18

There is absolutely no way of experiencing the truth of Torah except by practicing it for a while strictly on the basis of pure faith first. No secular person can understand the beauty of the Shabbath or the power of the laws of modesty until he keeps these laws first. So, too, it is with the duties of the heart. By making what seem like "insincere gestures" of love, forgiveness, saneness or courage, they will eventually become sincere.

If a man consecrates himself in a small measure down below, he is sanctified much more from above. — YOMA 39a

Understanding your resistance

At first, as you repeat these truths, part of your mind will create resistance with a wail of complaints and counterarguments to prove that these truths are wrong. Imagine complaining to a wise person about how awful you, your life, or someone close to you is (assuming, of course, that you are not being abused and are not facing a life-threatening event). Imagine the person telling a Torah truth to you, and your possible resistant response:

TRUTH: "You won't be so depressed if you see this situation as a challenging gift which God gave you for your growth."

PROTEST: "That's stupid! This illness (or spouse, child, job, boss, financial mess, etc.) is killing me! I don't want it, don't deserve it and won't grow from it!"

TRUTH: "You won't be so angry if you give people the benefit of the doubt and thank people for giving you the opportunity to perfect your *middoth*."

PROTEST: "I'd be stupid and dishonest if I forgave people who hurt me! I know they're deliberately being forgetful, insolent, incompetent, slow, stupid, cruel and inconsiderate! And I'm supposed to thank them? Are you nuts?"

TRUTH: "You won't be so anxious if you learn to ignore your nervous symptoms and refuse to become preoccupied with them. Your symptoms are distressing, not dangerous. If you learn to function with the discomfort, you will build self-confidence and self-respect."

PROTEST: "That's a lie! I can't cope! I hardly sleep at night. I'm nervous. I have scary thoughts all the time. I'm in terrible shape. I can't function like this! How can I convince myself it's nothing, when I believe something awful is about to happen? These nervous symptoms must be signs of a severe emotional disturbance."

TRUTH: "Most of life's problems are trivialities. If you want to cope more adequately, don't allow yourself to get upset about anything unless it is a major life-changing event or a sin."

PROTEST: "That's a lie! When the painter painted the room a

dark yellow instead of a light yellow, that was no triviality! I can't live with this! And when my best suit got stained, how could that be called a triviality? And when my son lost his bus ticket, that's supposed to be a triviality when we don't have money to make it through the month? And my washing machine is about to fall apart! My day is filled with one crisis after another. I can't help it that I get upset about everything — nothing feels trivial to me."

TRUTH: "Keep telling yourself 'with God's help, I can handle anything,' and you will! You don't realize it right now, but you have a wealth of undiscovered strengths."

PROTEST: "But the truth is I can't handle anything! I'm weak and high-strung and disorganized and really untogether."

TRUTH: "You're not crazy. You're just physically lazy and mentally undisciplined. Discipline yourself and you will get well."

PROTEST: "Being disciplined has nothing to do with mental health! That's simplistic! I need medication and years of extensive therapy! I am seriously crippled because of my past. Anyway, it's ALL the fault of my husband (wife, parents, etc.). If they would change, I'd be just fine."

TRUTH: "You can control your mind and your muscles."

PROTEST: "Obviously, you don't realize that it's impossible for a high-strung person like myself to practice self-control, especially with my family members and when I'm so poverty-stricken. If I had a loving spouse, health, wealth and a calm nature, I'd have self control. But with my background and my nervous system, it's impossible."

TRUTH: "Every person has the ability to rejoice with what God has given him [*Devarim* 26:11]."

PROTEST: "Well, you obviously don't realize how hopeless I am!"

TRUTH: "Your fears aren't always facts. Take risks! When you act with courage despite your fears, your muscles will show your brain that your fears are false."

PROTEST: "Wrong! My fears of being rejected and failing are real enough to keep me from trying anything new."

When a protester like this one begins working on self improvement, does he believe he ever will become calm and confident? Does he believe he ever will cease being terrorized and victimized by his moods, fears and nervous symptoms? No! But by practicing these spiritual truths, against his will, against hope, against fear and against inertia, he soon finds that discipline has everything to do with mental health.

Everyone who continues to repeat positive actions, even if they seem stupid or phony, will eventually achieve emotional health.

"Na'aseh v'nishma" — first you do the right thing, even against your will, and only then will you come to understand why it was important.

The ultimate application of "as if"

In his book, *Flying Without Wings*, Dr. Arnold Beisser describes how he fought despair when, shortly after graduating medical school in 1953, he was struck with polio. Inside his iron lung, he waged a battle to still experience himself as a worthwhile person and to experience life as enjoyable and meaningful. He wrote that acceptance of his paralysis was something he fought for not once, but daily. On his own, he came up with the most important mental trick of all: he decided to act as if he had chosen it all, including his own feelings, his paralysis and whatever happened to him there (see p. 102 and p. 127).

Arnold Beisser wrote: "On a ward full of disabled people, gloom can sometimes descend in a heavy cloud. Each patient feels uniquely victimized." Yet he found inner peace and courage by acting as if he chose to be in an iron lung! Is this not a lesson for all of us, especially those who feel "uniquely victimized"?

Accepting God's will does not automatically put us into a state of apathy or self-deception. Just the opposite is true! We see that everything really was created for a purpose. And with this realization, we become more accepting of everything God gives us. This enables us to confront people and problems in an assertive yet positive manner.

On an personal level, Arnold Beisser certainly did not want to be in an iron lung. But acting as if he had chosen God's will to be his own will, he was able to reach a level of consciousness which transcended his personal desires. This attitude motivated him to finish his degree in psychiatry and become director of a psychiatric hospital, and to serve as an inspiration for all those who came to him for guidance.

Speaking truth helps whether we believe it or not

There are numerous other truths which people can repeat to themselves when they're starting to panic or stew in anger (see the Spiritual Exercises in the EMETT example sheet, Appendix A). For example, the following mental disciplines create positive attitudes. The best way to retain contact with our Godly essence is to repeat these truths even though they seem like lies. Remember, they seem like lies only because they are such sublime truths that they cannot be made real at this moment, due to your resistance.

These truths are a kind of cosmic first aid in a crisis, miraculously lifting us beyond rage, resentment, jealousy and despair, and bringing us in contact with a transcendent reality which we were not aware of a few minutes ago.

Say the words and you will see small miracles begin.

TRUTH #1: "I will it to be this way. It is a gift."

When your will is in harmony with God's, you feel His presence, even though you may be in pain. Since God, in His infinite wisdom, wills you to have this particular challenge at this point in your life, then by your choosing it to be this way too, you become partners with Him instead of feeling distant from Him.

The "it" refers to any painful event over which you have no control: accidents, illnesses, insomnia, aggravating neighbors, financial losses, other people's bad moods and our basic personality make-up. By willing it to be this way, we stop arguing with God, stop fighting His will. We bring ourselves in tune with Him and His wisdom, love and strength by not opposing what He has chosen for us. Saying "I will it to be this way," is the opposite of saying "I can't stand it!" Willing it to be this way makes us partners with God! It's this sense of partnership which makes us feel we can cope with anything He gives us.

> Fulfill His will as you would your own will, so that He may fulfill your will as though it were His will; set aside your will because of His will. — AVOTH 2:4

Obviously, from the point of view of our personal will (sometimes referred to as the *ratzon tachton,* or "lower will") we do not want it to be this way! Who wants all these challenges? We all want comfort, tranquility, saintly neighbors, perfect health, adequate money and loving relationships with everyone. We don't want to be lied to or cheated. We don't want to see our children fail, or be rejecting or insolent. We don't want any pain. Who wants an emotionally crippled spouse, a handicapped child, or to sit in a hospital room watching helplessly while a loved one dies of cancer? Who wants to be sick, poor, lonely, rejected, cheated or abused?

But the minute we make God's will our will, we open ourselves to new awareness and understanding, and begin to pierce the thick cloud of what appears to be Heavenly injustice and absurdity. What we are piercing really is the veil we each wear, which prevents us from seeing God as manifest in this world.

The truth is that God blesses us with painful events so that we will be forced to develop a higher consciousness about God. When we first say "I will it to be this way," it may seem like a lie. But the truth is that His will *is* Truth. If He wills it, then we need this challenge. It's right and good and necessary for us, whether we like it or not.

◊ EXAMPLE: "The battery in my car went dead and I was frantic because I had to get to work. The night before, I had heard a lecture on 'it's a gift.' So, I said the words to myself though I felt stupid because they seemed like a lie. But the lecturer said to say them anyway, so I did. I mean, who wants to be late to work and get screamed at by a grouchy boss? But like magic, I calmed down and began to think about what to do. I told myself that whatever happened at work, I'd will it to be that way, too. The affirmations kept me calm and sane."

◊ EXAMPLE: "I just lost my job. Believe me, I don't want this situation. It's frightening and humiliating. The only thing which reduces my anxiety is to keep repeating, 'God, if this is the way You want things to be, then I will it to be this way, too.' Of course, I wish I had my job back or another secure job right this second — that's what I really want! But when I say these words, I remember that everything God does has a purpose, even if I can't see it at the moment. When I say these words, even insincerely, I know that things will turn out all right eventually."

◊ EXAMPLE: "I was engaged to a wonderful man who was killed in a car crash shortly before the wedding. I guess out of desperation and despair, I chose my present husband. He's not a bad person, just dry and passionless. There's no real relationship. For years, I yearned for my dead fiancé and couldn't make peace with my life. Perhaps I never will completely. But since I began to repeat this affirmation, I no longer get so paralyzed with sadness. I know that inner peace will come only if I will it to be this way, since this obviously was God's will. Sometimes, what started out as a lie actually does become true, and then I really do feel happy with my life, despite the pain. The words are slowly wearing down my wall of resentment and self-pity."

◊ Example: "My daughter is in her late twenties and not married yet. When I used to see her friends, some with five or six children already, I used to feel so terribly ashamed and miserable. Then I started using this phrase, 'I make Your will my will.' Now, each time I think about my daughter, I repeat the words and hope that God will help me make peace with whatever will be. I also accept her personality as God's will, which makes me feel less upset."

TRUTH #2: "I bless you for giving me the opportunity to perfect my *middoth*."

This phrase is to be used when someone has hurt you. It maintains love between you and others, and prevents you from stewing in rage and resentment. When your children are insolent, when a family member is critical or inconsiderate, when someone cuts in front of you in line or treats you disrespectfully, this phrase reminds you to judge every person favorably (*Avoth* 1:6) and to avoid being contemptuous and vindictive. It reminds you to work on your *middoth*, and will help you to stay calm even if others are not! You can sometimes even say out loud, "Thank you for giving me the opportunity to practice the mitzvah of not returning a hurt with a hurt" or "I'm glad that you're giving me the opportunity to practice self-control" (or patience, detachment, silence, etc.).

◊ EXAMPLE: "It was one of those hectic evenings when I was feeling overwhelmed by all the demands. Suddenly, my six year old spilled a glass of chocolate milk all over the floor. I wanted to throttle her. Instead I said, 'Thank you for giving me the opportunity to demonstrate self-control and to show you what a triviality is.' The funny thing was that even though I said the words totally insincerely, once I said them, I realized that it was true — that this is exactly what I need to demonstrate to my children. If I want them to be self-disciplined, I'm the one who has to be an example of that behavior to them. This was simply an opportunity to do so.''

◊ EXAMPLE: "When I came home from work, dinner wasn't ready again. I was about to explode, when I thought, I will it to be this way, that my wife is like this. Of course, it was phony at first because I don't like the fact that she is disorganized. But miracle of miracles, I calmed down. While waiting for my food, I practiced being patient and giving my wife the benefit of the doubt. I'm naturally a very hot-tempered person, but this trick of thanking people for not doing what I want is the first thing I've discovered to help me overcome my angry response."

◊ EXAMPLE: "A construction firm did a terrible job on an addition to our home and then demanded to be paid almost twice as much as the price they first quoted. The room leaks and has numerous other faults. We have to sue, which is going to mean months of time and money, and both physical and emotional anguish. I was so obsessed with the situation that I was unable to sleep. I was eating myself up with resentment. Then I decided to tell myself, 'I'm thankful that God is giving me the opportunity to demonstrate Torah ethics. We will respond in a dignified manner even if these people have been irresponsible.' I know we will grow from this if we keep using the experience to practice accepting God's will."

TRUTH #3: "I am a being of infinite value."

You say this to maintain your sense of your Godly image. Say this one when you feel like an idiot and a failure, or when someone tries to make you feel like one! Remember, most of us grow up thinking that our worth is determined by our appearance, popularity, intelligence, financial status and accomplishments. That's a lie. The truth is that our value is completely independent of human judgment and is determined by God alone, Who has created us in His image.

When you first say, "I'm lovable and capable," you might not feel it. If you were brought up in a critical environment, you may feel that you don't even deserve to exist since you're so imperfect. But say the words — especially when you are feeling depressed or are in the presence of critical people. It may take many years of saying this phrase before it sinks in. If you were abused as a child, you may not be capable of experiencing self-love at first. For you, the important thing is to give love to others, without thought as to whether it is appreciated or received. In time, your ability to receive will begin to develop.

At first, you may think it is impossible to stop bashing yourself for every minor mistake. You can't help but look around and see how inadequate and incompetent you feel in comparison to more capable types. But as you drop your condemnations against yourself, you will drop them against others. Soon, your relationships will improve, including the one you need most, with God.

> ◊ EXAMPLE: "My seven year old called me 'maniac' and refused to go to bed, while my five year old was punching the three year old, who was screaming. I kept repeating the affirmations I learned through EMETT — boy did they feel like lies, all of them! I felt like a total failure as a wife and a mother. But somehow, the words calmed me down. I started singing my favorite *Tehillim* while rubbing the seven year old's back and leading her to bed. After about five minutes, she calmed down and said, 'Ima, I love you.' Miracle. I got the other two to bed as well with the same technique — all the time singing *Tehillim* and saying the affirmations until I felt them as truth."

> ◊ EXAMPLE: "I went to pay a condolence call and suddenly blurted out something inappropriate. I wanted to die on the spot! I felt so awkward and stupid. But after a few minutes of self-bashing, I said to myself, 'Cut! Stop right now! It's not healthy.' I managed to stop that old negative tape recording from playing over and over in my mind by reminding myself that I am a person of value even if I don't always know what to say."

> ◊ EXAMPLE: "When a family member insulted me, I saw only two choices: either get angry and tell her off or suppress my feelings and be silently nasty. Then I thought of the words 'I'm a being of infinite value.' Even though I felt like a worm at the moment,

I experienced a glimmer of self-respect. Suddenly I saw that I had two other choices: to give her the benefit of the doubt and walk away or to confront her in a nonhostile manner. I decided on the latter course and said without malice, 'Do you realize that you hurt my feelings?' My response surprised her, and she said that she was sorry. I was amazed at my ability to stay calm, because ordinarily I would have been seething with hostility and convinced that I really was a failure.''

◊ EXAMPLE: "My husband and I were on the verge of a divorce and finally agreed to go for counseling. We arrived ready for battle. We both had a list of grievances which had built up over the last fifteen years. So I was really upset when the first thing the therapist did was to give us a pen and sheet of paper and say, 'Write down twenty things you like about each other.' I snapped back, 'That's not what we're here for!' But he said he found that his therapy was more effective if we did this first. So, I reluctantly went along. At first, neither of us could think of even one good thing about the other! But he made some suggestions — small things I wouldn't have thought of — which were true. Over the hour, we each came up with a list of twenty-five items. He said, 'Put this list in your *siddur*. After *daven*ing, read it over every morning before our next session.' I thought, This is crazy! But I did it. Sure enough, over the next few days, our attitude toward each other improved. When we sat down with the therapist the following week, we were more receptive to putting his practical suggestions into practice. Slowly our relationship improved. Yes, we still have our same old grievances, but they are counterbalanced by a sense of appreciation. Since then, I've tried this technique on some of my underachieving students. At first they all said, 'There isn't anything good about me.' But we always come up with a list of at least twenty-five things. When they repeat this list every morning, no matter how dumb they may think it is at first, their attitude always improves. I see now that positivity is a habit, just like negativity, even if it starts off feeling like a lie!''

Everything that happens is a Heavenly gift, tailor-made to bring our hidden potential into actuality. But there is no way that anyone who has put these truths into practice can convince a skeptic that he will be transformed, anymore than an Observant person can convince an anti-religious person that keeping the Shabbath, eating kosher or doing other mitzvoth will transform his life. One must jump in on faith, and practice saying these truths in order for the transformation to take place.

Now is the time to start practicing

Try the following exercises:

1. Think of a person or event in your life which you wish didn't exist. Now say to God, "I will it to be this way. This is a gift for my growth."

Note that when you stop resisting God, you calm down. And when you relax, you have a different perception of the situation. As long as you're fighting Him, you're creating so much noise that you can't hear His message as to why you've been put through these various heartaches and what you can do about it.

2. Think of someone who has hurt you. Imagine saying to this person, "Thank you for the opportunity to perfect my *middoth*." See what happens to your inner world.

Note that you are experiencing another internal miracle. You may still experience emotional pain from this person's presence, but you are no longer so hateful. Notice how the most obnoxious people offer you the best opportunities to strengthen your weakest *middoth*, such as patience, assertiveness and self-control.

3. Now, think of someone criticizing you and say to yourself, "I'm still a being of infinite value." Another internal miracle will occur. You will eventually begin to experience your Godly essence. You will feel that you have value, no matter what others think of you, no matter what your defects may be.

When you are in the midst of a painful situation, it may seem impossible to see the positive in it, but wanting to do so is enough to give you some measure of inner spiritual strength.

Overcoming inner resistance to these affirmations

The true service of God is built on a foundation of gratitude.

— STRIVE FOR TRUTH! vol. 1, p. 153

If you have trouble believing these affirmations, you may be able to overcome your resistance by filling in the following blanks:

"I must NOT accept God's will about this situation because if I do, I'll lose_____."

"I must NOT be forgiving and loving toward X, because if I do, I'll lose_____."

"I must NOT think of myself as worthwhile and competent because if I do, I'll lose_____."

You might find that you fear adopting a positive attitude because it means losing love, approval, pleasure, freedom, independence, identity, a relationship with another person, your sense of control over others or your excuse for avoiding adult responsibilities. Once you find that out, then it is your responsibility to achieve your healthy goals in a healthy manner.

> ◊ EXAMPLE: "My oldest son was very difficult. I'd often explode angrily and call him names. The last time I did this, I thought, I refuse to accept that God gave me this child for my growth because if I did, I'd lose... All I could think of was, I'd lose my excuses for being hostile. Then I'd have to work on myself! I had to admit that I don't put forth the effort it takes to relate to him in a more loving manner. Anger is a cover for laziness. It makes me feel I'm doing something useful, which I'm not. I'm basically passive and submissive. I'd rather just give up and say "it's useless" than invest the time and energy to help him. Now I see my *tikkun* — to fight to be a loving but disciplined parent instead of stewing in resentment and self-pity."

We are obligated to be grateful for all that happens to us, both the good and the bad (*Berachoth* 60b). When we make this supreme effort to appreciate what God gives us, we really do begin to see the hidden love which is behind all that He does for us.

> ...One who is "satisfied with his lot" [*Avoth* 4:1] is that happy person who has made spiritual attainments the goal of his existence...He therefore is able to thank God for every single item that God has given him to help him on toward his spiritual goal...the purer service of the Almighty. For him, everything is good...Nothing bad can possibly proceed from God, Who is the ultimate good...We may even hope that in time we will come to recognize the inner good in all that God does to us, so that we

retain our quiet confidence and inward happiness in any and
every situation.

— STRIVE FOR TRUTH! vol. 1, p. 43, p. 57, p. 61

When we awaken each morning, we say, "I offer thanks to You,
living and eternal King, for You have mercifully restored my soul
within me. Your faithfulness is great." Did those in concentration
camps always say these words sincerely when they awakened? Many
were grateful just to be alive. Others had to lift themselves out of
despair by repeating the words over and over again until they became
real.

So too, for us, when things are difficult. We can struggle to reach
the level of seeing each day as an opportunity for enlightenment and
growth, even in the midst of pain.

4 | The Gift of Lighting Candles in the Darkness

Chanukah, the Festival of Lights, arrives precisely when the days are shortest and there seems to be the greatest amount of darkness in the world. It is then that we are commanded to light candles. So too, in our own darkest times is it necessary for us to light spiritual candles which will illuminate our minds and encourage us to be strong. Even if we are not suffering from some major catastrophe, but simply trying to cope with the normal stresses of everyday life, there are moments when we feel overwhelmed with sadness and dissatisfaction, almost to the point of dispair.

Though we cannot change a *gezerah* (a Divinely determined occurrence), we can always, at any time, choose our attitude toward the event. Each act of choosing the healthy response is what produces spiritual growth. Whatever the hardship, the inner challenge is always the same: to bring light into our lives by making choices which will enhance us spiritually, or bring darkness by choosing thoughts which fill us with anger and sadness.

What differentiates those who are broken by life's difficulties from those who are strengthened by them is their strength of will: whether or not the person puts forth effort to practice the spiritual disciplines which develop true *emunah*. No matter what the situation — whether it is a sink full of dirty dishes or a major loss — we always have the power to choose our thoughts. Our power is the power to pray, to express gratitude to God for what we do have and to act in a loving manner toward ourselves and others.

Joining the spiritual olympics

Just as some people have natural athletic ability, others are more naturally calm, self-confident and optimistic. Whether or not one has natural spiritual talent, it still requires hard work to develop faith. In fact, the Hebrew word for faith, *emunah*, comes from the root which means "artist" as well as "exercise." Faith is a talent, and talents must be exercised continuously throughout one's lifetime.

Imagine an overweight, flabby person who never exercises coming to an Olympics coach and saying, "I want to win an Olympic medal." The coach will, of course, reply, "It takes hard work." Imagine the person saying, "I don't want to work hard. I hate to exercise. It's boring. I just want to win a pretty medal and see my name in the newspapers." Obviously, this would be a ridiculous request.

To participate in the Olympics, you must work hard. The same is true of the "spiritual Olympics." People often call a rabbi or therapist and say, "I'm depressed. I have no energy. I'm so discouraged. I have no friends. I have an eating disorder. I'm disorganized and undisciplined. Tell me how I can be happy." You can't be full of joy, faith and love without working hard to internalize Torah values.

The challenge

Anyone who reads Holocaust literature or books on others who have dealt with terrible traumas in their lives, will come up with a few basic principles, which I call candles, that can help bring light into the darkness of the moment.

A good blueprint for how to fight the war against despair is seen in the biography of Rabbi Yitzchak Shmuel Eliyahu Finkler, written by Rabbi Yechiel Granatstein, called *One Jew's Power — One Jew's Glory*. Rabbi Granatstein quotes Ephraim Rotenberg, who was in the slave labor camp at Skarszysko, Poland, with Rabbi Yitzchak'l,

> I watched him once during a roll call, when we were ordered to
> assemble and stand at attention, so that a selection could be
> made. All just stood there in abysmal despair, waiting for the
> Germans to make their random choice of whom to let live and
> whom not... I was standing near the Rebbe. I watched his lips

moving, murmuring, with a smile on his face. His pleasant
mood never left him! There he stood, whispering now to this
man, now to that one, rousing, heartening, consoling, pouring
into them his faith and trust in haShem... — pp. 108-9

Natan Sharansky, in his book *Fear No Evil*, describes his twelve
torturous years in various prisons in Russia. He was deprived of
contact with his family members, except for a few brief moments
every two or three years. He was kept in a freezing isolation cell for
longer than any other prisoner in the brutal Russian system. For three
years, he did not even catch a glimpse of the sun. He went into prison
weighing 145 pounds and, at his lowest point, weighed only 72
pounds. He almost went blind from lack of nourishing food, and
suffered permanent heart damage as a result of his brutal treatment.

Sharansky saw many people give in and go under: people who
committed suicide, who collaborated with the enemy or went crazy.
The day after he was released, he was asked how he kept his sanity.
He said, "A person must know what thoughts to put into his mind."

This is the key: a disciplined mind.

In the final analysis, what makes or breaks us in life is not the
losses themselves, but our attitude toward them. If we practice
Sharansky's tools, we will win against despair and develop real
emunah and *bitachon*.

Remaining emotionally honest

Candles which are lit in darkness are seen most clearly. But they don't
eliminate the darkness. Likewise, the spiritual truths do not necessarily eliminate emotional pain.

◊ EXAMPLE: "My husband has Alzheimer's disease. I felt guilty
whenever I got impatient with him or bitter about the fact that
my life has become so restricted. I can't leave him alone or invite
people over, not knowing what he'll do next. I kept telling myself
that I shouldn't be angry at him. It's not his fault that he's so
crabby or throws tantrums if he doesn't get what he wants
immediately. It's the illness. I had to give up my job, my classes
and my social life. He is often incontinent. He often doesn't
recognize me. I live with constant tension, not knowing what
he'll do next. Finally, I saw a counselor. She helped me to see

that I had a right to grieve for the loss of my best friend and my old way of life. Her guidance has helped me become more accepting and patient."

◊ EXAMPLE: "My two-year-old baby is dying of heart failure. He was born with severe brain damage and has lingered month after month in the hospital. I feel guilty for asking God to take him so that his misery will end and we can go on with our lives. I feel badly that I am sometimes consumed with envy when I see other mothers happily holding healthy babies. It takes constant effort to focus on my spiritual exercises. But there is no other way to deal with the pain."

There are no words which will take away the pain, no intellectual knowledge sufficient to stop the heart from aching. All we can do is acknowledge the pain and ask God for the strength to find meaning in life despite it.

The Torah obligates us to make our minds rule our hearts (*Guide to the Perplexed* III:8). When we fail to do this, we sink into negativity. Rabbi Aryeh Hilsenrad has provided an excellent *mashal* on how to relate to our negative emotional states. He said that just as there is a gauge in your car indicating when you are low on gas, so too, you can know that you're low spiritually when you are overcome with rage or despair. That's your indication that you need to fill up on Torah philosophy and mitzvoth (*The Jewish Press*, September 2, 1988, p. 22C).

You don't need to "trash yourself" when this happens. You simply need to make sure that these states do not become fixed, permanent attitudes.

Rabbi Granatstein wrote:

> In the times when the worst things were happening, the most horrible tragedies for members of the family and others, Reb Yitzchak'l would counsel and urge us not to become querulous toward the Creator, not to come to Him with bitter arguments and complaints. He would try to help people, including members of the family, to accept the Almighty's judgment in devotion and submission.
>
> — p. 207

To accept God's judgment may take a lifetime.

Lighting candles in the darkness

The following eight exercises are like candles. Although you will still be left with some pain, they will all banish the darkness to some degree.

1. FAITH: Develop a strong faith in God by talking to Him and praying, even if you don't feel the words sincerely at the moment. If you are angry or despairing, express these feelings to Him. Communicate. Repeat your prayers even if you do not believe the words when you say them. Say them anyway. Prayers have an effect, even if said insincerely at first.

Many people feel: I got a raw deal. God's punishing me for no good reason. This loss is absurd, unfair and meaningless. For the most part, these thoughts are normal. But they lead to despair if you dwell on them. Counter these thoughts with phrases like, "It's all a gift. I have to find out how to use it. Everything is from God, both the good and the bad. God will give me the strength to cope."

It is important to remind oneself constantly that every event has potential meaning, but that it is up to us to bring meaning into our lives by seeing how we can grow from it, how we should work on our *middoth* and make contributions to the world which we would not do otherwise.

Rabbi Ephraim Oshry's *Responsa from the Holocaust* is an amazing testimony to the faith and trust of the Jewish People in times of great tragedy. One would think that people would be less faithful during such traumatic times. To be sure, many were. Yet others became even more dedicated to Torah and mitzvoth because they knew this was the only thing they could rely on, the only enduring, permanent source of security in their lives. And they experienced this precisely because they were surrounded by so much pain, disappointment and tragedy.

Although Natan Sharansky started out his prison term as an atheist, it was in prison that he felt the sustaining power of God most powerfully. And his wife, Avital, who had to wage her own difficult struggle, became an Observant Jew during that time. When there was no one to turn to, no power on earth that could be of help, turning to God was their only resort! God knows what each of us needs to get us to turn to Him.

Sharansky starts his book by quoting from *Tehillim* (23:4): "Though I walk through the valley of the shadow of death, I will fear no evil for You are with me."

Each time he was taken down that long corrridor for an interrogation or had to face some new threat, he repeated these words over and over, and also added a prayer which he composed himself, asking for the strength to maintain his courage and dignity in the face of injustice and brutality. Certainly, he did not always feel confident or unafraid. No one could be free of fear under such circumstances. Keeping his spirits up was work!

A person in pain tends to become preoccupied with it, which intensifies the discomfort. This is why we must always have a focal point to our lives which reminds us of our higher purpose and helps us to go beyond our suffering. Our focal point is the spiritual goal of closeness to God.

> ◊ EXAMPLE: "I'm newly married and my wife is very critical. No matter what I do, it's no good. From the time I walk in the door, she's ordering me to wash, clean up, help with this or that. The other day, when I was putting up a *sukkah*, she started criticizing me. I got so angry that I was about to throw the hammer at her and say, 'Okay, you put it up!' But I didn't give in to the impulse. I started thinking about my goal, which was to make the *sukkah* no matter what the obstacles. I thought about how Jews tried to put up *sukkahs* even in concentration camps. They kept their humanity in the midst of inhumanity. So I calmly said, 'Let's focus on solutions. What exactly do you want?' That calmed her down and I was able to proceed. As I hammered those nails in, I cried silently for God to help me know how to treat her and to not be bitter and resentful. It's a tremendous struggle to believe that I really do have value, despite how I'm treated."

If God is your focal point in life, and you constantly reinforce your connection with Him whenever you face one of life's painful contractions, you will strengthen that bond immeasurably.

Faith is a choice which creates a sense of personal power.

2. PROTESTING AGAINST EVIL: Research has found that approximately 20 percent of humanity is psychologically disturbed. That means they have abusive tendencies toward themselves or

others. They need to crush all evidence of love and joy. However, since these people exist, then they are a necessary part of this world. When they come into our lives, we can grow in many ways. One of the major steps we can take is to realize that our sense of self-worth is not determined by man, but only by God. People and things do not give us value. We can internalize that awareness best when we are around critical, rejecting people who try to crush our spirits.

Rabbi Granatstein wrote of his beloved rabbi:

> His outward appearance was altered now. He no longer wore the traditional garments of a Rebbe that had graced him with dignity in the past. The peyos...no longer descended from his temples; nor did he wear his stately rabbinic hat or his Shabbos shtreiml anymore.... Yet the change was no more than in the outward guise... Nothing could alter the luminous nobility of his visage. There was an inner radiance in the man, that those about him could feel; and this, nothing could take from him. — p. 83

Protesting evil, either internally or externally, keeps our sense of self-worth strong. We protest internally by refusing to accept other people's negative opinions of us. Reb Yitzchak also resisted in other ways. He refused to eat the cooked food in the slave labor camps and refused to cooperate with the Judenrat (the Jewish police force in the ghetto). He told his followers, "We must resist at all costs, in every way we can. We will say fervently the holy words of *Sh'ma Yisrael*, to surrender completely to the Almighty's power and will — and then let them do what they want. Let them shoot us if they wish..."(p. 77).

Abusive people have no sense of remorse, guilt or anxiety about the terrible things they do to others. They enjoy terrorizing, humiliating and punishing others. Like all abusive people, their aim, said Sharansky, was "to separate me from everything and everybody I cared about, to deprive my life of its meaning, and to leave me without dignity or hope."

The bullies tried to paralyze him with fear: threats of a firing squad, reprisals against his elderly parents and various other punishments and tortures. (All those who, like himself, had been accused of spying, had been put to death.)

Sharansky maintained an independent sense of his own worth. He said, "The first time [I was arrested] when I was stripped and searched, I decided it was best to treat my captors like the weather. A storm can cause you problems, and sometimes those problems can be humiliating. But the storm itself doesn't humiliate you. Once I understood this, I realized that nothing they did could humiliate me. I could only humiliate myself. Once I had absorbed that idea, nothing, no searches, not punishments...could deprive me of my self-respect."

Sharansky refused to collaborate, compromise, bargain or even talk to the KGB. Being silent was a form of personal power. He quotes from *Tehillim*, "While the wicked man was in my presence, I was silent. I held my peace, while my pain was intense." He didn't deny his pain to himself, but he never let his abusers know of it.

Those who live or work with abusive people must work hard to maintain their self-esteem. They must also adopt a pretense of emotional detachment, because any show of weakness, fear or even joy— any attempt to communicate anything of one's inner world — brings even more ridicule, rejection and abuse.

Maintaining one's sense of self-esteem in the midst of external humiliation is a form of personal power. Maintaining one's sense of self-esteem despite an abusive past is an even more difficult act of personal power.

3. POSITIVE IMAGINATION: Your imagination is your most powerful tool for change. For example, you know intellectually that God exists. But how do you really experience that God is with you? In the beginning, you have to work with your imagination. You have the ability to imagine that you are not alone, that God has not turned His back on you, that He is punishing you for some valid reason. You can use your imagination to experience that He cares, that He is with you in this pain and this darkness. This is a mental exercise which must be done throughout the day in order for it to become a heartfelt reality.

Sharansky wrote, "The world I recreated in my head turned out to be more powerful and more real than the world of...prison; my bond with Avital [his wife] was stronger than my isolation; and my inner freedom more powerful than the external bondage."

To be able to harness one's imagination is one of the greatest forms of personal power.

Sharansky could have used his power of imagination to imagine himself going blind, rotting in prison, forgotten by the entire world. During those long and lonely years when he didn't hear from his wife, he could have imagined that she had forgotten about him. Likewise, Avital could have imagined that she would never see her husband again, that she would never have children (after all, the Russians had threatened that they would not release him until she was past child-bearing age), or that when he got out, he would be a broken man, no trace of the intelligent, exuberant person she had married.

Certainly any hopeful thoughts for this pair would have been considered completely irrational and unreasonable by most. The realistic approach would probably have seemed to be the most pessimistic view. But the two of them chose to think positively. Natan said that he kept a picture of Yerushalayim in front of his eyes at all times. Avital kept seeing him at the airport, free. And they did so against all odds.

By clinging to Torah principles in the midst of deprivation, one's spirit, which sometimes seems almost to be dying, can be kept alive:

> The survivors [of labor camps] avowed that they could find no words to describe what they felt in those moments. You simply had to imagine it, to see the scene before your eyes: Here were people on their way to a day of arduous slave labor, generally on an empty stomach... They would have to be prepared the whole time for the blows and beatings they could expect to receive in the course of the long working hours... On the way, against all odds, against all expectations, a bunch of Jews walk huddled together around the Rebbe, offering up *shacharis*, their morning prayer, as they go — to submit every day anew to the yoke of the sovereign kingship of Heaven! Every morning they bond themselves anew to their Maker, to yearn, hope and pray, 'May His great name be glorified and hallowed in the world' — in this earthly world where people of other nations were crushing the Jews, trampling them into the dust... And there they were, obstinate, determined in the face of all odds not to yield the ultimate mark of their identity. There they were, fighting, battling, struggling to proclaim morning and evening in the words of the *Sh'ma Yisrael* that haShem is the true God — their God.

> So it was that their bodies were in bondage...yet their souls, the

Divine element in the human being...they bonded and welded...to God.

— ONE JEW'S POWER, ONE JEW'S GLORY pp. 118-9

If you believe that you will always be sick, poor, alone, depressed, abused and powerless, then that is exactly how you will see yourself and how others will see you, as well. It is up to you to see yourself, with all the power of your imagination, as having a Divine essence which no human being can take away from you.

> ◊ Example: "I have been an *agunah* for eight years. In the beginning, I was terrified to leave my husband because I had no money. But when he continued to beat two of my children seriously, I knew I had to leave and take my children with me. Years of abuse had made me believe that I really was incapable of coping on my own, yet I began to imagine that I *would* somehow manage. This image gave me the strength to leave, to face endless, humiliating days in court and enormous debts. I feel now like a person who once had 'cancer of the spirit' and was cured, only because I began to imagine that a healthier life was possible."

Hope is rooted in the imagination. So is hopelessness. It is as easy to think a hopeless thought as it is to think a hopeful one. The choice is ours.

You are like an editor in a newsroom. Thousands of pieces of information come into your mind each day. What are you choosing to put on the front page? You make thousands of choices a day — consciously or unconsciously — to either focus on what is good in your life or to highlight the opposite.

4. GRATEFULNESS: Cultivate a spirit of gratefulness. Since we all have many unfulfilled desires, we could all easily become infected with the highly contagious emotional illness of bitterness. But how is it possible to be grateful in a prison cell or a slave labor camp or in the presence of an abusive relative? This can be done only by focusing on the joy of whatever mitzvoth one is able to perform in that particular situation. For example, in the slave labor camp of Skarszysko, Reb Yitzchak'l was able to obtain, at the expense of the inmates' secret valuables, a ram's horn, out of which another inmate, at the risk of his life, formed a shofar. A Chassidic Jew named Reb Avraham Altman *z.t.l.* described the scene:

> The Radoschitzer tzaddik...went scurrying about, his face
> beaming with joy, as his lips murmured endlessly... 'Baruch
> haShem, we will be able to keep the mitzvah of blowing the
> shofar!'
>
> By a bit of pure good fortune, shortly after, I managed to obtain
> two plums from some Polish laborer who worked in the camp...
> I ran at once to find Reb Yitzchak'l...and I gave him one plum
> for the *b'rachah* of *she-heche-yanu*... Out of sheer joy, the
> tzaddik embraced me. Tears of happiness ran from his eyes: he
> would be able to say the blessing... — IBID., p. 193

Natan Sharansky, who knew nothing about *frumkeit*, discovered
on his own the power of gratefulness. Gratefulness kept his spiri
alive. Over and over, he reviewed in his mind the good times in his
life. He kept expressing gratefulness even for what he had in that
dank, dark cell, like being able to see the sky on days when he was
taken out to exercise. When he was no longer allowed out, he was
grateful for being able to communicate with fellow prisoners, for
whatever kindnesses were shown to him, for reading matter, etc. He
focused on the good.

The very word Jew comes from *hod*, to be grateful. We start the
day with *Modeh Ani* because the words help to banish the blues. If
we keep saying *Modeh Ani* all day long, the very words reorient us,
keep us from drowning in self-absorption and focus our attention on
the fact that we have a purpose, a purpose which transcends personal
desires.

> ◊ EXAMPLE: "I used to be a terrible *kvetch*, always complaining and
> feeling deprived because of an unhappy marriage and a handi-
> capped child. Every Friday night, I'd light candles and pray, 'God,
> please teach me how to be grateful for what I have. Please help
> me to be less of a complainer and happier with my life.' One day,
> the answer came to me: to say every *berachah* with a real,
> heartfelt feeling of gratefulness for everything God is giving me.
> This effort didn't come naturally. It's like curvature of the spine,
> correction comes slowly. I have to change slowly, and constantly
> remind myself to be grateful. But little by little, I've become less
> negative."

Look around you this very moment. What is working in your life?

What parts of you are healthy? What did you manage to accomplish today? What can make you happy: a smile, a flower, a bit of music, the very fact that you are alive and conscious?

> ◊ EXAMPLE: "My husband, in his mid-forties, is dying of an inoperable brain tumor. We have a wonderful relationship and I'm scared to think of facing the world without him. We made a pact to make whatever time we have together as meaningful as possible and not to waste time on petty disagreements. We've become very close to each other and our children. We cry together when we need to, which relieves the tension somewhat. And we focus on what we have, not on what we don't have or won't have in the future. His illness taught us to live each moment to the fullest and to love each other to the best of our ability. In that sense, it's been a gift."

Even if 90 percent of your life is in darkness because of some devastating illness or loss, you can always find things which can bring joy into your life. You can be a fly or a butterfly. Just like flies are attracted to garbage and butterflies are attracted to flowers, you can focus on what is ugly in your life or you can take note of the beautiful, in yourself and in the people around you.

Choosing thoughts is an expression of personal power.

5. SELF-DISCIPLINE: Maintain a disciplined life. Reb Yitzchak'l said that apathy and despair were the greatest enemies. He constantly roused his fellow prisoners to *daven* on time, and to maintain whatever disciplines they were able to keep in those circumstances.

> In the winter in was impossible to say the morning prayers
> before going out to work...dawn simply came too late. Then the
> Rebbe would rise while it was still night, and put on his *tallis*.
> He put the *t'fillin shel yad* on his left hand, setting the leather
> box firmly on his biceps and winding the strap about his arm;
> and the whole thing would then go hidden inside the sleeve of
> his *kapotheh*... When he put the *t'fillin shel rosh* on his head, as
> the next step, he covered that well with his visored cap. With his
> overcoat on to conceal his *tallis*, he was ready to go out for the
> roll call, and from there to work — which meant a walk of a few
> kilometers to the factory. — IBID., p. 117

Our religious rituals raise us beyond ourselves, binding us to something greater than ourselves, helping us to overcome the illusion of being small and isolated. This attachment to God gives us greatness, power and dignity even when, to the outside world, we may seem powerless and crushed.

This tenacious determination to cling to healthy disciplines is essential when a person is in a traumatic situation.

Sharansky said, "Prison life encourages laziness." So, too, does any chronically painful condition. A depressed person may not want to do the simplest tasks, such as brushing his teeth or doing laundry. To avoid the tendency toward lethargy and depression, Sharansky exercised his body with whatever strength he had. He kept his cell spotless. And he kept his mind agile by playing chess games with himself. A chess prodigy as a child, he spent time figuring out new moves, proving to himself that he was still sane, that they had failed to break him.

When you are discouraged, think about what you can do now to contribute to the world, to your family, to yourself.

> ◊ EXAMPLE: "I have a strong tendency to depression. I am also very lazy and can sit and mope for hours. I've learned that the only way out of my doom-and-gloom state is to be very tough with myself. I force myself to go jogging for half an hour every morning despite my inner voice, which is screaming 'Go back to bed.' I force myself to pray and communicate with people. It's my muscles that overcome the defeatism of my brain. If I keep my actions and my words positive, my mood brightens eventually."

In his book *Survival in Auschwitz*, the author, Primo Levi, describes his constant battle "against exhaustion, hunger, cold and the resulting inertia; to resist enemies and have no pity for rivals; to sharpen one's wits, build up one's patience, strengthen one's will power. Or else, to throttle all dignity and kill all conscience... (Many become mussulmen) [sic] overcome before they can adapt themselves...beaten by time, the divine spark dead within them..." (p. 82).

Levi describes a fellow prisoner, twenty-two-year-old Alberto, who "understood before any of us that this life is war: he permitted himself no indulgences, he lost no time complaining and commiserating with himself and with others... He fights for his life... He 'knows' whom to corrupt, whom to avoid, whose compassion to arouse, whom to resist. Yet...he himself did not become corrupt" (p. 51).

To be surrounded by those who are unfeeling, hateful and cruel and to maintain one's self-respect is an incredible feat. It takes discipline. Levi describes L., an engineer, who had a survival plan:

> With his hands and face always perfectly clean, he had the rare self-denial to wash his shirt every fortnight, without waiting for the bimonthly change (we would like to point out here that to wash a shirt meant finding soap [of which there was almost none], time and space in the overcrowded washroom; adapting oneself to carefully keep watch on the wet shirt without losing attention for a moment [lest it be stolen], and to put it on, naturally still wet, in the silence-hour when the lights are turned out... L. had acquired in practice the whole appearance of a 'prominent' [someone singled out for special consideration] considerably before becoming one; only a long time after did I find out that L. was able to earn all this show of prosperity with incredible tenacity, paying for his individual acquisitions and services with bread from his own [meager] ration...

> His plan was a long-term one, which is all the more notable as conceived in an environment dominated by a mentality of the provisional and L. carried it out with rigid inner discipline and without pity for himself... L. knew that the step was short from being judged powerful to effectively becoming so, and that everywhere, and especially in the midst of the general leveling of the Lager, a respectable appearance is the best guarantee of being respected. He took every care not to be confused with the mass; he worked with stubborn duty... He avoided the daily struggle for the best place in the queue for the ration, and prepared to take the first ration, notoriously the most liquid [hence providing the least nourishment] every day, so as to be noticed by his Blockaltester for his discipline. To complete the separation, he always behaved in his relations with his comrades with the maximum courtesy compatible with his egotism, which was absolute.

> I believe that it was really due to L. that I am alive today; and not so much for his material aid, as for his having constantly

reminded me by his presence, by his natural and plain manner of being good, that there still existed a just world outside our own, something and someone still pure and whole, not corrupt, not savage, extraneous to hatred and terror...outside this world of negation. Thanks to L. I managed not to forget that I myself was a man.

— pp. 86-111

◊ EXAMPLE: "My husband was killed in a car accident a year ago, leaving me pregnant and with two small children. If anyone had told me a year ago that I would have to endure so much physical and emotional agony, not to mention financial disaster, I would have said that it would be impossible for someone like me to ever manage. No one can imagine the degree of self-discipline I need every waking hour not to fall apart. And I do not fall apart, at least not for long. I go on. I am finding strengths I never knew I possessed."

Self-discipline is an expression of personal power.

6. LEARN: Involve yourself in learning something new. There are Torah tapes for those who cannot get out to *shiurim*. There are endless opportunities to learn about the world, people, nature, etc. Learning is one of life's greatest joys. Sharansky learned Hebrew, learned about Judaism, reading whatever his jailors would give him when reading was permissible, and kept his mind vital by involving himself in learning something new.

Reb Chayim Pinchas Lubinsky, in writing about life in the Skarszysko slave labor camp, said, "In this camp all our possessions were taken from us, and we were left without a single volume of Talmud. How great was our happiness, then, when we found out that the Rebbe of Radoschitz had one volume hidden with him... He had it stowed away in his straw mattress. Our group...immediately arranged a regular learning period to study this tractate." (p. 116).

◊ EXAMPLE: "While convalescing from an operation, I decided to use my time to memorize as many chapters of *Tehillim* as I could manage. At first, I felt terribly inadequate because I could hardly retain anything at all. But little by little, I began to learn chapter after chapter by heart. What a joy this was for me! In spite of the pain, I was growing."

In addition to delving into the infinite world of Torah, people should also pursue their own personal interests, whether it be psychology, music or science. Those with emotional handicaps should read books on psychology, particularly self-help books to understand how to maintain sanity and avoid adopting the role of "co-dependent," i.e., one who takes it upon himself to rescue people or make them change, even though they don't cooperate or appreciate those efforts.

Those with physical illnesses must find out all they can about their bodies, various holistic treatments and the role of proper nutrition and attitude in curing illness.

Knowledge is personal power.

7. SOLUTIONS: Focus on solutions. Each and every day, Reb Yitzchak'l faced new problems; how to get kosher food, how to celebrate the holidays, how to find time to *daven*, how to raise the spirits of those who came to him for help, etc. Each problem was a challenge which he found some way to manage.

Sharansky also viewed every new loss or disappointment as the check move in a chess game — a challenge to be overcome. Instead of giving in to despair, he focused on how to outwit his enemies. In Russia, a man could be deprived of his freedom on the very day he was to be released, and sentenced to an extra ten years on the flimsiest pretext, such as lying down during the daytime hours when this was forbidden or talking after the bedtime hour. Sharansky had no power except the power of his own mind. He planned strategies so that he would be ready for all possibilities. He focused on constructive solutions and positive people (particularly his family members and fellow dissidents). No matter what his tormentors did, he figured out a game plan which would help him retain his sanity and his dignity.

You may not always be able to solve the problem in its entirety, but you can always do some small act which shows that you still have a heart and a soul. You can write a letter, smile, make a phone call, etc. Sharansky wrote that he was sure that the only reason the Russians did not allow him to die was because of the huge volume of mail which came to the prison, even though he did not see the letters himself. People all over the world took the time to sit down and write letters. How many of them thought that their single piece of paper would have a significant effect?

A man is known by his actions. It is not enough to think positive. We also have to act. And it's the little things that count the most. Make a decision to get involved, to care.

We each have our prisons. Though we are far more comfortable than those in actual prisons, we too are surrounded by internal barriers which keep us in spiritual darkness. Yet, by making healthy choices we bring light into our lives wherever we are.

> See, I have set before thee this day life and good, and death and evil...choose life. — DEVARIM 30:15-19

Without realizing it, we make choices every moment of the day as to how to think and behave. Most of these choices are automatic responses based on childhood patterns which need to be changed. That takes great effort.

During many of the long months of his imprisonment, there was no word as to whether Natan Sharansky was alive or dead. Yet Avital kept up her religious studies and spoke to countless heads of states and at numerous international rallies, despite the fact that she is a very shy, introverted woman. She kept her actions positive, which kept her spirit strong.

Action is power.

8. JOY: Cultivate a sense of humor and a spirit of joy in just being alive and having the ability to make choices.

Sharansky described how he would stand on his head while being questioned by a certain interrogator, giving the excuse that it helped him to think better. Once he was being escorted back to his cell after an interrogation with the only kindhearted guard he met during all those years. The guard's keys were clanking rhythmically. Sharansky began snapping his fingers to the rhythm, and soon the two were skipping down the hall "like a pair of Spanish dancers." He used every opportunity to make light of his situation and make fun of his tormentors until the very end. To focus on what is good in your life instead of what is terrible is a form of power.

Joy is power. Joy raises us above self-pity and despair. When I was in the most pain, that is when I looked for opportunities to make others happy. I was very selfish about this. I knew that the only way to lift my spirits was to bring others joy. That is how the Adahan Fund for the Poor began — because in bringing joy to others, I brought even more joy to myself.

I see the power of humor in the severely crippled people whom I have interviewed. They joke about their infirmities and smile. I know that inside they are often unhappy about their tragic fate, but even an insincere smile can fight the inner gloom. And they do manage, quite often, to be really, sincerely happy about life's small pleasures and their courageous accomplishments and successes.

In 1964, Norman Cousins, editor of the literary magazine *Saturday Review*, was diagnosed as having a very painful, crippling and often fatal disease called ankylosing spondylitis, which causes the disintegration of the connective tissue in the spine. He also had an allergic reaction to the prescribed medication so that he felt like his skin was "being chewed up by millions of red ants. The bones in my spine and practically every joint in my body felt as though I had been run over by a truck" (*Anatomy of an Illness*, pp.39-40).

Cousins decided that if he was going to die, at least he should die happy. He checked out of the hospital and into a motel room with round-the-clock nurses. He stopped all medication, took only megadoses of vitamins and organic fruits and vegetables and, most important, ordered copies of all the Marx Brothers movies and "Candid Camera" films he could get his hands on. He wrote: "It worked. I made the joyous discovery that ten minutes of genuine belly laughter had an anesthetic effect and would give me at least two hours of pain-free sleep. When the pain-killing effect of the laughter wore off, we would switch on the motion-picture projector again, and, not infrequently, another pain-free sleep interval followed. Sometimes, the nurse read to me out of a trove of humor books."

Mr. Cousins, who recovered completely from his illness, wrote: "The basic theme of this book is that every person must accept a certain measure of responsibility for his or her own recovery from disease or disability."

The shammash

9. LOVE: Finally we come to love, the *shammash* of this eight-candle menorah, the one which lights all the other candles. It is love

that makes a person really feel alive — love of God, of self, of one's fellowman.

When the Nazi beasts came to liquidate the slave labor camp of Skarszysko and transfer the men into Germany, the daughters of Reb Yitzchak, who had been with him in that camp, were devastated. Yet they continued their acts of love toward their father even in the final moments.

> While the men were being loaded onto the railroad cars, one of the daughters managed to throw a whole loaf of bread to him, so that he should have some food with him, wherever he might be going. With someone's help, however, he sent it back to them — so that *they* should have some food with them, on their way to their unknown destination.
> — ONE JEW'S POWER, ONE JEW'S GLORY, p. 171

Sometimes, of course, the circumstances are so overwhelming that one's spirit fails:

> We all said to each other that the Russians would arrive soon, at once; we all proclaimed it...but at bottom nobody believed it. Because one loses the habit of hoping in the Lager, and even of believing in one's own reason. In the Lager it is useless to think, because events happen for the most part in an unforeseeable manner; and it is harmful, because it keeps alive a sensitivity which is a source of pain, and which some providential natural law dulls when suffering passes a certain limit. Like joy, fear and pain itself, even [hope] can be tiring...We lay in a world of death and phantoms. The work of bestial degradation...had been carried to its conclusion by the Germans in defeat....[Then I] began to share these feelings with a friend, and by sharing, my sense of humanity returned.
> — SURVIVAL IN AUSCHWITZ, pp. 155-6

When Sharansky was denied mail privileges, he sent loving messages to his family members, if only telepathically. He went on hunger strikes and risked his life to get a few letters through to them and to show solidarity with other prisoners whose treatment was excessively harsh, even though that meant being deprived of letters from home and visits from family members and more weeks in a freezing punishment cell. He risked death to talk on the prison "telephone," which involved the men scooping the water out of their toilets in order to talk to each other. This is how he learned Hebrew! He risked death to leave a one-word message of hope carved in a piece of soap for a fellow dissident who followed him for their once-a-week shower. He wasn't passive! He loved people. He loved life. And he was determined to express that love whenever possible.

A loving person finds ways to love — no matter where he is.

In her inspiring book called *My Hundred Children*, Lena Kuchler-Silberman, who lost her only child and her husband at the beginning of the Holocaust, mentioned that what kept her going during those years was the hope that her younger sister, whom she managed to see from time to time, was still alive. Then Lena discovered that she had been captured and tortured to death by the Gestapo three days before the Russian army liberated Warsaw. Wandering around in total despair, feeling that she had nothing to live for, she found herself at a refugee center. Hearing cries, she walked upstairs and was confronted by the sight of seventy-five starving Jewish orphans, some on the verge of death. She made an instant decision to save as many of them as possible. She would be the mother to these orphans and give them the love no one else would. And in that moment of courageous decision making, her life took on meaning. She had found a noble purpose — to help others. Suddenly she felt full of life and excitement. The power of love.

To be able to love, even in the midst of so much hatred, is the greatest power we have.

> ◊ EXAMPLE: "I lost my husband and since my only child is distant both physically and emotionally, it often happens around evening time that my mental energy is low. I become nostalgic and depressed. The events of my life seem crushing. But somehow, the next morning, I wake up with renewed strength and an appreciation for life. I go off to my volunteer job with handicapped children, and once again, I welcome the day as a God-given opportunity to learn and grow and love."

We see how, even in darkness, one can always bring light into one's life, and often into the lives of others as well. At any time of the day, we can be grateful for something, we can show love, we can show we care, we can turn to God.

I have a little saying which I keep repeating to myself: "In the midst of apathy and indifference, I will care; in the midst of hatred, I will love; in the midst of despair, I will summon hope."

Faith, love, joy and gratefulness. These are powers which no human being can take away from us. Light these candles. Light them over and over and over throughout the day, every day of your life.

5 | The Gift of Being a Map Maker

A fool is one who makes petty things important and important things petty.

— VILNA GAON, MISHLEI 1:22

Few of us utilize the vast mental power which exists in our own minds. One of our greatest powers is our choice to lend importance to various people, events and objects in our lives or to minimize their importance or eliminate their significance altogether. In fact, it has been said that wisdom is knowing what to pay attention to and what to ignore.

You automatically make these choices all the time. For example, when you get an ache or pain somewhere, you have the choice of thinking (a) It's nothing. I'm not going to pay attention to a pain which will be gone shortly, or (b) This is the sign of a something serious. I'd better see a doctor.

When someone does something you don't like, you can think: Our relationship is too important to ruin it over a minor difference. (a) I'm going to focus on the good in him, or (b) This proves again that I really cannot trust this person and must keep my distance.

We are constantly making such choices. And these choices determine our emotional state.

Practice this skill

The ability to consciously maximize or minimize the importance of various people or events in our lives is a skill which can be developed and honed through constant exercise.

If you maximize the positive in yourself and your life, you will

89

feel hopeful, capable and loving. If you maximize the negative, you
will feel angry and despairing.

◊ EXAMPLE: "Yesterday a relative made a critical remark which
upset me greatly. Ordinarily, the impact of such an incident would
expand to the size of China in my mind and I would obsess about
this person's insensitivity for days or weeks. Instead I thought,
I'm not going to wait passively while this nasty mood drags me
down. I won't waste time on non-nurturing relationships. This
person used to be an extremely important part of my life, but
since these critical attacks aren't stopping, I'm going to have to
shrink this relationship down to the size of a dot. I took out a
world map to provide a visual counterpart to my plan. There, near
Hawaii, I found a barely visible dot called Gardiner Pinnacles. I
thought to myself, I'm going to make this person be Gardiner
Pinnacles and the good in my life to be the size of North America.
Each time I felt my anger return, I said Gardiner Pinnacles to
remind myself not to obsess. It was like playing with those
Shrinky-Dink plastic forms which shrink when baked in the
oven. As I shriveled the significance of the remark, my resentment decreased as well."

◊ EXAMPLE: "When my son came home for dinner, he very respectfully said, 'I want everything but the fish.' I was furious until I
thought to myself, He didn't speak disrespectfully and the fish is
Gardiner Pinnacles. That enabled me to endorse him for speaking
respectfully. Now the children and I all play Gardiner Pinnacles
with all our trivialities so that we keep things in perspective."

◊ EXAMPLE: "I asked my husband for money for a certain project
and he said he'd have to think about it. I was furious and started
thinking, He's so controlling and stingy. He doesn't care about
my needs, etc. Each time we have a conflict, I act as if he's a
monster, when in actuality, he is a very caring person. He simply
likes to feel that he is the one who makes the final decisions. I
decided to make Gardiner Pinnacles out of this trait and to focus
on the fact that our relationship is basically very good."

◊ EXAMPLE: "I had had a wonderful day with my children, staying
calm despite endless demands and emergencies. Then I had to
put them to sleep, and suddenly I lost it all and started yelling
and smacking. After they were asleep, I thought to myself, See,

the real me comes out when I'm tired. I'm really a 'smack addict,' smacking them when I'm under tension. All the good that I'd done all day was forgotten. But when I sat down with a friend and analyzed the situation, she said, 'It's not true that the real you is Griselda the Witch. You're like a seventy-five-pound anorexic who thinks she's fat, except in your case, you think you're awful if you lose control once in a while. Condemning yourself is just a bad habit. It can be changed by making your good traits into the big continents and Griselda the Witch into Gardiner Pinnacles.'"

The best way to get control of our bad moods is to focus on our life goals: i.e., to improve our *middoth* and perform mitzvoth. When we focus on this goal, then everything else becomes secondary.

Whenever you are upset, ask yourself, "Does this incident have anything to do with my ultimate values in life?" If the answer is no, then shrink it! Forget about what cannot be controlled and calmly solve the rest. You are the map maker of your life! This is your ongoing mental work, one you must do for your whole life.

Contraction and expansion exercise

Any emotion, whether positive or upsetting, can be expanded or contracted. Try this exercise. Think of something which produces feelings of jealousy, anger or anxiety. Now, take this feeling and make it grow bigger and bigger until it fills the universe. Then shrink it back to size. Now, recall a time when you felt calm, confident or loving. Expand that feeling. Make it fill the room, the sky, the universe... Now, shrink it back down. What you've just done is prove to yourself that you have power over your positive and negative mood states.

This expansion and contraction exercise can even be done with very young children. They love it. And it teaches them that they are not helpless victims of their moods.

For example, a woman whose husband had become ill was forced to go out and look for work. She was having a lot of anxiety about leaving her children and going from office to office to inquire about job possibilities. She couldn't sleep, had frightening heart palpitations and could barely eat.

I told her to imagine her anxiety growing bigger and bigger and filling up the whole room, then the whole sky and then the entire universe. When she had done that successfully, I told her to do the opposite — to shrink the anxiety down to the size of a tiny raisin. The ability to do both gave her a sense of control over her fear, which made it seem less overwhelming. By consciously choosing to contract the fear, she felt powerful and more in control of her life. By exercising this power over her fearful thoughts, she eventually developed the confidence to go out to work.

When you have to shrinky-dink yourself

A few years ago, a woman called me to ask what to do about her depressions because the medication she was taking wasn't working. She gave me a long report of all her distressing thoughts, feelings and physical pains. I sympathized for a few minutes. Then I gave her a homework assignment, which was to write down over the next twenty-four hours ten things that brought her some sense of pleasure and ten things which she did which required self-discipline. She called the next day, saying that she could not do what I asked because she was having even more alarming symptoms. I soon realized that the more I allowed her to talk, the more severe her symptoms became because we were paying a lot of attention to them.

This woman was not depressed because of any major tragedy. She had a caring husband who made a decent income and normal children. Her doctor said she was in good physical health, though she was taking antidepressants which made her anxious and tremulous, antianxiety pills which gave her insomnia, and sleeping pills to counteract the insomnia.

How could she break this cycle? Only by becoming less preoccupied with all her distressing feelings and physical sensations. Turning nervous symptoms into major continents only made them more intense and disabling, which made her more dependent on the pills with their distressing side effects.

I urged her to stop thinking so much about herself and get out of the house and find work, either paid or volunteer. I told her that meaningful activity was necessary to overcome mental inertia and emotional negativity. "But that's impossible," she cried back. "Awful thoughts just pop into my mind. I don't have control over them. They control me! How can I be expected to think about anything else when I'm not sleeping and when I'm having heart palpitations, stomach upsets, insomnia, headaches, fluttering in my eyes, twitches in my legs, and all kinds of aches and pains and frightening thoughts about possible future catastrophes? The tension is so great, and it keeps getting worse."

I told her firmly, "From the minute you wake up in the morning, you have the power to divert your attention and think about other things." I explained the concept of Gardiner Pinnacles and told her to make her nervous symptoms like tiny dots on a map. I told her, "At first it will take a lot of discipline to shrink these obsessive thoughts and fears into insignificance, but if you are determined, you can do it. Let's think of some worthwhile activities and make concrete plans to accomplish them."

At first, she was upset and accused me of not taking her seriously. She told me that she just needed to find the right therapist and get the right medication and then everything would be all right. I didn't hear from her again until two years later, when she called to say that she had been to three different therapists, but that her symptoms had gotten worse.

I said that I would speak to her only on the condition that she get a regular job or volunteer work. With nowhere else to go, she said she was ready to try my approach. Within a few days, she had found a volunteer job with immigrants and said that her spirits had improved. Within two months, she really saw that although she still had the same nervous symptoms, they were in the background instead of dominating her life. Whenever she became preoccupied with her symptoms again, she quickly turned them into tiny dots and pushed them to the back of her mind so that she could focus on her work.

Calming negative emotional reactions: It's easier than you think

What we do or do not value is a matter of culture and innate personality traits. A tone-deaf person, for example, will not value music as a musician does. A small child cannot appreciate religious values as one who has studied for many years.

What we value can also change in an instant. For example, if someone showed you a diamond and said that it was of the highest quality, worth millions of dollars, you would look at it as something of great value. Then if an expert came along and said it was a fake, suddenly it would just be a fancy piece of glass, no longer of value.

You can use the real diamond/fake diamond analogy in your life. You may have given some things real diamond value which don't deserve to be valued, such as certain people's negative opinions or having status based on material wealth. You can change this in an instant.

You are the jeweler of your life. You decide what's glass and what's a real jewel. This switch in perception is not as difficult as you may think. As you've grown older, you've discarded many things which you thought were of value when you were younger, and later realized were worthless. If you are a *ba'al teshuvah*, you saw your values change radically, in a relatively short period of time. Before becoming Observant, you valued certain politicians or movie stars, possessions, concepts and books which are no longer of value to you. Now you value learning, family, discipline, *chesed*, modesty, etc. You were able to make a major change in what you valued and what you did not.

You can use the same power to minimize critical remarks and minor disappointments. You can use the same power to maximize the beauty, love, and many blessings in your life.

◊ EXAMPLE: "Yesterday I mentally turned a non-Observant in-law into the size of a chocolate chip! Ordinarily, I would have been fuming for days at his remarks about *frum* people. Now it takes only a few seconds and my rage shrinks as I tell myself that my inner peace is more important than winning arguments. That's power!"

◊ EXAMPLE: "When I realized that my outfit was out of place at the wedding of a friend, I was mentally bashing myself over the head for not having worn something different. Then I said to myself, As long as I'm dressed modestly, what I wear is really insignificant in comparison to all the more important things in life. I'm not going to let how I'm dressed take on the importance of the size of China so that it spoils my evening, when I can let God fill my map."

Keep on shrinking

If you are the kind of person who has very strong emotional reactions, learn to shut off the flow of negativity to your mind by focusing on goals and gratefulness. Eventually, those enormous black clouds of depression, anger and fear will shrink way down in size. Each time the darkness threatens to expand, shrink it again by expanding the positive in your life in its place.

◊ EXAMPLE: "When my son said something *chutzpadik* to me, I felt like screaming at him. Instead, I showed him my world map. I said he was treating me like a Gardiner Pinnacles. That gave him a visual symbol he could relate to, and he said he was sorry. Then we were able to talk about what was bothering him in a calm manner."

◊ EXAMPLE: "I was screaming at my son for tracking mud onto my newly cleaned kitchen floor when I suddenly realized, Hey, I'm implying that I don't mind hurting his spirit because it's the floors that I treasure! That stopped me cold. I told him, 'I'm sure you didn't do it on purpose. You're more important than the floors.' He felt really bad and asked me if he could help me clean it up. If I had continued to be angry at him, he would have just been angry back."

◊ EXAMPLE: "It always drove me crazy that my kids wouldn't hang up their coats, or would leave their dishes on the table or not pick up after themselves. Then I realized that order is Gardiner Pinnacles to them, while it's China to me. I had to find a way to make this dot a little bigger in their minds because order really is an important *middah*. It may never be as big a deal in their minds as it is in mine, but I can do a lot to help them see the value of helping to keep things organized."

The failure of one partner to value to what the other one values is the basis for most marital disasters. For example, communication may be Gardiner Pinnacles to one and the entire world map to the other. So, make sure you do not make something insignificant out of what another values!

Also, be careful not to minimize things you should be paying attention to. People often ignore the symptoms of serious problems in their relationships, just as people often ignore the symptoms of a serious illness.

We have such a relatively short period of time here on earth, that we must invest our energies wisely and not waste them on anything which is outside the realm of Torah and mitzvoth. We won't have time for the important things if we're busy making mountains out of petty molehills.

If you want a quick test as to whether you should be putting your energies into a particular remark or event (including your own physical sensations and emotional responses), ask yourself, How will I feel about this ten years from now? If you are quite certain that it will be long forgotten by then and will have no significance in your life, don't give it significance now. It is, by definition, a triviality. And trivialities don't require an outpouring of emotionalism.

If there is a significant person in your life who is so emotionally disturbed that he or she cannot treat you respectfully, then you might have to reduce the entire relationship into a tiny island in your mind. Put that island off somewhere near the Arctic Circle! Then go on with your life and put your energies where they can do some good.

> ◊ EXAMPLE: "The heartbreak of living with someone who doesn't love you and whom you don't love is beyond description. The only way I can go on is to keep shrinking the relationship and making my involvement in *chesed* to others come first. That way, I feel that I am Gardiner Pinnacles and my goal of Torah and mitzvoth is as big as the entire world map."

PART II
Marriage

6 | The Gift of Knowing the Other "Facts of Life"

An unfulfilled expectation makes the heart sick, but a fulfilled desire is a tree of life.
— MISHLEI 13:12

How applicable this statement is to marriage! A marriage in which each partner is accepting of the other is truly a tree of life. But if they are constantly dissatisfied, their bitterness makes both of them sick.

The process of learning to accept each other is greatly helped by understanding that just as men and women differ physically, so too do they differ psychologically. Unfortunately, men and women marry with the belief that deep down the other person is just like them, with similar thoughts, emotions and needs. Hence they expect that married life will be harmonious until the end.

The fact is that they may have similar needs, but not in the same order of priority. Men and women often have conflicting needs within them: both for closeness and security vs. independence, control and respect. But women tend to put the need for closeness first, while men tend to value independence and control more, which puts their priorities in direct conflict with women's priorities.

In former times, women usually lived with an extended family around a courtyard. Many of their activities were done with other women, such as cooking in a communal oven and washing their clothes near the communal well, in almost continuous contact with other women with whom they were able to share their joys and woes. This courtyard lifestyle fit women's emotional needs for sustained personal contact so well. Unfortunately, in today's society few women have the ongoing emotional closeness which they crave.

Men, on the other hand, have not changed their tradition of leaving the home to go to work. Their contact with others always tended to be brief and impersonal, often involving giving or taking orders, exchanging facts or making business transactions.

Nowadays, women who still have their courtyard needs are often isolated in their homes and are lonely most of the day. So they turn to their husbands for the closeness and communication they would formerly have gotten from other women, a closeness which most men are unwilling or unable to satisfy. Not only does emotional closeness often threaten men's freedom, but few men have the same intense need for sustained emotional intimacy that most women have.

When men and women feel that their expectations aren't being fulfilled, they tend to think that their partner is deliberately trying to hurt them or spitefully withholding what would satisfy them. Thinking, If s/he really loved me, s/he'd be what I want, they become angry or withdrawn. Each time they get upset, they blame the other, assuming, Aha! This is proof that s/he doesn't really love or respect me!

Each begins to build a case against the other. Every grimace, bad mood, forgotten birthday or critical comment adds to their conviction that there is no love or respect.

The truth is that men and women often love differently and want to be shown love in different ways. This difference is compactly expressed by Byron, a famous English poet who wrote, "Man's love is of man's life a thing apart; 'tis woman's whole existence."

The following discussion should, hopefully, help wives and husbands give each other the benefit of the doubt. Knowing that these differences are normal often has a calming effect, as people realize, "I'm not alone. Other couples have similar frustrations. My spouse isn't doing this to hurt me on purpose." The next step is for both to figure out how to minimize the hurt feelings which can so easily result as a natural by-product of these differences.

Obviously, there is such a wide range of variations among men and women, that many of the following conclusions will be totally inapplicable to many couples. For example, there are many shy and emotionally sensitive males and many tough, aggressive females. Thus, please keep in mind that the following conclusions describe the general population, and certainly not every man or woman.

Understanding the differences

The important thing to remember about male-female differences is that they all have survival value. For example, considering the kind of work men have traditionally been engaged in throughout the ages, there is survival value in being combative, competitive, cool-headed, externally focused and out of touch with their own and others' emotional needs. In contrast, there is survival value in a mother being compassionate, adaptable, selflessly nurturing, and sensitive to subtle changes in her body and the emotional needs of people in her environment.

There is survival value in a man being less responsive and less receptive, while there is survival value in a woman being more responsive and more receptive. However, as they get older, many men and women do achieve a better balance between these two opposite poles, which enables them to live in greater harmony.

Other fundamental differences (which may not apply to specific people) are:

1. Men are more aggressive than women. Even when small, little boys play more aggressively, spend more time engaging in mock combat and competitive activities and enjoy using war-like instruments. When boys greet each other, they often give each other a hearty slap on the hand or back. Tenderness is not looked upon as a desirable trait, and they are often embarrassed to express it.

Boys pride themselves on their ability to trade physical punches without showing pain and, as they get older, throwing verbal punches in the same way. They perceive stoic indifference as a mark of maturity and strength, and see those who cannot achieve it as immature and weak. Thus, when men notice that women are not impervious to their gruff criticism or commands, they assume that women are inferior. However, women don't pride themselves on being impervious. On the contrary, women spend a lot of time practicing the very opposite — fine tuning their emotional radar to pick up on subtle cues as to whether or not they are liked, attractive or fulfilling others' needs.

The major emotion behind aggression and invasion is anger. Anger is a kind of umbrella emotion which hides a variety of hurt feelings. Men find it easier to express anger than face the emotions which anger covers, such as helplessness, fear or inadequacy. Much of this anger is aimed at impressing others or "psyching themselves up" so that they will feel less anxious and vulnerable in a tense situation.

Men express anger easily because anger signifies a willingness to fight and a way of declaring, "I'm in control. I'm superior." Women are often so frightened by men's anger that they become paralyzed and submissive, which feeds the man's sense of ego power, making it likely that he will use anger again to get whatever he wants. It also reinforces his belief that any expression of fear is womanly and must be suppressed at all costs.

When a man gets angry, he usually does not realize, or even lend importance to the effect of his anger on others. He thinks that his level of aggression is quite appropriate to the situation. She, on the other hand, experiences him as a steamroller. To him, she's overreacting; to her, he's insensitive.

The difference in their perceptions creates further conflict. He cannot understand why she is so devastated by his "little blowups" or his "helpful criticisms" which he thinks are so innocently aimed at improving her — her cooking, her organizational skills, her physical responsiveness, her intelligence or her social skills. To him, her "excessive" emotional response indicates that she is unstable and immature, so he criticizes her for being overly emotional, which shatters her further.

To a woman, a man's commanding voice, endless instructions and constant criticism are indications that he is insensitive, boorish, uncaring and cruel. Yet if she complains, he may dismiss her as weak and demanding. On the one hand, he wants to see her as weak so he can feel superior and in control of her. On the other hand, he may excuse himself by saying that he is merely trying to "toughen her up" by being so critical!

Partial solutions: Women can stop apologizing for being easily hurt. The desire to be loved is a real need. Emotional sensitivity is an inborn trait in most women, and is necessary for their role in life. Women can understand that the aggressive drive is an innate biological urge which is often necessary in the work world or a crisis. But it is not appropriate in the home. A woman can make her husband aware of the impact that his anger and aggression have on her by saying, "You probably don't realize the impact of what you said on me. But your words hurt me greatly." Or, "You may need to act like that at work, but you have to switch tactics when you come home." "You have a bad habit which is destroying our marriage."

The worst thing is for her to withdraw in silent hostility or pain, or to counterattack in fury. Rather, she must stand up to him in a firm but loving manner and tell him, clearly and factually, how his words or actions make her feel. She must let him know that the Torah obligates him to find nonaggressive ways to express his displeasure (*Vayikra* 19:18). A normal, caring man will, in time, learn to be more gentle. But an abusive husband will become even more abusive if she shows that he has hurt her.

Women can lessen the pain somewhat if they remember not to take men's anger as automatically indicating rejection. In many cases, women need to take men's anger less seriously, while men need to take the woman's feelings of vulnerability and pain more seriously.

Finally, a woman can realize that the anger is a cover-up and can try to help her husband identify the pain beneath it. A man who was . brought up in an abusive environment will often be highly aggressive, even cruel. Because he lacks object constancy (i.e., the security of knowing that others love him even if they are temporarily angry or unavailable), he will want to prevent what he unconsciously fears, i.e., certain abandonment by her, by controlling every aspect of her life. When he gets excessively upset, she can try to defuse his anger by reminding him, "I do respect you and care about you. I was just very busy/tired etc."

2. Men have a stronger need to feel superior, powerful and in control. One expression of the need to feel superior is the general practice for men to marry women who are less intelligent, smaller and younger than themselves. This seems natural.

> It is the nature of a woman to subordinate herself to her husband, but a woman will do so only if she feels her husband loves her.
> — THE RIVER, THE KETTLE AND THE BIRD, p. 90

From the time they are little boys, men relate to each other asymmetrically, either one-up or one-down. In any encounter, men quickly establish who is more dominant, powerful and successful. In

something my wife had borrowed. All afternoon, she told me, 'Do this and do that.' I don't think I'll ask again."

Men want to give orders, not take them. They feel a loss of power and status when demands are made on them to give, because the giving is not from their own initiative. Even when men believe, in theory, that they should share equally in the care of the home and children, they often have to be reminded and nudged to help with the chores or to spend quality time with the children.

Partial solutions: One way for women to be more successful in getting their husbands' help is to make specific, time-limited requests for individual, one-time acts, instead of expecting their husbands to always be available or to intuit their needs. For example, "I'd appreciate it if you would take out the garbage," or "...give the kids baths." They might also start helping when approached with noncommanding lead-in phrases like, "How would you like..." or "Do you think..."

> ◊ EXAMPLE: "I made a list of five easy things I wanted my husband to do, like to make sure that there are two pens that write near the phone, and to buy bread on Sunday and Wednesday. Maybe because I didn't ask for much, he went along with my requests."

Even then, you might not always get what you want.

> ◊ EXAMPLE: "I asked my husband to watch the kids while I went to take a nap. But all he did was sit and read while they screamed and ran in and out of my room. Then I asked him to help my older son with his math homework. He was so impatient that I decided for the sake of the boy's mental health not to ask again."

It is helpful for a woman to find out how her husband perceives his "givingness level." She might ask him, "On a scale of zero to ten, how much do you help me during the week?" In most cases, he will perceive himself as being far more helpful than she does, partly because giving is more difficult for him. He might answer "eight" when she feels that he rates a "two." If such a gap exists, it certainly is an indication that they need to talk about their different perceptions; both may be right. It would also be helpful for them to discuss exactly what their needs are and how they're being met. This is where a good marriage counselor can help both become more flexible.

4. Men's self-esteem is more career-centered. A man's wo
and this is just as true if his work is studying — is the focu
man's life, the central core upon which his sense of self and ι
built. Success in the world of work is essential for his sen
well-being. However, even when American women work outsic
home, they still report that their major source of fulfillment is
family.

Especially in his twenties and thirties, a man is preoccupied
proving himself, with "making it" and being successful in the
of society. He is devastated if he feels like a failure at wor'
learning, just as she is devastated if she feels like a failur
home. By the time they have reached their forties or fifties, r
are less success-oriented.

A woman's major preoccupation during these years is "making
it" by proving her fertility and ability as a homemaker.

This does not mean that relationships are unimportant to men.
They are very important. However, a man tends to feel devastated
and worthless if he lacks career success even if his relationships are
successful, while a woman, even if she has a successful career, feels
like she has failed if her relationships — especially her marriage —
are unsuccessful.

Unfortunately, this implies that there is often a gap in priorities.
If a woman's child or husband is ill, she usually does not hesistate to
stay home. If a man's wife is sick, he will generally ask, "Are you
sure you need me to stay home? Can't you manage?"

As a consequence, the woman may get enraged, thinking, "Look
how intensely he cares about his studies." Or, "Look how devoted
he is to his business. In contrast, I hardly rate second place. I'm just
an accessory in my husband's life. I'm not really meaningful to him.
He doesn't really care about me as much as I care about him. I'm
doing most of the giving. He's not investing as much in the family as
I am. All he talks about or worries about is his work."

Meanwhile, men often complain that their wives do not really
grasp the tremendous importance which work has for them. "Making
it" not only has survival value in terms of putting food on the table;
it also has tremendous ego value.

Possible solutions: Women can avoid feeling unnecessarily hurt,
rejected or disappointed if they accept the centrality of career

achievement to a man's sense of self-worth. It may be difficult to play second fiddle to a husband's work or studies, but women should be aware that it is also difficult to be married to an unambitious man who is so depressed and lazy that he fails to seek or hold a job.

5. Men have more difficulty with the spontaneous expression of loving emotions. Men tend to be less aware of their emotional needs, just as women tend to be less aware of their physical needs.

"Women are merciful" (*Megillah* 14b). Even in early childhood, the differences are often apparent (except for tough-natured girls and sweet-natured boys). Boys often laugh at expressions of tenderness and sympathy, seeing the one who needs it as weak and the one who gives it as having allowed himself to be manipulated. "Aw, poor thing," they'll laugh, not taking each other's pain seriously.

Boys are not usually rewarded for being emotionally expressive. On the contrary, during their formative years, they are likely to be ridiculed for it. On the other hand, little girls are urged to talk about their feelings and are sympathized with. Boys are more likely to be told, "It's nothing." "Don't be a sissy." "Go out there and fight." "Don't bother me with that nonsense."

In general, men's emotions are less accessible to them. Women tend to express empathy and engage in self-disclosure far more easily and naturally than men do. Men often fear that self-disclosure will cause others to think less of them.

What makes this situation even more frustrating and confusing for women is that the average man usually does open up emotionally during the courtship period, when he has a specific goal in mind, i.e., marriage. He may express fears and doubts, talk with great emotion of his love for her, and speak very openly about his childhood hurts and disappointments. However, with the marriage ceremony over, such self-disclosure is usually reserved only for very special occasions.

Many women complain, "I don't have the emotional closeness I want with my husband." "My husband treats me like a stranger." In fact, there is a physiological basis for this complaint. Numerous research studies have confirmed that the brains of men and women are organized quite differently. One major difference is that the emotional center in a man's brain is located specifically in the right hemisphere. In contrast, women's emotional capacities reside in both halves of the brain. In other words, in men, there is actually less brain space devoted to feeling, while more space is given over to other matters, such as spatial, visual and conceptual skills.

These facts have enormous implications. For example, since the verbal and emotional centers in women are more diffuse, spreading across both hemispheres of the brain, women can more easily identify their feelings and talk about them at the same time. They are also better at picking up emotional nuances in voice, gesture and facial expression. In contrast, because the emotional and verbal responses of men are segregated into separate hemispheres, men are better able to detach from their emotions when they speak, but are less sensitive to emotional cues. For women, their feelings are aroused at the same time that their thoughts are activated.

Although there are men with female-type brain structures and women with male-type brain structures, the average man and woman fall into the above patterns of response.

The corpus callosum is the bundle of fibers connecting the two hemispheres of the brain. In women, the corpus callosum is thicker in the area which allows for the flow of information between the verbal/reasoning centers and the emotional centers. This is why many women say, "If I'm feeling strongly about something, it's hard to think straight."

The more connections a person has between his left and right hemispheres, the more articulate and fluent he will be. If a man has trouble expressing his emotions, it may partly be due to the fact that information is flowing less freely from the right side (the emotional center) to the left side of the brain, where the ability to express feelings verbally resides (*Canadian Journal of Psychology*, pp. 144-92).

Thus, instead of thinking, "My husband doesn't love me because he isn't talking to me right now," a woman can depersonalize the situation and tell herself, "He has less interest in feelings that I have because his brain is organized differently. I will give him the benefit of the doubt and tell myself that he is not trying to hurt me deliberately. If I don't get angry and I remain patient and loving, he will develop greater facility in making connections between the two halves of his brain." Likewise, instead of thinking, "My wife is hysterical," a husband can tell himself, "If I get angry, she'll feel threatened. Then she'll become even more emotional. However, if I am loving and supportive, she'll calm down. Then it will be easier for her to separate reason from emotions. In time, she will become more skilled at doing this."

Men and women also relate to the world differently. Women are more interpersonally oriented. They are far more sensitive to and concerned about people and their feelings. Men are more impersonal. Their fascination is with things which can be explored, used, assembled, disassembled or figured out. Even as babies, girls maintain eye contact for longer, are more interested in communicating, more sensitive to sound and touch, and more responsive to faces and soothing words. Boys are more active and will jabber away at things which are dangled in front of them with as much delight as they do faces (*The Real Differences between Men and Women*, pp. 38-49).

In general, a woman gets angry because she feels hurt about not getting enough emotional closeness. If she asks her husband to help and he refuses, it's not the loss of an extra pair of hands which hurts her so much as the thought that "this proves that he doesn't really care."

In contrast, a man tends to get angry if his wife does not provide the services or the ego enhancement he seeks from her. His anger involves a certain degree of depersonalization of the object of his wrath, i.e., his wife. She becomes a thing to be shouted at or pushed around. Things don't feel, so there are no feelings to be taken into account except his own. In fact, he is usually quite surprised to discover that his anger has had such a devastating effect on her and he cannot understand why. He thinks she should be able to compartmentalize her feelings as easily as he does his own, that she should be reasonable and forget what happened as quickly as he has. She will then say, "I resent having to explain why I feel so hurt! He should know! How can a smart man be so stupid?" She must realize that the male-organized brain is less emotionally sensitive and does not take feelings so seriously. Such people do need to have things explained to them, over and over again, starting early in marriage.

Because men relate more abstractly and impersonally to people, they may not ask for details about their wives' thoughts and feelings, which, to them, is the major sign of caring. Instead, they tend to show caring by actions rather than words; solving problems, fixing things around the house, shopping, going on outings, learning with the children and paying the bills.

Obviously, a man who has grown up with the idea that the expression of emotions is a sign of weakness cannot be expected to respond positively when his wife tries to share her fears and doubts with him. Having spent his life training himself to be insensitive to his own inner world, he cannot suddenly be sensitive to hers. His emotions have long since been made inaccessible, locked away in another part of his psyche so that he can prove his masculinity. When she has a strong emotional response, he may act cold and sarcastic as a defense, in order to keep himself from being infected by the intensity of her feelings. Emotional suppression easily becomes a fixed, automatic response because it is so pleasurable to feel powerful and manly by doing so.

The one emotion men have no trouble expressing is anger, an emotion of aggression. Women are trained from childhood not to show anger, or at least not to show it openly. Passive-aggression (subtle sabotage, hostile withdrawal, etc.) is much more common among women, while a man's anger is often expressed, tolerated and excused. A man will tend to think of his anger as justifiable and appropriate, but think of his wife's anger as unjustified and controllable. He has the right to explode because dinner isn't on time, but she has no right to feel hurt that he exploded or explode back. After all, it was her fault that he exploded.

A man often thinks that the fact that he gets angry, criticizes and argues proves how much he cares, how involved he is with his wife! But that's not the kind of involvement she wants! She assumes, "If he loved me, he wouldn't behave like this. So he must not love me!" Men often become impatient and irritated when women react emotionally to their outbursts or criticism. They wonder, "She's so emotional! What's wrong with her? I hardly said anything!"

A positive interpretation of a man's resistance to the expression of intimate emotions is that it is due to his anxiety over the actual depth of his love for his wife and the extent to which he needs her. He would rather deny this bond, for to recognize his dependency on her would make him feel vulnerable, and consequently, anxious. A woman has no such conflicts about being aware of how much she needs and wants her husband.

When a man distances himself, the wife is likely to feel terribly hurt. But her demands for closeness push him even further away. The more she pursues, the more he distances. If she probes for information, he tends to close off even more tightly.

It is normal behavior for a man to withdraw when a woman comes on too strong emotionally. Unfortunately any expression of emotion is too strong for an emotionally suppressive, insecure man. No matter how toned-down and mild she may try to be, he may react defensively and with hostility.

Partial solutions: Women can save their strongest emotions for special occasions or sympathetic women friends. Otherwise, every time she expresses a strong feeling, he thinks she is just "crying wolf" again — i.e., overreacting with an excessively dramatic display of feelings — and should not be taken seriously.

Instead of waiting for a husband to express his love verbally, a woman should consider a man's actual behavior in order to evaluate his level of caring. If he comes home regularly from work, helps at least occasionally with the chores, shows concern for you, and can be relied on in a crisis, then he is a basically caring person. All these behaviors are indications of caring. He may not be able to say, "I love you," but he may be expressing it in other ways. Occasionally you can say it for him by using words like, "I know this means you love me."

Also, women can let their husbands initiate conversation. When the pressure to talk if off, men may become more communicative. If a man is emotionally unsupportive, a woman may feel hurt, but she does not have to be enraged and think he is doing this purposely to hurt her. Instead, she might consider that he needs time to learn communication skills and develop the neural connections between the left and right sides of his brain. If she shows genuine pleasure at his expressions of positive feelings, however rare that might be, this will eventually reinforce his desire to continue.

Wives cannot be patient teachers if they are condemning their husbands for not satisfying their needs. If the atmosphere is positive, most women find that their husbands do mellow with age and become more expressive. One evidence of this is how much more most men enjoy their grandchildren then they did their own children. In the meantime, caring friends, loving family members and fulfilling work can ease the frustration and loneliness to some degree.

Finally, mothers can try to prevent problems by encouraging their emotionally inhibited children to share their feelings from an early age. This will help develop the nerve connections between both halves of the brain so that the flow of information will be less restricted. If sharing is a normal and enjoyable experience in childhood, children are more verbally expressive when they marry. On the other hand, mothers can teach their highly emotional children to focus on solutions and develop their reasoning capacities so that they are not so easily overwhelmed by feelings or devastated if they are criticized or rejected.

Nurturing vs. non-nurturing marriages

Every person has a shadow or non-dominant side to his personality. Thus, even the coldest type has the ability to develop some degree of communicativeness. And the most hysterically emotional type can develop the ability to be more reasonable and rational. However, this must be done with positive pressure (love, positive feedback, etc.) and not negative pressure (criticism). In a negative atmosphere, people become even more polarized toward their innate tendencies.

Thus, in a caring marriage, love for one another grows steadily as the partners become more accepting and appreciative of the other and more and more focused on the other's needs rather than their own selfish desires. In this atmosphere, their love transcends the disappointments which are inevitable in any relationship. If they focus on what the other does give, they automatically minimize or ignore what is lacking.

Sadly, in a non-nurturing relationship, their differences are magnified instead of minimized. As time goes on, there is greater distance and deeper despair. They become cold, cruel and bitter. Every effort to be loving, supportive, or positive is rebuffed and rejected, and both are miserable. The only way out of this sad state is to focus on loving, giving, forgiving and appreciating one another.

> Where do we need more protection, more curtains and more privacy than in our weaknesses? To look at your spouse's weaknesses is the same as passing judgment. It's an invasion of

privacy. You can't build an intimate relationship if you don't respect your spouse's borders as well as you do your own.
— DOESN'T ANYONE BLUSH ANYMORE, p. 3

The fact that your spouse isn't perfect shouldn't be your problem. If your husband or wife were perfect, then you wouldn't need any talent or wisdom. The [goal] is that this person isn't perfect, and it doesn't bother you. It's not your problem because you accept your spouse unconditionally.

We are not talking about dangerous misbehavior or physical violence, just normal, human imperfection...it's not enough simply to tolerate your spouse's faults. You have to be like the sons of Noah and not see them. [As it says]...'and their father's nakedness they did not see' (*Bereshith* 9:22). They saw that he needed to be covered...You see what needs to be done, but you don't look for faults...see the condition, but...don't judge the person. The reason you don't notice is not because you're so kind, so wise, and so magnanimous that you overlook your spouse's faults. It's not overlooking; it's having respect for your mate's privacy.
— Ibid. pp. 6-7

Hopefully, by understanding the essential needs and basic nature of the other, two spouses can build an atmosphere of appreciation and acceptance despite their differences. Those women who long for closeness and are married to men who have little need for intimacy should form support groups with others in the same situation so that they can learn to survive in their "emotional Siberia."

Note: Those involved in arranging *shidduchim* should not assume that opposites always complement each other in a positive manner, or that the mere fact that a man is a brilliant scholar is enough to ensure that he will be a compassionate mate. When a person with strong emotional needs is married to someone with minimal emotional needs, the marriage is often a tragedy for both.

The gift of understanding will hopefully strengthen the gift of foresight: it is valuable to see who the person really is before the relationship becomes established, and this, in turn, will enhance the gift of appreciation of that person afterward.

7 | The Gift of Understanding Different Communication Styles

Domestic discord is probably the most widespread form of human misery.
— THE RIVER, THE KETTLE AND THE BIRD, p. 7

The difference in men's and women's natures affects the way they communicate at the most profound level. If the couple also has completely opposite personality traits (see *Appreciating People*), the lack of understanding can lead to an abyss of loneliness for both.

Of course, those most affected by a lack of emotional responsiveness on the part of their partner are likely to be those who react strongly to the loss of love and approval [referred to as Feeling types]. Men and women who are more emotionally aloof and less concerned about emotional closeness are referred to as Thinking types.

Before marriage, Feeling types are attracted to Thinking types because the latter seem so knowledgeable, confident, strong, imperturbable, "together" and sophisticated. Afterwards, they often experience Thinking types as aloof and insensitive. Likewise, Thinking types are attracted to Feelings types because of their warmth and demonstrative natures. After marriage, they then complain that they are needy, weak, immature and unstable.

When a Feeling type marries an emotionally distant Thinking type, the result is often disastrous, unless they learn to become more like the other one.

Unfortunately, the opposite usually happens. The Feeling one makes what seem like normal requests for closeness, but which seem, to the Thinker, to be excessive, suffocating demands. The more the

Thinking one disregards the validity of the partner's feelings and distances him/herself, the more frantic the Feeling one gets. This is especially true of the highly emotional types, who tend to feel threatened when they are not able to connect emotionally.

If this pattern continues, the wall of hostility and mistrust can become too thick to penetrate. This is why it is so important for partners to understand each other's needs and appreciate the type of person they have married.

Intimacy vs. independence

[The following discussion provides a general picture of the differences between men and women, and will not apply to every reader.]

The most basic problem which both men and women face is their conflicting needs for emotional intimacy and independence. Men and women want both. But for women, to be loved is more essential than to be independent; for men, the priorities are reversed. Men will often sacrifice closeness to achieve a sense of independence, while women will sacrifice their independence in order to feel loved.

> ...a woman's nature is to find favor in her husband's eyes... giving a woman the feeling that she is unloved is akin to spilling her blood.
>
> — IBID., p. 47

Women, especially Feeling types, constantly worry, "Does he care?" They need reassurance that they are loved. A man constantly tests to find out, "Do I still have my freedom and independence?" If she puts on a new dress and he doesn't notice, she may be shattered, for she feels, "I'm not cared about." If he wants to go someplace and she tells him to do something before he leaves, he may explode, for he hears a metamessage [what he hears between the lines] of "I'm not free to do as I please."

This is not to say that men don't want emotional intimacy or that women don't want freedom. Not at all. Many women become depressed if they are confined to the house all day long, with no freedom to develop their own interests or talents. A woman may explode if she wants to go somewhere and is told that she cannot, for one reason or another. But her primary urge for closeness is usually stronger than her craving for independence, unless she is very unhappy with her marriage. Likewise, a man may explode if his wife doesn't give him a decent meal because he takes this to mean that she is saying, "You're not important to me. I don't respect you." He, too, wants closeness. But that craving is secondary to his desire for power and independence, unless he has a cold, undemonstrative wife, in which case he may become preoccupied with her lack of emotional warmth.

The desire for intimacy vs. independence is even seen in the differences betwen male and female body language. For example, researchers have found that from the age of two or three, girls sit closer to each other and look into each other's eyes more often and for longer periods of time than boys. Boys sit at angles and avoid looking in each other's eyes; even at this young age, they are avoiding closeness.

A couple's conflict between their two basic needs for independence and intimacy is evident throughout the day. For example, if he helps with the chores, he may worry that she'll expect him to do them everyday, and thereby he'll lose his freedom. But if he refuses to help, even though he may not necessarily have something more important to do, he thinks he will be showing his independence.

In general, men see life as a competitive battle in which their goal is to maintain power, status and independence, and avoid failure. Women's goal is to achieve intimacy, validation and support, and avoid isolation. For women, the most important thing is to feel liked and close with others. For men, it is crucial that they be respected. Being disliked is usually the most devastating for women, because their primary need is for love. Being insulted is usually the most devastating for men because of their primary need for status.

When women choose careers, they often choose nurturing professions, e.g., social work, nursing and teaching, whereas men do not.

Closeness is an end in itself for women, while for men closeness means being "tied down," and is therefore a threat to their freedom of movement. Even at a young age most girls are concerned about maintaining harmony and closeness. Thus, they will often give in or even lie to preserve closeness. They may avoid confronting others or asking questions directly. [Note: this may not apply to teenaged girls and their mothers!] Having to use tricky, indirect "women's wiles" to get what they want is a reality few women manage to escape. Boys and men are more blunt and aggressive about stating their desires.

Thinking types, in particular, tend to see others as adversaries, as potential or actual enemies. If a man has to call in a neighbor to fix the plumbing because he's botched it up, he may feel one-down to that neighbor, turning the neighbor into an adversary. If his wife talks to a friend and shares information she hasn't shared with him, her friend becomes his adversary.

Most men are embarrassed by open displays of affection. Instead they express their need for human contact indirectly in an oppositional manner, for example by disagreeing and criticizing. Men often maintain this oppositional format around women as well, disagreeing, opposing and resisting.

Men relate hierarchically, unconsciously sizing up the competition and responding accordingly. In any encounter with another person, they instinctively jockey for status, evaluating themselves according to where they stand in a hierarchical social order. They are either one-up or one-down. And what they want most is to be one-up.

Girls relate to each other more as peers on an equal footing, so many are uncomfortable with giving orders. With men, they tend to take a one-down position. Some girls are still taught, "Don't be too smart or no one will marry you. Be invisible. Stay in the background." Women are often treated like children: they are expected to take orders, to be in need of protection, to be always available and ready to jump when someone makes a demand and to have no right to set firm limits or state demands.

In view of these differences, how is it possible to have a good marriage? The degree of satisfaction in marriage is directly determined by the extent to which both partners overcome their natural selfishness and focus on giving, not taking. Ideally, as both mature, they stop measuring how much independence or intimacy they are getting, and strive only to be sensitive to the other's needs and to do what will bring joy to the other.

> The third and highest level of peace in marriage...is [when] ...neither of them conceives of himself as a separate entity. Each is as keenly sensitive to the other's needs as if they were his

own. Each is as happy to give to the other as he is to receive
from him. There is no separate sensation of 'I' — there is only
'we.'— IBID., p. 5

Building status

The Sages commanded us that a man should honor his wife
more than himself, and love her as himself... Similarly, they
commanded the woman to honor her husband very much... She
should consider him as a prince or a king, follow his desire, and
remove everything hateful to him.
—RAMBAM, MISHNEH TORAH, 15: 19-20

Unfortunately, there are many obstacles which stand in the way
of achieving this goal of mutual love and respect:

Man's *yetzer ha-ra* drives him to concentrate on his own
physical desires, power and prestige — in other words, to
become a servant of himself rather than God.
— THE RIVER, THE KETTLE AND THE BIRD, p. 11

Overcoming the desire for honor through control and domination
of others is the most difficult of all, for "the desire for honor tugs at
a person's heart more than any of the other longings and desires in
the world" (*The Path of the Just*, p. 171). But when ego becomes
more important than communication and consideration, it threatens
the marriage.

This craving for honor is deeply ingrained in the male psyche. It
can be observed even in young boys. From childhood, they achieve
status in similar ways, such as by giving orders, refusing to take
orders from others and pretending to be indifferent to pain.

Women are lower status in all societies. Unless a man is quite
sensitive and emotionally developed, it's very tempting to put women
down because this provides a quick way of attaining a pleasurable
feeling of superiority.

Status can be attained in many ways, such as by:

1. Criticizing. Put-downs are everyone's favorite way of maintaining a one-up position.

2. Not asking permission. For a man to consult his wife about
whether or not to buy something out of the ordinary is, to the man,

akin to being like a child who has to ask his parent permission first. If she consults him about buying something or going somewhere, she considers this to be evidence that she cares enough to consult him. For a man, it means his wife is not independent, like a child who can't act without first asking permission.

3. Stalling when a request is made or refusing the request. If giving orders is a sign of status, resisting them makes the man feel one-up. A man doesn't want to feel like he can be ordered around by a woman, and he certainly does not want others to get the impression that his wife orders him around.

So, what does he do? When he is asked to do something, he waits until he feels he is doing what she wanted as a result of his own initiative. For example, if she says "Will you please take out the garbage," he'll wait until he feels that taking out the garbage was his idea. So, after she asks, he will say yes, but then wait a good while until it looks like he is doing it of his own accord. But before that happens, she usually asks again. Again, he will say yes, but delay to keep from feeling that he's being ordered around.

This is the source of men's tendency to see women as nags. Because he says yes but delays so that he won't feel one-down, she asks again and again, not understanding what the problem is. And she, feeling put off, is left wondering whether or not the job will ever get done.

> ◊ EXAMPLE: "It was a terribly hot day. I got into the car and asked my husband to turn on the air conditioner. He said, 'In a few minutes,' and kept driving. I asked again, and he said, 'Soon.' All the grief of my marriage surfaced in that moment. I was so deeply, gravely wounded by his response that I felt that if I didn't have three kids in the back seat, I would have thrown myself out of the car. Life just didn't seem worth living."

A similar situation occurs when children become teenagers and their drive for independence from their parents outweighs their drive for closeness with them. Many teenagers resist taking orders from their parents and put their parents down in order to achieve a sense of independence and status.

4. Not saying where he's going. He doesn't want to be hemmed in by having to report his whereabouts. He wants to protect his one-up

position by acting as if he's independent.

5. Not asking for help. Asking for help or advice is seen as a lack of independence and as synonymous with incompetence and insecurity. Many men will drive around for quite a while looking for a street rather than risk feeling one-down by asking for directions. Thinking types resist going to doctors, no matter how badly they feel, and refuse to see marital therapists no matter how bad the marriage is. Women feel comfortable seeking help and showing gratitude for it.

> ◊ EXAMPLE: "I was sure that something my husband told me was not *halachically* correct. So I told him that I wanted to call our *rav*, but he got angry. I called when he left, and it turned out that my husband was wrong. I told him when he came home, and he had a fit!"

6. Not giving or accepting sympathy. Men often feel one-down when others express sympathy. Men and women often have opposite interpretations of the same sentence. For example, if a wife says to her husband, "I'm sorry things didn't work out," she feels as if she's being sympathetic, while he senses condescension, that she is looking down on him and thinking, The poor jerk. On the other hand, she would like very much for him to express such sympathy when things don't work out for her. She would not hear a metamessage of "you're a failure" if he would express sympathy.

7. Being the problem-solver and the advice-giver. Both put the man in the position of being one-up. The advice-giver is more knowledgeable, reasonable and in control. When a woman expresses pain, she usually wants reassurance, support and validation. However, he is likely to give advice instead, thereby taking a one-up position.

For example, a woman said to her husband, "I hate my big nose." What she wanted was reassurance that he loved her despite her nose or that he thought she was beautiful. However, what he said was, "Maybe you'd like to ask a *rav* if you can get a nose job." She got upset because to her, his response confirmed to her that he thought she was ugly. He didn't understand why she burst into tears. He was relating to her statement as a request for a solution. She, however, heard a metamessage saying "I think you're ugly." He completely denied having this metamessage in mind and insisted that he was merely providing a solution.

Women are much more attuned to metamessages having to do with a threat to their sense of closeness, while men are more attuned to metamessages having to do with loss of status.

8. Displaying expertise. Giving advice also provides a pleasurable sense of superiority. Men's talk is often aimed at impressing others. Being able to display their achievements and skills is a way of feeling one-up. Women, on the other hand, tend to play down expertise in order to make men feel one-up.

For example, a woman asked the clerk in a camera store how to work her VCR. The clerk kept saying things like, "It's really simple," while speaking too quickly and giving so much information in such a short period of time that she felt totally confused. She left feeling like an idiot. The clerk's feeling of superiority was enhanced when she did not understand what he was saying! Sadly, many teachers do the same thing. They give low marks to reinforce their own feeling of being one-up, to the detriment of their students.

When encountering a man with a strong status problem, a woman would be better off asking another woman to explain the equipment to her.

9. Arguing. Very often, a woman will make a suggestion to go somewhere, buy something, or make some change, and the husband will shoot it down by saying, "It's not needed," or "It's too expensive," etc. What women don't realize is that this is simply an opening bid in a negotiation and not necessarily a final answer. Instead of walking away feeling crushed, she should make some kind of counter-bid to keep the negotiations going. For example, she might say, "Please think about it for a day and perhaps you'll come up with a different answer." Or, "That's one opinion. Does my opinion count in your eyes?"

10. Ridiculing or dismissing others' troubles as trivial and insignificant. Telling people "it's nothing" is a very one-up act. Studies have shown that doctors, too, tend to take women's complaints less seriously than men's.

Laughing when others are in pain is a sure way to achieve distance and dominance — and destroy the possibility of closeness.

11. Not giving reasons for their decisions or demands. Men give commands they expect to be followed without their having to explain

why. Women often tack on some explanatory statement. For example, "Brush your teeth so you won't get cavities," or "Drink your milk so you'll have strong bones." However, for men, giving reasons is like having to account for their decisions, a one-down position!

> ◊ EXAMPLE: "I picked a warm, Feeling dentist because he gives me a running account of what he's doing, how long it will take, how things are going, etc. I love getting feedback. But when I had to have root canal treatment, he sent me to his Thinking partner, who worked on me for an hour and a half without one word of feedback! I hope I never have to go to him again!"

> ◊ EXAMPLE: "I had my learning-disabled son evaluated by a stern, Thinking-type woman who made her recommendations in a total of three minutes. When I asked for more information as to how to implement her recommendations, she got very upset. I just wanted information! But she viewed me as challenging her authority. I really tried to be very submissive and respectful, but she couldn't take being questioned. She wanted me to do everything she told me to do without understanding why. I walked out of her office in tears. I then had to do all the testing over again with a warm, sympathetic man who gave me all the information I needed to understand my son's problems."

12. Not apologizing and not taking the blame. Men have more trouble admitting to being wrong. Men don't apologize as much because that makes them feel one-down. Women apologize much more than men, even if they've done nothing wrong!

For example, a man who had been very critical of his wife or who consistently ridiculed her when she expressed her feelings, could not understand why she became distant and depressed. Rather than apologize and face what he had done to push her away, he justified himself by saying, "She's just crazy."

Hurt people are more insecure

The more insecure a man is, the more likely he is to become obsessed with making others respect him. He sees disrespect in the most minor disagreement or lack of obedience and gets enraged in order to make himself feel in control again. In contrast, the more insecure a woman is, the more obsessed she tends to be with pleasing others and winning their approval. She fears disapproval and abandonment, and tries to reestablish closeness.

Insecurity can stem from numerous sources: verbally abusive parents, parental neglect, failure to achieve in school, physical handicaps which were the source of ridicule when the person was young, or major catastrophes such as death or divorce. Those coming from such a background have a need to overcontrol the environment because they felt so helpless and out-of-control as children. Knowing this fact can help others be more compassionate to those with obsessions and compulsions.

Building distance

According to Deborah Tannen's book, *You Just Don't Understand*, men's talk is "report talk" while women's talk is mainly "rapport talk." Men talk for a purpose: to get information, to impress others, to hold center stage and to maintain their status. Women talk as an end it itself, to create closeness.

Men who fear intimacy will maintain distance in the following ways:

1. Not listening. Many men believe women should be seen and not heard. Any amount of talk by a woman will seem like too much to such a man. When women do talk, men perceive them as talking more than they actually do. Some completely ignore what their wives tell them. Others devalue what they say, no matter what is said.

> ◊ EXAMPLE: "I had waited the whole year for the few weeks my husband has off from *yeshivah* after Tisha b'Av, when I thought my husband and I would have time to talk. The whole year I try not to bother him so that he can devote himself to learning. Well, the time came for a vacation, but there wasn't any talk. My husband was willing for us to go places together, but he was so uncomfortable whenever I tried to talk to him. I just felt like crying all the time from loneliness."

Partly, this gap is due to the fact that boys' relationships are held together primarily by activities. They don't want to talk, they want to do something together. For girls, what holds relationships together is sharing feelings. For women, sharing is an end in itself. Men want to do something: learn, fix things, exchange information, etc.

◊ EXAMPLE: "I'm a Feeling type with a very Thinking-type wife. Whenever I wanted to talk to her, she'd say, 'Go learn. Talking is a waste of time.' It was only after she learned about the different personality types that she realized that I have a legitimate need to share. Since then, she listens a little more, but she still tends to get impatient after what seems to me to be a short time. I get the feeling that she looks down on me for having this need.

◊ EXAMPLE: "I asked my husband, who is an extremely anti-emotional Thinking type, to take care of things at the bank because we're overdrawn. The sentence took perhaps three seconds, but he answered, 'Don't lecture me.' For years, I've tried to keep my sentences down to eight words or less, because more than eight words sounds like a lecture to him. I find him to be extreme, but I go along with it because I want to keep up the communication, limited as it is."

2. Not showing feelings. Almost universally, the feeling man is seen as weak and unmanly. Observe how a young boy will cry if he receives a blow at home, even a minor one. The same boy receiving a far more serious blow will stoically keep his emotions to himself if other boys are around.

Women create closeness by sharing secrets, especially their troubles. This is evidence of friendship. Women who don't share details about their personal lives are often seen as cold and arrogant. To men, telling secrets means exposing their weaknesses. To admit to having a problem is to be one-down, incompetent, inferior, weak and stupid. A man feels as though his privacy has been invaded. Having one's privacy invaded is not always as threatening to women. They are able to see it as the price they have to pay for gaining closeness.

Thus, the proverbial complaint of women, that "it's like pulling teeth to get him to talk," has much truth to it.

A man spends his life either dismissing his feelings as unimportant, or keeping them to himself. Silent men are seen as powerful, deep and having tremendous self-control. Unfortunately, silence makes women feel like their husbands are treating them like strangers. Men don't realize that silence is far more painful than anything else they can do to their wives. Women see this "emotional stinginess," as though their husbands are purposely withholding closeness in order to hurt them.

> ◊ EXAMPLE: "Our son was having a lot of difficulties in school. He was ten and still not reading or concentrating. He was always getting kicked out of class. I kept begging my husband to let me take him to a specialist in learning disabilities, but he kept saying, 'There's nothing wrong with the kid. He's just lazy and stubborn!' I finally had to borrow money to go."

> ◊ EXAMPLE: "If the state of our marriage could be compared to the state of a physical body, then we have terminal cancer of the relationship! But my husband won't think of going to a therapist!"

Feeling types can easily keep up a kind of stream of consciousness monologue to their friends about what they are thinking and feeling throughout the day. Men rarely do this. They don't tell their fleeting thoughts or relate the feelings they experience throughout the day, because they don't seem important to them.

> ◊ EXAMPLE: "A friend told me that my husband's *chavrutha* was getting married. I asked my husband why he hadn't told me and he said that it hadn't seemed important."

3. Calling a woman over-emotional implies that she has nothing to be emotional about, and therefore that she is irrational, stupid, out-of-control and crazy. With that metamessage in the air, it's no wonder that a woman gets even more emotional when told that she shouldn't be!

The tendency to not take women seriously is part of men's general tendency to look down on any display of emotion as a sign of stupidity, weakness and incompetency.

> ◊ EXAMPLE: "I used to get even more hysterical when my husband would tell me, 'You're just being hysterical.' Those words made me feel like killing him or myself! Then I began to realize that my strong emotional response frightened him, made him fear that maybe I was going to go off the deep end one day. With effort, I learned to mask my external response so that he wouldn't lose

confidence in me. Now, when I'm feeling out of control, I keep my mouth shut until the strong initial impact fades, or I leave the room so he won't pick up on the emotionalism which I radiate! I no longer put myself down for not being unflappable. That's not the portion God gave. My emotions don't make me inferior or crazy — it just means I have to be more self-disciplined."

4. Talking about impersonal, not personal matters. When Observant men get together, they generally talk about religion, politics or business — all impersonal subjects. A woman feels loved when her husband shares personal details of his life and asks for personal details of her life. This is how women feel close. In fact, when a woman does not have problems to share with a friend, she may feel distant from her.

When a woman wants to establish status and distance, she does so by consciously not sharing personal details of her life.

Men don't think they have to work at marriage or do anything to reinforce closeness. They think that the very fact that they are present in the home is enough to get this message across. If a husband doesn't remember birthdays or anniversaries or even what color eyes his wife has, it's not that he doesn't care. It's just that he's not focused on the intimate, personal aspects of the relationship.

◊ EXAMPLE: "When my children are at camp, I write them chatty letters. My husband tells me to write at the end of the letter, 'Hi from your dad.' If he does write anything, it's usually to tell them to be sure to bring home the insurance forms from the hospital if a child had an accident, or to make sure to keep a copy of the amount spent and to bring back whatever money is left over."

◊ EXAMPLE: "I was very unhappy in my marriage and my husband wouldn't see anyone with me. So I finally went myself. When I told the therapist that my husband never tells me he loves me, he suggested that I tell my husband that I need to hear these words. Well, I told my husband and he said, 'But I told you last year that I loved you.' I had to explain why it wasn't enough."

Women often focus on what they perceive to be a personal metamessage, while men tend to focus on the impersonal message. For example, the husband very innocently relays an impersonal message such as, "There's too much salt in the soup," or "I'd like to have my shirts ironed instead of tumbled dry." The wife then bursts into tears because she hears a personal metamessage of failure and rejection. She'll tearfully say, "You think I'm totally incompetent. You don't love me." He says, "I don't know what you're so upset about. I just don't like so much salt in my soup," or "I just like the feel of ironed shirts."

◊ EXAMPLE: "When my husband asked if there was any mayonnaise in the house, I said, 'No, I forgot to buy it.' Inside, I was sure he was thinking, She must be totally incompetent. So I checked it out and asked, 'When I said there was no mayonnaise, were you implying that I'm incompetent?' And, surprised, he replied, 'Absolutely not! I can use margarine. It really doesn't matter.' I was so relieved."

To ask questions is, like the wise son at the Pesach *Seder*, a sign of caring. When women ask about the details of other people's personal lives, it is a way of showing they care and are involved. Men don't usually want to hear a running account of their wives' feelings. In fact, it may disgust them. When a man asks how your day was, he'd probably prefer a general reply of *"baruch Hashem."*

◊ EXAMPLE: "A distant cousin of my husband's visited us. She is a Thinking-type lawyer. For two hours I racked my brain trying to think of questions to ask about her and her work, to which she gave only brief replies. She never even asked me anything about myself. It was obvious that she was in total control, maintaining an impersonal distance by not asking about me. I got a headache from the strain!"

◊ EXAMPLE: "My husband has to travel overseas two or three times a year for two or three weeks at a time. When he comes back and I ask him how things were, he usually says, 'Fine.' That's all. If I go away to visit my family, he never asks me what went on there. During the first few years of our marriage, it used to drive me crazy that he never asked any details about my life. I just wanted to die most of the time because I felt so unloved. Although I realize that this impersonal way of relating is common, I've never gotten used to it. It's still painful after thirty years."

◊ EXAMPLE: "When my doctor suspected I had a possible malignancy, he took further tests and said I'd have the results in two weeks. I was terrified. Since my husband doesn't like me to talk, I told him only briefly that there was a slight suspicion and when I'd have the results. Well, I lived on pins and needles waiting for that day to come around. When the doctor called to say that everything was fine, I was so relieved. Just as a kind of test, I decided not to say anything and see if my husband would bring up the subject. He didn't. Days passed and he didn't mention it. I felt overwhelmed with doubts about him and our relationship. When I finally broke down and told him how unloved and scared I felt, he was shocked. Tearfully, he told me he loved me very much but didn't know how to show his concern. I suddenly realized the depth of his feelings for me. That was a turning point in our lives and since then we have become closer."

5. Not listening. The role of listener may feel to many like being forced to assume a one-down position. To listen to someone who rates a lower status (i.e., female) may make many men feel like they are lowering their own status position, just as people don't listen to their servants.

◊ EXAMPLE: "When my husband wants to talk, I have to listen with rapt attention. At first, some of what he tells me is interesting. But after a while, I start to get bored. The more impersonal his talk becomes, the more trapped and oppressed I feel. Often, our conversations somehow and mysteriously turn into lectures by him."

◊ EXAMPLE: "I'm from a family of four girls and three boys. I feel like I grew up invisible. The boys got the attention. Whatever they said was important. I was happy when I married a man who appreciates my intelligence and encourages me to study."

It makes sense that if a man sees his wife as subordinate, then to talk to her or listen to her would put them on an even par. If he thinks of her as weak and incompetent, then only another weak and incompetent person would take her seriously.

Women show that they are listening by keeping up a running feedback support system during a conversation. They'll say "yeah," "that's right," "mmm, uh-uh" far more than men. Women smile more and respond more positively and enthusiastically by agreeing, laughing or saying words of sympathy. Women expect the listener to be active, to show signs of interest and support. Men who don't respond in this way are perceived of as being uncaring. However, a man may be listening when he seems not to be.

> ◊ EXAMPLE: "As a joke, I sometimes take my husband's pulse when I'm talking to him, and say, 'Are you still alive?'"

If asked to give more signs of support, a man may feel as though he is being asked to aid someone who is defective in some way. Don't be ashamed of your needs; it'll help him to grow.

Men dominate conversations by talking more, interrupting more, sidetracking, diverting and controlling the topic, and changing the topic. Women generally talk about what the man wants to talk about. He also wants to control when the conversation begins and when it ends.

The only solution to this problem is for men to become conscious of their need to become more sensitive, more empathic, and less concerned with status and honor.

[Much of the information in this chapter was taken from *You Just Don't Understand*, by Deborah Tannen.]

Some helpful hints for women

Don't judge harshly.

1. Be honest about your feelings from the beginning of the marriage. If you lie and withhold information because you think it's not nice to speak up or that if he loved you he'd know what you wanted without you having to say it directly, you'll end up hurting the marriage. Men are not mind readers. Ask directly for what you want; if you can state your need calmly and clearly, and your husband is the type of person who does want to have a healthy relationship, he will respond appropriately. If he doesn't care, you will have to resort to more indirect tactics.

2. First try the direct approach of stating your needs calmly and distinctly. If that doesn't work, then fight for your rights — in an assertive, non-hostile manner. Don't argue aggressively. Men fear aggressive, argumentative women, for they threaten their sense of power, status and self-esteem. Whenever appropriate, write notes when you want your husband to do something. That might lessen his

feelings of being nagged or hemmed in. If you keep reaching impasses, get counseling, see a *rav*, or let him know in some other way that your needs are legitimate and need to be respected. Even so, if he is emotionally disturbed, he may not care how you feel.

3. If you really need something, don't take your husband's initial no as a final no. The initial no is simply the opening bid in a negotiation process. When you need to have a picture hung, a shelf put up, the heat turned on or help with a child, first try to identify and allay his fears about his possible loss of freedom and status if he complies with your request, and ask for suggestions as to how he would solve the problem. Always try to work things out in a peaceful atmosphere by validating his needs as well as your own.

(In extreme situations, you may have to go to a *rav* to make him fulfill his obligation to provide even minimum heat, food and clothing. However, if your husband is highly emotionally disturbed, you won't be able to work things out with him and he will probably refuse to see a *rav*.)

You might also run into opposition when you express a desire to take a class or go to work. He may put up incredible resistance because he wants total control over you. If so, you will have to fight for your right to do things which bring you fulfillment. Otherwise you, like many women, will end up very depressed.

4. Speaking of negotiating, be aware that women do something similar. When she says, "I'm so depressed, I could just die," this is her opening bid in the process of becoming closer. She probably doesn't want to commit suicide. She simply wants to feel that someone cares by hearing their words of sympathy and support. If your spouse consistently ridicules you or ignores you when you try to talk, you can tell him that all you need is a few seconds of sympathy once in a while, and that it is an important mitzvah to provide this compassion.

If you are a strong Feeling type, explain to your husband that when you complain or say you are depressed, it doesn't necessarily mean that you're headed for an imminent nervous breakdown. You are not trying to frighten him, manipulate him or prevent him from being independent and doing what he wants to do. You just want to feel cared about by getting him to show a personal interest in you. If he is a withdrawn, cold type, however, you may not achieve the feeling of being cared about in this personal way that you want.

5. Practice being in a non-hostile assertive mode so that you can see what it feels like.

> ◊ EXAMPLE: "We have one car and I rarely get to use it. I wanted to prove I loved my husband by being nice and accommodating. I'd get resentful and blow up at him, instead of stating what I wanted clearly. I've finally learned to negotiate, and either give in or stand firm depending on how badly I need something."

> ◊ EXAMPLE: "My four boys were fighting. It was the end of the day and I had no more strength to deal with them. I thought to myself, Okay, let them just tear the place down. I give up! But then I thought of how my husband would respond if he were there. I went into his tough mode and started giving orders just like he does. I firmly instructed one to go to his room, another to go to my room, a third to the kitchen and a fourth to the laundry room. I told each one what to do in each room. I made myself impervious to all their tears and entreaties, and remained insistent. When I need it, it's important to act this way. My image of myself as a fragile, hot-house orchid will just have to go if I'm going to bring these kids up properly. At other times, I can switch to a less demanding mode."

6. Many men want less emotional intimacy than women, especially if they are Thinking types. If you have a strong need for emotional warmth and intimacy, you will feel very lonely and you'll definitely need fulfilling outside activities.

However, don't assume that a Thinking husband doesn't care. Most men do care very deeply, but are simply unable to express their feelings. Let him know that it is to his benifit to learn to express love in words because this develops him spiritually, as a person who can also express love for God.

If your husband fits the above description, believe it or not, you have an average marriage. Your husband is not deliberately trying to hurt you. The angrier you become and the more you pressure him to relate, the less he will be able to develop this side of himself.

7. If your husband is an emotionally aloof type, use the "loving, yet silent treatment" as opposed to the "hostile silent treatment." That is, wait for him to take the initiative in communication and don't flood him with a barrage of accusations. Make the interchange

pleasant and endorse him happily for sharing. Over the years, with loving appreciation for his good qualities and patience, he may develop a desire for more contact.

8. Avoid the aggravating spiral by which your response to your husband's withdrawal provokes you to be more clingy or angry. For example, when your husband withdraws and your alarm goes off signaling a threat to intimacy, don't try to get closer because that will aggravate his fear of losing independence and cause him to pull away even more. Let go. He's not depriving you of closeness on purpose. He's scared. Be patient. Your effort to be joyful, loving and self-disciplined creates the environment in which growth may take place.

9. Realize that Thinking types may see conflict as a sign of caring. Although Feeling types want harmony and closeness, Thinking types enjoy teasing and arguing. It's not only pleasurable, to them it's evidence of involvement, though it's probably not what you envisioned when you thought about a loving relationship!

10. Don't allow yourself to be physically or verbally abused in the hope that this will make your husband love you more or to prove to him that your love for him is so unconditional that you'll do anything. If your husband isolates you from family and friends, criticizes you constantly or is physically violent, he has a severe personality disturbance which may not change radically. Such men can be taught to restrain their aggressive tendencies only if they really want to fight this addiction. They rarely become truly loving. Nor can you expect to love them as they are. My book *Living With Difficult People* can provide suggestions as to how to cope with this painful situation.

11. Let your husband know that he doesn't have to prove himself or impress you, that you love him as he is, even though you want him to improve his level of emotional sensitivity. In most cases, I have seen tremendous improvement over the years if the woman demonstrates positive *middoth* while insisting on considerate behavior. It turned out that these husbands saw this greater openness and sensitivity as a gift from their wives.

12. Sensitize your Thinking-type children so that they will want to share with their future spouses. Feeling-type (both male and female) children naturally want to share feelings with you. However, you will need to take extra time to sensitize your Thinking types so

that they do not grow up to be cold and impersonal. One way to do this is to set aside a few minutes for caring communication each night before they go to bed. If they don't know what to talk about, ask the best-worst questions (i.e., "What was the best thing that happened today and what was the worst thing that happened today?"). Let them experience pleasure in the exchange of personal information. It will become a lifelong habit. In so doing, they will develop positive feelings about sharing emotions and their Feeling side will be strong enough to overcome their natural tendency toward noncommunicativeness.

God created men and women to be different. He gave us different sensitivities and different tasks. See these differences as offering opportunities to develop the gifts of greater understanding and compassion.

8 | The Gift of the Marital Midbar: Creating Your Own Oasis

And Adam said, "This is now bone of my bones, and flesh of my flesh."

— BERESHITH 2:23

Adam's expression of supreme oneness is every normal person's dream — to feel at one with someone who cares about you so deeply that you are as precious to him as he is to himself. Unfortunately, many couples do not achieve this ideal. Only a minority describe their marriages as the ideal "best friend relationship." For some, marriage may feel like a lonely *midbar*, a desert without nourishment, protection or closeness.

Sometimes this is due to simple incompatibility — two basically good people who are so different that they cannot understand the others' needs or feelings. But most involve one seriously troubled partner who more than likely represents one of the following categories:

(1) Distancers: these spouses are withdrawn, secretive, suspicious, uncommunicative, rigid and basically cold.

(2) Dominators: these spouses are hot tempered, tyrannical, overly controlling and sometimes violently abusive.

(3) Clingers: these spouses are weak, passive, unambitious and dependent.

Many people have a combination of all three categories, manifesting all of the above negative traits at different times. Many have severe mental problems. They may be paranoid, passive-aggressive, phobic, sociopathic, obsessive-compulsive, manic-depressive or emotionally autistic.

While disturbed people have moments of normalcy, they are incapable of sustaining loving bonds of mutual respect on a consistent basis and tend to be chronically unhappy and hypercritical. In most cases, they deny that they have a problem and blame their spouses for their unhappiness. Most refuse counseling. Any attempt to get them to admit to a problem usually ends with vehement denial and often an intensification of their destructive behavior.

To live with a disturbed person means prolonged agony which always involves abuse, both subtle and obvious.

◊ EXAMPLE: "My wife has only one interest — money. She thinks that because I don't have a big salary, I'm nothing. I don't get beaten physically, but I feel whipped by her angry looks and critical remarks. She is always annoyed with me, as though I am a bothersome insect. This is slow torture."

Unloved women may see themselves as married widows.

◊ EXAMPLE: "There is only one woman in my husband's life, and that's his mother, who hated me even before I married her son. She makes all our decisions including what to buy, what to eat, what to name our children, and where we must spend the holidays. He is so passive and weak that he agrees. She kept telling my husband that I'm crazy. Now no matter what I say, he tells me that it's because I'm nuts. I don't have a husband or a marriage. I am totally alone."

◊ EXAMPLE: "Life is torture with an abusive person. The children are either bullies like him or passive and depressed like me. They treat me with the same disrespect that he shows me, criticizing and ridiculing me constantly. It's so hard to go on."

◊ EXAMPLE: "How does a woman stay sane with a man who won't study, won't go to work, won't communicate and won't help? I don't know how long I can take this! He can listen to the news or drive around for hours. When I try to talk to him about how serious our money problems are, he walks away. He's completely wrapped up in his own world."

The plight of the unloved wife is mentioned more than once in the Torah. It is even the source of a special law: "If a man has two wives, one beloved and the other hated...if the firstborn be hers that was hated...[that son] shall...be given a double inheritance" (*Devarim* 21:15-17).

Being hated is a reality which many people must live with. Just as some people must live with physical handicaps, others must live with people who have serious spiritual handicaps, and being in a constant state of resentment is the greatest handicap of all.

Although there is nothing in the Torah about the hated husband, this is a reality which many men face as well.

Divorce or stay?

Obviously, the thought of divorce arises often in the minds of those suffering with an emotionaly disturbed mate. They may continually weigh this option, especially after an abusive incident. What is best for the children, for you?

The mother, in the majority of cases, is afraid to leave an abusive man because of the likelihood of impoverishment, and because after years of abuse, she herself is likely to be so anxiety-ridden and depressed that she does not believe she can manage alone.

Once there are children, there is no such thing as a complete divorce because parents must consult each other about support payments, visits, holidays, etc. The rancor and bitterness don't end with a *get*, if one is lucky enough to get one. Court battles, custody battles and financial battles all continue to make life *gehinnom*. On visitation days, you worry about the children being hurt or having their minds poisoned by your spouse saying terrible things about you. When the children return after a visitation, they may be hostile and have trouble readjusting to you.

It is also humiliating and frightening to put your life in the hands of the courts. It is the abusive parent who usually has the money to hire the best lawyer. Abusive people are excellent liars, and judges often believe the lies. Custody may be given to an abusive parent. In court, it is the abusive parent who is apt to be smiling calmly and confidently while the normal parent is nervous and distraught. If the normal parent has been to a therapist for help, s/he may be seen as the crazy one while the one who refused to go is seen as normal. Blackmail of wives over a *get* is common; she may be required to pay an outrageous sum in order to obtain it.

Is it better to live in a home full of hatred and conflict or in a single-parent home which is calm and safe? Children tend to imitate the disturbed parent's worst traits. Therefore, if a parent is physically abusive, it is far better to protect the children by getting as far away as possible. Otherwise, they will become abusive themselves.

The following symptoms are manifest after a divorce, or after years of abuse or seeing one's parents fighting all the time prior to the divorce:

(1) There is an increase in misbehavior. If children have seen abuse in the home, they have learned that this is normal and acceptable behavior. Abuse makes children feel terribly helpless and worthless.To compensate, they may try to prove that they are powerful and cover their hurt and anxiety by misbehaving or engaging in anti-social behavior, such as stealing, torturing animals, hurting younger children, being truant from school, destroying public property, etc.

(2) They entertain reconciliation fantasies, hoping the parents will get back together. They may long for the noncustodial parent, and may idealize him, seeing him as really good and loving despite all that happened.

(3) They tend to become more anxious and guilt-ridden. Young children blame themselves when their parents divorce, assuming "they got divorced because I was bad." They may feel guilty for not having been able to prevent the divorce and for not being able to bring the parents back together.

(4) They may be consumed with worry over the distressed parent. They feel responsible for their parents' unhappiness and feel guilty if either of the parents is depressed.

(5) They also fear that their parents will "divorce" them, too. They are afraid to form attachments, for fear that everyone will eventually abandon them as well. They are more cynical about relationships, and either avoid commitments or bond superficially.

(6) They tend to regress in behavior, becoming more clingy and demanding of reassurance.

(7) Children ages 6 to 12 often fall behind in school for at least the first year following the separation.

(8) They may be hostile toward the custodial parent for not doing more to keep the marriage together. Children's anger most often is

directed at the mother. They blame her for not having done more to make things work. If the father was abusive, they blame her, not the father, for not having protected them.

(9) A chaotic, undisciplined home atmosphere produces children without internal discipline, structure and stability. This can be seen in disorderliness, inability to follow through on tasks, lack of pre-planning, impulsivity, procrastination, etc. Or, they may become compulsive about external order to overcompensate for their sense of internal chaos and lack of control.

(10) If a parent remarries, they may refuse to shift their loyalties to the step-parent and do everything to break up the new marriage and bring the original parents back together.

(11) They are likely to feel defective and unlovable.

Symptoms may be worse if:

(1) There is no contact with the noncustodial parent.

(2) There are no siblings.

(3) The parents use the child to get back at each other. The higher the level of hostility between the divorced couple, the more problems the children have.

(Taken from *Journal of Child Psychology and Psychiatry, Journal of Development and Behavior Paediatrics,* and *Ontario Medical Review.*)

When a spouse is mentally ill, the abuse may not stop after the divorce. Abusive people will continue with attempts to hurt their ex-partners emotionally and financially. This is why it is so important to be physically distant from an abusive person after a divorce.

Certainly, if the custodial parent has a positive attitude and a decent income, the children are better off away — far away — from the abusive parent. In sum, once one has had children with an emotionally disturbed person, the bonds with that person can never be cut completely. Whether one stays married or gets divorced, there are many difficulties to be overcome. You alone can decide if it is more harmful to stay than to leave. The decision is never easy.

Keeping your spirit alive and staying sane

Whether you choose to remain with your spouse or not, there is inevitably some degree of physical and psychological damage to you and your children. Stress-related illnesses are common. Even worse is the erosion of your spirit. If you live with a violent person, you may become violent yourself. If you live with someone who is emotionally repressed and uncommunicative, you may find yourself becoming more and more withdrawn as the years go on.

People will tell you: "Make an independent life for yourself," or "Don't let his/her behavior bother you," but this advice does not tell a spouse how to deal with the effects of emotional abuse on oneself and one's children. It does not answer the question, "What do I do with the pain of wanting to love and be loved by my spouse?"

It is incredibly difficult to create an oasis of love, joy and meaning in the midst of pain.

You may never change your spouse, but you can be the kind of person who contributes to the world despite adversity. To do so, you must focus on the gifts which the marital *midbar* can offer:

(1) The gift of love. Love is sanity. You may never feel love for your spouse, in fact, you may feel profound disgust and hatred. For your own sake, you must work to at least achieve some level of acceptance of the other person, unless he or she is violently abusive. The more abusive the person is, the harder you have to work to avoid drowning in despair.

Ultimately, happiness is determined by the degree to which you devote yourself to Torah, *avodah* and lovingkindness (*Avoth* 1:2), all of which can be done at any time, in any place. In other words, you must get very busy physically and become very disciplined mentally.

No person or activity can ever substitute for the lack of a loving partner. But you can find ways to express love to others. You can express love toward God, your children, friends, family members, etc. Don't try to love an abusive person! The loving thing to do is to keep your distance!

> ◊ EXAMPLE: "I went to numerous therapists until I finally realized that there's only one thing to do: stay busy! When I feel most hopeless, that's when I force myself to give to others and fight my tendency to withdraw in despair. When I feel unloved, I find ways to make others feel loved. When I feel most unhappy, I try to make others feel happy. Sometimes I feel that I have lost it, that my heart has dried up and withered like an unwatered plant. But then I give to someone and I see that my spirit has not died."

(2) The gift of gratefulness. This is best done by playing the *Neshamah* Game. To do this, you state your case and then listen for the response from your own inner voice of wisdom. Be willing to listen for the answers which will come from the depths of your own soul. These are the most satisfying. From within yourself, you will hear what you need to hear at this time in your life, taking into account your particular personality, needs and present level of awareness. No one can do this for you as well as you can. (Note: it is helpful for someone else to play you and plead for understanding from the Godly part of yourself.) For example:

You: "Tell me, *neshamah*, why do I have to suffer this torture? All I've wanted from my spouse is to be loved. But what I've gotten is indifference and cruelty. It's not fair! I'm so miserable! I hate my life."

The following answers were given by people who are struggling to survive in loveless marriages:

(A) "You've been to an endless variety of therapists and advisors, hoping for miracles. You needed this spouse so that you would learn to stop waiting for others to change and so that you would turn your attention to developing your inner resources. You're the one who must change and grow."

(B) "It's easy to be loving and joyful when things are going your way. But if you can remain loving and joyful in the midst of so much pain, your *neshamah* rises to a much higher level."

(C) "All your life, you've depended on people and things to make you happy. You needed this particular spouse so that you would finally realize that the source of happiness is within yourself. You've learned to create an atmosphere of joy independent of external circumstances. The lesson has been painful, but it was the only way to help you gain this awareness. Realize that it was God's love for you which created this situation so that you would be forced to grow in this way."

(D) "You would never have understood the meaning of unconditional love if you had married the perfect spouse. You've learned the hard way to be accepting of people as they are and realize the limitations of your control over others. You've learned the hard way what it means to love another person only for the sake of loving, without expectations or demands."

(E) "Without this pain, you would have gone through this lifetime without a shred of sensitivity. You would not have turned to God for help. You would not have become so giving. Of course, you'll protest that you'd be far more giving if you had a loving spouse, but the truth is that you might be just as selfish and self-preoccupied, with little compassion for those suffering from emotional distress. Now you are a much more understanding and compassionate person. Many people do things for others out of a natural desire to give. But you needed to be forced to run around doing things for others because of your pain, which is something you would never have done if you'd been happy."

◊ EXAMPLE: "For years, I was angry and depressed, thinking that God had deprived me of the thing I wanted most in order to punish me. When I played the *Neshamah* Game, I realized that God brought me this particular mate to force me to turn to Him. It was out of love that this happened. This realization brought me a sense of inner peace and joy, which eventually affected everyone in a positive way, including my spouse."

◊ EXAMPLE: "The realization that I was in a loveless marriage was devastating until I started taking gratefulness seriously. Every day, I forced myself to write down the things I had to be grateful for. I realized that only by writing things down would I make a real impression on my brain. I wrote that I was grateful that I could make a meal for my children or help them with their homework, grateful for being able to help someone or appreciate a flower. I started noticing little things, like a child's smile or freshly laundered clothing. Gratefulness is the only thing that keeps a person from being bitter. When I get sad, I read my Gratefulness Notebook and that raises my spirits again."

◊ EXAMPLE: "My wife is very abusive, yelling at me frequently and even sometimes throwing things at me. I used to be insanely jealous of people with warm wives and normal lives. But over the years, I've made peace with the fact that no one can have another person's reality. It's futile to be envious. It's like rejecting God when you reject the portion He's given you (*Shemoth* 20:14). I used to get very depressed until I saw this situation as a gift which enables me to grow spiritually by demonstrating self-control and not responding to her in kind."

(3) The gift of letting go of the compulsion to control.

◊ EXAMPLE: "I was constantly trying to rescue, heal, change and control my spouse to get the closeness and approval I wanted so desperately. I dragged him to therapists and gave him articles and books to read in the hope that he would become more insightful. It took me years to stop this co-dependent craziness and overcome my compulsion for closeness. Once I stopped trying to force communication, I felt much more sane! Now, I simply try to keep the atmosphere as polite as possible. And when he begins to get nervous, I get very quiet and don't talk. I just try to get the children out of the house. I talk to God all the time, asking for His help to get me though the day without anger or bitterness."

(4) The gift of accepting the grief.

◊ EXAMPLE: "I see myself as belonging to a special, unofficial club of people married to disturbed spouses. Only those who have been through this can understand the pain I'm in. For a long time, I thought my sorrow was not legitimate. After all, I seem to be healthy and have healthy children, so what do I have to be sad about? But this is a legitimate pain. It's like being paralyzed in a part of your body. My grief is reignited every time I see that angry, sour face or hear those same critical remarks or see the children being insulted or abused. I used to think I'd get over the pain, now I realize that I simply have to live with the heartbreak and go on with my life and my own *tikkun*."

(5) The gift of mental and physical discipline.

◊ EXAMPLE: "Being in an abusive situation is very debilitating, even if it's verbal abuse. To be told day in and day out that I'm incompetent and stupid made me violent and hysterical. I lost my will to live and was depressed for a long time until I began to build some sense of self-control and self-esteem by becoming an exercise teacher. Exercise not only pulls me out of the dumps, but it helps the other women in my classes as well. They walk in with pinched faces and slumped shoulders and walk out with a feeling of pride. It's really true that when you force yourself to do something positive with your muscles, your brain becomes more positive as well! It's your muscles that teach your brain that you can go on. As I became more disciplined with my body, I also became more disciplined in my thinking. Self-discipline has brought me more self-respect."

(6) The gift of joy.

◊ EXAMPLE: "I used to obsess constantly about my marriage until I just wanted to die all the time. I felt like a hostage held by terrorists, terrorized day and night and not able to cry out because no one would care. I felt totally alone in the world and emotionally deadened. Then I met a woman who was also in an abusive marriage. She taught me ways to keep my spirit alive by taking me to classes and folk dancing. She calls this her 'joy therapy.' She says two hours of dancing is better than all the therapists she's been to. Now, when I start sinking into rage or despair, I divert my attention and ask myself, What would make me happy this very second? Abusive people want their mates to be stuck in despair. It gives them a feeling of control, which encourages more abusive behavior. That's why I'm so determined to be as joyful and independent as possible despite this insanity. I've finally started to take control of my life and, with the encouragement of my *rav* to make certain decisions which will protect me and the children. I don't want to encourage abuse and I don't want my children to grow up seeing a depressed mother, which I went through as a child. I want them to see me as strong and able to retain my joy in life no matter what happens. It's not easy, because I'm so used to being sick and depressed. I faithfully keep a Happiness Notebook. When things are tense, I read it to myself or to my children to remind us that we are basically good and that we have had good times and will have them again."

(7) The gift of assertiveness.

◊ EXAMPLE: "My wife was always screaming about something. Finally, I bought an *EMETT* book and told her that every time she exploded, I'd give her some tool from the book which would help her control her temper. We learned to call petty things trivialities. We learned to solutionize and see mistakes as learning experiences. Little by little, not only did she gain more control over her temper, but I've improved as well!"

◊ EXAMPLE: "My husband wanted full control over my life. He wanted to know every move I made and every thought in my head. Then he would criticize me for everything. Little by little, he made me cut off all my relationships with friends and family members. No matter how much I tried to please him, things got worse. Finally, I went to my *rav*, who told me very emphatically, 'Only share what is absolutely essential. Don't talk to him so much. It only makes him nervous. Find activities which nourish your soul!' And I did! I resumed contact with friends and family and went back to school for a teaching degree despite his objections. He tried to punish me in many ways, but I kept pursuing my goal of normalcy. Giving in to crazy demands only feeds people's insanity! A mentally disturbed person can never be pleased, no matter what you do. That's what insanity is all about. I see that he respects me more now that I don't let him tyrannize me!''

◊ EXAMPLE: "Before I got divorced, I thought of myself as weak, incompetent and unstable. I don't know how I had the courage to end the marriage, except that the physical and emotional abuse were crushing me to death. Getting a divorce taught me that I was a strong person with much courage and ability to handle things I didn't think I could handle before, including being exploited by lawyers, bosses and just about everyone I came into contact with. I am now married to a wonderful man who told me that he was attracted by my positivity and strength, which was developed by going through those hardships. I was lucky in having financial resources at my disposal. My friends who are trapped by poverty have it much harder. They have to find other ways to assert themselves."

(8) The gift of silence.

◊ EXAMPLE: "After many years, I realized that no matter what I said, my husband would argue, criticize, invalidate or ridicule me. So I decided to stop talking to him except for absolutely essential matters, like 'I need the car tonight' or 'The phone bill needs to be paid.' I shared nothing of a personal nature. If he talked to me, I either nodded silently or mumbled a two-word response. I thought that after a day or two of this, he would beg me to start talking again. But he didn't. In fact, he seemed to enjoy the silence. I thought I would die of grief. It was like being buried alive. Day after day, I kept hoping that he would show some real concern about me. But there was no change. He simply has no interest in being close to anyone. Years have passed like this. I've dealt with everything on my own, a stillborn baby, a daughter's wedding, the loss of my parents, etc. I've learned to go on. There are times when my defenses are down and I weep for the love I never had. But then I pull myself together. The atmosphere is usually calm, which is far better than the tension of our early years. Silence keeps me from trying to get through, which only leads to terrible frustration. Silence keeps me from saying things which can only turn a cold war into a conflagration. We have an emotional divorce. I deal with him as I would with a broken leg: it's painful but I go on with my life as best I can."

(9) The gift of perspective.

◊ EXAMPLE: "It's amazing how adept crazy people are at making sane people feel crazy! They try to make you feel that it's you who's incompetent, unspiritual and insane. Thankfully, when I started working, I got an entirely different perspective, because I was with people who appreciated me and treated me with respect. I'd always let others define me. I don't give them that power anymore. I keep my perspective; I'm the normal one! I keep my spiritual perspective as well, that everything is a gift in life if we use it for growth."

(10) The gift of self-sufficiency.

◊ EXAMPLE: "I don't share friends, plans or experiences with my husband now because he'll only make comments which will sour the experiences which bring me joy. I get away from the house as much as possible and keep my activities to myself. Yes, it is lonely, but there is satisfaction in feeling that I have faced reality and conquered my obsession with needing approval and close-ness."

(11) The gift of pretending.

◊ EXAMPLE: "I have to pretend to be polite, sane, detached, happy and confident because the pretense pulls me up out of my rage and depression. If I were to be sincere about her petty cruelties, I'd be out of control, and then the kids would have no one to model proper behavior."

With some bullies, you have to pretend for the good of the other family members involved. With other bullies, pretending may only make the situation worse.

◊ EXAMPLE: "For years, every move I made aroused a critical comment; I couldn't cook, clean, sew, wash the dishes, do the laundry or take care of the baby adequately. I pretended that I was able to bear the pain and that it wasn't bothering me. But after years of this, I was ready for an insane asylum. I saw myself as a total failure, nothing but a fat, incompetent, unlovable slob. Finally, I told my husband, 'I will not take this any longer. Abuse is evil and I will fight it. I was wrong to pride myself on my ability to swallow my pain! It's only made things worse.' He was shocked. He said he thought everything was fine! I told him, 'From now on, don't criticize how I do things unless there is some real danger or sin involved.' Of course, being so addicted to criticism, it wasn't easy for him to stop, especially since he can put almost anything I do into the category of a sin. He is used to using religion in an abusive way. But when he falls back into his old ways, I remind him that he's hurting me. I don't pretend anymore. I firmly let him know when he's hurting me or being mean to the kids. He really had no awareness of the effect of his anger on anyone!"

(12) The gift of endorsements.

◊ EXAMPLE: "I endorse myself constantly for doing as well as I am doing, despite feeling grief-stricken some of the time. I flood my home with endorsements. I keep a paper on my fridge for each family member and write down the things I have accomplished despite the pain, as well as things my spouse and children do which are positive. Focusing on the negative is easy! Positivity takes work, especially for someone like me, who comes from an abusive background. I had no idea what it meant to be loved or loving until I started out by endorsing myself for every tiny step toward health."

(13) The gift of imagination.

◊ EXAMPLE: "Each night before I go to sleep, I imagine myself responding to criticism with silence or calm assertiveness. When I do this before an attack takes place, I'm much more able to maintain my dignity when it actually happens. I've programmed myself to think, I bless this situation, as it is giving me the opportunity to perfect my *middoth*. Every time I do this, I react more calmly and sometimes more effectively to my spouse's annoying behavior."

(14) The gift of faith.

> ◊ EXAMPLE: "I've learned that when you think that there is nothing, absolutely nothing to live for, that's when you really discover God! It's from the pits of desolation and death that I rebuilt myself. God gave me an abusive spouse so that I would be forced to cry out to Him and turn to Him. God might have chosen some other way to force growth, such as some terrible illness or other difficulty, but He knew I needed this test, that it was the only way to force me to seek Him and find my own inner strengths."

The pits

From the pits of despair, "You will seek the Lord your God and you will find him if you search after Him with all your heart and with all your soul" (*Devarim* 4:29).

Many of our forefathers had "pit experiences." Avraham was thrown into a dungeon by Nimrod for ten years (*Pirkei D'Rabbi Eliezer* 87) and, afterwards, into a fiery furnace (*Sefer HaYashar* 10). Yosef was thrown into a pit by his brothers (*Bereshith* 37:24) and by his master (Ibid. 39:20). Moshe was also thrown into a pit for ten years by Yithro (*Yalkuth Shimoni* 8:1). The Jewish People, as a whole, spent 210 years in Egypt (*Shemoth* 12:40), and then another forty years in the desert. So it seems that experiences of terrible hardship and isolation are prerequisites for spiritual growth.

When we are denied our heart's desires, we can overcome the pain by either developing an attachment to the spiritual dimension, or we try to numb ourselves with destructive addictions which constitute spiritual death. This is why the Jewish People's bonds with God were first forged in the *midbar*, where there is little or no external source of sustenance, and where there are no tempting material charms to ensnare a person. This is why the *midbar* is a gift; it is the place with the greatest potential for spiritual growth.

In most cases, when one spouse puts forth the supreme effort to strengthen him/herself spiritually, the other spouse makes some improvement, however slight. Even if there is no change in your spouse, the important thing is to focus on your mitzvoth and *middoth* — no matter how badly you are feeling or how others are acting. This is when the greatest spiritual growth takes place.

You cannot really know the reward you get for a mitzvah done in darkness, pain and uncertainty. But knowing that there is a reward for your efforts provides a measure of comfort in the midst of this darkness. Your personal life may seem to be in a shambles, but your spiritual life can be very fulfilling. It is sad not to be loved. But it is worse to be unloving.

PART III
Relationships

9 | The Gift of Forgiveness: Clearing Our Cosmic Debts

Each night before retiring, we say a prayer: "Master of the universe, I hereby forgive anyone who has angered or vexed me or sinned against me, either physically or financially, against my honor or anything else that is mine, whether accidentally or intentionally, inadvertently or deliberately, by speech or by deed, in this incarnation [*gilgul*] or any other...."

What a powerful prayer! But let's be honest. How can we say these words with heartfelt sincerity, when we've all been hurt by numerous people thousands of times in thousands of big and little ways? How do we let go of the resentment we feel toward those who have harmed us, who have treated us with contempt, spoken *lashon ha-ra* against us, caused us to lose large sums of money and caused us mental anguish with their meanness or indifference?

An answer to this question can be found in the following;

> Cast your bread upon the waters, for after many days you will find it. — KOHELETH 11:1

In other words, whatever we send out — both the love and the hate — we eventually get back. Those who send out hate, get it back. Our challenge is to not get sucked into their web of negativity by responding with more hatred.

An extraordinary incident illustrates this point beautifully. The saintly Rabbi Aryeh Levin *z.t.l.* slipped one rainy day in one of Jerusalem's narrow alleyways and fell in the mud. A member of a rather extreme group, which opposed his close friendship with a certain religious leader whose politics they didn't agree with, happened to be passing by and yelled at Reb Aryeh, "It serves you right! That is just what you deserve! This should be the fate of everyone who follows [that Rabbi]!" Reb Aryeh picked himself up and, wiping the mud off himself, went over to this man and said in a gentle voice, "I see that you are vexed and angry. Perhaps you have some complaint against me. Maybe you were once hurt or injured through me? If so, please forgive me."

The man was so surprised that he continued on his way without another word, feeling ashamed at his outburst (*A Tzaddik in Our Time*, p. 96).

Rabbi Levin was at such a high spiritual level that he automatically assumed that whatever happened must be necessary for his own spiritual growth. Anger was inappropriate for, in his eyes, this man was giving him the opportunity to correct some mistake or sin which he had committed either directly or indirectly. He saw human beings merely as agents of God, providing us with challenges to stimulate our spiritual growth. Certainly the man had acted in a most despicable manner attacking him while he was down, but Reb Aryeh knew that man's existence resembles a closed circle, and that his response would determine whether or not he perpetuated a negative cycle of hatred.

In Hebrew, the word *gilgul* comes from the word "circle." If we could look at our lives from the perspective of the World of Truth, we would see that all the trials and tribulations which we must endure are well-deserved and make perfect sense. We would see that we needed each of these thousands of losses and disappointments we experienced to give us the opportunity to perfect ourselves. We would also see that everything we have given out has returned to us eventually — both all the acts of *chesed* we have done as well as the pain we have caused.

If the saintly Reb Aryeh had responded to that insult with an insult, he would have hurt himself more than the other person! He liberated himself from that strongest of all natural responses, i.e., to return a hurt with a hurt.

> Those who accept insult and do not mete it out, who listen to their disgrace and make no reply, about them Scripture says, 'Those who love God are as the sun rising in its might.'
> — SHABBATH 88b

Forgive: for your own sake as well as the other's

The famous researcher, Hans Selye, "showed how the body, in effect, could manufacture its own poisons, when under siege by negative emotions, especially protracted frustration" (*Head First*, p. 21).

It's hard to think of thoughts as having power, because they seem like fleeting abstractions, without real substance. But the truth is that thoughts have tremendous power. Thoughts are the most powerful weapon which mankind possesses, both for building and destroying. If we understand this, we understand how even silent, unexpressed love can heal, and how unspoken resentments can destroy.

With every thought we think, we create either a positive or negative energy field around us. For example, imagine a woman who awakens in the morning and says with real sincerity, "*Modeh ani!* Thank You, God, for the gift of life and for all the challenges of the coming day." Then she says her morning *berachoth* with heartfelt thanks for sanity, for sight, for freedom to choose good over evil. No doubt, this woman will be in a pleasant mood and feel loving toward her family members.

In contrast, imagine a woman who awakens thinking, Yich, another day of tension and torment. When she gives commands to her muscles, such as "Get out of bed," or "Make breakfast," they will balk and refuse to carry out these commands because they feel heavy and lethargic. She will snap angrily at her children and they'll be grouchy and unpleasant in return. She'll think, See, it's true. My life is awful! No wonder I'm so depressed. Who wouldn't be in such a negative atmosphere? She's not likely to realize that it was her own attitude, i.e., Yich, another day, that set her up for one failure after another.

What is the cause of her slothfulness and her gloomy morning? The children? Certainly, they're not perfect. But the real reason she feels bad is her own attitude. Her thoughts are mirrored back to her in a world which seems depressing and gloomy.

> The Kotzker once remarked: The time to eat is in one's youth; the time to sleep is in the grave; for sadness and depression there is no time at all. You may call it depression but I call it escape from obligation and a rejection of the yoke of Heaven.
> — AND NOTHING BUT THE TRUTH, p. 39

Unless you are in a truly abusive situation or suffering from extreme pain or a major loss, depression is the result of not making the effort to be grateful. It results from the habit of focusing on what you lack instead of on what you have.

Negative thoughts create a negative magnetic energy field around us. Like a magnet, condemnations attract more condemnatory thoughts. The people you interact with pick up on your negativity subliminally. Unless they are either very dense or at a very high spiritual level, they may also start complaining or responding to you negatively, thus proving that your negativity is justified.

> ◊ Example: "I came back from a class late at night and saw that my children had left a mess in the kitchen. I was furious, thinking, They don't respect me. Furthermore, I haven't trained them properly, so I'm a failure as a mother. Not only that, but I'm not doing well at anything. My negative thinking became so pervasive that in a matter of seconds, I was condemning myself, my husband and my children and seeing my whole life as bleak and miserable just because there were a few dishes on the table. I would have gone to sleep angry and been angry at everyone the next morning if I didn't stop the vicious cycle by telling myself, Give them the benefit of the doubt! They simply are less aware of the mess than I am. Leaving dishes on the table does not automatically signify lack of love. There is so much that is good and positive in my life. Mood is a matter of what a person focuses on. Since I have a tendency to focus on what's wrong, I have to work hard to change my bad habit."

Self-perpetuating cycles

> Even in your thoughts do not curse a king...for a bird of the skies may carry the sound and some winged creature may betray the matter. — KOHELETH 10:20

Our attitude toward life is the result of what we choose to focus on from the 10,000-odd thoughts that pass through our minds in an average day. The ones we choose to focus on seem to come from some external place. In actuality, they are simply the result of thoughts we have programmed ourselves to think. For example, if you spend a lot of time thinking about the negative in yourself, in life and in the people around you, you eventually become a bitter person, disgusted with everything and everyone. The world will look like a hostile jungle to you; people will seem incompetent and uncaring. This is the inescapable, circular effect of being hypercritical. You'll be convinced that you're seeing the truth — that people are untrustworthy creeps and that life is disgusting. But what you are really seeing is the result of your own thoughts being thrown back at you in mirror image.

Thoughts — both positive and negative — not only feed on themselves, they create strong emotional bonds. Your hateful thoughts automatically tie you to the person you are thinking about. Since thought leads to speech and speech leads to action, you are also likely to hurt that person in some way, perhaps by speaking *lashon ha-ra* about him or sneering or grimacing in his presence. When that happens, he is likely to hurt you back, which causes you to want to hurt him back, thereby keeping the vicious cycle going. In other words, when you condemn people or hurt them in any way, you bind yourself to them in this repetitious pattern of negative responses.

The only way to break this cycle is with forgiveness. When you forgive, you cut the ties and free yourself from the hatred which would have bound you to him forever.

So, the next time you are having vicious thoughts about someone who just hurt you in some way, think: Do I want to tie myself to this person? Do I want to poison my mind and body with this negativity? True, you're enraged. Your blood is boiling. You feel you have a perfect right to be angry. But do you want to create a spiritual defect in yourself which will need to be corrected at some future date, or do you prefer to keep yourself mentally and spiritually strong?

The Chofetz Chaim said that a man who had stolen had to come back in another lifetime to repay the debt (*Sefath Tamim*, ch. 4). What about those who "steal" people's peace of mind? Is that not also stealing? If we apply the same principle to those who "steal" from others emotionally, then we arrive at the inescapable conclusion that by hurting people, we create a debt which must be paid back at some future time.

So, let's say you're furious with an in-law, spouse, neighbor, a sibling, boss or co-worker. You gnash your teeth and condemn that person mentally for being such a stingy bully, or an irresponsible bum, or a lazy slob. Even though you're not expressing your disgust in words or actions, you are poisoning your mind and body with your accusations. You don't think you're doing anything wrong because your silent condemnations are unspoken.

If someone told you that by being so angry, you'd be forming an invisible psychic bond to this person, you might let go of demanding that the person give you what she cannot or will not give. It might even help to think that every time someone lies, cheats, disappoints, rejects or hurts you, the Teacher is testing whether or not you can use this painful experience for your spiritual growth. And if you flunk, He'll simply retest you until you pass.

On the other hand, if you knew that by achieving a state of heartfelt acceptance and forgiveness of the people who hurt you, that you would be finished with this test, would you still want to hold onto your anger? No! You would let go of it like a burning hot coal that had been placed in your hands. You would get rid of your anger by immediately diverting your mind to some positive thought.

The inescapable conclusion is that we must examine our thoughts just as thoroughly as we examine food for bugs. We don't want *traif* in our food! Why would we want it in our minds? So, we must tell ourselves very sternly: I refuse to think about him/her except to feel compassion or indifference. Forgive so that the bond will severed.

> ◊ EXAMPLE: "One day my eight year old came home from school and told me, 'Mom, the mind isn't a *machsan* [storage area] where you can just dump all your old things. You have to be very careful what you put in there.' How true! I have to be very disciplined about what I think and read and look at in order not to fill my mind with junk."

A silly mind trick?

Hope and forgiveness are methods of strengthening ourselves spiritually. Norman Cousins, who cured himself of a crippling and usually fatal disease, wrote at the age of 74:

> Life is an adventure in forgiveness. Nothing clutters the soul more than remorse, resentment, recrimination. Negative feelings occupy a fearsome amount of space in the mind, blocking our

perceptions, our prospects, our pleasures. Forgiveness is a gift we need to give not only to others but to ourselves, freeing us from self-punishment and enabling us to see a wider horizon in life than is possible under circumstances of guilt or grudge.

— HEAD FIRST, p. 111

Forgiveness may seem like a mind trick. But it is a powerful one. It forces us to realize that our thoughts have power and that we have to be in control of this power or it will destroy us.

◊ EXAMPLE: "A relative is a very fastidious perfectionist whose visits were agony for me. But the last time she came by, I was able to stop my usual poisonous thoughts just by thinking that if I didn't control myself, that maybe she'd be my mother or my daughter in a future lifetime. I don't care if this is a mind trick. It's working! I forgave her. I had compassion for her. And I got through her visit without feeling like I was going to crack up!"

◊ EXAMPLE: "I signed as a guarantor on a home loan for a couple whom I regarded as close friends. Suddenly, they picked up and left the country. I had to find a second job to pay off their debt. When I found out where they were, I tried every legal means to get them to pay, but to no avail. Whenever I start gnashing my teeth about the damage they've done to me, I tell myself that I'm probably paying off some debt to them which won't become clear to me until I'm in the World of Truth. This calms me down and keeps me from letting them destroy my mental health all over again each and every day. I hope forgiveness will sever the bonds between us forever."

Canceling debts

Forgiving does not mean that you're being a weakling or a coward. It means that you are being self-protective by keeping non-nourishing people at a distance. By forgiving, you calm down and can look at your options: counseling, a lawyer, stoic resignation, etc.

◊ EXAMPLE: "I always prided myself on being able to get along with everyone, until I worked for a doctor who bullied everyone on the staff. I tried talking to him, but nothing worked. I finally had to admit that I couldn't handle being around him and quit. For months afterwards, every time I began to obsess about him, I'd have to tell myself sternly, CUT! That word reminds me to forgive myself for not being able to get through to him and to avoid bearing a grudge that would continue to tie my life to his.''

◊ EXAMPLE: "My oldest daughter and I had a terrible relationship because she didn't think of herself as a child, but rather as a second mother in the home. She would tell me what to wear, what to cook and how to discipline the younger children. Although I read *Raising Children to Care*, I didn't want to use any of the suggestions because I had no desire to even be close to her. But then I started thinking about the ramifications of our hostility toward each other. If I stayed angry, then maybe we'd have to repair this relationship in a future lifetime — and maybe it would be worse next time. That scared me into taking action. Every time she did something upsetting, I first forgave her. Then, to arouse positive thoughts and feelings in myself, I started to endorse her throughout the day for anything I could think of that I appreciated about her. When she is nasty, I forgive, which allows me to calmly say, 'We don't shame people in this house.' When she tries to dominate, I first forgive, then calmly say, 'You have overstepped your borders again.' I'm no longer trying to change her or create a closeness that may never exist, but things are now more bearable. Believe me, I was nice to her for my own sake, not for any altruistic reasons. But even so, our relationship has improved greatly.''

Forgiveness helps us realize the truth: that our *middoth* are independent of the people and events in our environment. People can highlight certain defects in ourselves, but the work to overcome those defects is ours alone. Our *middoth* are our own doing and no one else's. Other people may be rude, crude and cruel, but that is no excuse for us to respond in kind. People can be terribly disappointing and events can be painful and tragic, but our response can always be in keeping with the values of Torah.

◊ EXAMPLE: "My husband has great difficulty giving. It doesn't matter whether it's time, money or information. Even after many years of marriage, when I ask for just a few seconds of his time and he refuses or calls me names or explodes, I still feel crushed inside. It may take me two or three days to get over the sadness and get back to myself. During those days I pray, 'God, help me not to condemn him. Help me to forgive. I know that this is the best he can do right now. Help me to accept what You have chosen for me. Help me to continue to function and be happy despite my sadness.'"

Some people might view the effort to forgive as a mere mental trick, without any real significance or power, but this is not true. We have to constantly throw out the garbage which accumulates in our minds, just as we have to do a daily garbage run. These efforts are meaningful, even if they are in the abstract realm of the mind.

Almost everybody, even those we are closest to, will disappoint us at some time. In order to respond properly, it is very helpful to program our minds ahead of time by imagining a disappointment, and seeing ourselves responding with forgiveness and compassion.

Thoughts, though unseen, have great power. Whether we are restraining negative thoughts or negative impulses, we are rewarded for that effort with a sense of God's actual presence, for,

> If a man consecrates himself in a small measure down below, he is sanctified much more from above. — YOMA 39a

10 | The Gift of Accepting the Limits of Our Control over Others

One of mankind's most driving passions is the passion to fix, modify and change the people around us. Our Godly desire to improve the world is often manifest through annoyance and hostility toward people's imperfections.

Ideally, it would be best to notice these imperfections with a neutral "oh," like a dermatologist who looks at a skin disease without condemning the patient, and then decides if medication would help or if it would best be left alone. Instead, we tend to get hostile and anxious that the person is not as caring, organized, ambitious, honest, intelligent or capable as we would like. We wish we could be tailors, "Ah, if only I could make a few alterations. I'd take a snip here and a tuck there and have the perfect mate (or parent, child, friend, teacher, etc.) Then I'd have the closeness I seek. Then I'd be happy. Then I'd never feel alone or unloved. Then life would be perfect."

This desire is based on the erroneous belief that it is possible to find the "perfect match," and that only when you find that person can you be truly happy. The truth is that even in the best of relationships, people will inevitably disappoint you at times. There is no such thing as perfect understanding at all times.

Certainly, there is a unique joy in finding someone who speaks your same "soul language." However, trying to force closeness is dehumanizing. Whenever you try to control others for the satisfaction of your own needs, whether by bullying them, flattering them or pleasing them to the point of losing your own identity, the end result will eventually be greater distance.

When this happens, it is important not to indulge in a popular

159

pastime, whose theme might be summed up as, "I'm going to make you love me. I'm going to get control of you! I'll find the magic key which will turn you into the spouse or child of my dreams."

You may run to parents, rabbis and therapists asking:

"How can I get my scattered, disorganized, spaced-out spouse to be more focused and organized?"

"How can I make my cold, critical spouse be warm, accepting and affectionate?

"How can I get my passive, weak, unconfident spouse be more aggressive, confident and ambitious?"

"How can I get my learning-disabled child to love learning, get my domineering oldest to be kind and compassionate, get my disorganized youngest one to be more assertive and responsible, and get my spacey middle one to be more mature and focused?"

It is difficult for many people to accept their inability to change the God-given traits of their partners and children. Unrealistic hopes and excessive drama over this reality prevent people from loving others as they are.

Criticism polarizes

Most people assume that if they just get angry, critical and depressed enough, the other person will turn into whatever they want him to be. Despite repeated failures, it is amazing how few people realize that criticism does not work. In fact, constant criticism polarizes people because it implies, You must change, but I know you can't.

A person who is subject to constant criticism feels, I really am a failure. In a hostile environment, the tendency toward extreme behavior intensifies, for what we mention, we strengthen. Thus, criticism causes people to become even more locked into their negative habits because they feel hopeless. Furthermore, the more we focus on a person's negative points, the more upset we get.

> ◊ EXAMPLE: "I wasn't the neatest person in the world when I got married, but I wasn't the biggest slob either. I was a very competent and skilled teacher and felt pretty good about myself. However, after a few years with a very fastidious spouse, I feel like I can't do anything right. With those eagle-eyes on me, I get

all discombobulated and really mess everything up, which only proves that I really am totally untogether."

◊ EXAMPLE: "The angrier I got about my wife being so shy and undemonstrative, the more withdrawn she got!"

The same principle holds for children.

◊ EXAMPLE: "I kept screaming at my teenager that she only cared about her looks. She spent hours doing her hair and was always demanding money for clothes. I keep telling her to take a *sefer Tehillim* in her hands instead of a hair-brush. Well, with all my yelling, she got even more obsessed with her looks!"

Attempts to control people always end in the destruction of the relationship. All you can really do is model the behavior you want and encourage improvement with positive feedback and constructive suggestions. You cannot force change against a person's will. You may be convinced that your criticism is a sincere attempt to improve the person and your relationship. But if you are angry and resentful, you will get the reverse of what you want. Your hostility indicates that your desire is for your good, not the other person's.

Recognize what can and cannot change

So what can you do with the pain you feel when you see that a family member does not meet your standards and expectations?

It helps to make a few rules for yourself. For example:

Rule 1: I will not agonize over things I cannot change, including people's God-given predispositions.

People can be taught good manners, but they cannot change their basic nature. For example, people who express little need for emotional intimacy during the first few months of marriage are not likely to change much over the years. You may not get the romantic closeness you crave. But you may be able to achieve appreciation and consideration for each other.

Rule 2: When I think about someone who has brought a lot of pain into my life, I will not continue obsessing about him/her unless I can improve the relationship in some way. If not, I will forcefully divert my attention from this person and think of constructive things

I can do with my life.

Rule 3: If I start condemning someone, I will switch gears and focus on my own *middoth* which need changing.

Rule 4: I will state my needs honestly, with love in my heart. If the other person doesn't respond positively, I will accept that God does not want me to have what I want right now.

What can and cannot be changed

Pain about a relationship is greater if your hopes are based on demands which the person is incapable of meeting. Thus, it is essential to recognize what can and cannot be changed.

We all have inherent predispositions which remain basically unchanged throughout our lives such as:

* temperament and sensitivities
* talents (e.g., basic intelligence and natural skills)
* tempo (slow or fast) in thought, speech or action

These three Ts form a kind of basic foundation of the psyche, similar to a person's basic body structure. Even the best plastic surgeon has to work within the limits of that structure. Similarly, the most skilled psychologist cannot change the basic sensitivities and predispositions of another person.

It is often difficult for people to honestly face their God-given limitations. Few people really know themselves. They will naively say,

"I know I've always been quite bossy and not very sensitive to people's feelings, but I'm sure that when I get married, I'll be completely different."

"I've always been rather clumsy and disorganized, but I'm sure that when I read that book on home management, I'll be able to get it all together."

"I realize that my spouse has been cold and uncommunicative for the last forty years, but I keep hoping for change."

Recognizing your innate characteristics does not mean condoning harmful behavior. It simply means being honest about your innermost drives, needs, values, strengths and weaknesses.

By the time a child is six or seven years old, the basic foundation of the personality is pretty much established and does not change drastically throughout life. Certainly maturation brings many welcome changes in many people, but these changes have to do with the development of better *middoth* rather than any radical change in one's innate personality.

There is a great deal of scientific controversy as to what constitutes a person's nature. The Rambam sums up some of the major categories of inborn dispositions in *Hilchoth Deoth* (I:1). These include the tendency to be:

1. Easily-angered vs. naturally calm
2. Vain vs. humble
3. Coarse vs. refined
4. Greedy and materialistic vs. satisfied with little
5. Stingy vs. generous
6. Light-hearted vs. melancholic
7. Cruel vs. merciful
8. Timid vs. courageous

Of course, these are not strictly separate catetories. Even the cruelest person can be merciful at times and timid people often express great courage. However, we do all have certain preferred modes of behavior. By recognizing our inherent, God-given tendencies, we see what weaknesses must be overcome. We can then achieve mental health by finding a balance. This requires that we consciously choose a middle path between each extreme (except when it comes to humility; here we should strive for the extreme).

Thus, for example, a hot-tempered person can certainly learn to be more patient and self-disciplined. He remains basically hot-tempered, but has learned to control himself. A bossy type can try to restrain the desire to tell others what to do, but she may always have to fight her basic desire to control others. A high-strung type can learn to calm himself down with special breathing exercises and secure thoughts, but his nervous system will still react more emotionally than that of a less sensitive type. In other words, even if, as the Rambam recommends, a person goes to the opposite extreme in order to balance himself, he still retains the original tendency. This is similar to a person who has been overweight from childhood and then loses weight. The tendency to gain weight easily may remain for a lifetime.

Eight other inborn, God-given dispositions are described in

depth in *Appreciating People, Including Yourself.* These are:

1. Introverted vs. extroverted
2. Sensory (pleasure and interests derive mainly from the material world) vs. intuitive (pleasure and interests derive mainly from abstract ideas, ideals and theories)
3. Feeling (sentimental, warm, people-oriented, forms bonds with people) vs. thinking (analytical, objective, fact-oriented, tends to keep emotionally aloof).
4. Perceiving (option-oriented, curious, spontaneous, fun loving, independent) vs. judging (closure-oriented, structured, restrained, traditional, proper, obedient)

Although people can and must develop their weaker side in order to achieve a mental balance, their essential predisposition retains its dominant influence throughout life.

Not recognizing your innate predispositions can cause needless suffering.

> ◊ EXAMPLE: "I am a very introverted, intellectual person with a passion for learning. When my daughter turned two, I opened a nursery in my home for other two year olds so that I could be at home with her and still have an income. But the truth was that I really didn't like being with children. I'm not demonstrative and really hated all the noise and commotion. I could never think of what to do with them. I was afraid to admit that I'd rather be pursuing my intellectual interests, so I spent a miserable year with them and made them miserable too, rather than admit that I wasn't much of a group leader and nurturer. I see now that I can work on myself to be more affectionate, but it's not realistic to think I can be what I am not."

> ◊ EXAMPLE: "My husband loves using his hands. But in our society, this is considered to be lower-class work. I nagged and nagged him to learn all day until my *rav* said I was pushing him into an emotional breakdown. It's true. He got more and more depressed until I finally realized that if I really loved him, I should encourage him to develop the talents God gave him. Now that he learns part-time, he is so much happier."

Other major dispositions, which are largely innate and not subject to drastic change, include:

1. Fastidious and meticulous vs. easygoing and unexacting

2. Oppositional vs. peace loving and approval seeking
3. Emotionally sensitive vs. thick-skinned
4. High-strung vs. placid, tranquil and unperturbable
5. Domineering and control-oriented vs. submissive and people-pleasing
6. Ambitious, action-oriented vs. unambitious and slow moving
7. Creative vs. conformist

Each person is a combination of hundreds of such traits which make up his unique personality. Honesty about our basic predispositions is the first step to being able to control our negative tendencies and balance them by developing the opposite side.

Unhealthy extremes are more likely to be found in those who suffered from childhood abuse or are now in abusive situations. Thus, in a hostile atmosphere (whether from oneself or others), people become more extreme in their innate predispositions because these conditions prevent the flexibility and hopefulness necessary for growth.

◊ EXAMPLE: "My husband was very uncommunicative during the early months of our marriage. I thought he'd never open up. But as time went on, he became more talkative. He's from a stiff-upper-lip family which looks down on any expression of feeling as a sign of weakness. In order not to be ridiculed by his family, he adopted this cold, unfeeling front, but actually he was a kind of hidden Feeling type. As we grew closer, this side of him began to flourish because, as a Feeling type, emotional intimacy was very important to him. His sister, on the other hand, who really is an essentially cold person, got colder as time went on."

◊ EXAMPLE: "When my son was in the second grade, I would look in his book bag and feel such despair at what a mess it was. It seemed to me that his book bag presaged a future of total failure. I was always nagging him to be more organized, but he only got worse. Finally, I decided to let go and let him deal with his problem in his own way. My secure thought was that since he could be very organized when he really wanted to be, he would become more orderly as he got older and realize on his own that this made life much easier and gave him more self-respect."

◊ EXAMPLE: "When my daughter was in second grade, I realized how severe her disorganization was. Her handwriting was very confused, she was also extremely scattered mentally and had difficulty concentrating. As she got older, things didn't improve. In fact, they got worse. Everything was always a mess — her room, her schoolbag and her appearance, and I was always angry. I thought she was simply lazy and stubborn until I went to a specialist in learning disabilities. He discovered that she had mild brain damage which manifested as a problem with coordination and organization. I was blaming her for something she had no control over. She has now had years of occupational therapy and special help in developing organizational skills.''

◊ EXAMPLE: "My husband is very absent-minded. He's lost thousands of dollars because of misplaced scraps of paper on which he jots down orders. I've bought him every kind of memory aide you can think of, but he loses those too! We spend half our lives looking for his keys, his wallet, his checkbook and whatever else he needs at the moment. I hate the chaos and confusion. We're always in debt. But nothing I've done has helped make him any less absent-minded. I used to be furious with him all the time, but I've learned to accept that this is the way he is. He's a good-hearted person and that's what I focus on.''

Encouraging improvement: focus on the positive

The second rule in dealing with a family member who does not meet your expectations is to create an atmosphere which will encourage improvement. This doesn't mean that you will eliminate what's bothering you, but it may reduce the severity of certain problems.

1. Give positive feedback: catch the person doing what you want and praise him for it. Acts which are endorsed will occur more often.

◊ EXAMPLE: "My son is married to a extremely meticulous woman who spends most of her time straightening the closets and scrubbing everything spotless. It breaks my heart to hear her yell at the children for breaking one of her thousand and one rules about what they can and cannot do. All I can do is try to get through to her by showing appreciation for what I do like about her. It was very phony and mechanical at first, for she has so little awareness of people's emotional needs. For her, being clean and obedient are primary values. Her basic tendency is to withhold affection and choose the path of strictness and punishment. However, whenever she overcomes this pattern, even for a few seconds, I endorse her warmly and hope that there will be even some slight growth as time goes on."

◊ EXAMPLE: "It was hard to accept that my oldest son had such a cruel streak. Whenever he was mean, I'd scream at him how cruel he was. Then, one day, he gave a dollar to *tzedakah* and got a receipt. I purchased a little frame and put the receipt in it and hung it on the wall. Every time he showed even a speck of generosity or kindness toward someone, I wrote it down on an endorsement sheet that I have on the refrigerator. The written word is so much more powerful than anything I say. In time, he really has become less nasty."

2. Value what the other person values. If you live with someone who really values neatness, learn to value it more, even if you don't become as fastidious as that person. If the person values emotional contact, learn to listen and validate.

◊ EXAMPLE: "I was always upset that my husband wanted to talk to me in the evenings. To me, this was *bittul Torah*. Then I read *Appreciating People* and realized that he's a Feeling type and needs this emotional connection, while I don't feel this need as strongly. Once I understood his need, I resolved to spend more time listening. I admit that this was very mechanical and awkward at first, but I found that I enjoyed this closeness. I'm developing a compassionate part of myself that had been dormant before."

◊ EXAMPLE: "I used to think of my son-in-law as cold and unsociable. Then I realized he's just an introvert who is very shy and uncomfortable in crowds. That made me feel much more positive toward him, which improved our relationship."

3. Model positive behavior yourself: help others grow by being a model of Torah values in your own life.

◊ EXAMPLE: "We are a rather disorganized household, lacking in structure and discipline. For the most part the children appear to be doing well in spite of it, but I always have felt bad that we aren't as efficient and orderly as other families appear to be. Finally I realized that I have to accept my nature rather than condemn myself for being this way. But at the same time I have to force myself to be more diligent about putting Torah principles into practice. Since I'm not naturally organized, I'll have to take extra time to make things more orderly and plan ahead, since self-discipline is the basis for all good *middoth*. Then if a stressful event arises, I'll be able to demonstrate Torah values and keep things from falling apart. I've noticed that when I condemn myself, I get paralyzed into inaction."

4. Accept what cannot be changed — with love in your heart.

   ◊ EXAMPLE: "I went to about a hundred different doctors and therapists and wasted thousands of dollars and a lot of time in an effort to overcome my high level of anxiety. After years of trying everything from acupuncture to psychotherapy, I finally accepted that I must learn to live with being high-strung. Now, when I get nervous, instead of feeding my fearful thoughts, I think calming thoughts and do calming breathing exercises. I have to live my life despite my nerves. I used to hate myself. Now, I see that fear is the opposite of love. Love of God and myself calms me."

   ◊ EXAMPLE: "My husband is a very passive, simple person with little ambition in life. I thought that if I just get him to the right therapist, he'd turn into a deep-thinking, ambitious go-getter! It was pretty stupid. I was just young, so I thought that with effort, you could make people be anything you wanted them to be. Now I know better."

Remember that children are far more flexible in their ability to improve *middoth* and imitate new behaviors. However, just as people's bodies get stiffer as they get older, so do habits become more resistant to change.

Accepting our innate deficiencies awakens humility and compassion. The next step is to take responsibility for diligently practicing the disciplines which keep these tendencies from becoming destructive extremes.

The destructive effect of nonacceptance

Many people feel they cannot love someone unless the person undergoes a major personality overhaul. In other words, they want a different person altogether. Let's take a man whom we'll call Avi. He complains, "I want my wife, Suri, to be like Mrs. Cohen. Mrs. Cohen has eleven children, is always cheerful, calm and beautifully groomed and her house is spotless. My wife is disorganized and can't handle the few children we do have! She says that she hates housework and that being home all day is boring and stifling. Well, she'll just have to learn to be a *balabusta* and like it!"

Why can't Suri be like Mrs. Cohen? Well, Mrs. Cohen is an extroverted optimist who loves being with children on an ongoing basis. She is also blessed with greater physical stamina, partly because she is a confident, cool-headed type who rarely has a severe response to stress. She can manage on little sleep and is less unnerved by any noise or commotion in the house. She has a natural talent for order and discipline, and a system for everything, from when to change the towels to when to visit the dentist, so that she generally feels in control, both within and without.

On the other hand, Suri is an unconfident, hypersensitive introvert who reacts strongly to stress, including noise, fighting, messes, criticism and lack of sleep. Her nervous system is more reactive, so she gets sick more often and is distressed by her frequent lack of sleep. Good-hearted, but not authoritative, she feels at a loss when it comes to setting limits and disciplining the children. They know it and take advantage of her blurred boundaries, inconsistent rules and overly good-hearted nature. She also finds housework boring and she craves intellectual and spiritual inspiration, without which she feels empty and dead. She lacks innate organizational skills, so that the numerous tasks of cooking, cleaning, bathing children, shopping, menu planning, etc., often seem overwhelming.

Yes, Suri can learn to be more organized. She can develop some ability to systematize. But she will never be naturally meticulous or as methodical as Mrs. Cohen is, any more than a tone-deaf child can achieve the same greatness at piano as one who has a natural gift for recognizing and playing musical nuances.

As angry as Avi is with Suri, she is equally bitter about the raw deal she got in marriage. She hates his emotional coldness and his need to dominate others. Like many women, she bonds by sharing feelings, while he considers such sharing to be a sign of weakness and stupidity. She likes things neat and clean, but is not obsessed by disorder, while he sees a messy kitchen as threatening to his sense of well-being. She thinks of him as stingy, while he thinks of himself as generous.

Avi's wife is weak in the very areas he values most, and vice versa. If their marriage is to be anything other than a continuous battle, she must work extra hard to be more orderly and disciplined and, at the same time, find fulfilling outlets for her creative talents. And Avi's *tikkun* must be to develop compassion, generosity, patience and listening skills and let go of his ego desire to control people. That will require as much work from him as it will for his wife to get more organized and authoritative.

Avi and Suri can be more openly appreciative of the other's positive traits and become more sensitive to what the other values. Whether or not they will be willing to do so is the question.

Modeling positive behavior

We can never be all things to all people, nor can others give us the perfection we would like. We must learn to accept, respect and appreciate our own and others' talents, needs and limitations. Often, the best thing we can do is simply model good *middoth* ourselves.

> ◊ EXAMPLE: "My wife is a very emotional person who used to overreact to everything. If she would start screaming, I'd get upset and often started screaming, too. I finally realized that the only thing that calms her down is for me to stay calm and remind myself, She's just insecure, she's not deliberately trying to hurt me. Sometimes I say to her, 'Tell me what I can do to help. I'm not your enemy.' Her ups and downs are very painful, but we're both learning to ride the roller coaster without panicking or getting angry at each other, so that her moods pass more quickly now."

You can make someone stop smoking in your home, but you cannot make the person want to stop smoking. The same thing is true in terms of personality. The big question is always: Will this person want to make an effort to change? A shy person can try to be more outgoing, but will he ever feel really comfortable in crowds or with strangers? He certainly won't have the same drive to be with people that an extrovert has. A stingy person can make the effort to be more generous. But will he want to be? And what will be his definition of generous? When he gives a minute of his time to talk to his wife or child or gives a dollar to *tzedakah*, he may feel that he has been extremely generous, but in comparison to a spontaneously generous person, these acts of giving may hardly seem worth noticing.

Likewise, a cold person with very little need for emotional intimacy can learn listening skills, but will he want to? A person's ability to bond emotionally is fairly well determined early in life.

Just as a diabetic must discipline himself to avoid eating certain foods, the person who has a tendency toward any extreme must be extra disciplined to stay on the middle path. However, not everyone is interested in doing so.

The one thing we can all work on is to love people as they are. If growth is possible, it will happen in an atmosphere of real acceptance and appreciation.

Miracle of love: let it go and let it grow

We all, no doubt, indulge in a bit of "If only he/she were more/less _____ then I'd be so much happier." This kind of thinking only leads to much bitterness and despair.

Unless you are dealing with an abusive person, in which case you must be aggressively self-protective, it is important to be encouraging and compassionate toward others. If you cling to romantic dreams of radical change or have a strong desire to control others, you'll be bitter and angry much of the time, constantly blaming others for making you unhappy.

> ◊ EXAMPLE: "I was constantly making comments about my wife's weight until I realized that this made her even more likely to turn to food as a source of comfort. When I finally stopped criticizing her and began to say words of appreciation and love, she became less obsessive and even joined a Weight Watchers group. I admit that, at first, my compliments were insincere. The truth is that I don't like fat people. But the more I made these forced gestures, the more I realized that she is a good person despite her weight. I began to focus on her good points. I don't know if I'll ever feel as physically attracted to her as I would like, which is painful to me, but I do appreciate her."

◊ EXAMPLE: "I was always on my eleven year old's back to get up early and *daven* with his father. Each morning was a struggle which often ended up with my husband screaming at him, too. But the child only got more and more hostile. Finally, my husband said, 'I give up.' I then told my son that prayers were his responsibility. If he wanted to get up and go with his father, we'd be very happy, and if he didn't, he could pray at school. For two months, he didn't get up on time. I didn't say anything. What I did do was tell him, 'When I *daven*, I feel happy that I have the privilege of talking to the King. I'm so grateful to be able to stand before the King of the entire world!' After two months, he got up on his own and left the house on time with my husband. And he's kept it up because the choice came from within him and not from us coercing him."

◊ EXAMPLE: "My four year old is very clingy and unconfident. He cried so much in *cheder* that the rebbe finally sent him home. I was hysterical because I didn't want him and the two younger ones with me all day. I was so angry at him for not being more independent that I was quite mean to him for the first week. Then I let go of wanting him to be other than who he is, and I started giving him extra love and attention. After three weeks, he decided on his own that he wanted to go back to *cheder*! When he did, he was a different child and was happy and cooperative!"

◊ EXAMPLE: "I'm proud of the fact that my husband learns full time, but it was terribly hard to accept that he was unwilling to deal with worldly things, like helping me with chores or taking care of bills. I was inwardly very resentful. At some point, I stopped fighting reality and faced facts. I would have to take over the financial responsibilities and set certain limits, like getting a phone which could receive incoming calls only. The truth is that sometimes I wish I had married someone more competent to deal with financial realities, but I don't want to spend my life grieving over what I don't have. Instead, I can be proud of developing strengths I never knew I had, including a capacity to be respectful and accepting of people as they are."

Our disappointment in ourselves and others can lead to endless hours wasted in self-pity and resentment. Or, we can recognize our limitations and practice unconditional acceptance. Whether or not improvement takes place, our *avodah* is to constantly practice our "duties of the heart," including the humility to accept our limitations in changing others.

Two helpful exercises

When you are heartbroken or enraged, try the following statements to calm yourself down:

"S/he's doing the best s/he can with the tools s/he has."

(You may have to say this statement thousands of times under your breath until the hatred in your heart is erased.)

"The more resentful I feel toward this person for being this way, the more I will try to relax and accept Hashem's will with love."

"The more uptight I get around her, the more I will endorse myself for bearing discomfort with good will."

"The more I want to change him, the more I will be aware of the need to surrender everything beyond my control to God."

"The more emotion-flooded I become, the more I will relax and become solution-centered."

After repeating these phrases, you will then be able to see more clearly whether it is best to take assertive action or divert your attention from what is outside your realm of control.

The second exercise is to imagine a conversation with your *neshamah*. Have someone play you, and you play your *neshamah*, which is in touch with the truth. Have the person ask you, "Why did You bring this person into my life?" Then, imagine what this Godly part of you would reply. The person playing you can protest, "I don't want this person in my life! S/he makes me miserable and makes me feel like a failure! If s/he weren't around, I could accomplish so much more! I'd be so much happier. So why did I have to go through this?" The answers that come to you are the ones you need to hear.

You will find yourself realizing that the most difficult people can be the greatest blessing because they are the ones who force you to work on the humble acceptance of your limitations, on assertiveness, on silence, self-control and the entire list of *middoth* found at the back of this book.

11 | The Gift of Emotional Tzedakah: Empathy

If you really want to express your love in a meaningful way, bring greater understanding and closeness between you and others and reduce tensions and conflicts, you must learn how to listen — not just with your ears, but with your heart.

Listening is emotional *tzedakah*, for it requires that you give of yourself in the fullest sense possible. People think of listening as a passive act. It isn't. To really listen, one must allow oneself to actually experience the emotions of the person who is talking to you. That means allowing yourself to feel both the depths of their pain and the heights of their joy. Listening means that you give up your own self-involvement in order to invest your attention in the other person's world. That takes time and effort. That's why it is considered an act of real love.

One of the forty-eight ways by which a person acquires a true Torah personality is the willingness to "bear the yoke of one's fellow" (*Avoth* 6:6). Empathy is one way that we can do this.

I witnessed a good example of how not to "bear the yoke" in a family medical clinic. Near the waiting room was the nurse's station, where a three-year-old child was howling in pain as the nurse tried to clean his badly scraped knees with antiseptic solution. He kept screaming, "It hurts! It hurts!" while the mother kept screaming even louder, "It doesn't hurt! It doesn't hurt!" The louder she screamed, the angrier he became because she was not validating his distress.

What the child needed to hear was, "I know it hurts. What a brave boy you are! Yes, it does hurt. A lot. I know. Soon it will be all over. Such a brave boy you are."

The mitzvah of loving others is best fulfilled by trying to understand how they think and feel. This is what creates a feeling of closeness and unity.

The truth is that we cannot really understand another's pain until we have experienced the same thing ourselves. Even then, there are always individual differences. In many cases, we are limited by lack of experience. For example, can a woman with children really know the pain of being childless? Can a person who has never lost someone close really know the pain of a loved one dying? Can the healthy have any idea of what it is like to live in chronic pain or can the wealthy really understand what it is like to be impoverished? Can the young know what it is like to be old and lonely? Ultimately, we struggle with our losses pretty much alone. Yet we have an obligation to help people feel less alone by doing our utmost to enter their reality and feel things from their point of view.

What is empathy?

> *Chesed* is not merely giving material goods to others. A person must learn to understand others in order to fulfill the obligation of doing *chesed*. He must try to sense their problems and feel their suffering.— Paraphrased from ALEI SHUR, pp. 93-94

Empathy comes from the words *em* (in) and *pathy* (feeling). Empathy is simple because you don't have to do anything! You don't offer advice, don't try to uplift the person, calm him down or find a solution for him. Empathy means sharing in another person's emotions, getting inside his heart and mind for a few seconds so that you can have some understanding of what he is experiencing.

Empathy is the essence of love. It's the first step in good communication, the first step in a crisis — and often the only step which is needed to calm down an explosive situation. And it often is something we can accomplish successfully in the time span of ten seconds or less!

Empathy implies, If you are in distress, then I am in distress with you. You are not alone. If this is important to you, then it is important to me too, important enough for me to take the time to understand what you're going through.

R.E.A.C.H.

Empathy consists of the first three steps of the REACH process:

R: *REFLECT* the other person's feelings in your face and awaken the same feeling in your heart.

E: *ENCOURAGE* the person to share more by saying, "Oh, I'm so sorry," or "Tell me more about how it happened," or by asking questions which show interest.

A: *ACCEPT* and validate the person's right to feel whatever he is feeling, whether it is bored, overwhelmed, insulted, rejected, afraid, lonely, helpless, hurt, disillusioned, despairing, cheated and angry, or loved, enthusiastic, confident, generous, forgiving and calm. Don't condemn the feelings or try to change them. Simply acknowledge, "You're really upset" or "You're in a lot of pain."

Often, REA is all the other person needs in order for him to feel better. If not, he might need and want more help.

Logic and philosophy cannot penetrate if a person is experiencing intense emotions. "Head talk" (e.g., "Things will work out," "Count your blessings," etc.) will sound superficial and even cruel if you haven't had any "heart talk" first. So it is usually best to do a minute or two of REA before going on to C:

C: Ask the person to *CONSIDER CHANGES* in attitude or behavior that might solve the problem, or help the person bear the pain of what cannot be changed. For example, you might say, "What can you learn from this experience?" "What solutions have you thought of?" "Why do you think God brought this sitaution (or person) into your life?"

H: *HONOR* the person for having shared and for trusting you enough to share his pain with you.

The importance of reflecting

> This is my God and I will glorify Him. — SHEMOTH 15:2

Abba Shaul commented on this verse: "Emulate Him. Just as God is compassionate and merciful, so too should you be compassionate and merciful" (*Shabbath* 133b).

Reflecting means feeling in your own heart what the other person is going through. It means allowing your facial expression to mirror their pain. It doesn't have to be anything major: the washing machine broke; the eggs burned; there was a critical remark; an illness; an incompetent clerk; a disappointment at work, etc. We can all try to identify with the feelings that arise from these situations because we've all had them. When we empathize, we pull out of our memory banks similar feelings which accompanied our own experiences. If we've never experienced what another person is going through, we can still attempt to feel what he or she is feeling. This very effort creates a greater sense of closeness.

The results of not empathizing can be disastrous for a relationship.

◊ EXAMPLE: "I am undergoing chemotherapy. Every time I try to tell my husband how bad I feel, he says, 'But you look terrific. Everything's going to be fine.' I no longer have any desire to talk to him."

◊ EXAMPLE: "Once, when I was eleven, I came home devastated because the girls in my class had decided to ostracize me because my parents were divorced. I poured my heart out to my mother, explaining what had happened, and she patted me on the head, flippantly said, 'This too shall pass,' and walked out of the room. I felt so rejected that I decided never to share anything with her ever again. And I didn't."

Empathy doesn't have to be about major issues. You can have a toothache, a sprained ankle or a stain on your favorite suit. When you share a feeling, you want someone to share the same emotion with you. You can practice "bearing the yoke" with another person just by acknowledging that the person is in pain and has the right to show it.

Encouraging more

> ...true love [is] to realize what others are lacking and to feel
> their suffering. — LOVE YOUR NEIGHBOR, p. 306

To encourage a person to share more, you also need to avoid "roadblocking" him with invalidating statements. Note the following encouraging vs. discouraging statements:

1. Encouraging: "You must feel awful about getting laid off, and after so many years at the company. What happened?"

Discouraging: "I knew this would happen! Every time you try something, you fail! You're so irresponsible!"

2. Encouraging: "Oy, the car was totaled? You must feel terrible. How did the accident happen?"

Discouraging: "You're so careless!" "I've told you a million times to be more careful. What a disaster!"

3. Encouraging: "I know how awful it is to feel fat, to be fighting this never ending battle of the bulge."

Discouraging: "Who cares about your weight problems? You don't think about anyone but yourself. Don't you have anything more important to think about?"

4. Encouraging: "Oy, that must have been so embarrassing!"

Discouraging: "Don't take it to heart." "You always make mountains out of molehills." "It's not that bad!"

5. Encouraging: "Oy, I'm sorry it got lost. I'll help you find it."

Discouraging: "You're such a scatterbrain! You're always losing things!"

6. Encouraging: "I know how it is to be bored. You sometimes feel like screaming! Let's brainstorm about things to do."

Discouraging: "Bored again? You ungrateful brat! I'm not your entertainment director! Get away from me."

Avoid pat answers

> If there be among you a needy man...you shall not harden your heart nor shut your hand from your needy brother. — DEVARIM 15:7

Pat answers are impersonal, trite statements made with a "hardened heart" and no real show of concern. These statements make the other person feel wrong, bad, inferior, petty, immature or stupid for feeling bad. For example: "It's nothing," "Count your blessings," "Don't take it to heart." A pat answer conveys the message: "You and your problems are of no significance to me." "You don't deserve to be taken seriously." That is why it feels so bad to be "pat answered" with some trite cliché or facile advice.

If one says, "*Baruch Hashem*, you still have so much to be

thankful for" after a few minutes of sincere sympathy and with real love in your heart, the words will usually have a positive effect. If said flippantly, the words will seem to be an attempt to get the other person to shut up. It's all a matter of what's in our hearts.

It doesn't matter whether someone has a terminal illness or has just stubbed his toe, the important thing is to feel with the person and validate his right to express his pain.

We cannot always help those in pain, but we can always "bear the yoke" by showing sensitivity to their feelings. This is not to say that every minor ache and pain should be the occasion for serious attention. That would be just as disastrous as being indifferent, for it would train the other person to be self-preoccupied and to make mountains out of molehills. However, real pain calls for a show of concern, even if there is little we can do to help.

There is a famous joke about the inscription on a tombstone which said: See, I told you I was sick! It's a joke — but the pain of feeling that no one is listening to you or taking you seriously is the very real and obvious metamessage beneath the humor.

The feedback loop

When you show the person that you care by trying to understand what he or she is feeling, you create what is called a feedback loop. Trust between people is built when they can share their deepest feelings and know that they will be understood and accepted.

To create a feedback loop, you have to take the time to listen to the other person's perceptions. People can have completely opposite emotional reactions to the same experience. Unless you know how the person really feels, you cannot respond correctly. For example, X finds it relatively easy to accept her miscarriage since she is in her early twenties, with three children under the age of three. But Y is devastated by her miscarriage because after trying for years to conceive, she fears that she has lost her only chance for a baby.

Empathy means being where the person is, not imposing your own judgments or feelings on the other.

Or, let's take criticism. Because X is secure about her husband's love for her, she wasn't shattered when he mentioned the mess in the living room. However, Y's husband suffers from Abusive Personality

Syndrome. She is crushed whenever he puts her down, because she knows his remarks reflect a basic contempt for her and a belief that she is a totally incompetent failure. X can shrug off an occasional critical comment or reply, "You're right! I'd better get my act together." But Y won't welcome someone telling her, "Don't take it to heart."

X was glad he was fired because he was looking for an excuse to do something he really wanted to do. He had some money saved up, and was confident that another job would turn up eventually. He didn't mind hearing someone say "it's all going to work out" because that's what he believed. But Y just lost his job and doesn't have any savings. With winter coming and a car payment due and another child on the way, he knows that the loss of the job means the loss of a car, no heat during the long, cold winter months, no shoes for the seven children, and tremendous hardship for everyone. He is an insecure, unconfident person, and this has been a terrible blow to his already low self-esteem.

As you see, you must know the context of the event for the individual before you can know how to respond. You should also be aware of the fact that people can feel invalidated by those who are overly sympathetic.

Empathy builds relationships

A woman consulted me about her oldest daughter, age fifteen. Despite punishments and slaps, this child continued to be insolent. For weeks, I helped the mother understand the concept of empathy and encouraged her to practice on the minor losses and pains in her children's lives. Then came a major test. A few weeks before the mother was to give birth to her eighth child, the daughter needed a new dress. When the mother offered to go to town with her, the girl yelled at her angrily, "I don't want to go with you. You're fat and you're ugly. I don't want this baby and I won't help you after it's born!" Normally, the mother would have slapped the child for being so *chutzpadik*, and I'm sure many readers would justify this response.

However, in keeping with her newly adopted attitude to use every stressful event as an opportunity to model good *middoth*, the mother said, "I see that you're in pain. I love you. Tell me what's bothering you." With that, the child burst into tears and, hugging her mother, said, "I'm sorry I was so mean. It's just that we don't have any time together and we'll have even less time after the baby comes." As they talked, it turned out that the child, at fifteen, was experiencing major fears about the whole subject of pregnancy and childbirth, as well as having the burden of the household chores on her shoulders while her mother recuperated, and feeling upset that they would have less time together. By sharing these feelings, the two were soon laughing and feeling better.

Without empathy, the daughter's outburst would have intensified their emotional deadlock. With empathy, their relationship became closer than ever.

When communication has ceased: The best-worst game

Sadly, all too often lack of empathy causes family members to stop communicating with each other. If this has happened in your family, you can often renew a relationship by asking the person each night, "What was the best thing that happened to you today?" When s/he has told you, ask, "What was the worst thing that happened?" No matter what the person says, listen with all your heart. Validate. Accept. Don't give advice.

> ◊ EXAMPLE: "I had felt very cut off from my husband for years. We had stopped communicating because we both felt the other had no understanding. After learning about empathy, I decided to try again. Once a week, I tried the Best-Worst Game with him. I listened. I didn't offer any advice, which was my big weakness. I used to tell him what to do, which, especially for a man, was very demeaning. In time, he started asking me the same questions. Little by little, by sticking to the rules of REA, we were able to re-establish a relationship which I thought had died."

> ◊ EXAMPLE: "Because I was feeling so estranged from my son, I started playing the Best-Worst game with him. Suddenly, one night, he blurted out that he had been molested by a neighborhood pervert three years earlier. I was so upset — not only about this horrible incident, but about the fact that he had held this in for three years, three years of pain for all of us, during which his

marks went down and his behavior had deteriorated. It made me realize how much we had hurt him by not being empathic toward him when he was small. Thankfully, thanks to my new empathy skills, we were able to deal with the problem openly and get the help our son needed as well as start a court case against the man involved."

Empathy helps people to bear the pain

Empathy awakens and maintains love. Just knowing that someone cares about your feelings helps you to accept what cannot be changed or find the courage to take action when needed. In an atmosphere of acceptance, your mind unfreezes and you can think of the *berachah* in the event.

> ◊ EXAMPLE: "Being divorced, with three small children, and no money to pay the bills, I just can't take the pressure sometimes. Sometimes, I get so depressed I want to die. Then I call the one good friend who has been with me through all of this. For some reason, when she sympathizes with me and lets me talk about my desire to die, I invariably brighten up and have a desire to go on again, despite the pain. I don't know how it works, but she makes my life bearable."

Our ability to be close to others is developed as we face our own losses and disappointments. In fact, this is sometimes the only benefit we may be able to think of at a time of loss, i.e., Now I know what it's like. Now I can really sympathize with others. Empathy is one way we can put our pain to good use.

The gender problem

Many times women complain, "My husband isn't sensitive to my needs. He doesn't seem interested in my life or seem to really need an emotional relationship all that much. He says he loves me, but there is no real closeness or understanding." Many times, men complain, "She's forever nagging me. She's always on my back. She doesn't understand my needs or respect my feelings."

Men and women tend to communicate differently and have

different emotional needs. Typically, what women want most from any personal interchange is empathy, while men want factual information or to engage in problem-solving discussions.

Men and women often react quite differently to the subject of empathy. Men (in particular Thinking types) are more sensitive to issues of respect, hierarchy, status, power and independence. This leads to difficulties in both giving and receiving empathy. For example, many Thinking-type men (and Thinking women) may believe:

1. A person who empathizes is being condescending. For example, if someone says, "I'm sorry you lost your job," to a woman, she is likely to hear that statement as an act of concern and involvement, while a man may take it to imply that the person considers him to be a loser. The same sentence — two opposite reactions.

Because men often interpret an expression of empathy as an act of putting the other person down, they may refrain from empathizing in order not to appear condescending.

2. Expressing feelings implies that one is needy and lacking control of a situation. Men are more comfortable expressing anger, for anger gives an illusion of power and control. To express unhappiness or seek support, on the other hand, implies weakness and lack of competency to many men. Because men are more status conscious, they often deny having any deficiencies and think no one else should either.

If a person associates the expression of feelings with the lack of control, then to encourage someone to express feelings is to encourage the person to be weak, incapable and out of control.

3. Empathy creates emotional closeness, and emotional closeness threatens their independence and autonomy, i.e., "If I listen this time, I'll be sucked into the slime pit of emotionalism with this person forever and never have any time for myself." It's true that empathy requires some investment of time, but if men don't invest that time, they may find that their wives complain more, not less, or that their formerly loving wives become surprisingly cold and distant.

4. Listening passively puts one in a subordinate position. Thus many men feel uncomfortable and feel a loss of status when they are "talked at," lectured to or taught by a woman. No matter what the content of the conversation, the position of having to listen to some-

one else can be painful.

5. The expression or existence of feelings is of no value. When a Feeling type begins to talk about feelings, even in a very controlled manner, a Thinking-type person may experience the other as overly emotional and overly talkative, even if he or she is merely reporting an event or speaking briefly. Hence the quickness with which many men accuse women of being hysterical and their feelings exaggerated and unwarranted. This judgment, often rendered, makes women furious, which then makes the accusation of hysteria seem true.

Those who pride themselves on being able to turn their own feelings on and off at will don't understand why Feeling types cannot do the same.

6. Listening to someone's problem requires the listener to do something about it. Men prefer to be in the position of respected advice-giver and teacher, as this maintains the one-up, superior position with which they feel more comfortable.

When a woman (or a Feeling-type man) shares feelings, she does not necessarily want the problem solved. Usually, she is simply trying to establish rapport. She wants a sympathetic nod of the head, or a verbal expression such as, "Oh," "Yeah," or "Hmmm."

Unfortunately, what often happens is that an unhappy wife approaches her husband to report her feelings and establish rapport. His first reaction is not to empathize, but to give advice or to wave her away like a pesky fly. If he gives advice, he gets the pleasure of feeling superior, but he's missed the REA, which is usually all his wife really wanted. Jumping to C (problem solving) cuts her off from achieving emotional closeness. If what she wanted was advice, she'll go away pleased. But if what she sought was closeness, she'll be very frustrated.

Men talk mainly to gather information, solve problems and impress others. Sharing feelings as an end in itself may seem absurd to them. Women tend to share feelings as an end in itself, because that is how they achieve a sense of closeness and feel less alone. A complaint is often simply the opening move in an attempt to connect. They gauge the degree of caring according to the response. If closeness is achieved by hearing words of support or sympathy, the interpersonal tension vanishes. However, if a man attacks or pushes her away, the woman may be highly distressed because that is the only way women know to achieve closeness, which is the average woman's greatest need.

Ironically, men (and Thinking women) often believe they are showing involvement when they criticize, give orders, give advice or lecture! But Feeling types interpret these behaviors as attempts to put them down and keep them subordinate.

Giving support is more natural for women because they have stronger needs for affiliation. They don't experience loss of status, power or independence when they do so. Even if they do, the loss is worth it in order to experience closeness. They don't associate the desire for emotional support and closeness with being inferior, stupid or immature.

Bridging the gender gap

It is extremely painful for a person who longs for closeness not to get it. It is cruel to say things like, "Stop complaining and be happy with what you have," "Most women are in the same boat, so don't feel so sorry for yourself," "Count your blessings." In fact, to jump in with such responses is to deprive her of the very closeness which she is craving. Lectures don't fill empty stomachs, nor does philosophizing fill an aching heart.

Those who feel sad and lonely need someone to empathize with their pain. The closeness which is lacking in the marriage is then somewhat compensated for by closeness with another human being who listens without judging, analyzing, advising or preaching. And it often enables someone in an emotional Siberia to go on with her life.

Women can more easily bridge this gender gap with Feeling-type men who have a greater innate desire for emotional closeness. Those with Thinking mates, however, are far more frustrated, since Thinking types often simply do not understand why empathy is of any value or importance. With patience, however, many Thinking types eventually come to see the value of empathy as an act of *chesed*.

In dealing with an unempathetic husband, the following may be helpful:

1. Don't assume that your husband is deliberately being insensitive just to hurt you. Most men are just not as sensitive as women.

They spend far less time developing interpersonal skills as children and have far less interest or experience in these skills.

2. Men's needs for status and power often create conflicts with their needs for affiliation. Be aware of that conflict.

3. Without anger, demonstrate the effectiveness of empathy. This is especially effective with children. Say to your child when your husband is in the room, "I feel so bad along with you." When they see how well empathy works, they may be more willing to employ this tool.

4. Without anger, state precisely what you want. E.g., "I don't want advice. We may not attach the same degree of importance to this matter. I don't want you to maximize or minimize what's bothering me. I just want you to hear what I have to say and to feel my pain."

5. State clearly, "If you continue to criticize or show indifference, you will kill the relationship, because I will lose all desire to relate to you."

6. Limit your demands and complaints, or write them down and give them in written form to your husband, or work through a third party such as a *rav* or a counselor.

7. Model empathy. Say to your husband, "Seems like you had a hard day," "That was very embarrassing," "I see how upset you are."

Although few husbands are like best friends, many do become more empathic with time. As Thinking-type men reach middle age, they often mellow. They may no longer be so obsessed with status and independence or feel their masculinity is compromised or threatened by listening or sympathizing or by wanting emotional closeness.

However, if Thinking types have gotten the impression that Feeling types are hysterical, unreliable and out of control most of the time, they become less sympathetic. What can you do?

1. Stop nagging. If your husband experiences your emotional demands as a bottomless pit which he cannot possibly fill, he'll be discouraged by the threat of certain failure with you. He'll think, Why let her talk? If she starts, she'll go on and on and tell me how I've disappointed her and caused her so much pain. I don't need to hear this!

2. Let go. No one wants to be constantly pushed into doing

something distasteful. Find ways to make yourself happy. Wait patiently for him to show a desire to communicate. When he does, make it pleasant! Don't tell him or even hint through body language that "it's not enough, you creep!"

3. Be thankful, truly thankful, for whatever you get. Remember, he's reached a point where he's had enough criticism. Now is the time to encourage. It may not be all you want, but positive reinforcement is the best way to get people to respond positively. You can only create a more loving atmosphere if you have love in your heart and show it whenever you can.

When marriages go sour, they may be saved with empathy

He was angry about his wife's desire to move from their fourth-floor flat to a more expensive ground-level apartment. He kept saying to her, "You're just a *kvetch*. If you were really spiritual, you would accept what you have and be happy to make sacrifices because your husband is learning full time."

She kept saying, "I can't talk to him. In fact, we haven't talked about anything other than superficial things for years. He has a pat answer to every problem. I could have a conversation with him in my own mind beforehand and save myself the trouble of hearing him tell me again, 'Everything will be just fine,' or 'You're over emotionalizing.'"

He kept saying, "I feel I have to protect myself from being attacked by a litany of complaints and poor-me stories every time I walk in the door. I just turn it off."

The colder he got, the more desperate she became. By focusing only on the negative in each other they lost sight of the total picture: he saw her as one big sore thumb, and she saw him as an emotional iceberg. To break the deadlock, their counselor had them switch roles. He role-played his wife and she role-played him. Then the counselor had them both practice saying empathic statements, such as "I hear you," "I'm sorry you're in so much distress," "I see your point of view." Like many emotionally suppressive people, the husband feared, If I show I care, the complaints will go on and on forever. He changed this belief once he realized that by being empathic, her complaints decreased because then she was getting the closeness she wanted!

Empathy changed his perception of his wife. He realized that she was not such a *kvetch*, but simply lonely. He said, "I guess I'd also feel depressed, overwhelmed, frustrated, discouraged, unappreciated, inadequate and cooped up in solitary confinement if I were home all the time with three small children. I guess I really do need to take the time to understand her world a little."

Empathy also changed his wife's perceptions. She realized that her husband was a basically caring person, who was afraid of being overwhelmed by her demands, however minimal she felt they were. Every demand of hers made him feel like less of a man and more of a child being nagged by a domineering mother. When she stopped being so angry at him for not fulfilling her demands, and began to find ways to make her life happier independent of him, she appeared less needy, which made him feel less threatened and more sympathetic. They often filtered their requests through their *rav*, who was able to present them to each in a manner which, being devoid of emotional overtones or threats, was easier to accept.

She was advised to keep her communications positive and upbeat for the next few months. This made him want to listen to her, since it was now an enjoyable experience rather than a painful one. With the pressure off him to perform emotionally, he softened. As their communication improved, she could talk to him about the effect of pat answers in a general way without making him feel attacked. True, she had to suppress her anger and jump to the opposite extreme of positivity in order to balance her years of negativity, but little by little, they developed a more honest relationship.

Two months later, the husband came and told her that he was taking out a loan in order to find a ground-level apartment. He wasn't as insensitive to her needs as she had thought.

When not to empathize

Empathy is not always appropriate or necessary. For example:

1. When the person in pain asks for help in changing his attitude or behavior. When someone has lost his way, he doesn't want anyone to tell him, "Oh, you must feel so bad about being lost." He wants

directions! If people want advice or help in solving a problem, they'll be annoyed by your sympathy. It often helps to ask, "What do you want — advice or sympathy?"

2. When the person is carrying on excessively. Sometimes it is best to divert a person's attention away from his pain, to get him out of the house or involved in other interests. When my children were little and would be excessively upset about some trivial matter, I used the diversionary tactic of talking about their next birthday party, even if it were months away.

3. When the person has done something wrong. Then you must sternly say, "This is wrong. This is unacceptable!" There is also a time to give *mussar*, such as when the person is really on the wrong path or has adopted the wrong *hashkafah*.

4. When the person suffers from Abusive Personality Syndrome. These people get pleasure out of hurting others. No matter what you say, they will crush you by attacking your statement as insensitive, stupid or irrational. Many of these people are truly evil. Stay away from them.

5. When you don't have the time or are in too much pain yourself. If so, it is better to tell the person, "It's not a good time for me to talk. I'll be free in an hour."

Chronic complainers

Listening to endless complaints is like giving alcohol to an alcoholic. A chronic complainer will go on and on, getting more depressed and bitter. Chronic complainers believe that if they stop *kvetch*ing, they will have no way of bonding to people and will be isolated and alone. Give a few seconds of empathy, but realize that it won't help to let them go on and on. Neither will it be helpful to say, "You're such a *kvetch*! You're so wrapped up in yourself!" Instead, give homework assignments. For example, tell the person:

1. "From now on, every time you put a piece of food in your mouth, say a *berachah* out loud, with real gratefulness. Do this for two days, then call me back and let me know if it hasn't brought a little joy into your life." The people who just want to *kvetch* will not call back. But those who want to improve will be grateful to you and will do their work diligently.

2. Tell the person, "Buy a little notebook. On one side of the page write down ten things that required you to exercise self-discipline. On the other side, write down ten things that brought you joy. Call me back tomorrow and report your list." This will teach them how to bond in a healthy manner. (Children with a tendency toward self-pity can reverse this trend with a Happiness Notebook.)

3. Encourage the person to read books on the Holocaust. That may give them some perspective.

4. Keep saying, "So what are you going to do about this problem?"

5. Say, "I also complain more than I should. I don't always handle my own losses and disappointments well. I'm not always thankful for everything I have in life. Let's work together on being more grateful."

> ◊ EXAMPLE: "I used to be full of self-pity and looked for people who would sympathize with me. I loved telling about my horrid childhood, my unhappy marriage, and my inability to 'find myself.' I used to revel in the slime pits of self-pity. Finally, a friend gave me real *mussar*. Whenever I started to tell about my tragic plight, she'd say, 'I feel badly that you had to go through all that, but there must be a reason why Hashem wanted it to happen. Tell me what you've learned from what you went through. Now tell me ten things you have to be grateful for.' I was resentful of her at first. I thought she was not empathic and completely superficial, but I knew, even in the darkness of my despair, that she was right and that she alone could help me. Thanks to her, I learned not to be so dependent on outside circumstances for my feeling of well-being and now I find joy in being grateful for what I have instead of always focusing on what I lack."

People who really want to get better will do these assignments. Those who don't, won't. Disturbed people, if given a sympathetic ear, will take more and more of your time and turn more and more negative.

When empathy is the correct response, it is a great gift to let others know you care. When empathy is not called for, it is also a gift to disconnect from that person or to help him grow by teaching him to direct his thoughts and his behavior in a healthier manner.

12 | The Gift of Recognizing Invalidation

Do not comfort [your fellow] while his dead lies before him...

— AVOTH 4:18

Rabbi Shimon ben Elazar's advice has great psychological insight. And it holds true not only in situations of actual death. The opposite of empathy is invalidation. Invalidation is what happens when you express an opinion or a feeling and someone replies, "That's ridiculous", "How could you be so stupid?", "Oh come on, you don't really believe that!"

Unfortunately, few people heed Rabbi Shimon's advice, as the following scenes indicate.

Scene 1: A top cardiologist from Moscow made *aliyah* with his family. At the absorption center, he expressed his disappointment at not being able to find a job in his field in Israel. He had finally taken a job delivering groceries for the local supermarket. As he spoke with me, a cheerful volunteer made continuous invalidating statements.

C (cardiologist): "Boy, it sure is rough to go from being a respected doctor in a large hospital to being a delivery boy."

I (invalidater): "How you make a living isn't important. The important thing is that you're living in Israel."

C: "But I'm not using my mind the way I want to. I'm not keeping up with the literature. I'm losing my skills. And there's so little money that I just can't make ends meet."

I: "Oh, don't feel bad. Everyone lives on overdraft here."

C: "Yeah, but I can't pay the bills. I'm not making it. And when the manager of the supermarket tells me to take a broom and sweep up, I find it very difficult."

191

I: "Don't worry. Everything will be fine."

C: "But I can't live on hope. I want to work in my field."

I: "Hey, come on! Cheer up!"

Scene 2: A friend's eight-month old baby was undergoing treatment for cancer. I sat with her for hours, hearing one visitor after another say, "Don't worry. He's going to be just fine." When we were finally alone, she looked at me through tearful eyes and said, "Don't they know how much their optimism hurts me? Don't they realize that they aren't letting me talk about what's most on my mind — that he may not get better? It's like someone putting a hand over my mouth and suffocating me. I have to lie and smile and say over and over, 'Of course, everything's going to be fine,' which only makes me feel worse. Why can't these people stop with their optimistic drivel and just listen a little?"

Scene 3: Two grandmothers were talking at a bus stop about their children. Number 1 was telling Number 2 how sad it was that her son and daughter-in-law had left Israel for America. "It's so sad," sighed Number 1. "We were so close. I don't have the money to see them and since my son is a teacher, he won't be able to visit me often." "Don't worry," Number 2 replied, "They'll be back soon."

A look of pain flashed across the face of Number 1. Instead of commiserating, Number 2 was giving her false hopes. Nevertheless, Number 1 tried again, saying, "It'll never be the same. A visit to see my children and grandchildren for a few days every few years is not the same as having them live on the same block and having them run over each afternoon for a few minutes' chat with Bubbie. I miss them so much already. It's devastating."

"But look at all you can do with your life now. You won't be tied down. You can do whatever you want now," Number 2 replied. At that, Number 1 fell silent, her shoulders slumped in sadness and isolation.

Scene 4: When a young girl got a poor mark on a test, she told her mother how badly she felt about it. Her mother said, "It's just a test. It doesn't mean anything." The girl continued, "But it's important to me." Her mother replied, "Don't make such a big thing out of it. There are so many worse problems in the world." The daughter tried again. "But I might not get into Seminary if I don't do well." The mother said, "It's your own fault! You don't study enough!" The daughter left the room looking very discouraged.

Scene 5: A young mother complained to an older woman about feeling trapped in the house all day long. She told her, "I'm so depressed. I resent my children and snap at them when they make demands. I think about death all the time." The older woman said, "Nonsense! These are the best years of your life! What's wrong with you? Don't you appreciate how wonderful it is to have healthy children? You're ungrateful, selfish and spoiled." The young woman fled the home in tears.

Scene 6: A young woman had a miscarriage. When she burst into tears at hearing the confirmation of her fears, her doctor said, "Come on, be strong. You'll have more." His voice and manner were so impersonal and flippant that she felt he was saying, "Forget that this happened. It's nothing." By not validating her right to grieve, he intensified her grief. He was implying that her baby's life, short as it was, was of no significance.

My daughter had to undergo a painful medical procedure. As she was writhing in pain, the doctor kept saying, "This doesn't hurt." If only he would have said, "I know this hurts, and I'm sorry to have to do this, but it will only take a few more seconds" — anything but that invalidating statement, "It doesn't hurt." The gift of that experience was that it reminded me to be extra careful not to invalidate others.

Notice that in each of these examples, there was no REA, no attempt to share the other person's pain. Instead, the sufferer was belittled. You may not think the other person's pain is all that bad, but if you care about someone, then you'll make the effort to take seriously what she takes seriously.

When we fail to fully grasp another's pain and do not share their burden, then instead of a moment of mutual intimacy, there is only disappointment and distance.

Recognizing invalidation

> A wicked man hardens his face... — MISHLEI 21:29

Most people don't mean to be cruel when they give pat answers. They simply don't have good communication skills. They do not realize that by minimizing people's pain, they maximize it, or that by maximizing, they make the person feel worse than he did when he began speaking. However, some people are truly abusive. The best way to know if you're with a truly abusive person is to ask yourself if he or she is constantly trying to make you feel like you're crazy, stupid or totally incompetent.

Invalidation is similar to having someone pull the chair out from under you when you are about to sit down. That is what it is like to be hit with an invalidating statement. It is important to recognize these statements in order to understand why you feel bad after hearing them and so that you can avoid making them yourself.

Note the communication roadblocks which make the other person feel stupid, isolated and misunderstood in the following scenes.

Scene 1: A person says, "I don't feel good. I'm falling apart. I need help."

Shaming: "Other people manage. Why can't you?"

Ordering: "Shut up! Stop complaining. Just keep on going!"

Implication: There's something wrong with you! You're really inadequate.

Scene 2: The person says, "I feel so fat." Or, "I did a lousy job." Or, "I'm not happy with our marriage." Or, "I think one of our children really needs help. He's very unhappy."

Denying, arguing: "I think you're thin! But you did a great job. That's the stupidest thing I ever heard. Everything's fine! There's nothing wrong with this family!"

Implication: There's something wrong with you. You have lousy judgment. You're stupid for feeling what you're feeling. You're crazy.

Scene 3: A person says, "I'm so depressed. I don't feel like living." Or, "My husband/wife is so difficult." Or, "I'm having a lot of problems with my oldest. She's so insolent."

Advising: "Just take a hot bath and you'll perk up." Or, "Just show your husband/wife more respect and everything will be wonderful. Just give that girl a good smack!"

Implication: There's something wrong with you. After all, the answer's so simple. You must be stupid if you can't figure it out yourself.

Scene 4: A person says, "We lost all the money we'd invested." Or, "I have a terrible headache." Or, "My son is stealing, running away from home and breaking windows."

Minimizing: "Stop crying. It's not the end of the world. Don't take it to heart. It's only money! I don't understand why you're so upset. It wouldn't bother me one bit! It's just a phase he's going through. It'll pass."

Implication: There's something really wrong with you. You're petty and immature. You have no right to feel hurt. Your feelings are inappropriate.

Scene 5: A person says, "I just lost my job." Or, "My daughter's been married six years and has no children."

Philosophizing: "Just have *emunah* and *bitachon*. Count your blessings. This too shall pass. It will all work out."

Implication: There's something really wrong with you. You're not a really spiritual person. You're just a *kvetch*.

Scene 6: A person says, "I lost my ticket. I flunked the test. The cookies burned." Or, "I can't control the kids."

Name-calling and put-downs: "You careless idiot! You stupid jerk. You're completely untrustworthy! Next time you'll burn the house down! I can't leave you alone for a second! You're such a marshmallow! You're a wimp, a *kvetch*, a feminist, a jerk or a nag. Better you should never have been born! You're going to be the death of me! You've ruined my life."

Implication: There's something really wrong with you. You're so horrible that you don't deserve love or respect.

Scene 7: A person says, "I'm falling apart. I can't go on." Or, "Every time I think about losing that job (person, house, etc.) I feel terrible."

Smoothing over: "You'll feel better tomorrow." Or, "Don't worry. Time heals."

Implication: There's something really wrong with you for complaining when you have nothing to complain about.

Scene 8: A person complains about some mistake or failure.

Warning, threatening: "You're going to end up a bum/an old maid/irreligious, etc. I'm going to beat you black and blue. You'll be the death of me. You'll cry over my grave."

Implication: There's something really wrong with you and if I don't take charge of your life, you'll ruin everything.

Often, invalidating statements are not so blatant. They can begin with a subtle lead-in such as:

"Why don't you just...," as if all problems can be easily solved.
"If only you had..."
"How could you have been so stupid?"
"You always..."
"You'd better..."

When a person reveals his pain to another, he is testing whether or not he can trust the listener. If he doesn't get support, trust can never be established, which is the major reason why so many relationships die and why so many marriages end up in silence or divorce.

Of course, minimizing can be useful at the right time and place. For example, saying "It's nothing" can be helpful to a person who has accidently torn a page in a book he's borrowed or spilled something on your tablecloth. On the other hand, you might need to warn or threaten if someone is in real danger. You often have to command children to follow your orders. And philosophizing is often helpful, as is denying a falsehood. There is a time and a place for everything.

Taking children seriously

The Vilna Gaon describes the fool (*kesil*) as someone without a heart (*chasar lev*). One of the signs of someone lacking a heart is that he ridicules those who are in pain (*Mishlei* 1:22).

Some parents interact with their children almost exclusively by giving orders: "Brush your teeth!" "Say a *berachah*!" "Don't hit your sister!" "Go to your room." "Take a bath." "Clean up that mess!" "Get out of here." While such orders are, to a certain extent, unavoidable, there must be something more to the relationship. If all children hear from you is orders, they will never form a relationship with you of any depth or meaning. The lack of closeness can cause them to become hostile, depressed and insensitive.

Children are often the victims of invalidaters who frequently tell them, "It's nothing," before even knowing what the problem is or the extent of the damage. Many parents are so afraid of spoiling their children that they think they should automatically deny, minimize or ignore the problem whenever a child is in pain in order to toughen him up for the "real" world. This does not toughen the child up. It teaches him not to care about people's feelings.

Children do not have the intelligence or understanding to deal with sibling jealousy, failed friendships, physical handicaps or the thousands of other pains they encounter. They need tools to deal with these situations. They need to know someone cares.

Love means giving significance to the things others take seriously, even if you think it's petty nonsense. Rabbi Yisrael Salanter (*Michtav MeEliyahu*, vol. 1, p. 99) says that a parent should have the sensitivity to realize that the loss of a toy boat to a child is like the loss of a real boat to an adult. When a younger sibling tears up an older child's work of art, it's no different than discovering that someone has smashed something which you worked very hard to create. When a child loses his trading cards, breaks a favorite toy or is rejected by a friend, an adult may be tempted to see his loss as trivial and his pain as unjustified. But it's a major loss to the child. If we remind ourselves that we, too, have mourned our own trivial losses, we will be more compassionate.

Furthermore, many of children's seemingly petty problems are serious; they may have an emotionally disturbed teacher, parents who argue all the time or unruly peers to contend with every day. After all, bullies do need to be stopped. Some teachers do need to be removed from the school system. Some aches and pains, if ignored, do get much worse.

To a large degree, parents determine whether a child will become an empathic or non-empathic adult. If the parents view their child's problems as so trivial that he is not worth listening to, they should not be surprised if, in the future, the child is insensitive to the parent's feelings. When a parent invalidates a child's feelings, he misses out on the opportunity to create closeness with the child and to model good listening tools.

To you, his little problems seem nothing compared to your own major pains. But to the child, they are major. Feelings need to be respected for that person to feel respected. And empathizing doesn't take long, usually only a few seconds.

To understand this further, use the above scenes to identify the communication roadblocks used in each following exchange.

1. Child: "I don't like this. It tastes yuck."

Invalidating response: "Eat it! It's healthy! What do you think this is, a restaurant? I stood with my varicose veins a long time to make you this meal and you turn your nose up? You ungrateful little brat!''

Communication roadblocks: _____

Validating response: "You don't like how it tastes? I'm sorry, but this is what I made. Do you want to make yourself something?''

2. Child: "I'm scared.''

Invalidating response: "Nonsense! Don't be scared. There's nothing to be afraid of. Stop being such a sissy.''

Roadblocks: _____

Validating response: "It's okay to be scared. I get scared myself sometimes when I have to do something new or go to the doctor. I feel the fear, but I do what I have to do anyway! That's called courage. Doing the things you fear to do is what builds confidence!''

3. Child: "I'm stupid.'' (Or, "I'm ugly.'')

Invalidating response: "Nonsense! You're wrong. You're smart.'' "You're a girl, so being smart isn't important!''

Roadblocks: _____.

Validating response: "Wow, that really hurts. I remember being laughed at in school, too. It felt awful. Tell me more about what's going on. Maybe this calls for some solutionizing.''

4. Child: "I flunked the test.''

Invalidating response: "It's your own fault. You didn't study! You're going to end up nothing but a bum, that's what!

Roadblocks: _____

Validating response: "I see how bad you feel. Do you want me to help you think of some solutions?''

5. Child: "I'm hungry.''

Invalidating response: "It's your own fault for not eating more at the last meal. Now you can just suffer.''

Roadblocks: _____

Validating response: "Hmmm...we're not eating for another hour. How about some fruit or veggies until then?''

6. Child: "I hate you!''

Invalidating response: "You ungrateful, *chutzpadik* little brat, you deserve such a beating!'' Roadblocks: _____

Validating response: "I'm very sorry you feel like that. Beneath anger is pain. You must be very hurt to say something like that. Tell me what I could do to improve our relationship.''

7. Child: "I hate him!"

Invalidating response: "You go over there right now and tell your brother you love him!" Roadblocks: _____

Validating response: "It's hard to have an older brother (or sister) who is acting like a bully (or a younger one who is annoying you) or who always gets good grades. I really sympathize with you."

8. Child: "Daddy (Mommy) criticizes me all the time. I can't stand it! I want to run away from this place!"

Invalidating response: "That's not true! Your Daddy (Mommy) loves you very much. It's all your fault. You're the one who's provoking him (her)." Roadblocks: _____

Validating response: "I feel terrible that you're being criticized so much. I see how hurt you are. I wish I could get him (her) to stop. Tell me what I can do to help."

9. Child: "I didn't do my homework! Oh no, my teacher will kill me! And I can't find my books!"

Invalidating response: "Serves you right! You're such a scatterbrain! No one will ever want to marry such an irresponsible idiot like you!" Roadblocks: _____

Validating response: "I also have a problem following through and keeping things in order. Let's solutionize. How can we work on this problem together? We have to help each other to make lists and stick to schedules and put reminders up."

10. Child: "My bike was stolen."

Invalidating response: "How could you have been so stupid as to have left it unlocked! I can't believe how stupid and careless you are! You could cause a major disaster with such a careless attitude." Roadblocks: _____

Validating response: "I feel so bad for you! You loved that bike so much. It brought you so much pleasure. I wish we had the money to get you another one. This is a big disappointment. Maybe we can think of some way for you to earn money to get another one."

11. Child: "A kid at school keeps hitting me."

Invalidating statements: 'You must have provoked him! Just forget about it. It can't be that bad. You're a *kvetch*! You complain about everything! Grow up! I have no time to listen to this nonsense. I have more important things to do. Go away! Just hit him back."
Roadblocks: _____

Validating statements: "Oy, I see how hurt you are." Suggest solutions such as: "Do you want me to talk to the principal or the boy's mother? Would you like to take a self-defense class?"

12. Child: "I hate my teacher. She screams at us all the time. School is torture!"

Invalidating response: "You're just talking *lashon ha-ra*. I don't want to hear about it. I've heard that she is a very fine teacher. You're just complaining." Roadblocks: _____

Validating response: "Oh, I know how hard it is to sit there hour after hour while your teacher yells. I'm sorry you're having such a rough time. Maybe I can talk to her, and if that doesn't work I'll go to the principal."

Try one yourself. Child says: "I have nothing to wear."

Invalidating response: "_____."

Validating response: "_____."

Of course, empathy is not always the right tactic. Obviously, parents must also give orders and impose solutions, such as: "Go to bed!" "Clean it up now!" "I am getting you a tutor!" However, in many situations our empathy as well as our help are necessary.

When you make invalidating statements, you miss out on an opportunity to model empathy and, even more important, to show your children that you care enough to take action to protect them.

By validating children, you teach them that the healthiest response to pain is to first share it with someone who cares. Then, if there is no solution to the problem, they will be more able to bear it with stoic dignity. And if the situation requires assertive action, they will have more courage to take it.

Sometimes all we can say is, "I wish there were something more I could do. But all I can do is say that I love you."

◊ EXAMPLE: "Each time my son complained that his bed was too small, my husband would get angry and yell, 'Just be grateful for what you have and stop nagging.' When I explained the concepts of empathy and validation to him, he replied, 'If I validate him, then I'll have to buy him a new bed.' 'Not at all,' I told him. 'Just tell him you're sorry his bed is so uncomfortable, but that we just don't have the money for a new one. Let's see if he stops nagging.' And that's exactly what happened. However, by validating the child, my husband suddenly saw his point of view and told him that he would try to think of ways to save up and get him a bigger bed."

◊ EXAMPLE: "My five year old had tantrums whenever he didn't get what he wanted. When he screamed, I didn't want to empathize with him over the fact that he couldn't have all the candy he wanted, or get the window seat, or the leg of the chicken or new shoes. I just wanted to hit him! But the angrier I got, the bigger his tantrums grew. Luckily, I learned to empathize before he got even more violent. When he's really upset, I just hug him and tell him I'm sorry I can't give him what he wants. He gets upset for a while, but if I keep saying how sorry I am that I can't give him what he wants, and really empathize with his pain, he eventually calms down."

◊ EXAMPLE: "I take care of a nineteen month old each morning. This morning, when his mother forgot to leave his beloved security blanket, he started whining and looking all over for it. *Baruch Hashem*, I had learned about empathy in my EMETT class the night before, so I hugged him and said, 'You really want your blanket. You miss it a lot. It's hard not to have your blanket with you.' I was amazed that he calmed down and didn't ask for it again! I couldn't believe that empathy would help in a child so young."

We adults may know that children are notorious for getting "divorced" from their best friend and getting back together the next day, but the loss of a friend — even temporarily — can be very traumatic for a child. We know that children often exaggerate the pain they're in, but they have no means to distinguish between the feeling of danger and true danger. Almost any loss may feel catastrophic.

Children don't turn into demanding little monsters, spoiled brats, sissies or hypochondriacs if we offer a few seconds of sympathy when they are hurt. In fact, the opposite happens. When we take a few minutes to empathize, they become less demanding because they feel loved and secure. They also become more responsive to us, because we have modeled responsive behavior to them.

This is particularly true of high-need level children who really do need more time and attention. They are more anxious because they experience the world as a threatening place. This can be due to birth trauma, marital strife between the parents, a learning disability, or verbal and physical abuse. Unless the adults around them are sympathetic, they will conclude that they are hated and unwanted. As a result, they will try to protect themselves from further pain and anxiety by becoming more violent or withdrawn.

No matter what a child is upset about, the fact is that when he talks, he's reaching out to us by expressing his feelings. And that reach-out reflex will wither and die if it is not encouraged.

When sympathy isn't necessary or appropriate, adults can often avoid excessive drama by saying the following:

1. "Let's measure it objectively on a scale of zero to ten."

> ◊ EXAMPLE: "My kids can turn anything into a major event. So I taught them how to measure discomfort on a scale of zero to ten. For example, since the little girl next door got run over by a car and broke her pelvis, I've used that as a 'nine.' But when the cookies burned, that was a 'one.' I also tell them how I work my own emotionalism down. I'll tell them, 'This feels awful, but it's just a little uncomfortable.' I don't measure for the kids. I let them decide the number, and if it's a high number, then even if the event seems trivial to me, I respect their feelings."

2. "Let's focus on a solution." (This works for spilled juice, minor squabbles, etc.)

3. "What did we learn from what just happened?" For example, a child got a poor grade on a test, lost his keys or forgot to take something important to school, etc.

Note: Adults also respond positively to these non-threatening, nondramatic sentences.

Children's doctors and dentists can have an egg timer on hand for frightened children. Before a medical procedure, they can say, "I know this isn't pleasant, but watch the sand go to the bottom of the timer. I'll be done by the time all the sand stops falling!" By empathizing with the child and diverting his attention, they'll have more cooperative children — and teach empathy at the same time.

Why invalidaters invalidate

Most people invalidate others because they simply don't know any better. They think they're being helpful. Such people are usually very responsive to being taught effective communication techniques. However, chronic invalidaters are emotionally wounded and invalidate because they believe :

1. "People who express feelings are inferior and the ones who remain cold and impersonal are superior."

2. "Advice giving is pleasurable! It puts me in a one-up position. I can solve even the most serious problems in seconds."

3. "I'm strong because I can suppress my feelings. I wouldn't be able to function if I didn't. If everyone suppressed their feelings, they would feel better and be more functional."

4. "If I listen to others' pain, I'll encourage it."

5. "If I listen to someone and can't do anything for the person, I'll feel inadequate and incompetent."

6. "I have it so much rougher than s/he does. S/he has no right to complain." For example, when a young person complains to an older person about a problem, the latter may think, "He's young. His problems are so petty compared to mine." If a married woman complains to a widow about her husband, the latter may snap back, "Be grateful you're married! Any husband is better than none!" If a wealthy person complains to a poorer person about a problem, the latter may want to shout back, "Money makes everything easier!" When a childless woman hears a new mother complain about being deprived of sleep, she is sure to think, I'd never complain about lack of sleep if only it were for the same reason."

7. "I'm the one who should be in the spotlight!"

Those who are unable to empathize are unable to love. If nothing else, we can have compassion for such people. Think of what they are missing.

The pain of emotional unresponsiveness

One famous instance of tragic invalidation occurred when two young men escaped from Auschwitz under a pile of clothing which was being carted away from the death camp. They had seen the packed cattle cars arrive, seen the terrified, naked people being driven with whips into the gas chambers. They heard the screams. They saw the smoke. They escaped to warn their fellow Jews of what was going on. Yet wherever they went, whenever they tried to tell their story, people told them that they were crazy, that it could not possibly be that this was happening. No one believed them. The few who did were silenced as being crazy or lacking faith in God. Eventually both men committed suicide.

Suicide or homicide are often on the minds of people who live with invalidaters who meet any expression of feeling with scorn or ridicule. For example, one mother said very smugly, "My rule is that whenever a child comes home and complains about a teacher, I say that the teacher is right and the child is at fault. As a result, they don't complain about their teachers." Her children don't talk to her about anything else of importance to them either. They have no real connection to their own mother.

It doesn't take some tragic event to make us feel humiliated when we are pat answered about it. Any time we make a mistake, forget something, break something or just feel a little blue, it is likely that someone will pat answer us.

Giving *chizuk* is an important *chesed*. But don't blithely reassure people, "Everything is going to be just fine," unless you are a prophet or have information that the other person does not have. For example, don't say, "Oh, I'm sure you'll have children" to the woman who has tried every treatment available and is still childless. Don't tell a battered woman, "Just respect him more and he'll be calm and loving." Don't tell an unmarried woman, "I'm sure that special man will turn up soon!" Don't tell someone in chronic pain, "I heard about this man who found this miracle cure. I'm sure it can work for you. You just haven't knocked on enough doors yet."

Lack of empathy is one of the major reasons for so many divorces and so much anger and depression today.

◊ EXAMPLE: "After going to many doctors, most of whom told me that my pain was all in my head and that I needed a psychiatrist, I finally found a doctor who discovered that I had severe nerve damage which has been causing me excruciating pain for the past five years. He said that there was little that could be done. I was devastated by the news. But what was almost equally devastating was when, on the way home, I burst into tears and my husband said, 'I don't know why you're getting so emotional. You're not going to die.' What he didn't understand and what I couldn't get across to him was that living with so much pain has got to be worse than death. Dying isn't the problem here. Living is. I don't know how to go on when all that stretches in front of me is a lifetime of pain and no one to share it with."

The pain of the pat answer adds to one's pain

The pain of being pat-answered was brought home quite starkly during my recent hospital visits with a young mother who had inoperable cancer. She told me, "While I've been lying in this bed, I've had plenty of opportunities to evaluate people's reactions to me. Most people keep a safe emotional distance. It's like they're on a different planet emotionally. Doctors look at the chart, not at my eyes. They examine my body, but never concern themselves with my feelings. They ask how I feel, but they don't want to know how I really feel. When friends ask how I feel, they want me to say that I feel great and that I'm sure there is going to be a miracle quite soon. They come and chat about everything other than what is uppermost on my mind, and maybe their minds too — which is death. That's what I want to talk about — the loneliness and the fears, about how my children will grow up without me, who will be there for them and how alone they'll feel without me and how difficult it is to say goodbye to them. When I try to talk about my fears, these people tell me things like, 'Don't listen to these doctors! They don't know what they're talking about. You're going to be fine. Why, I know this man who was told that he had inoperable cancer ten years ago and he's managing a business now!'

"When I think of the people who help me the most, they are those who care enough to just be there for me. They don't give advice, don't try to cheer me up by talking about miracles, don't try to make me into a saint because I express a positive attitude or make me feel like I'm sinning when I talk about my fear of dying a slow, agonizing death and leaving young children behind. They just come and hold my hand gently and listen to me talk. I'm not always down. Sometimes I am very accepting and philosophical, sometimes I'm even funny. Sometimes I'm very scared or angry or depressed. I have very few true friends — people I can be real and honest with. With real friends, I can be silent, share my insights, my jokes and my despair. True friends cry when I cry and laugh when I laugh. They let me feel whatever I am feeling at the time, so I can go in and out of different moods, without feeling wrong or bad for being down, or like I have to put on a performance and cheer others up by being cheerful.

"True friends just listen and share. They don't act as if they know the answers to my questions. They let it be okay not to know or understand everything. They don't put on a brave or cheerful front for me, so I don't have the burden of having to do that, for them. The result is that with them, I can face the reality of my helplessness. All the others with their glib answers only make me feel more alone, more isolated and afraid because I cannot be real. I have to pretend. I can't communicate with them. This is very painful. Yes, miracles do happen, but I wish people would stop telling me that I'm bad for feeling that I'm not going to be one of those miracles.

"I like it when someone can say, 'I'm scared too.' That makes me feel so much less alone. I'm glad when someone can say, 'It's so hard to go through this.' Why pretend to hope when it is so much more real and honest to accept that hope can sometimes keep you from coming to terms with the truth? I hate the pretense, hate seeing those people walk into the room, knowing that they will say the same thing over and over and that I will have to waste time being phony."

Using religion to cover up insensitivity

Many people pride themselves on their faith, when, in actuality, they use religion to justify their impatience and their lack of real concern. They imply that it's easy to, "Just accept your lot in life and be happy." Consider our Patriarchs and Matriarchs, who expressed great anguish on many different occasions, such as the grief of being childless. Why couldn't they just accept? Because philosophy doesn't erase heartbreak. The heart has a life of its own, and must be respected.

It is true that *emunah* and *bitachon*, i.e., the awareness that everything that happens is ultimately good and necessary, make us feel less bitter and angry. But a person doesn't get to that level of awareness by putting himself down or having others put him down for being emotionally honest.

If you want to help someone grow, you must first form a close emotional bond by accepting him as he is and allowing him to express his feelings. That often creates a desire to consider a change in attitude. The heart must be allowed to unburden itself before the head can accept disappointment philosophically.

Being *b'simchah tamid* (always happy) is a great mitzvah. But it is also important not to lie to ourselves about what we feel. People who jump in with spiritual phrases too soon belittle others.

The following phrases, which are true and valuable when used in the right time and place and with real love and concern in your heart, will be experienced as suppressive if said flippantly or to people who are feeling deep pain about possible mental or physical collapse, divorce, severe disability or death.

"Your *emunah* and *bitachon* are weak. If God gave you the test, He will give you the strength to bear it."

"*Gam zo l'tovah.*"

"Everything's going to be just fine!"

"You deserve this. It's a punishment."

These phrases may upset those who not only feel bad about the situation, but feel bad for feeling bad.

Staying calm around invalidaters

Being invalidated hurts, especially if it comes from someone whose love you want. Many times, all you can do is remain silent. Don't feel badly for staying distant from them or wanting to keep things P.S. — polite and superficial.

Whenever possible, it is a great *chesed*, both to invalidaters and those who must deal with them, to tell them that their responses are hurtful. Most chronic invalidaters will continue to invalidate by saying things like, "You're just touchy." Or, "You're the one who's insensitive, not me!" However, you may be able to get through to others.

To a clerk: "I know you're busy, but it would not take much of your time to treat your customers in a more humane way."

To a doctor: "I am not just a body. I also have feelings."

To stay calm, the following steps may help:

1. Identify the underlying implication beneath the comment. Invalidating remarks generally fall into the main accusations that: You are stupid, crazy, selfish, unspiritual, incompetent, uncaring or

just plain insensitive.

2. Take a deep breath. As you let your breath out, let go of your desire to change the person's opinion. Imagine putting the person's opinion in a balloon and seeing it fly into outer space. Imagine untying your self-image from the image that person has of you, as you would untie a knot. Someone's opinions are not the Absolute Truth.

3. Decide how damaging the opinion is. If it belongs to a family member, does it mean the person doesn't love you? Is it the end of the relationship? How would that affect you? If it's a boss, does this mean the loss of your job? If it's a minor slight to your honor, you can probably cool down quickly. If it's a major break in an important relationship, then even if you get hysterical, your negative behavior will only reinforce the person's negative opinions.

4. Catch the person off guard by making a nondefensive statement in a calm voice which identifies the person's underlying accusation:

"So, you think I'm incompetent and can't handle finances?"

"So, you think I am selfish and uncaring because the meal wasn't ready on time?"

5. Ask, "What would you like to do about this?" Stay nondefensive. Remember, you're dealing with mere human opinion, not an Absolute Truth.

6. Ask yourself, "Is it true that I am incompetent? Am I crazy? Am I really an insensitive, uncaring clod?" (That is hardly likely if you are reading a book of this sort!) If it's not true, put the person's opinion in a balloon and let it go. If it is even partially true, you can say:

"True, I am sometimes selfish." Or, "True, I am incompetent in this area. I'm doing the best I can to improve myself." Or, "That's true. I'm not the most together person in the world, but I still deserve love and respect even though I'm not perfect."

If it's not true, you can ignore the person or say, "I disagree. I am not a selfish, uncaring person."

7. Distance yourself emotionally or physically from the person. Don't suck off empty bottles. Trying to get nourishment when there isn't any, even if it is your own mate, parent, child or sibling will only frustrate you and enrage the other person.

The gifts of invalidation

One of the gifts of invalidation is that it reminds you not to act like the invalidater by being insensitive to others. Each time you are invalidated, you can think, "The gift in this is that I've been reminded of the importance of listening, really listening with my heart as well as my head, to what others are feeling."

Another gift is that it reminds you that perhaps there is some truth in what the other person is saying. You can look within, and ask, "Am I complaining needlessly? Am I really as grateful as I could be for all I have? Am I staying in pain in order to gain attention, control, protection or an excuse to escape responsibilities? Is there some better way to get my needs satisfied?"

A third gift is that it reminds you not to allow yourself to be externally determined and defined by the opinions of others. And when the pain of being invalidated seems almost too great to bear, you have the gift of moving your muscles and staying busy with positive activites.

A fourth gift is that being invalidated is humbling. It reminds you of your limitations — that you cannot get through to everyone, cannot be liked by everyone and cannot make some people like you no matter how hard you may try. You cannot control others' opinions or always get what you want from people. You're left with the humbling realization that the only person you can really change is yourself.

13 | The Gift of Anger: Revelations about Our Need for Growth

Be not easily moved to anger...
— AVOTH 2:15

Let all thy deeds be done for the sake of Heaven.
— AVOTH 2:17

Who is mighty? He who subdues his passions.
— AVOTH 4:1

Researchers have found that when people get angry, their bodies pump out stress hormones such as adrenaline. When this happens on a continuous basis, the surge of these hormones can damage the heart and lead to cardiac arrest and death. Adrenaline causes the body to release fat into the bloodstream to provide energy when a person is under attack. That's often necessary when there is a real attack. Chronically hostile people tend to have high levels of cholesterol in their blood because they feel under attack all the time (*Superimmunity*, p. 29).

In addition to physical damage, we all know how harmful anger is to us emotionally — how it blocks our ability to think and act constructively, how it causes us to commit numerous sins against both God and man, including hatred, vengeance and grudge bearing. And yet we all get angry! Why? Because anger makes us feel powerful and is often a very effective tool for getting our immediate needs satisfied. We're afraid we'll turn into easily exploited doormats if we lose this source of protection and control. Since it is difficult to get rid of it, our job is to deal with it positively.

Anger is an attempt to avoid facing the truth about the extent of our inability to control people and life. The gift of anger is that it offers us the opportunity to practice self-discipline and discover the truth about our innermost needs and limitations.

The steps to avoid anger are as follows:

1. First, validate your feeling that something is wrong. Anger is essentially a way of saying "I care!" or, "I'm in danger!" or, "My essential needs are not being met!" or, "My rights are being violated!" Anger may be the only thing keeping you from being apathetic or despairing about a situation which demands action. However, once you are aware that something is wrong, don't keep the internal sirens blaring. You need to think constructively and rationally.

> ◊ EXAMPLE: "I spent four hours in a hospital emergency room in terrible pain before a doctor came to examine me. I was furious about the poor care. But I don't just want to stew. I want to improve the situation by writing letters to the hospital director and others who are involved and even contact the newspapers."

2. The next step is to ask yourself honestly, "Am I really under attack? Is there a real threat or danger to my physical, mental or emotional health at this moment? Has a real injustice been committed against me or others? If so, then I do need the energizing hormones produced by my anger to rouse me out of passivity. But once I have the awareness that action must be taken, I don't need to stay angry. I simply have to take action."

It is true that the environment is being destroyed, that many politicians are liars, that the Jewish People is under constant threat, that hospitals and school systems rarely give the services they should, and that there are people posing as professionals who are incompetent or cheats, etc. And we do have to take action whenever possible against these real threats.

However, our feeling of danger often has no basis in fact, such as when somone cuts in front of us in line, leaves dirty dishes on the table, eats without proper table manners, loses a bus ticket, monopolizes the conversation, doesn't come to our *simchah*, etc.

Whether we are dealing with real danger or a minor inconvenience, our challenge is to uphold Torah values when we respond.

Since most of our everyday stresses do not involve major, life-changing events or sins, why do we often react to minor events as if they were catastrophes? Because from the time we were children, we confused danger with discomfort! And we continue to do this unless we learn to objectively examine whether or not our responses are appropriate. Each time we get angry over a non-threatening situation, we can remind ourselves to use this opportunity to re-program our brains by telling ourselves, "Calm down, there's no actual danger here," or "Whatever the event, it's an opportunity to perfect my *middoth*."

> ◊ EXAMPLE: "I excitedly called my daughter in Israel to tell her that we were coming for a visit. She paused at the other end of the line and said, 'To tell you the truth, Ma, we're so broke that I'd rather have you send the money you'd pay for the tickets instead of coming, as much as I'd love to see you.' Well, I was enraged. I wanted to yell back that she wouldn't be seeing her parents or the money! Thankfully, I have a very strict rule with myself not to talk when I'm enraged, so I made an excuse to hang up. Then I thought about it. She was only being honest. She really must be desperate. I hadn't taken the hints in her letters seriously. She really does love us, so there is no real danger of losing the relationship. As I became more rational, I calmed down. Then I called her back and told her that we'd come and also try to help financially."

If you live with someone who criticizes you from morning until night, there is real danger. You are being constantly attacked, and the attack is no less harmful than if you were being slashed with a knife. Those who live or work with critical people do have a higher risk of stress-related diseases, including heart disease, ulcers and cancer. You may fall into suicidal despair. This is real danger.

When there is no real and actual threat, don't call all the engines out of the firehouse! Firmly tell your brain, There is no real danger here, so be quiet! This reminder is important because as children we perceived many people and events as threatening, which were not really dangerous from an objective point of view, such as being ridiculed for how we dressed, getting a poor grade, getting yelled at for not finishing our food or not cleaning our room, being hit, etc. In addition, we saw adults who exploded angrily when they felt irrationally threatened by spilled juice, dirty floors, uncooperative kids or misplaced keys. From them we learned that it is right, good and necessary to explode when we are upset.

But we are adults now, and as adults we can distinguish between a feeling of danger and its actual existence.

3. Ask yourself, "Is this really worth getting excited about? Is this so important that I must display my entire arsenal of weapons and commit numerous sins against man and God by exploding angrily or harboring silent hatred in my heart?"

> ◊ EXAMPLE: "I babysat for a neighbor and when she paid me, she gave me less than what I felt I deserved. I was furious until I realized that it's not worth losing my mental health over two dollars. I can calmly tell her that there's a difference of opinion or forget it. I used to eat myself up for days over these petty incidents until I realized that since I'm a high-strung person, fury is a luxury I simply can't afford."

> ◊ EXAMPLE: "I was in the middle of giving a *d'var Torah* when my wife started clearing off the table and asking the kids to pass their dishes to her. I was so furious that I was on the verge of saying something really nasty. Then I thought, Wait, maybe she did something impolite, but that's no excuse for me to commit the sin of *ona'ath devarim* (hurting people's feelings with one's words)! So I became silent. She then realized what was going on, apologized and sat down. I shared with everyone how I had controlled myself, which was probably the best *d'var Torah* I could have given!"

4. Ask yourself, "What problem am I trying to solve?" As children, when we got angry, someone came along and provided a solution. So, the belief is programmed into our brains that we must get angry and then a solution will eventually emerge. That's why many of us still think that we must STAY angry until the problem gets solved! The juice spills, the child loses his bus ticket or there is an unexpected outburst from a neighbor. It seems that it is proper and even absolutely necessary to get angry in order to get the ball rolling so that we, or someone else, can then work things out.

> ◊ EXAMPLE: "I hired a crew to seal the roof, but with the first rain, it leaked all over the furniture. I was furious, but instead of letting

my anger get the better of me, I focused on a solution: get another company to fix the roof, warn people not to use this crew and write a letter of complaint to the Better Business Bureau.''

◊ EXAMPLE: "When I found out that my oldest son was hanging around stores in the afternoon instead of being in *yeshivah*, I was furious with him for weeks on end. I kept thinking that if I got angry enough, he'd start to love learning. Of course, he didn't. The problem to be solved was how to get him to enjoy learning. That meant getting him a tutor who could impart a lot of emotional warmth and transferring him to a different *yeshivah*.''

◊ EXAMPLE: "My oldest daughter is just three, but she's been driving me crazy with her defiance and tantrums. I kept thinking that if I just got furious enough, she'd calm down. But my anger didn't solve anything. She just got worse. So I defined the problem: neither of us could tolerate frustration. I needed to take assertive action without getting violent and she had to learn that tantrums wouldn't get me to give in to her. As I was able to tolerate her tantrums without breaking down, they eventually stopped.''

We all grow into adulthood with thousands of irrational responses already stored in our mental computer. We may still react to present events as if we were two years old. This is why it is so important for us to examine our present responses. Each time we get angry, we can remind ourselves to use this opportunity to break away from our childish initial response and find a mature, rational one.

Don't get angry, get smart

In order to wean yourself away from chronic anger, you will have to change your language. It is extremely helpful to share your anger-reducing techniques out loud with your family members so that they see the importance of avoiding anger. Your positive attitude can even render it fun and exciting to think of constructive responses to minor problems. By saying the following phrases out loud, you are not only turning what may, at first, seem like lies into truths, but you demonstrate to others how to do the same. The following phrases should be used throughout the day:

1. "I am giving you the benefit of the doubt. I'm sure you didn't mean to do this." Giving the benefit of the doubt is like first aid in an emergency, akin to applying a tourniquet to a person who is bleeding profusely. Taking away the *davka* (the presumption that others are deliberately and intentionally trying to hurt you) stops you from bleeding emotionally. It stops the flow of hatred, vengeance and grudge bearing which is so poisonous for you spiritually.

Before you do anything else, assume the person is innocent, immature, in pain, unaware, preoccupied, etc. This will calm you down so that you can think clearly about how to respond most constructively. Keep whispering to yourself, "S/he's doing/loving the best s/he can with the tools s/he has right now." The purpose is not to make you passive, but to help you think more rationally about whether you need assertive action or stoic acceptance.

Emotionally disturbed people, who are chronically angry and bitter, are in a kind of spiritual coma, preoccupied with their own needs, and often oblivious to and uninterested in the effect of their anger on others. Treat them as you would treat someone in a physical coma: try to awaken them, but don't expect miracles! As for evil people — those who take pleasure in hurting others — stay away from them! There is not much else you can do!

However, the vast majority of people can be taught to use anger-reducing tools if you demonstrate them often enough.

2. "This is a triviality. In this house, we don't emotionalize trivialities, because if we do, we'll be angry all the time. My priority is my mental health, so I'm not wasting my time getting upset about something I can't do anything about (or something that just needs to be solved)."

3. "This feels dangerous, but it's not. It's just a fear, not a fact."

4. "I am rebuking you with love in my heart." If a person has committed a transgression, he deserves rebuke. But this must be done according to the Rambam's Rules of Rebuke (*Hilchoth Deoth* 6:7): (1) in private, (2) with a gentle, tender voice, (3) with love in your heart, pointing out that you are doing this only for the person's good. Otherwise, remain quiet.

> ◊ EXAMPLE: "I left instructions with my maid about what to do while I went to teach. When I came back home, very little had

been done. I was very upset, as we are on a very tight budget and this once-a-week help is very important to me. It was difficult for me to speak because I felt betrayed and had lost trust, and also because I didn't want to hurt her feelings, since she has so many problems of her own. So I started by saying that it looked like her heart just wasn't in cleaning today and that she hadn't done much. When she protested, I showed her what hadn't been done. I kept saying that I really cared about her, but that she would have to do better."

◊ EXAMPLE: "I invited three couples to dinner in honor of my husband's birthday. I worked hard preparing the food and making everything nice. Then no one showed up, or even called to cancel. I was so furious! I couldn't stop thinking about it. How was I going to talk to these so-called friends in a loving voice? I thought about it for days. First, I gave the benefit of the doubt. They all have numerous small children; they didn't know how many people were coming and probably thought that their absence wouldn't make a difference; they didn't realize how important it was to call. With this in mind, I called each one of my friends and told them, for their own good, that if they ever cannot make a date with me or someone else in the future, to please call and let me or the other person know. I'm glad I waited until I had calmed down so that I could think only of their benefit when I called."

5. "Let's play this scene again." Redo the scene, calmly this time.

◊ EXAMPLE: "When my son said something to me in an angry voice, I immediately told him to go out of the room, close the door, and then come back in and speak to me in a civilized tone."

6. "In this house, we crush flies, not people." Shame is appropriate if someone has committed a deliberate sin. If that is not the case, simply solve the problem. If you, like many people, were brought up in a condemnaholic home (one filled with continuous harsh and unwarranted criticism), you will have a strong urge to criticize and will be somewhat insecure, paranoid and untrusting of others. Building trust requires that you be consistently loving and determined to focus on the good in others and yourself. Your aim should be to bolster egos, not to destroy them.

7. "Hm...this is an interesting challenge. How can we turn this

touchy situation into a learning experience?"

◊ EXAMPLE: "I had waited all year to have some vacation time with my husband when he was off from *yeshivah*. But all he wanted to do was to rest at home. I was so resentful that I walked around with a sour expression on my face, which only made him withdraw even more. Finally I thought, How can I turn this into a learning experience? What I need to learn is to be more self-sufficient. I decided to go out with the three little ones on my own. I left with tears in my eyes, *schlepp*ing a double stroller and a heavy bag of supplies. I was determined to have a nice day and to give him the benefit of the doubt. I came back with a happy face and no resentment in my heart. I told him how hard I had worked to understand his needs and that's why I came back in a good mood. The next day, he decided to go out with us!"

8. "I am/you are as precious as a *sefer Torah*. You wouldn't step on a *sefer Torah*, would you? I'm a *ben Melech* and so are you!"

9. "What a wonderful opportunity you are giving me to perfect my *middoth* and demonstrate self-control! I'm thinking of the tremendous spiritual reward I'll get if I don't respond in kind!"

◊ EXAMPLE: "After years of not visiting my son, I finally got the money together to fly there. Well, I'm not a meticulous person at all, but I've never seen such a pig sty. I felt like I was going to throw up when I walked in and saw food and ants all over the floor, and dirty diapers scattered here and there. I told myself, Okay, calm down. Focus on solutions. So I offered to help my daughter-in-law and decided to be as nice as possible. I hoped that by showing love to her, perhaps we could become closer. Then I'd be able to find out if she realizes she has a serious problem and, if so, whether she wants help in overcoming it."

10. "In this house, we focus on solutions, not theatrics." One of the best ways to create a feeling of closeness is to say, "I have the same (or a similar) problem. Let's work it out together."

◊ EXAMPLE: "I was feeling very hateful toward my oldest daughter because she is such a whiny child. Then I realized that I'm not so pleasant to be around myself! One day, I told her, 'Look, I also need to work on being more grateful and less of a *kvetch*. Let's work on it together. We'll both keep a Happiness Notebook and at the end of the day, we'll tell each other what we wrote.' It's helped our relationship and our outlook on life tremendously."

11. "I trust that everything God does is for our good. We may not realize it right now, because we're not yet in the World of Truth, but when we get there, we're going to see how it all makes sense."

◊ EXAMPLE: "I was furious when my wife came down with a serious illness. I had married her, expecting that she would work and support me while I learned. I felt so betrayed by her, because I thought I had married someone strong and healthy, and she wasn't. I had to get a job, help with the kids and the cleaning, which infuriated me even more. I felt like my very spirituality was endangered. I was very resentful that I no longer had the status or the fulfillment of a man who learns full time, and I walked around with a chip on my shoulder. But after that first year, I saw the gifts that accompanied this major disappointment. I became a much more giving person, and much more understanding of others with problems. It gave me a push to break through many barriers, especially my arrogance."

◊ EXAMPLE: "I was so upset because I saw that we wouldn't have enough money to send the kids to camp this summer. Then the car wouldn't start and I came back into the house and was hit again by the realization of how small it is and how junky everything looks. I was so bitter! So I told my husband, 'God isn't unfair! He's doing this so I can see what inner strengths I possess! He's doing this so I will turn to Him more and really make Him part of my life!' Soon I began to feel better."

Your response when you are angry or others are angry at you is the best test of your spiritual level. When you respond in a loving manner, you pass the important spiritual test. Continuous acts of self-discipline increase self-respect and a feeling of closeness to God. Your ego may take a beating. But the fact that you have overcome your natural desire to get angry is rewarded with a higher level of conciousness. This is the gift which anger brings.

12. "Isn't it wonderful that we can have a difference of opinion and still love each other?"

◊ EXAMPLE: "My husband and I both wanted to use the car. I could see a tense battle ahead, so I told him, 'It proves how strong our relationship is that we can fight about the car and still love each other.' That took the edge off our anger, and we worked out a compromise."

The more often you say these phrases out loud, the calmer your home life will be.

Responding to normal people's anger

People get angry at you because they want to control you. Adult anger is very similar to a child's tantrum. Respond to adult tantrums the way you do to a child's tantrums: remain calm (even if it's only a pretense!) and resolute about your decision not to give in. If you give in, they will keep getting angry whenever their needs aren't met.

The following may also be helpful:

1. Ask the person, "What are you hoping to accomplish by saying this?" Then see if you can help him achieve his goal. He may only want you to put less salt in the soup or to be on time. Agree!

(However, beware of evil people. Their goal is to crush you. You do not want to help them reach this goal!)

2. Tell the person, "Please check the *hechsher* on what you just said."

3. Tell the person, "You have the right to make a request; it's the anger which is harmful. So tell me specifically what you want."

4. Say, "I'll write down your request and we'll work on it." Validate the other person's ego need to feel noticed, important, understood, approved of, etc. Acknowledge these needs. If you agree with the person, say, "You're right. I have been inconsiderate of you." If you don't agree, say, "You have a point." The latter is a neutral statement that conveys an acknowledgment without obligation on your part.

6. Reassure the person that you love him/her. Most people are surprisingly insecure about whether or not they are loved. In particular, young children and those from abusive backgrounds are paranoid, certain that others are out to deliberately hurt them. So use anger as an opportunity to reassure people of your love.

◊ EXAMPLE: "When my three year old kept saying, 'I want to kill you,' I was so enraged that I lost control and poured black pepper on his tongue. Boy, did he scream! But the next day, he said the same thing again. Again I resorted to the pepper. But he kept saying those same words. So I tried washing his mouth out with soap. Finally, in desperation, I called my EMETT leader and she said, 'As the oldest of three children, he's probably feeling quite left out. He's not hateful, he's just in pain. Don't respond to the words; only respond to the pain.' She advised me that the next time he says he wants to kill me, I should hug him and tell him, 'Even if you want to kill me, I love you more than anything in the whole world.' When he calmed down, she said to try to find out what's bothering him. I tested out what she suggested and he hasn't said the words since."

◊ EXAMPLE: "My husband was upset that I had bought something without his prior consent. I was about to attack and yell back at him that's he's a stingy rat. Instead I said, 'You're right. Neither of us should make a major purchase without first consulting the other one. I'm really sorry. I didn't intend to hurt you.' End of argument. End of anger."

◊ EXAMPLE: "I was furious when someone came into my store just before closing time and wanted to see my entire stock of dresses, and then walked out without buying anything. Then I thought to myself, 'Did I lose anything really essential? Was there any real danger to my physical or spiritual well-being?' No! I lost time, that's all. The word *triviality* puts things in perspective and calms me down."

◊ EXAMPLE: "I bought an expensive cordless telephone which broke after one week. I was furious until I realized that the phone is a triviality in comparison to my mental health. I just got a bum phone and will demand an exchange or a refund."

Emotionally disturbed people will continue to be enraged, vengeful, cold, withdrawn, spiteful, hostile and abusive no matter what you do and say. Try to get away from them as much as possible. Leave the house. Go to a class, a store, a friend, etc. Do not try to get through to them.

7. Say, "Last time this happened you got a lot angrier. You're making progress." Even if this isn't true, saying these words may calm the person down by complimenting him and giving him the

feeling that he is capable of improvement.

8. Say, "Being upset is not an excuse for not having self control."

Distinguish between ego wants and spiritual needs

We have many needs, which can be classified as personal ego wants (which foster a sense of separateness between God and man) and spiritual needs (which promote a sense of closeness and oneness).

Our *neshamah* needs are for: closeness to God by being loving and joyful, learning Torah, doing mitzvoth and working on our *middoth*. In contrast, our ego wants are for: *kavod* (self-importance, respect), control and power over others, comfort, convenience and pleasure at the expense of spiritual principals and values, approval and security (physical, financial, etc.).

The ego takes a pounding in this world because it's needs are insatiable. It wants us to feel fearful so that we will cling even more passionately to the people and possessions which give us an illusion of security and *kavod*. The more the ego is crushed, the more the *neshamah* rejoices at the opportunity to prove that only God, Torah and mitzvoth are important. The *neshamah* knows that what we need is control over our own thoughts, speech and deeds.

> ◊ EXAMPLE: "A relative snubbed me at a social event. I felt terrible until I asked myself, 'What's the threat? Is there any real danger?' No, the only thing hurt was my pride, my feeling of self-importance. There was no real danger, just inconvenience and discomfort. With that frame of mind, I was able to ignore her and enjoy myself."

There is no real danger when ego needs aren't met

As you develop your ability to distinguish between essential *neshamah* needs and nonessential ego needs, you will find yourself reacting to stressful events more calmly. You will realize that only the ego is bruised when the clerk yells at you for not bringing the right forms, or you ask him to consider your request and just get a blank stare in return. Only the ego is hurt when you don't receive the *aliyah* to the Torah that you wanted or someone takes your parking place or pushes in front of you in line.

When it's only the ego which has been hurt, don't take it so seriously. Don't emotionalize ego losses. Ignore the situation or speak up assertively.

For example, identify the ego losses involved in the following examples:

1. I dropped in at a friend's house and she barely acknowledged my presence. She spent most of the time talking with her other guests. Ego loss: _____

2. I waited the whole day for the service man to come, and he never showed up. Ego loss: _____

3. I asked a relative a question and he barked back that he wasn't in the mood to talk. Ego loss: _____

4. I asked a child to do a chore and he said, "Later." Ego loss: _____

5. A friend dropped by and my three boys spent most of the time she was there fighting with each other and otherwise acting unruly. Ego loss: _____

6. I waited almost three hours for the doctor to see me! Ego loss: _____

7. I asked my brother for a loan and he refused. Ego loss: _____

8. I prepared what I thought was an excellent meal, but no one said a word of appreciation. Ego loss: _____

9. I tried to organize a fund-raising campaign, but everyone had an excuse as to why they couldn't help. Ego loss: _____

10. I asked for what I thought was a fair price and the other person said I was a cheat. Ego loss: _____

As soon as you identify the loss as only an ego loss, you will not become so angry because you know that the satisfaction of this desire is not essential for your spiritual growth.

When you let go of needing others to satisfy your ego needs, you are no longer devastated by their negative opinions. If someone likes you, great. If not, you can respond non-defensively, aware of the fact that a crushed ego is humbling, not devastating. Your self-worth is determined by God, not man.

Overcoming childhood programming

It takes time to train yourself to avoid getting hostile when others disappoint you. At first, you will often fall back into your old childhood pattern of trying to force other people to meet your ego needs. But with practice — lots of it — you will learn to either confront assertively or ignore trivial pains.

> ◊ EXAMPLE: "I was about to have a nervous breakdown when I added up our debts. I couldn't sleep and could barely function. When I finally called my parents to ask if they could help, they started yelling that I have to stand on my own feet and must stop expecting them to help. I was so angry. I wanted to yell back at them. Thank God, I'd made myself promise on Rosh Hashanah to keep my mouth shut whenever I feel emotionally poisonous. So I hung up and started thinking. What's been hurt? Only my desire for comfort and understanding from them. If I'm not getting either, it means God doesn't want me to have these ego pleasures right now. I saw that when there's no one to turn to, there's only God and my own resources. That's what I had to learn — to be more self-sufficient. I calmed down and was no longer angry as I began to think of ways to deal with our financial problems on my own. Now I see myself as an independent, courageous person instead of a victim."

> ◊ EXAMPLE: "My fourteen-year-old daughter is going through a very hostile phase. In her eyes, nothing I do is good enough. I don't dress right, don't cook right, don't clean enough and I'm too restrictive. She's forever rolling her eyes or grimacing in disgust. I was exploding and imploding in anger, until I finally identified my losses as ego losses — for approval and closeness. I decided to view her as a smoker, spreading noxious fumes whenever she 'lights up.' Just as I am firm about not allowing anyone to smoke in my home, I was just as firm in telling her to leave the room and not to spread her poison around me. When I manage to stay firm but calm and non-judgmental, she eventually calms down and apologizes."

The gift of anger is that it allows us the opportunity to overcome our automatic, knee-jerk responses and develop the self control it takes to respond to frustration in a Torah manner.

PART IV
Understanding Oneself

14 | The Gift of Defeating the Mad/Sad/Bad Genie Syndrome: Part I

> *The greatest service of God lies in the purification of motive.*
> — STRIVE FOR TRUTH! vol. 1, p. 99

Most children are familiar with the story of Aladdin, a poor boy who found a magic lamp. When he rubbed the lamp, a genie emerged from it who granted the boy all his wishes. Children who often feel so helpless and weak love this story, for it gives them in fantasy the powers they can never have in reality.

Feeling powerful is an essential need. No one likes to feel helpless. One way children get a feeling of power is to get into a bad mood. They see that when they act mad, bad, sad, sick or crazy, they often get what they want. Adults often don't realize that they do the same: going around for months or years feeling angry, inadequate, depressed and anxious in order to gain some sense of power. Prolonged negative moods are primitive expressions of an unconscious hope that by staying in these states, one will gain love, attention, protection, respect, financial security, or a dramatic improvement in one's own or someone else's *middoth*. For example, "If I just hate myself enough for yelling at my kids/being lazy/sloppy, then I'll get it together faster." Or, "If I get angry enough at my spouse, he'll become more ambitious in learning/make more money."

The fact that we spent so much time being in bad moods during our formative years, and thus getting protection or attention, makes these moods difficult to give up as adults. After all, from the time we were born we screamed when we were uncomfortable. And then someone (usually mother) magically seemed to appear out of no-where and give us the nourishment and attention we wanted. Anger and sadness were our main survival weapons, the only ways we had to satisfy our two most fundamental needs for love and protection.

The "scream response" becomes a magic genie, making children feel potent and bringing the promise of the fulfillment of their desires: get depressed and get pampered; have an explosion and get immediate attention; cry and get a new bike, a new pair of pants, a day off from school, a special treat, a new schoolbag etc. Act mad, sad, bad, sick or crazy and get what you want. This syndrome is terribly seductive because it works so often!

What brought you comfort as a child may bring you grief as an adult

The idea that being in pain will cause someone to magically appear and take care of our problems is so deeply ingrained in us that many people think, The genie of unhappiness isn't doing his job. It must be because I'm not feeling bad enough! I guess I have to get even angrier, sadder, more anxious and sick. Then I'll get what I want!

Small children can be excused for this behavior because they do not have the skill to express their needs in words, or the ability to find alternative sources of gratification. When they are rejected or hurt, they don't know how to be lovingly assertive, delay gratification, accept suffering philosophically or internalize a sense of self-worth which is independent of others. Their impulses are intense and overwhelming. Their sense of worth and of security are totally determined by others. They must rely on others to get their needs satisfied. What else can they do but cry angrily?

Loving and being loved makes children feel good. But being angry gives them a sense of power. A smile connects, but a hateful frown gives them a sense of protection and potency. You can feel this sense of power now, as you think hateful thoughts about someone and feel that you have created a protective distance. It is an illusion, but one which works for children, who often feel so vulnerable and powerless.

As they mature, healthy children discover that hostility obeys a law of diminishing returns. They find that if they sulk and have tantrums too often, they are scolded, ignored or rejected. Eventually, they discover that they must stoically accept many losses and give up their childish demands to have all the love and material things they dreamed of. They find constructive ways to deal with pain and disappointment.

However, many adults remain like children, insisting that the path to potency is bad moods. They grimace, get depressed, stew in resentment, lie, nag, criticize, hit, scold, slam doors, panic, lecture, punish, insult, scream, throw things, stomp out of the house, withdraw in silent resentment for days, sulk, threaten to hurt us or threaten to have a nervous breakdown (or worse) to get people to change their thinking or behavior. Like children, they think it's the job of other people to make them happy, secure or worthwhile. So it makes perfect sense to be angry when they don't deliver.

> ◊ EXAMPLE: "When I was a child, every time I didn't want to go to school, all I had to do was get a headache or a stomachache. I still use illness to get out of doing things I don't want to do."

> ◊ EXAMPLE: "When I was little, my father used to hit me and then send me to my room. I'd sit there and sulk for hours and wouldn't come out even when my mother bribed me with sweets. She'd be frantic and then my father would lay off for a while. Now I'm in my twenties and still have the same response when people aren't nice to me. I go in my room and sulk and stew!"

It takes much effort to uncondition ourselves, for the memory of having used these coercive tactics successfully is deeply ingrained in our psyches. The tendency to use unhappiness to achieve happiness is especially strong in those who grew up in or now live in abusive homes where there is a great deal of physical violence or criticism. Such abuse teaches the victim that getting mad, sad, bad, sick or crazy really is the path to power.

If you think your worth, happiness and security depend on others, you'll get stuck in these five negative states to get what you want. You'll be angry at people who don't make you feel good. You'll try to bully people into being what you want because you think your happiness is dependent on them and you'll be miserable when you don't get everything you want.

Misery provides an illusion of potency

Obviously, there are times when we might have to act mad, sad, mean or even crazy to get what we want or even to survive. King David had to feign craziness (*Tehillim* 34). Some situations require force. In times of danger, anger can motivate us to take action. Grief is an appropriate response to a major loss. The Rambam states that we must sometimes make a show of anger (*Hilchoth Deoth* 2:3). When a tragedy strikes, grief, even depression, is normal.

However, staying mad, bad, sad, sick or mentally unbalanced is destructive. Many people employ their old childhood "scream response" when they feel hurt:

"I MUST stay depressed. It's the ONLY way to get my husband to pay attention to me."

"I MUST be mean. It's the ONLY way to get respect."

"I MUST obsess anxiously about this problem. It's the ONLY way it will get solved."

"I MUST criticize my children all the time or they'll be irreligious, irresponsible, lazy, spoiled *chutzpadik* brats!"

"I MUST keep hating myself. It's the ONLY way I'll improve."

"I MUST eat myself up with guilt. It's the only way I can show what a caring person I am."

No wonder people stay so anxious, angry and depressed! They think it's the only way to get what they want! Misery not only provides the illusion of power, it often works! So, it is no wonder that people explode at family members to get a few minutes of peace and quiet or some cooperation, or scowl at neighbors and think that will improve their behavior, or use illness as an excuse to avoid certain chores or get extra attention. They're certain that they could never accomplish so much so fast by being nice, calm, happy and healthy.

Don't expect instant changes if you've spent a lifetime using these mood states to protect you from pain. It's not easy to give up these patterns if you think they are serving you!

Identifying insecure thoughts and goals

You can figure out why you get into certain negative mood states by making your unconscious goals conscious. Each time you get stuck in a bad mood, see it is an opportunity to identify your insecure thoughts, i.e., what you fear losing if you stop being unhappy.

First, think of a situation which you are miserable about: e.g., your weight, a nasty neighbor, a difficult child, a grouchy spouse, a stingy relative, a crummy job, your own bad *middoth*, etc.

Now, say the first thing that pops into your mind, even if it seems silly. Write down as many responses as you can think of.

"I must continue to stay very angry (or sad, silent, anxious, panicky, hostile, passive, etc.) because it's the only way I can get _____."

"If I stop being so angry (or depressed, etc.), I'll lose _____."

"If I act loving, kind, healthy and strong, I'll _____ (or, people will think I'm _____)."

The most common answers have to do with the fear of losing:

1. Love and attention. "I must stay miserable to show people how much I need their love, how much I want their closeness. If I were happy, people would think I'm fine and ignore me." "I must stay miserable about this or people will think I'm heartless and irresponsible! Being miserable shows that I take my problems seriously." "I must be a doormat or I'll be rejected."

2. Sanity. "I must show how miserable I am or I'll go crazy from suppressing my feelings." Or the opposite: "I must deaden myself emotionally because if I show my feelings, I'll get violent and hurt those who have hurt me or crack from the pain." "I must have a minor nervous breakdown. That will prevent a major nervous breakdown. People will see how overwhelmed I am and help me, so I'll remain sane!"

3. Power. "I must get angry to get people to change." "It's the only way to keep people from hurting me." "I have to stay anxious. If I stopped, then terrible things would happen. This way I'm prepared for the worst."

4. Protection. "I must stay resentful to remind myself to keep my distance from this person. If I were to be nice and loving, I'd forget how much he's hurt me and I'd fall into his web again." "If I suddenly became loving, people would step all over me. Anger is survival." "I must stay numb to protect myself from the pain."

5. Freedom. "Anger is the only way to show people that I don't

need them. It makes me feel independent, like I'm my own person."
"If I get depressed enough, my husband doesn't object to me going out. Then I have an excuse to get away."

6. Self-respect. "Any self-respecting person would get angry! Anger shows people that I'm not a doormat!"

7. Respect from others. "Getting angry is my way of getting people to take my feelings seriously. If I stopped being enraged, people would walk all over me and go on hurting me."

8. Motivation. "If I stopped being miserable, I wouldn't do anything about my problems. I'd become an apathetic, complacent slob with no desire to change. People would think I'm selfish and self-centered and don't care about anything or anyone." "If I get depressed enough, I'll hit rock bottom. Then something is sure to happen to get me out of it!"

9. Favor and approval from others. "I must stay miserable to show people how overwhelmed I am, so they'll pity me and be nice." "Being a doormat is the only way to prove that I'm really unselfish, spiritual and good. If I stopped being a doormat, I'd become an aggressive and demanding witch and everyone would reject me." "If I stopped being guilt-ridden I'd be rejected as heartless, mean, crazy, uncaring, immature, unspiritual, phony, cold, selfish, stupid, arrogant, etc. They won't like me."

10. Self-control. "Being depressed keeps all my feelings frozen. By staying numb, I'm less likely to express the rage I feel toward certain family members who have hurt me so much."

11. Self-importance. "I must stay miserable. If I'm a normal, happy person, I won't be unique or special anymore!" "If I'm happy despite all the disasters that are taking place in the world, people will think I'm insensitive and stupid."

12. Success. "If I were healthy, I'd have to get a job. I'm sure I'd fail and I can't bear failing."

13. The feeling of solving the problem without having to take any action. "Stewing in anger makes me feel like I'm doing something about the problem."

14. Olam Ha-ba. "If the righteous suffer in this world but are happy in the next one, then it means that if I'm happy here, I must be bad. So, by staying sad, I'll be happy later." "I must be miserable to show God how hard I'm working."

15. One's child-like status. "If I'm depressed, people won't make demands on me. I won't have to invite guests over or go to work. I can remain a child and be taken care of. If I were healthy and happy, people would ask me to do things for them. I'd get frazzled, drained and worn out."

16. Control of God. "If I'm miserable enough, God will give me what I want, like health, love, money, etc." "If I acted happy, God would think I'm satisfied with what I have and He wouldn't give me what I want!"

17. The ability to punish others. "I must be miserable to punish my husband and children for not loving me enough. When they see my grouchy, gloomy face, they'll feel guilty and will be nice to me."

18. The ability to punish oneself. "I must stay sad to punish myself for the bad things I've done. If I enjoyed life, it would seem as if I didn't care about the bad things I've done."

19. The ability to avoid punishment. "I must stay in pain to prove to God that I'm good and that He shouldn't punish me." "By suffering so much, God will see that I can't handle any more and He won't add to my suffering."

20. The feeling of self-righteous truthfulness. "I must get angry or I'd be dishonest. After all, the truth is that I'm furious!" "Why shouldn't I be depressed? I hate my life. I'm proud that I don't lie about my feelings!"

21. Touch with one's feelings. "If I stopped being in so much pain, I'd lose touch with myself, with the fact that I am really unhappy. Then I'd just be numb and frozen, like a robot."

22. An important relationship. "Staying angry gives me hope that I can make the relationship be what I want it to be. If I stopped being angry, the relationship would die." "Staying grief-stricken, enables me to hold on to this person that I loved so much. It's my way of saying, 'I haven't forgotten you. I won't betray you by allowing myself to laugh or love ever again.'"

23. One's identity. "I am a depressed person. I wouldn't know myself if I suddenly had a more positive outlook." "I'd lose my sense of self if I changed."

24. The ability to survive. "I have to be angry and depressed. Somehow, it's the only way I can stay alive." "I must stay horrible to my children. Then they'll leave me alone. That's the only way I'll

survive motherhood and have some peace and quiet."

These insecure thoughts are usually totally unconscious. Initially, you don't realize why you are afraid to let go of the negative moods. You're simply feeling angry or sad. It seems beyond your control. You don't realize that these moods once brought you attention and power or, if you were abused as a child, that they meant survival! You just know that you fear being healthy, loving, compassionate and joyous.

So it is no wonder that people can go to therapists for years without getting well if they continue to believe that to get people to like them, they must be guilt-ridden, unhappy or overly accommodating. Unconsciously they're certain that if they give up the Genie of Unhappiness, they'll be even more miserable!

Reality testing: does it work?

When you get stuck in a bad mood, you usually don't know what your insecure thoughts are. This is why filling in the blanks on p. 230 is so important. It makes you conscious of your fears as well as your goals. Usually your goals are perfectly healthy and legitimate: love, approval, security, protection, sanity, respect and growth. Nothing wrong with that! It's just that your methods of getting there are at best ineffective and at worst harmful.

The first step out of this quagmire is to do some reality testing by asking yourself:

1. Are my insecure thoughts realistic? Will I really lose status, money, love, attention, protection, identity, etc., if I let go of this nasty mood?

2. How devastating will it be if I don't get what I want? Will I have a physical or mental collapse if this happens? Will I be able to go on with my life? What if my spouse is never the brilliant *talmid chacham* or the communicative, warm person I always wanted? What if I never become the success I wanted to be? What if this relationship dies?

3. Are my goals realistic? Will anger turn my unambitious, insensitive and disorganized child/parent/spouse into a calm, loving, organized go-getter? Will self-hatred transform me from a high-strung, extremely emotional person to someone calm, coolheaded

and unflappable?

4. Are my tactics working? Is my behavior getting me what I want? Does insanity bring sanity? Does unhappiness bring me more happiness? Does anger give me real control? Am I a better person? Are the people around me less critical, stingy, selfish, disrespectful, dishonest and inconsiderate? Am I more motivated when I am miserable?

The truth is that you block your growth by constantly berating yourself for your imperfections. Hating yourself does not keep you from being lazy, irresponsible, unspiritual and undisciplined. Instead, it discourages you until you sink into inertia. Growth through self-torture doesn't work!

You think you get more cooperation and can control people with anger? In fact, you'll only increase their negative behavior! You think your hatred keeps you safe from manipulative people? More likely, you simply isolate yourself. You think people will pamper you if you're miserable? More likely, people will get sick of your negativity and reject you.

◊ EXAMPLE: "I was furious about being cheated by a salesman. My insecure thought was that my anger showed that I wasn't a wimp or a pushover. Being angry felt like an act of self-respect. Then I asked myself, By staying furious, will it keep him from cheating others? Not likely. True self-respect will come from doing something to fight this injustice, not just getting into a foul mood."

◊ EXAMPLE: "I was furious when my wife bought something I thought was unnecessary. My insecure thought was that if I don't explode, she'll waste all our money. Then I asked myself, By being miserable and vengeful, will she spend less? Maybe. But on the other hand, she might get so angry herself that she will spend more just to get back at me. So I spoke gently to her about staying within the budget, and she didn't take offense. She agreed that she would consult me in the future before making a purchase over a certain amount."

◊ EXAMPLE: "I've been furious at my husband for years for being so uncommunicative. When I asked myself what would happen if I stopped, I was surprised to find that the answer was, There will be no relationship. It will be dead. Then I realized how I've been deluding myself. Anger gave me the illusion that I'd one day get the love I crave if I just put enough pressure on him. When I dropped the illusion, I went through a period of grief, but then I went on with my life in a much healthier way."

5. If I accept the portion God gave me and become loving and joyful with my life as it is, what am I afraid of losing — respect, identity, power, freedom or control?

Breaking the illusion of potency

People will not give up behavior which they think will bring them pleasure or protect them from pain. Weaning oneself away from the genie involves the willingness to do what is most difficult. When you see that your old methods are really harming you, you feel bereft, even panicky, but if you persist in your struggle for mental health, you'll eventually find a more constructive way of relating to people.

> ◊ EXAMPLE: "I have a very clingy ten year old who would follow me around all afternoon. It was driving me crazy that she had no friends and wasn't more independent. I was afraid that if I didn't push her away, she would never grow up, never get married and always be draining me. I was getting more and more hostile to show her that she had to grow up. From my childhood, I learned that anger is power and hostility protects. But after talking it out with my EMETT leader, I decided to take her advice and do the thing I feared to do, which was to show her my love for who she was right then at that moment. So I did. I spent an hour hugging her and cooking dinner with her while we chatted. Next thing I knew, she took her coat off the hook and said she was going to visit a classmate. I was flabbergasted. All my fear and hostility had only brought about what I feared the most, instead of bringing me the relief I thought I would get. Love works!"

A young woman was distraught because her husband wasn't diligent in his learning. Married only a year, she had expected him to run off enthusiastically to learn first thing in the morning and return late at night happily exhausted from a day spent in rapturous delight with the wisdom of the Torah. When he began to get up late and wanted to talk or help with the dishes, she became frantic with fear that she would lose the one thing she wanted in life: to be the proud wife of a brilliant *talmid chachim*. Whatever love and respect she had for him was disappearing fast.

So, what did she do? She believed, If I show anger, he'll change. If I'm super-ambitious and go briskly off to work, it will show him I'm responsible and doing my part. Then he'll be ashamed and do his part. When asked to fill in the blanks on p. 230, she said: (1) "I must be angry or he'll think learning isn't important to me. Anger is the only way to show him how seriously I take his learning. (2) If I stopped being angry, he'd lie around and I'd lose respect for him and I'd lose standing in the community. (3) Since my *avodah* is to encourage my husband to learn, if I don't do my job, I'll lose my portion in *Olam Ha-ba*. My whole purpose in life will be lost. I'll be a nothing! A nobody! I'd rather die!"

Was her anger working? Obviously not. In order not to feel impotent, she had turned into a nag, bullying him in the name of Heaven. A session with her husband's *rosh yeshivah* convinced her to take the pressure off him and work on her own *middoth*, especially unconditional love. She realized that her love was conditional on him being a diligent learner. If she continued to think like this, then when she had children, her love would be conditional on their being perfect angels. The result would be an atmosphere of terror and abuse. She was lucky that she was still young and had learned an important lesson: If you don't have love in your heart, even the holiest of goals becomes destructive.

She recognized that her compulsion to control was abusive. A person can persuade, influence and urge gently. But force is dehumanizing and destroys people's spirits.

It's not always easy to get in touch with such deeply buried beliefs. But when we do, it is very liberating.

Next step: finding your real potency in solutionizing

Don't fall for the illusion that anger or depression means that you're doing something about the problem. For example, stewing about being overweight feels like a solution. At least you care enough to stew! But it's a poor substitute for going on a diet and beginning a regular exercise program.

Stewing about an uncooperative child feels like action. It's not! Perhaps the child has learning disabilities and needs testing. Perhaps he needs a play therapist, a tutor or a new school, more time with you, more positive feedback, a criticism-free environment and a discipline program based on behavior modification techniques. The possibilities are vast.

Instead of waiting passively for a genie to drop out of the sky and fix your problems and make you happy, you have to take control of the only two things you can control in life: your mind and your muscles.

Therefore, once you have defined your goal, the next step is to ask yourself, What constructive tactics can I use to motivate myself and others to change? For example, you might consult a *rav*, write a letter, be empathic, use "I" messages (e.g., "I feel very frustrated when you're late"), have family conferences, use the suggestions in *401 Ways to Get Your Kids to Work at Home* to motivate children to help, see an expert, or face reality and accept that God doesn't want you to have what you want right now.

If you cannot do anything to get the other person to change his ways, ask yourself, "If the people around me can't give me what I want, what specific things can I do to make my life joyous and meaningful nevertheless?"

You can avoid being resentful and bitter only if you spend your time engaged in meaningful activities or practicing compassion, forgiveness and gratefulness. The time you spend being in a bad mood is time you can't spend living and loving fully!

The Genie of Unhappiness seduces you by making you believe you have the power to change people or change yourself instantly and easily. This genie makes you think that happiness is out there somewhere.

The truth is that self-respect is built on using self-control, not on losing it! People repeat any action which ever brought them any kind of pleasure or power. So, if you scream like a maniac, have panic attacks or get depressed and thereby receive the love, attention or protection you've been craving, then over the years, you'll have more and more of these episodes. In time, you'll become more abusive toward yourself and others.

It's not easy to escape the clutches of the magic genie because it appears so powerful.

The genie of anger

A condemnaholic criticized his wife constantly. Whatever she said, cooked or bought was wrong. He constantly accused her of not being religiously strict enough, of being selfish, wasteful and uncaring. He believed anger would force her to change.

He thought his motivations were perfectly legitimate and noble! He wanted to feel powerful, and he went about it in the same manner he had learned from his parents: crush with criticism. Having had this done to him as a child, he felt it was perfectly legitimate to do it to others as an adult.

Did anger get him what he wanted? Of course not! His wife tried to protect her sanity by opposing him. She eventually despaired of ever being able to get his love and withdrew physically and emotionally. She became cold and numb and kept hoping that she would catch some fatal disease so that she could leave him by dying. Force never brought him the love or control he wanted.

In another situation, a woman said, "I'm always angry at my husband because he's so weak and passive. I hate having to be the strong one! I can't turn to him for support, because he often gets depressed and falls apart."

When asked to identify her insecure thoughts and goals, she said, "I must continue to act resentfully toward my husband because it's the only way I can get him to be more aggressive, strong and confident, and keep the children from turning out like him." Was anger accomplishing what she wanted? Obviously not. Feeling attacked and inadequate, her husband's response was to withdraw into his shell even more.

What she needed most was to love and accept her husband as he was. That would allow whatever strengths he had to blossom. But she couldn't do that unless she gave up the belief that anger was the only way to make him change and the only way to maintain her self respect. Her chronic resentment only intensified the behavior she hated most in him. It gave her an illusion of power, but brought only failure and despair.

Anger doesn't change people. It only reinforces bad habits — of the one who is angry as well as of the victim.

The genie of depression

A woman called me in a suicidal depression. Pregnant, with six young children, she felt that she had lost control of her life. Although she knew she would never actually commit suicide, she kept thinking about taking an overdose of pills. I asked her, "Let's imagine what would happen afterward. There you are on the hospital bed, hooked up to an intravenous drip, finally able to tell people what's bothering you, and this time they'll listen because they finally realize how desperate you've been all these years. What would you say to them?"

She had no difficulty replying, "I'd tell my husband, 'I had to do this to get you to listen to me! I've been trying to tell you for years that I was unhappy, but you never took me seriously! You took me for granted and ignored me and never showed any appreciation for me until I wanted to die. I'm a failure at everything — as a wife, a mother and a homemaker. I can't bear another pregnancy right away. I need sleep! I'm always exhausted. I can't give all the time. I look at all the women who manage to do more than keep up with their households and I feel like a failure. I used to be so enthusiastic about life. I can't stand being cooped up in the house all the time. I need to get out, to learn, to grow. There is nothing to look forward to but more work. I feel trapped and lonely."

I asked her to fill in the blanks on p. 230. During the course of the next hour, she came up with the following: "I must get depressed because (1) it's the ONLY way I can get my husband to give me attention, (2) if people see how depressed I am, they won't blame me for neglecting my children, (3) it's an excuse to scream and hit because a depressed person can't control herself, (4) it's the only way to keep my mother off my back — she doesn't make demands on me if she knows I'm in a deep depession, (5) it makes me feel hopeful that maybe something will change."

Then she said, "If I stopped being depressed and got strong and healthy, I'd be all alone. Plus, people would think I'm just fine and would make demands on me, which I wouldn't be able to live up to."

Since her depression was doing so much for her, no wonder she had been clinging to it for so many years! Imagine getting identity, irresponsibility, cooperation, self-esteem, protection and power! How could anyone let go of such a "treasure"? Yet little by little, she learned to achieve her goals in other ways. She soon realized that her desire to be dependent would not bring her the greatest pleasure, i.e., self-esteem and consideration from others.

This woman is typical of many who think that depression will bring relief. True, she may get her husband's attention for a while, but as soon as she gets stronger, he'll probably withdraw again because most men do not have as strong a need for emotional intimacy as women do. However, because getting severely depressed got his attention once, she keeps doing it, hoping to see that worried look of concern on his face instead of his usual indifference or annoyance. What he gives her is called negative attention, and for a lonely woman, it seems better than no attention at all.

However, depressed women find that it takes more and more to get their husbands' attention! In the meantime, depression keeps them from finding nourishing activities and relationships which would fulfill some of the emotional needs which their husbands cannot satisfy.

The only way out of this trap is for a woman to take responsibility for her own happiness! She can start this process by thinking of five practical, attainable things that would make her feel loved and happy, such as a job, *shiurim*, crafts, exercise classes, etc. The next step is to pursue them! In order not to lose contact with her husband, she can ask for minimal time together: a night out with him once a month, five minutes of help from him each evening or that he join her family get-togethers once every two or three months.

You will not be able to get everything you want, but you can figure out how to get at least some of your needs satisfied right now. This is called taking charge of your life. Stop waiting passively for someone else to make you happy. This only causes more anger and depression.

Every person has his own particular *neshamah* needs which he must discover for himself. Whatever brings you joy is what your *neshamah* needs. When you assert your legitimate, healthy right to do the things and be with the people who bring you joy, you won't need the genie to get a phony sense of power. You'll have true power.

Avoiding the drama detour with children

Getting mad, bad, sad, sick or crazy to get what you want is like going from New York to California via Europe. These drama detours waste a lot of time and energy, and rarely even get you where you want to go.

Small children have no choice but to dramatize their feelings because they can't put their needs into words. They can't say: "Love me! Protect me! Make me feel important, secure, special and cherished." Or, "Leave me alone! Let me control my own body! Don't invade my borders. Let me be independent and autonomous."

Help children express these needs in words. When you define their goal, both you and they become more realistic about how to achieve what they want.

◊ EXAMPLE: "I used to hit my two year old whenever he failed to cooperate. Then he started calling me names like 'ka-ka face.' Again I hit him. Then he started hitting other children. I figured he needed MORE force. Unfortunately, the child came to the same conclusion! He was even more determined than ever to call everyone 'ka-ka face,' while I was even more determined to break his spirit. Finally I realized that hitting was like a drug. Though sometimes necessary, I had to use it with tremendous caution. I thought that hitting was good *chinuch* and that I was obligated to take every wrong thing he did very seriously and to respond immediately with tanks and heavy artillery. A few sessions with a child therapist helped me to consider my choices, such as letting him say his nasty words alone in the bedroom or letting him say them into a tape recorder and playing it back until he himself said, 'Enough! I don't want to hear it any more!'"

◊ EXAMPLE: "My teenager stormed into the kitchen and said he wanted peace and quiet so he could study. 'Can't you keep things quiet?' he snapped at me. I wanted to slap his face for talking to me like that. Then I realized what my erroneous belief was, that I had to get angry to make him act respectfully. Would it work? Of course not. Instead, I replayed the scene and told him to state in a calm manner what he wanted, beginning with the words 'I would like.' He looked at me with amazement, as if to say, Who needs words? If I just scream, I'll get what I want! But he left the room and came back in and said, 'I'd really appreciate it if you could try to keep the little ones quiet.' Then he looked embarrassed and said, 'I'm sorry I spoke to you like that.' What a victory!''

You have thousands of opportunities to teach children how to avoid the Genie of Unhappiness. And every disappointment is an opportunity to practice being loving, honest and compassionate.

If a child is disrespectful, give *mussar* only if you can do so with love in your heart or in a calm, but authoritative policeman-like mode. Otherwise be silent or focus on a solution during the moment of crisis. People hear words spoken with love.

◊ EXAMPLE: "My teenage daughter was very angry about all the work she had to do in the house. Thank God, we have a large family, but I'm often in bed because I have difficult pregnancies. Plus, I'm rather disorganized, while my daughter is naturally orderly. She cleans while I seem to be having a grand old time lying in bed — at her expense. The last time she complained, instead of getting angry, I just said, 'You are not allowed to speak to me like that. You don't have to get angry to get me to listen. I'm sorry you have so much work. I appreciate all you do very, very much. I know it's hard for you. Let's work out some kind of solution.' My empathy calmed her down. I promised to use baby sitters more often if she would help the other days without acting grouchy. She happily agreed.''

Overcoming the initial response of impotency and frustration

At first it is terrifying to let go of the mad/sad/sick syndrome. You may feel at a loss for what to do with yourself, like a smoker who has given up cigarettes. You may think, My greatest pleasure has been taken away. Now I'll never get my husband/wife to be what I want! Now the kids will never cooperate! Now no one will notice me or take me seriously! I'll be isolated, helpless, misunderstood, unprotected and miserable!

True, in many cases you will have an initial sense of loss. But this will soon be offset by the joy of gaining self-respect and inner tranquility, and having more harmonious relationships.

For example, a critical mother learned to be silent or leave the room when she felt an urge to criticize. At first, she thought she would burst from keeping her rage inside. But she was not just being passively hostile. She kept repeating to herself, "He's doing the best he can with the tools he has" and "Hashem must not want me to have my desires fulfilled right now," until she calmed down and used the silent time to define precisely what she wanted. Then she returned to the scene and simply stated her goal without all the name-calling which used to accompany her words. For example: "Dishes must be removed from the table after eating" or "You must be in bed by eight o'clock. You can read until you fall asleep." She was learning to motivate with love, not hostility.

In another situation, a mother was constantly criticizing a learning-disabled child for being spacey, disorganized and hostile. The result? All three traits intensified. She felt, "I MUST continue to be very hostile toward her because it's the only way I can: (1) make her become a responsible, successful person, (2) make her respect me, (3) show people how much I care about my child. If I stop criticizing, I'll become apathetic and uncaring, and she'll end up a total failure!

Her goals were positive, but her bullying methods were not. She thought anger would save her child. But it was counterproductive. When she stopped trying to motivate her daughter through hostility, she was able to see more clearly that her daughter needed firm guidelines stated in a loving manner. It all took time and energy to formulate and put into action. Hatred had seemed so much easier. But in the long run, it caused grave damage.

With the help of a therapist, the mother developed a behavior modification program. She wrote down her short-range goals and endorsed her daughter whenever she did something positive during the day. She put a sheet of paper on the refrigerator and wrote down all the good things her daughter did throughout the day, and then read them back to her each evening. She substituted endorsements and compassion for the malice which was hurting them both. In a more loving atmosphere, the child began to improve.

Accepting our impotency over others

Perhaps the hardest thing for us to accept is our essential impotency over anything other than our own minds and muscles. As children, we wanted to control the universe. We performed to get others' approval. We dressed in a certain way to win admiration. We did what we were told to win others' love. We got angry in order to feel that we were in control. Everything we did was aimed at affecting others. Now, as adults, we must switch the focus of attention to our own *middoth*. Nothing else can be controlled.

Just as we gave up the childish toys we played with when we were younger, we have to give up the Magic Genie of Unhappy Moods. Each time we get into a bad mood, it's an opportunity for us to give up certain childhood myths, such as:

1. Satisfaction of my needs comes from others.

2. I must first get extremely angry or depressed before I can motivate myself to change.

3. It is dangerous and catastrophic not to get the love and approval I want.

4. If I don't get what I want, it means I am a failure and deserve to be punished and rejected.

5. If I stop being angry, anxious and depressed, people won't see how unhappy I am and will never give me what I want.

6. It is my obligation to hurt the people who hurt me or don't live up to my standards of efficiency, religiosity, intelligence or sensitivity.

7. My best protection against those who hurt me is to hate them and thus put distance between us.

Maturity means accepting that:

1. No one can make me feel secure, worthwhile or fulfilled. That's between me and God. I am essentially impotent when it comes to changing other people. All I can do is model Torah ethics.

2. The best motivation to change is not fear, but simply my desire to be closer to God.

3. My job is to love others; whether or not they love me back is in God's hands.

4. If I don't get what I want, God doesn't mean for me to have it. I can still be loving and have much joy in my life.

5. My goal is to work on my own *middoth*, nothing more. Jealousy shows a lack of gratefulness. Resentment shows a lack of compassion. Anger means a lack of forgiveness.

6. Hostility doesn't change people. Hurting people only gives me an illusion of power.

7. My best protection against those who hurt me is to pray for them and close the mental door so I don't obsess about something they said or did.

15 | The Gift of Defeating the Genie Syndrome: Part II

There are three steps in defeating the Genie of Unhappiness:

1. Identify what you want.
2. Get your message across to the person.
3. Pursue your realistic goals with zeal and give up the impossible ones without bitterness.

> ◊ EXAMPLE: "My car stalled on the freeway. For a few minutes I sat there fuming about the fact that I have to drive an old wreck and don't have money to get a new car. Then I laughed to myself, because I wanted to say to God, 'Please, let a new car drop out of the sky. Let me arrive at the bank this afternoon and discover that someone has deposited a million dollars in my account.' So much for romantic dreams."

However, many times, these realizations are more difficult to achieve and implement.

For example, a woman complained, "I want to be Superwoman. But I'm completely overwhelmed, especially now, before the holidays. I feel like I'm having a nervous breakdown. The children's demands drive me crazy. I get hysterical when I don't get enough sleep. I can't take being poor. As hard as I try to be a good mother, I often hit and scream."

When asked to figure out her goal, she said, "I want to be a Superwoman because it's the only way for me to get love and respect." She had a high-strung nature which was made worse by her belief: I shouldn't be this way. She thought, If I just try harder I'll be like my calm, confident neighbor who has a high-paying job as a learning disabilities specialist, a baby almost every year and a house as neat as a pin. She knew that her frequent explosions and depressions were creating an unhealthy emotional atmosphere for the children. But she felt she could handle the same burdens as someone with a stronger constitution. She couldn't accept having an emotional handicap. She wanted to be a superstar. So she pushed herself to her limits, and felt exhausted and on the verge of a nervous breakdown.

Having suffered abuse as a child, she had unrealistic expectations of herself, which is typical of abused children who grow up blaming themselves for the abuse and thinking, "If only I were perfect, then I'd be loved."

She had to do a great deal of re-programming in order to calm down and stop being so abusive to herself, her children and her husband. The first step was to state her messages.

What did she want? Love. However, like many people who were brought up in dysfunctional homes, she felt she didn't deserve it. So the message she had to give over and over to herself was: I may not be a superstar, but I still deserve love. It took a few months to internalize this concept, but she made it a reality by repeating it to herself often.

She had to give up the erroneous belief that needing help was a sign of failure. She found that if she reached out in a loving manner at her first signs of panic, she didn't have to resort to a full-blown state of hysteria in order to dramatize her needs.

Although it felt uncomfortable at first, she gave her children the message, "I love you and treasure you" by giving them positive feedback throughout the day. This was in stark contrast to the message she had been giving them (which she herself had received as a child), i.e., "You're pests and burdens and you make me miserable." The negative message was a form of psychological abuse which only made her children more defiant and hostile.

She learned to keep her lips locked when she felt like attacking, and to wait patiently for her nasty moods to pass without condemning others or herself. With positive reinforcement she was able to get her children to take more responsibility in helping with the chores. However, she gave up the unrealistic demand that they become perfectly obedient little robots who would jump whenever she gave an order. She found that by stating her messages calmly, she was able to get far more cooperation. And when she didn't get what she wanted, she sought a constructive solution instead of attacking with name calling or slaps.

Face the grief

Another woman was constantly resentful and angry because she perceived her husband as sloppy, passive and lacking in ambition. In her mind, her belief was: I must be angry because it shows how desperately I want him to change. If I stop being angry, he'll have no reason to change. Anger gives me hope. It makes me feel powerful. If I loved him and accepted him as he is, I would not only be dishonest, I'd be in dispair.

This woman's desire for control only alienated her husband and intensified her anger and his passivity. Being angry made her feel powerful and self-respecting. Anger protected her from experiencing her helplessness at having married someone she perceived to be a failure. When she stopped being so obsessed with his negative traits and let go of her dreams of having the perfect husband, she was free to suddenly realize that he had many positive traits. What followed was a realization that one of the gifts her husband gave her was an opportunity to learn to accept God's will and to be accepting and appreciative of people as they are. The new positive atmosphere made him more willing to improve as well.

Avoid the drama: state your message clearly

We cannot always act calm, cool and collected when a stressful event occurs. Although it's true that some people are so heavily armored that they don't take us seriously unless we express the depth of our feelings in a very dramatic way, what we want to avoid is stirring up unnecessary drama over trivial situations. Then we can focus on solutions.

At first, you may feel terribly vulnerable and helpless when you give up your childhood control tactics. For years, you've used the Genie of Anger to make yourself feel powerful and protected. You've used the Genie of Gloom to get pampered and excused from obligations. Until you build an arsenal of positive communication tactics, plus habituate yourself to forgiveness and acceptance, you might still crave an occasional "fix" of an explosive outburst or depressive setback. When you realize how destructive this is, you'll search for more constructive solutions. For example:

1. You want to put distance between yourself and non-nurturing people? Don't get hostile. Just stay away from them. Or keep the relationship P.S. — polite and superficial. Make it clear to yourself that you don't spend time with people who put you down. It may be appropriate to tell chronic criticizers: "Chronic criticism is evil, since the goal is to crush others and deny their *tzelem Elokim*. Please stop."

Children use hatred to make themselves feel emotionally distant, and to feel powerful and protected. But prolonged resentment is a poor tactic because it binds up your energy with that person. If the person is a stone wall, save yourself the time and effort you spend being resentful and become compassionate instead.

Many people fear compassion because they think of it as an emotion which connects them to people. But you can also use compassion to distance yourself. It is a better distancer than hostility because it enables you to disconnect from the person with love and go on with your life without investing your energies in a non-productive relationship.

2. You want respect? Respect others and they will usually respect you. Respect yourself for who you are and others will respect you. If appropriate, say, "I want you to consult me when you make a decision which affects my life."

Don't expect respect from chronically critical people.

3. You want help? Ask for it! Say, "I need ten minutes of your time right now." Or, "Let me know when you can give me some time and how much time you're willing to give." "I need your help right now, and that doesn't mean I am incompetent or incapable."

4. You want to feel loved? Act loving, even if others don't. It might help to ask your spouse or child, "Tell me what you think would improve our relationship."

You might have to face the truth that this person cannot give you what you want. This may be terribly painful, but it is better to confront the truth than to waste time hoping for the impossible.

5. You want less criticism in the house? You can say:

"This relationship will die if you continue to criticize me."

"I feel confident that I can make a responsible decision on my own."

"True, I do admit to having imperfections. But the only way I can build my confidence is by making my own choices. So, I thank you for your advice, but my way is working just fine for me."

"I value our relationship, so please don't give me advice unless I ask for it."

"Your way is different from mine, but both have validity. I'm confident that things will work out."

6. You want someone to get rid of a bad habit? You can't make anyone change a habit they don't want to change. But you can say:

"I can't control what you do outside this house. But inside, you are not allowed to smoke."

"I don't want to be on your back, but I hope, for your health and the sake of our relationship, that you will see a doctor" (or, "Take the time to listen to me").

Don't nag people about major personality problems, such as being slow, lazy, selfish, insensitive, etc. If possible, give them small tasks and show them that they have the ability to be different. If this is impossible, focus on their positive traits or distance yourself emotionally.

7. You want more appreciation? Get into the endorsement habit, mentioning the good that others do. Others will imitate you if they're mentally healthy.

8. You want space? Say, "I need time to be alone right now." "I love you, but I have to tell you honestly that I can't have you staying with us for such a long visit. I can try to find a room for you to rent nearby if you'd like." "When I come home from work, I need a few minutes by myself to relax. Then I can talk."

9. You want to set limits? Say no with love. Make rules and regulations about things that upset you. For example:

"I love you and want to help you, but doing X comes first."

"You're infringing on my rights."

"You can have guests once every two weeks, not every week."

Logical consequences are especially effective for setting limits. For example:

"If we can't stay within the budget we set, we'll have to cancel all our credit cards."

To a child: "If you wake me up when I'm taking my nap, I won't have the energy to take you out later on."

With children, it's especially helpful to include them in the decision-making process. For example, "If you lose your bus ticket again, what extra chores can you do to pay me back for it?" Or, "What privilege do you want to give up if you fail to do your homework?" "What should the consequences be if you don't do your chores?"

Stating messages directly often takes courage. After all, some people may ridicule you for speaking up and imply that you are incompetent for wanting help and selfish for thinking of yourself.

You also risk discovering that many people cannot give you the love, understanding and level of intelligence or competency you want. You risk finding out how empty or abusive the relationship may be. By being direct, you may suddenly realize that this is a relationship which you want to end or limit to only superficial encounters.

So, state your desire. But remember: Effort is up to you, but the results of your efforts are up to God and man.

Anti-tantrum training

By threatening or punishing, we often do get children to stop what they are doing, hang up their coats or finish their food. But anger doesn't work on deep-rooted habit patterns and it doesn't foster love. Furthermore, the use of shame and punishment as control tactics is what destroys spirits and relationships.

> ◊ EXAMPLE: "My eight year old was misbehaving, so when I took my other children out for pizza, I told him he had to stay home as a punishment. I then left the house, crossed a busy six-lane highway with my other children, and hailed a cab. As the driver was pulling away, I looked around and was horrified to see the eight year old dash across the middle of the highway in an attempt to stop me, almost getting killed in the process. By the time we had all gotten out of the cab and crossed the street to go back home, the child was nowhere to be found. He had run away. When he finally turned up late at night, he got a good beating to teach

him a lesson. The next day, he ran away again. Finally I realized that we would have to find some other way of reaching this child.''

While a show of anger is often necessary, many parents are convinced that anger is the only way to stop misbehavior. And if anger doesn't work, they assume that they simply aren't getting angry enough. They are so blinded by this conviction that they often don't realize that the child is becoming more violent and despairing. In fact, running across the highway in the middle of traffic was a suicidal act.

Anger doesn't make people more "spiritual," considerate, mature, loving or responsible. What does work? Anti-tantrum training.

Anti-tantrum training can begin when a child is very small by teaching him to use words to express his desires directly. From the age of two, parents can say, "Hold my hands, look into my eyes and start a sentence with 'I want.' Then we'll see if it's something I can do for you." Focus on solutions.

The same anti-tantrum training can be tried with adults, too! The results are often gratifying.

Ask: what are your (my) insecure thoughts?

The next time you get upset, ask yourself: What are my insecure thoughts? They fall into two categories:

(1) MINOR INSECURE THOUGHTS: I will temporarily lose approval, closeness, respect, control, sleep, comfort, a small amount of money or some momentary satisfaction of an ego need.

(2) MAJOR INSECURE THOUGHTS: I (or someone else) will lose a significant relationship, will have a mental or physical collapse, will become immoral, irreligious, will lose all trust in myself or others, will die, etc.

If you are having only minor insecure thoughts, you can probably deal very calmly with the situation. However, expect to be agitated if your insecure thoughts are in the second category.

◊ EXAMPLE: "Whenever I'm upset, I demonstrate to the kids how to calm down by saying out loud, 'Hmm...let me think why I'm so upset. What are my insecure thoughts?' Usually, it's something minor and they see that I quickly calm down. By sharing this out loud with them, they get used to doing this themselves."

◊ EXAMPLE: "My oldest daughter is having real 'teenageritis.' She's so nasty to me that I don't know whether to act cold or nasty back to her. I finally identified that my main insecure thought is that we'll never have any real closeness between us. Once I identified this insecure thought, major as it is, I knew that I could deal with her only by staying loving and giving rebuke calmly. Yelling certainly won't get me the closeness I want. I can only pray that the years will soften her."

◊ EXAMPLE: "For years, I didn't invite Shabbos guests because my two active children were so incredibly obnoxious. But I gave it another try last week and invited a newly married couple. Well, my kids did their whole bit: refused to sing, refused to sit still, refused to eat what I served and hit each other constantly. I was so mortified that I just wanted to die. My insecure thoughts were: My guests will think I'm the worst mother in the world. I'm losing status and comfort. When I identified the loss, it became more bearable. My goal is not to get someone else's approval, but to act like a *mentsch* no matter how my children act. That helped me to keep my cool."

◊ EXAMPLE: "My husband was very upset when I came home late from a meeting. I asked him, 'What is your insecure thought?' He thought for a while and then said, 'That you don't really care about me.' As soon as he said it, he realized how untrue it was and he laughed. The next day, when the baby was screaming, he picked her up said, 'What are your insecure thoughts? Do you think you have to scream to get my attention? You're right! But in a few years, we're going to teach you some other methods!'"

The endorsement principle

If you are feeling positive about people, they are more likely to respond positively. Therefore, awaken positive feelings in yourself by thinking of the good things this person has done before you start talking to him. The most important psychological principle you need to know is that: when you endorse yourself for the positive steps you are taking today, no matter how small those steps may be, you will automatically take bigger steps tomorrow. When you crush yourself or others for being failures today, you will do worse tomorrow.

The following stories are examples of this principle.

◊ EXAMPLE: "One of my children has a tendency to be very messy. I used to constantly nag him to clean up after himself. But I finally realized that this was only making him feel hostile toward me. So I decided to program his mind positively by giving him success experiences in neatness. For example, I mixed up all the knives, forks and spoons in the drawer and asked him to put them in their proper compartments. While he was working, I kept saying to him, 'I see that you are a person who likes to see things in place. Look how happy it makes you to make things beautiful.' After a few days of this, he was much more responsive to me when I asked him to clean up the messes he made. Each time, I would say, 'I know that it makes you happy to put things in order, so would you please...'"

◊ EXAMPLE: "I was always resentful of the fact that my husband was so unhelpful and indifferent toward me and the children. I found myself becoming angrier as time when on. But when I learned about the endorsement principle, I decided to endorse him for any act of consideration, no matter how minor. It took a few years, but he has become more involved with us."

◊ EXAMPLE: "I was always knocking myself for not being more self-disciplined. I procrastinated and lost my temper a lot and didn't follow through on plans. Every day, I'd tell myself, 'I have no self-control!' So of course, every day I'd feel more out of control. The situation didn't improve until I started using the endorsement principle. I endorsed myself for the times that I did demonstrate self-control and did follow through on decisions, no matter how minor they were. Little by little, my self-esteem rose. My image of myself as an incompetent and undisciplined person changed as I celebrated the times I succeeded. I am now much more in control of myself and my life."

◊ EXAMPLE: "My oldest girl, who is seven, is very bossy and also extremely active. I disliked her so much that I couldn't stand to be in the same room with her. Whenever she acted mean toward one of her younger siblings or was insolent to me, I slapped her. Finally, I went to a counselor who told me to empathize with her and praise her whenever she was good. Well, that was the last thing I wanted to do, but the situation was so bad that I tried these suggestions. Lo and behold, they often worked! Our relationship still isn't what I'd call great, but I don't feel so hostile, and probably as a result, she has calmed down."

The endorsement principle was stated very succinctly almost two thousand years ago by Hillel, who said:

Be of the disciples of Aaron, loving peace and pursuing peace, loving your fellow creatures and bringing them near to Torah.
— PIRKEI AVOTH: 1:12

Draw people close with love, even if you have to force yourself at first. It's the only thing that works in the long run.

Each of us has a wellspring (*ma'ayan*) of faith, self-worth, joy and inner strength which can be discovered whenever we look for constructive solutions to problems. Keep telling yourself, "This person (or situation) will force me to develop creative capacities that would not have been developed otherwise."

Our goal is to motivate ourselves and others to improve in reaction to our love; and when that is not possible, to accept the unchangeable with love.

16 | The Gift of Escaping from the IRS

*Any love that is dependent upon a specific
consideration, when that consideration vanishes,
the love ceases; but if it is not dependent upon a
specific consideration, it will never cease.*
— AVOTH 5:16

Just as there are many levels of artistic or muscial talent, so too are
there many levels in one's ability to love others. The highest level is
unconditional love, a love of man and God which is not dependent
on getting anything in return. However, the ability to love unconditionally is developed only by overcoming our inner resistance to the
spiritual disciplines necessary to reach this level.

To understand why this resistance exists, it is important to realize
that our minds work according to two different and usually opposing
systems: The Infantile Response System (IRS) and the Spiritual
Response System (SRS). The hallmark of a person who is stuck in
the IRS is that he is preoccupied with satisfying his own physical
desires. He has a "gimme" and a "make me" attitude, i.e., "Gimme
attention and love — right now! Make me feel happy, important and
successful." And when he doesn't get what he wants, he blames
others and stews in anger or depression.

In contrast, the hallmark of a person who is functioning within
his SRS is that he blames no one for his moods and takes responsibility for his thoughts and actions. He bears his disappointments with
dignity and knows how to serve God with joy, even in the midst of
pain.

However, we must go through a process of disappointment and
disillusionment with the material world in order to appreciate what

the spiritual world can give us. Unfortunately, many people remain stuck in the IRS.

To break out of this mental prison requires identifying our false IRS beliefs. At first, we don't realize that these beliefs are irrational. After all, we've lived with them since childhood, so they seem normal and correct. Luckily, unlike the Internal Revenue Service, this is one system we can escape from!

Stressful events: endless opportunities for enlightenment

> Of all that Hashem created, not one thing was made without a purpose. — SHABBATH 77b

One of the purposes of stressful events is that they enable us to identify and eliminate the erroneous beliefs which keep us from experiencing Godliness in this world.

1. IRS Myth: I have no choice but to be angry. I must have control over people and make them love me, respect me, submit to me and make me happy.

SRS Truth: I can only have true mastery over my own thoughts, speech and actions. I can try to influence others to do good by demonstrating good *middoth*, but trying to control their freedom of choice is evil. Control is the opposite of love. Love means wanting what is best for others; evil is wanting others to serve my own selfish ego desires for pleasure, comfort or *kavod*.

2. IRS Myth: I have no choice but to feel alone and isolated. God is distant. All I see is injustice, unfairness and cruelty in all the tragedies surrounding me. He doesn't see or care about me.

SRS Truth: It's my choice to experience God as close or distant. I can't come close to Him by waiting for Him to make all the moves. I create closeness by nullifying my will and carrying out His will as if it were my will (*Avoth* 2:4). I trust that "God is close to all who call upon Him" (*Tehillim* 145:18). My task is to feel His presence by turning away from sin and by speaking with Him like a child to a father.

3. IRS Myth: I have no choice but to be depressed. I'm not getting all my heart's desires for comfort, control and *kavod* fulfilled.

SRS Truth: The material world will always disappoint me in the long run. Its pleasures are fleeting and ultimately unfulfilling. I'll never get all I want on an ego level; but I'm getting precisely what I need for my spiritual growth. Only spiritual growth is truly soul satisfying. I will always feel deprived from a materialistic point of view. "No man dies with even half his heart's desires fulfilled" (*Koheleth Rabbah* 1:34). My goal is to strive to be loving and joyous with whatever God gives me.

> There is no happiness in the world in material things; there is only happiness in spiritual concerns. The one who enjoys a rich spiritual life is happy. — STRIVE FOR TRUTH! vol. 1, p. 29

The very fact that Hashem sustains me from moment to moment and gives me life, sight, speech and the ability to make choices and grow in understanding is enough reason to be constantly grateful. This material world is not all there is to life. It's not the physical pleasures which are so important, but the SRS pleasures which are the most fulfilling.

> There is no bliss that is sweeter and more delightful than that which is earned by subjugating one's base instincts.
> — THE CHAZON ISH, p. 161

I am in this world for Torah, prayer and acts of loving-kindness (*Avoth* 1:2), which I can do at any time or in any place. If I focus on what I'm lacking, I'll always feel deprived and angry at man and God. If I focus on what I'm getting and giving, I will feel loving and loved.

4. IRS Myth: I have no choice but to hurt those who hurt me.

SRS Truth: Since human relationships inevitably involve both deliberate and unintentional slights, snubs and misunderstandings, I can always have an excuse to inflict pain on others. Instead, I focus on the tremendous spiritual reward I receive when I give the benefit of the doubt and overcome hatred, grudge bearing and vengeance (*Vayikra* 19:17-19). When I rid my heart of these three barriers, I can see the hand of God in all my encounters with people.

> I will strive to be like those which the Talmud praises as able to be humiliated, yet do not humiliate in turn, who hear insult and do not retort, who perform out of love and are happy in affliction... — SHABBATH 88b

I welcome opportunities not to react negatively to someone who has hurt me, for then my sins are forgiven...
— ROSH HASHANNAH 17a

5. IRS Myth: I have no choice but to feel inferior and superior. If someone has more than I have (e.g., money, children, degrees, possessions, etc.), s/he is more worthwhile and deserving of more respect. If I have more, I'm more worthwhile!

SRS Truth: I recognize that envy, lust and the desire for honor will destroy my life (*Avoth* 4:21). I cannot love others from a position of superiority or inferiority. Both positions isolate me. Love is based on mutual respect and appreciation for others as they are right now.

Envy is the result of believing in the illusion of separateness. It is this illusion which makes us feel resentful toward those who have more or arrogant toward those who have less. In truth, the Jewish People is one. The good deeds that a person does are a credit to all of us.

6. IRS Myth: I have no choice but to withhold, withdraw and refuse to share. Giving to others diminishes me.

SRS Truth: In giving to others, we are actually giving to ourselves. Giving is the source of the greatest joy. Giving to others is a way of imitating God, which makes me feel close to Him.

7. IRS Myth: I have no choice but to feel anxious about getting approval since my happiness, sense of security and self-worth are determined by others."

SRS Truth: It is attachment to God that brings happiness, security and self-worth. If my value is externally determined, I will be continuously angry that others aren't doing enough to make me feel good. If my value is internally determined, I will not feel threatened by what others think of me or give me. In this way, my relationships will be based purely on love.

8. IRS Myth: I have no choice but to look down on those who don't live up to my standards.

SRS Truth: God created each of us in His image, with infinite value. He gave each of us the precise talents, personality, parents and physical circumstances needed to fulfill our special mission. My spiritual work is to love others and myself as God loves me, as I am, with my imperfections.

From the above, we can see how children may often be unhappy no matter how loving their parents are because they think their inner state is determined by external conditions. If they think their worth is determined by others, they will always be anxious about what others think. If they think their happiness is determined by how much they're getting, they'll always be jealous of those who have more and blame others angrily whenever they feel unhappy.

It is only when we transcend the IRS that we can understand how it is that we can create love and joy no matter what the stresses may be.

Conditional love

> A person comes to love the one to whom he gives...
> — STRIVE FOR TRUTH!, vol. 1, p. 130

In the IRS mode, only conditional love is possible, because one is focused on one's own ego needs. Such a person sees others as a threat because he fears that others will fail to give him what he needs to make him feel respected or worthwhile.

People who love conditionally usually love only those who meet their needs and standards. If they are fastidious, they love and respect only fastidious people. If they are brilliant, they love and respect only intelligent people. If they are image-oriented, they despise those who do not flatter them.

To love people who are exactly like oneself is easy because it is actually a form of self-love; after all, one is loving others because they are like oneself. When the fastidious person walks into a home which is not up to his standards, he will grimace, and purse his lips and make some derogatory statements. The intelligent person will honor only people he can talk to at his level. When he hears a statement which does not meet his level of profundity, he will smirk arrogantly and perhaps write the person off in his mind as a stupid fool who is not worth the time of day. And the person who is pious only on the outside will feel hatred and disgust in his heart when he meets someone who does not follow his exact same customs.

It is far more difficult to love those who are different from us. Yet this is the real test of how loving we are, because then we are loving not out of self-love, but purely, in order to fulfill the commandment to "Love thy neighbor as thyself" (*Vayikra* 19:18). True, selfless love is *ahavath chinam*, love which is given for the sake of honoring another's *tzelem Elokim*, regardless of what that person has achieved or what he or she gives in return.

The only way to clear our hearts of hatred, grudge bearing and vengeance is to practice the unconditional love which is a natural result of thinking according to the SRS. This is what transforms us from selfish, self-centered takers into spiritually mature givers.

The mitzvah is not, "Love your neighbor who is kind, considerate, intelligent and polite." It says, "Love your neighbor" (*Vayikra* 19:18). If He had meant this to be an easy mitzvah, He would have made everyone wise, good-hearted and competent. But that is not how He created mankind. Our task is to fulfill this mitzvah when it is most difficult. This is when the greatest spiritual growth will take place and when we earn the greatest reward.

◊ EXAMPLE: "I put my son in a high-pressure *yeshivah* where he did not belong. He is not an academic type and was always behind, always feeling bad about himself. I realize now that it was my desire for *kavod* that made me keep him there because I wanted to say, 'My son goes to this *yeshivah*.' At the time, I erroneously believed that only brilliant people deserve respect. Meanwhile he got more and more depressed and withdrawn. He hated learning, hated us, himself and life. When I switched mental systems, I began to love him as he is, and found a low-pressure *yeshivah* where he is treated with love."

◊ EXAMPLE: "When someone else got the promotion I had expected, I was stunned and furious. From my IRS mode, the world seemed like an unfair and totally unjust place. When I moved into the SRS mode, I accepted that since God willed this, then I could will it, too. Whenever I'd move into my IRS mode, I'd feel profound disappointment and hatred for the person who got the job, and disillusionment with life in general. When I moved into the SRS mode, I felt sane and at peace because I knew my *neshamah* begged for this for my growth."

◊ EXAMPLE: "When my older son wouldn't share a computer game with his younger brother, the younger one got violent. I hate when the older one is mean and selfish. I hate seeing bad *middoth* in my children. I was about to grab the game away from the older one when I thought that my goal was to get the older one out of the IRS idea that giving would diminish him. That meant that I had to be in my SRS, and not my IRS. I mentally switched gears, and a few seconds later an idea struck me: I told the older one, 'When you give, your heart gets bigger and then more of God can come in. And when you don't give, there's less room for God.' It worked. That's all I had to say. The older one thought for a minute and then gave willingly, happily."

◊ EXAMPLE: "Each time I suffer a major disappointment, I move into my SRS and think, 'Thank you, God, for making me less attached to the pleasures of this world.'"

Each time we break through the IRS, we experience tremendous joy, like the joy of one who has been liberated from prison. This is the joy of self-transcendence. And the only way to experience it is to move out of the IRS and into the SRS. To get out of a bad mood, you have to get into a good mode!

17 | The Gift of Loneliness

Though my father and mother have forsaken me,
the Lord has taken me in.

— TEHILLIM 27:10

It is not good for the man to live alone.
— BERESHITH 2:18

Loneliness. It's one of the emotions people least want to experience. They will do almost anything in order not to feel alone, including trying to fill the vacuum with mind-numbing activities. They will get furious and criticize others to mask their sense of isolation. They will bend over backwards and please everyone in order not to be rejected. They will spend hours searching for fancy clothing and furnishings and agonize over their public image and try to outdo everyone else in the race to be noticed and admired — anything to avoid the sense of existential aloneness which can be so terrifying. But no matter what we do, loneliness is something we cannot avoid for long.

◊ EXAMPLE: "I wanted to say something to my spouse. But instead of the closeness I wanted, I got the usual grimace and an impatient, 'Don't bother me.' It's always like this. When I attempt to communicate, I feel I'm alone in an echo chamber. It's like living in an isolation cell."

◊ EXAMPLE: "I asked a family member for a small favor, and the person said, 'I'm busy.' Enraged, I wanted to scream back, 'I've done so much for you and you let me down like this? You selfish rat!' I bit my tongue, but the incident burns in my heart."

◊ EXAMPLE: "It was my birthday. I expected a call from my married daughter, maybe even a visit. But there was no call. I've given so

263

much to this child. Now she barely thinks of me. I felt so rejected that life seemed to have no purpose anymore."

◊ EXAMPLE: "I was invited to a wedding where I didn't know anyone except the mother of the bride, and she was busy chatting with her other guests all the time. I sat at a table, surrounded by people who wouldn't respond much to my attempts to converse. I felt rejected. I felt invisible. My feelings of unreality were so strong that I wanted to pinch myself to feel real again. I left early and when I came home, I ate all the sweets I could get my hands on."

◊ EXAMPLE: "I was being wheeled into the operating room. I felt like crying. I wished someone would take my hand to reassure me and let me know that I'm an individual who is cared about. But everything was impersonal and sterile, including the hearts and minds of those taking care of me. The aloneness was terrifying."

At such moments the aloneness is like a terrifying abyss. When you reach out again and again to someone who is not there for you, you wonder if you can ever trust anybody again, if anyone really cares. Sometimes you attack that other person angrily. At other times you withdraw, grief stricken, your mind numb, your heart turned to ice.

It's often like this with relationships. One minute you are full of love and hope, wanting to reach out and make contact. The next second, you are enraged, hating the very people you want most to love. You don't know what to do with the pain. You may even be angry at yourself for needing people, for being so shattered by these slights, snubs and rejections. You don't like feeling emotionally dependent. You may castigate yourself, "Why can't I be stronger, tougher, less needy?" Or you may castigate others, "Why don't people care more, show more concern?"

Such incidents are painful because they threaten our deepest emotional needs for closeness, understanding and belonging. To be noticed is to exist. To be loved is to feel alive. To be rejected is to feel diminished, threatened, even dead.

Some people need more emotional contact than others, but hardly anyone is immune to the pain of rejection and loneliness.

Facing reality

It is an inescapable fact of life that we will not always get the understanding and closeness we crave, surely not on a continuous basis. There are times when we feel more alone, and there are people with whom we feel more alone. And there are inevitable moments of distance and disappointment with friends. When we are sick or are dealing with a traumatic situation, few people can really understand what we are going through as we strive to retain our sanity and faith.

Loneliness is the price we pay for caring. After all, if the postman doesn't remember your birthday, you don't feel badly. When a salesman acts like you don't exist, you don't take it seriously. But when your spouse or child snubs you, you feel terrible. The more emotional energy you have invested in a person, the greater the sense of loss when that person seems not to care.

Loneliness is also the price we pay for being self-aware, for this self-awareness leads us to realize that no one can really understand us completely. The extent to which we can share our lives with even the most understanding person is limited. Here and there we connect and communicate, but even these treasured moments do not alter the fact that most of our thoughts and feelings remain unshared.

Furthermore, when we do attempt to share, the response we receive is sometimes criticism, impatience, invalidation, misunderstanding or a blank stare of incomprehension — leaving us feeling even more isolated than before we attempted to reach out.

Intuitive types, in particular, suffer more intensely from a sense of loneliness, not only because there are relatively few Intuitive types in the world for them to communicate with, but because their emotional needs are more difficult to satisfy. They don't want to just chatter away; they want real depth and understanding. It is rare for an Intuitive type to find that depth with anyone. In fact, when he shares his deepest feelings, others think he is rather odd, even unbalanced. Furthermore, the Intuitive-type person, by definition, is acutely aware of his essential aloneness.

Those who suffer from BPS (see Chapter 20) feel particular anguish because they already have a tendency to feel totally alientated and estranged from humanity. Certain of being abandoned, they do not form stable, trusting relationships. When they are with caring people, they constantly fear that support and love will be withdrawn at any minute. When they do not feel loved, whether justifiably or not, they feel so painfully isolated that they may become suicidally depressed. They often sabotage their relationships and intensify their sense of loneliness by breaking off their attachments almost as soon as attachments are formed.

No matter what his personality type or problems, each person must find positive ways to cope with loneliness. Those who do not will attempt to escape from this pain with addictions and compulsions which only reinforce distance and hostility.

When aloneness becomes isolation

No normal person likes to feel isolated from humanity. Psychological disturbances result from the inability to bond to others. Children will provoke others to beat them just to feel noticed. Our very sense of having an existence is connected to the presence of others. So it is no wonder that isolation is experienced as being worse than death.

In her brilliant study of a community of elderly Jews in California, the late Barbara Myerhoff wrote of those who had no relatives to care for or care about them. They would come to the little community center and, "On seating themselves...their eyes would search desperately for the gaze of another person...It seemed to me that they needed to reestablish human contact, to be certain that someone else saw them. They knew this was not a dream, they were awake and still alive. All their losses — of strength, energy, sensory stimulation and physical contact — fused into a bedrock of fear of losing their awareness of existence — something different from the fear of death. These people no one spoke to, no one greeted or touched.

"Periodically, they came back to life, in a short, sharp outburst of singing, dancing, praying, fighting or eating, emerging from behind a veil as fully realized presences. Seen from outside, the contrast was shocking. What it felt like from within was impossible to know.

"Even the very active, energetic people came more completely alive when looked at...In their collective life, they showed themselves to themselves and proclaimed their continuing reality...The opposite of honor was not shame but invisibility. Being neglected was more unbearable than disgrace...[One woman] would harangue on any subject as long as possible to make up for her neglect and to demonstrate her existence in no uncertain terms" (*Number Our Days*, pp. 143-145).

This life-in-death experience is what we all want to avoid. The terror of being unnoticed, alone, neglected and forgotten is worse than death because it feels like death without the "blessing" of unconsciousness.

The stages of loneliness: death and resurrection

When we feel lonely, we are apt to go through the following stages:

Stage 1: Anger. Anger always arises from a sense of threat, either real or imagined. The threat you fear could be anything from the loss of your life to the loss of closeness. When people don't react with the understanding or sensitivity you want, you may become furious, accusing the person of not caring.

Anger may be an attempt to keep you from seeing how empty a particular relationship is. Because anger creates a lot of commotion, the turbulence gives an illusion of a relationship with the person with whom you are angry. Anger feels like a connection because you are interacting with the other person, but it is nothing more than a pseudorelationship. Anger gives an illusion of power, an illusion of connection. It keeps you from experiencing that you are alone. It makes you think that you are definitely going to get this person to give you what you want if you just persist long enough: love, honesty, sensitivity, closeness, great achievement in society, a perfect home life, obedience, submission, etc.

The terror of existential aloneness can be easily triggered whenever you feel rejected. In response, you may blow up at people, hoping you can make people care. You get angry because: the soup is cold; he used up all the hot water; she didn't get the car back on time; he went without asking you to go along; she bought it without asking you; he left his dirty socks on the floor; she didn't remember your birthday; he refused when asked to help; she arrived late; he was in a bad mood, ad infinitum.

You get angry because you don't want to see: that maybe the

person whose attention you want doesn't really care all that much; that maybe you don't really care all that much; that you are essentially powerless over people; that no one, even the most wonderfully understanding person in the world, can ever understand you totally. Anger helps you to avoid the truth.

Beneath the angry response is the demand: Prove you care by taking care of my needs immediately! Make me the center of your life! Be available at all times! Make me feel that I matter to you, that I belong. Otherwise, I am dead.

> ◊ EXAMPLE: "I had had a very hard day at work and wanted to talk to my wife, but she was on the phone when I got home. I was so angry that I ripped the cord out of the wall. That'll teach her not to be on the phone when I get home!"

Anger may keep his wife off the phone, but it certainly won't get him the closeness he really wants! His anger gives him nothing more than an illusion of having the power to keep her close. In reality, he's distancing her even further.

> ◊ EXAMPLE: "I was in the middle of speaking to my husband when he got up and walked out of the room! I was so furious that I got a bucket of water and dumped it on him when he wasn't looking!"

Her anger will definitely make him pay attention. He will, no doubt, get furious in return and even strike her. The turbulence will feel like they have some connection. But in reality, it keeps them from really connecting.

Anger, an attempt at closeness, always destroys that goal. However, it may feel a lot less painful than the next stage.

Stage 2: Depression and despair. You wait in passive, silent hostility for the other person to make a gesture of concern. You stew and brood resentfully, hoping, "If I get depressed enough s/he will see how awful I feel and will start caring more about me."

Depression is a kind of "negative bonding." Like anger, the obsessive brooding makes you feel connected to the person you're upset with. In reality, there is no connection.

Some depressed people become compulsive caretakers or people pleasers to avoid being alone. They often accept abuse, hoping that eventually the object of their desire will change. They see abuse as preferable to being alone. This is true especially of those women who think, The only way to keep from being abandoned is to always be accommodating, pleasant, compliant, submissive, nonassertive and available. When, despite all their efforts, they are rejected anyway, caretaker types become deeply depressed.

Other depressed people develop addictions and compulsions. Having failed to achieve satisfying bonds with people, they bond to objects: food, books, cigarettes, money, possessions, etc. Or they develop compulsions for working, cleaning, shopping, dressing fashionably, or compulsive rituals to fill the vacuum where human bonds should be. These are all attempts to escape the feeling of isolation.

The attempt to hurt oneself in order to feel real or make contact with others is especially likely in those with dependent personalities, for they unconsciously want to remain children and be taken care of. They believe that the only way to do so is to be sick, either physically or emotionally. To them, being strong, healthy and successful means being alone. So they resist all efforts to become more independent or adopt healthier attitudes and actions. They cling in an attempt to get others to rescue them and stay close, which inevitably drives everyone away.

◊ EXAMPLE: "A relative calls at least five times a day to tell me how depressed she is and how awful the world is. I have four small children and a home business, and her calls drag me down and make me very nervous. I can't say I'm too busy to talk, because then she gets furious and tells me that I'm selfish and bad. Complaining is her way of feeling close. She doesn't realize that her sad, whiny voice is alienating me, that she is getting the opposite of the closeness she says she craves."

◊ EXAMPLE: "My wife is extremely critical. I come home prepared to hear the latest insults. It's like having garbage dumped on me. I hate my life. When I think about her, I get so depressed!"

Yet people still cling to unsatisfying relationships with mournful despair because the next stage seems even more frightening.

Stage 3: Coldness and apathy. You've gone past the threshold. You simply stop caring about the other person — or about life.

◊ EXAMPLE: "During the early years of my marriage, how I bent over backwards to please! How I pulled teeth to get information out of my spouse or carry on a conversation. But after a while, I just got tired of the effort because nothing ever changed. I remained alone. When I felt angry, I still had hope. But this coldness feels worse; it's like being dead. I don't care about anyone, even myself."

◊ EXAMPLE: "I lost my husband last year and soon after, my only child moved away. I had no idea that loneliness could be so unbearably painful. I find myself asking my husband what he would like for dinner, and whether I should get a new battery or fix the roof, and how he's feeling and whether he wants to come with me to the store. And at the store or the doctor's office, I am always consulting him and feeling his presence. At home, I find myself braiding my nonexistent granddaughter's hair and holding a nonexistent grandchild on my lap as I tell her a story. Alone at my Shabbos table, I see nonexistent family members smiling at me from their chairs and hear their nonexistent laughter as we talk about our week. If anyone knew that I live part of my life in this other dimension, they'd think I was crazy. But I'm not. It's just that the lines between various realities have blurred, and this is the way I comfort myself and avoid that awful coldness which used to grip my heart and make me feel afraid to be alive. I don't want my ties to life to be severed. I just want to hold on to everything that has ever brought me joy."

A person can stay stuck in any of these stages for years. Only rarely do people make it to the fourth stage.

Stage 4: Rebirth. Like a seed which can only sprout after going through a process of transformation, so, too, do we come to new understanding and awareness after going through the above stages. Rejection, criticism, abandonment, illness, unfulfilling relationships and loneliness give us the opportunity to destroy our attachments to the materialistic world. We are not left totally bereft if we have a sense of purpose or commitment to improving ourselves and forming bonds of love.

From the pain and heartbreak of life can come a new realization that God is all there is, that nothing else matters except to help others see this truth.

◊ EXAMPLE: "For years I had a terrible relationship with my oldest daughter, who was often very hostile. I'd get so furious that she was so mean to me. After she moved away, I just detached from her. It was awful at first. But after years of this, somehow new buds of caring started to grow. I started to appreciate her personality, as different as it is from mine, and she acted nicer toward me. It's a whole new relationship now, based on a kind of mature, quiet acceptance of each other, without wanting the other to change."

◊ EXAMPLE: "After my son died, I was sure I would never laugh or love anyone again. I hated being alive. It was many months before I noticed a flower or could bear to hear music. Then slowly, without my even willing it, I came back to the land of the living. It was an awful, long, cold winter. I've learned that when I fall into despair again, which inevitably happens from time to time, especially when I light candles or a holiday comes around, I now know that I will come back to life eventually if I just wait patiently."

We are all going to go through these stages thousands of times. Getting to Stage 4 is not a one-time achievement; we get there over and over again after going through the other three stages. The only way to speed the process is to get rid of our illusions about being able to control others and our belief that we can love only if we are loved in return.

What do you do with the pain?

Thus, what we do with these moments of loneliness spells the difference between mental health and mental illness. In fact, mental illness has been defined as a state of isolation from others. To love, reach out and care are all signs of mental health.

So there you are, reeling from the shock of a critical remark or a snub or simply feeling lonely. How can you lessen the pain and turn this experience into a gift? By using it as an opportunity for growth. Here's how:

1. Surrender to the pain. Don't fight it. That only makes it more intense. Validate your grief.

◊ EXAMPLE: "Since my wife died, I have experienced many moments of intense aloneness. It's awful. When this happens, I let myself feel the full intensity of the pain. Sometimes I have a good cry. Then I pick my head up, pull my shoulders back and think of what I can do for someone else. Giving helps me."

◊ EXAMPLE: "I'm an Intuitive type. When I go out in the afternoons with my baby and meet other mothers at the park, I feel so intensely alone and self-conscious. They're chatting away about things that don't really interest or excite me, like recipes or how to get things clean, while I want to share my deepest feelings or learn something which will deepen my love of Torah. We're on different planets. Part of me longs to fit in, to be part of their world. But I've learned to accept that I can't. My world is different from theirs. It's only when I'm with other Feeling types that I feel sane and loved. When I'm not, I don't have to feel unreal, crazy or unwanted. I can be at peace with this reality instead of fighting it. If this is the personality God gave me, I can appreciate this gift and use my special sensitivities to help those who can value what I have to give."

2. Think of something pleasurable you can do at that moment. "Who is rich? He who rejoices with his portion" (*Avoth* 4:1). We're not supposed to accept our portion in life stoically; we're supposed to find some way to be happy with it!

◊ EXAMPLE: "I don't think anyone can imagine the loneliness of an unmarried woman whose friends are all married and having one baby after another. The pain was eating me up until I decided that I was going to find some way to make every hour of my life as pleasurable as possible. Now, when I start to feel that excruciating loneliness, instead of wallowing in it, I immediately ask myself what would make me happy. It might be learning Torah, gardening, visiting a friend, doing a *chesed* or doing something creative. Whatever it is, I pretend that I am lighting a small candle in the darkness. It doesn't make the pain go away completely, but at least I'm not stewing in resentment and bitterness."

3. Use loneliness as an opportunity to reconnect to God. If you aren't getting the closeness you want from someone, see it as a "busy signal" on a telephone; hang up and "dial God."

◊ EXAMPLE: "My mother was in one of her moods and started yelling at me, 'You can't do anything right!' Her words were like a knife in my guts. It seemed that there was no comfort or love in my life. It was so painful. I wanted to numb myself and not feel anything. But I went into my room and let the pain rise in intensity until it began to fall and fade away. I was left with a very empty, sad feeling. But at least I hadn't given in to the impulse to scream back at her. I kept muttering, *b'yado afkid ruchi* (in His hands I place my soul) over and over."

◊ EXAMPLE: "I was lying in my hospital bed, unable to sleep. The nights were so long and I felt so alone. The only way I could cope with the pain was to surrender my thoughts, my pain, my fears, my very life into His hands. I thought to myself, Every moment is a gift. Everything that happens to me, I will see it as a gift. Each time this exercise brought me a measure of relief."

◊ EXAMPLE: "I've suffered an unusual amount of loneliness in my life whether with my parents or with friends. I married late and didn't realize until afterwards that my husband has absolutely no need for emotional intimacy. Finally I spoke to my *rav* who said, 'Think of yourself as having a Ph.D. in loneliness. It's one thing you certainly know a lot about. So, take your Ph.D. and do something with it. You have a need to love and be loved. So love people who need it.' I started volunteering at an old age home, where loneliness is the biggest problem. This has changed my life. I feel so needed and appreciated for the first time in my life. I forget about myself when I'm helping others and the pain goes away for a while."

4. Use loneliness as an opportunity to break a negative habit pattern. When you feel alone or disappointed in someone, consciously make a decision not to indulge in an addictive emotion (e.g., rage, depression or bitterness) or a compulsive habit (e.g., shopping, criticizing, overeating, etc.). Instead, think of something positive you can do at the moment: share your pain with someone who cares, do something for someone else, say *Tehillim*, call a friend, take a walk, etc.

◊ EXAMPLE: "I went to my wife's family for Pesach. Since she is from a different culture and was surrounded by her numerous family members, I felt very left out. I tried to be pleasant, but when my feeling of alienation became overwhelming, I excused myself and went outside for a walk. Normally, I would have started complaining to my wife about how left out I felt and I would have criticized her family's customs and behavior in order to make her so miserable that she would agree to leave early. Instead of blaming her for my unhappiness, I had a pleasant time outdoors. By taking responsibility for my moods and behavior, I am overcoming a negative pattern."

5. Seek people who are nurturing and nourishing, and stay away from those who aren't. Stop sucking off "empty bottles." If you came from a non-nurturing background, it will feel normal to turn to non-nurturing people, even evil people, for nurturance. This is one of the most common neurotic patterns. But it can be broken by avoiding the impulse to get through to non-nurturers. Instead, put your energy into developing nourishing relationships.

◊ EXAMPLE: "I have only one close relative who lives in the same city. For years I tried to have a relationship with her and only became a target for her constant criticism. Yet I persisted, inviting her over, having her children come, listening to her attacks in silence, etc. Finally, I realized I was trying to get something from her that she can't give. It was so hard to give up the relationship at first. It was like an addiction. I'd been running after her so I wouldn't feel so alone in the world. I had to wean myself away and accept that I would have to deal with my loneliness in a positive way, by finding nurturing friends."

6. Accept the gap between what you want and what you have. The effort to make a relationship work is up to us; but the success of those efforts — i.e., whether people like us or not — is up to God.

No one can get through to everyone, but if you're the kind of person who tries to do so and feels like a failure if you don't, you may still be clinging to a childhood belief: I can't stand rejection; I should be able to make everyone like me; if people don't like me, it's my fault. Trying to make people like you won't foster closeness and will probably have the opposite effect. Recognize that there will be a gap of understanding in all relationships at some point. When you experience it, smile, breathe out slowly, tell yourself that this is God's will, and find the gift in the situation.

◊ EXAMPLE: "My favorite teacher is brilliant, but rather cold. He's critical of me for not thinking logically enough. This hurts me terribly, especially when I see him giving so much attention to his favorites and not even taking the time to answer some of my questions. I used to try to show him how smart I was, but I always ended up feeling like a jerk. The truth is that I just don't have his brilliance. I am not an outstanding *talmid chacham*. It's hard to accept this because brilliance is what I respect most. I must work to humbly respect myself as I am. When I feel inferior, I take a deep breath and say to myself, 'God, this is what You gave me and I will rejoice in it.'"

7. Don't isolate yourself. You may feel alone, but that does not mean that you have to be bitter and hostile about it. If you can't make contact, you have the opportunity to practice experiencing God's sustaining love. Ultimately, that awareness is what will give you strength to bear your most difficult and lonely times.

◊ EXAMPLE: "I felt so isolated when I moved to this neighborhood. I was always complaining to my husband about how cold and indifferent people were. Finally he told me, 'God didn't give you this gift of loneliness for you to sink into despair. He meant it to be a catalyst so that you would accomplish your mission of helping others.' I was angry with him at first. I thought, He just doesn't understand! But little by little I began to give, instead of expecting others to give to me. I'm the one who had isolated myself by being so self-preoccupied. When I became more concerned about others, my life changed. I host classes in my home, coordinate a *chesed* committee that distributes meals to the elderly, and give as much as I can."

8. Send love telepathically to those whom you perceive to be rejecting. Silently talk to them on a supra-rational, nonverbal level. This may sound strange at first, but the truth is that nothing we do is lost, even in the realm of thoughts. The good that we send out has an effect on the world, if only on a very subtle level. As you talk to the person, imagine the point of oneness which unites us all, our common *tzelem Elokim*. Our external differences give us an illusion of separateness, but we can relate to our true oneness whenever the external differences seem to block all hope of normal contact.

◊ EXAMPLE: "I offered two friends a ride to the pool. Since neither has a car, they accepted happily. But once we got there, they ignored me completely. I swam alone while they had a good time laughing and swimming at the other end of the pool. For the entire hour and a half, they didn't even wave or smile to me. At first, I was so furious I could hardly swim. Then I got depressed, thinking about how this is the story of my life — rejection from everyone I try to be close to. Then, I started repeating to myself, 'If this is what God wants me to experience, I accept His will.' The more I let go of wanting things to be my way, the more I relaxed and was able to enjoy myself. As I drove them home, they continued to ignore me. I silently sent love to them, accepting God's will so I wouldn't be eaten up by jealousy. It worked. When I dropped them off, they smiled sincerely, thanked me for taking them to the pool and invited me in for coffee."

9. Teach teachable people to validate you. For example, let's say you have a complaint and the other person says, "You're just *kvetch-ing* again," or "Don't let it bother you." Tell the person, "It would be more helpful if you would just validate me." Then teach him phrases which would help him to do so, such as:

"I'm sorry you have to go through this."

"This must be so difficult for you."

◊ EXAMPLE: "My doctor suspected a malignancy and took a biopsy. When I told my husband, he said, 'I'm sure everything is going to be fine.' I kept saying, 'But I'm scared.' But he kept denying the danger. Finally, I told him, 'Your attempts to be cheerful just make me feel more alone. If you would validate me, I'd feel better.' Then he said that it was hard for him to accept reality and that's why he tried to deny it. Once he validated me, I felt he was on my side, and that made it easier to get through the difficult days which followed. Both of us felt less alone."

Few people are so open to change. It's worth a try to keep a relationship viable, but with many people the best you can do is keep things light and superficial. Tell yourself that it is a bearable, not unbearable, discomfort.

If, after repeated attempts to get people to understand you, you see that they are only getting more hostile, tell yourself, "If God wanted me to have understanding and closeness now, I'd have it. Since I don't, He wants me to find some other source of satisfaction for my need to connect with others."

In this way, if you do get the closeness you want from people, that's great. Enjoy it. And if you don't, it's still a gift because now you have the opportunity to experience God's sustaining love. Ultimately, that awareness is what will give us strength to bear our most difficult and lonely times.

A ninety-two-year-old man, who had spent many years in exile in Siberia, told a friend of mine, "I'm glad I spent so much of my life alone. I learned to talk to Hashem. That's all I had. It was good preparation for old age. Now I never feel alone."

Those who have experienced an unusual amount of rejection and isolation can see this as God's way of making sure we know how important it is not to isolate ourselves from Him, not to treat Him as a stranger or abandon Him. Our painful experiences can be used to remind us, every minute of the day, to bring Him into our lives in some way.

> ◊ EXAMPLE: "Because I experienced so much rejection and isola-
> tion as a child, I'm extra careful to make sure that my children
> feel that I cherish them and I try to help them feel that both I and
> God care about them. I constantly tell them things like, 'What a
> wonderful mitzvah you did. You made God so happy!' 'You just
> hurt your brother! Is this how a *ben Melech* acts?' I'm constantly
> quoting passages from *Pirkei Avoth* and other works to keep the
> atmosphere elevated and to keep a sense of God's presence
> always on our minds."

When we feel alone, rejected or unwanted, we can use it as an opportunity to repeat over and over, "*Ein od milvado* — There is none except God" (*Devarim* 4:35). The gift of loneliness is that it reminds us to reconnect to the only One who can be relied on to make us feel less alone.

18 | The Gift of Good Mourning

When I faced the sudden death of a much wanted last baby late in pregnancy, I plunged headlong into an abyss of grief which I had never experienced before. I have faced many losses in my life, but never before had I experienced such overwhelming, intense, numbing, crushing sadness for months on end.

And yet there were gifts in that experience. I can now empathize much more honestly with others who have faced such losses. Before, my empathy for others who were grieving lacked depth. After, I clearly understood what grief does to a person: the nightmares, the struggle to stay functional and keep from shattering despite the awful emptiness, the loss of all joy, and the pain that never stopped for very long.

Mourning is not a time during which pain fades and dies away, but it is the time when we learn to live with pain.

I learned that grief has a life of its own. It comes and goes when it wants and there is nothing, absolutely nothing we can do to make it go away faster. All we can do is be patient as we internalize the Torah perspective which enables us to live with the pain. This process takes longer for some than for others.

I learned what it means to wage a fierce battle to attain an attitude of acceptance of God's will on a minute-to-minute basis. When I found myself sinking into bitterness, I had to consciously force myself to concentrate on all that God had given me, instead of on what I felt I lacked. Being someone who tends to focus on the latter, it was an uphill struggle to go against my nature.

I learned that it is not really possible to comfort a mourner, except by sharing his pain. Each mourner wages an essentially lonely battle to find a way of staying afloat in his stormy sea, especially during the long nights and difficult times when there is nothing to distract his attention from the pain.

I also learned that there is a certain closeness which develops between people who have undergone similar losses, which would not otherwise exist. I am certain that one reason Hashem puts us through various hardships is because they enable us to experience a precious closeness with certain people which can come only between those who have struggled with identical losses.

I also learned a lot about faith. During those moments of anguish, I realized in a way I had never experienced before, that there is only one true source of security and solace to which we can turn in times of loss, and that is God. And if not for my faith, I would have felt totally lost and in despair. Thus, my faith was strengthened.

I used to think people "get over it." Now I know that people simply learn to live with their grief, just as people live with all kinds of painful physical illnesses. I learned to go on, to find a measure of joy in little things. More than anything, I learned to cultivate the art of gratefulness as a means of staying sane and retaining my *emunah* and *bitachon*.

Emotional scars don't disappear, but they are proof that we have triumphed over adversity.

A grief response can occur over any loss

Grief is not experienced only when loved ones die. We grieve about small deaths as well as major ones. We may grieve over the loss of a relationship, a job, self-esteem, financial security, fulfillment, etc. If we live long enough, we may lose most of what we held precious in this physical world. So it is important to learn to face loss with dignity and faith.

> ◊ EXAMPLE: "In an unhappy marriage, each day brings its share of wounds. Every time the spouse withdraws when you try to talk, or criticizes and calls you names or walks away when you ask for help, you grieve all over again."

> ◊ EXAMPLE: "I have a brain-damaged child. The grief over what he might have been, had he been normal, never goes away com-

pletely. For years, I'd come home from work and open the door hoping maybe he'd suddenly become normal. I often have to struggle to accept him."

◊ EXAMPLE: "I've been divorced for three years. Since my husband takes my children two days a week, I constantly re-experience the grief of being alone and abandoned. The day before they go, they're anxious and upset, and when they come back, they're so depressed or hostile that I can't get through to them. It takes them a day or two to get back to themselves so that we can share our feelings and be affectionate again. Then it's time for them to go back to him. They're grieving too. Even though he was physically violent, in their young minds having a father at home would probably be preferable to having him away. They're too young to understand that I had to save us all from his insanity by moving away. All they know at this point is that they're hurting. And they often blame me for their pain. One thing I've learned is that it's essential to express the grief to each other and not to hide the pain."

Stages of grief

Psychologists have identified five major stages in the grief process. However, we do not necessarily grieve according to this order. In fact, our initial response may be a feeling of acceptance of God's will with perfect faith. Then suddenly, we may go into one of the other stages. We may then go back to acceptance again and then, when we are tired, go into depression or anger.

1. Shock, denial, and disbelief. At this stage, we still don't believe it is true. We fight the reality. We hang on to any possible shred of hope that it didn't really happen. Our mind plays tricks on us, making us think that the loss will somehow be restored and everything will return to the way it was.

◊ EXAMPLE: "I had put down a deposit on my dream home, when the person who was providing most of the money called to say he could no longer help us. I'm still in shock. Mentally, it was as if I was already living there. Knowing we'd be moving made it easier to bear our tiny apartment on a high floor with no space to move or breathe. I still can't accept that I'll never live there. I keep thinking that the money will come through somehow. I even think of the people who bought the house as living in my home."

◊ EXAMPLE: "After my husband died, I still looked for him behind the steering wheel whenever I saw a car like his. Mentally, I talked to him, asked his advice, asked him what he wanted for supper, saw him sitting across from me..."

Each time we are confronted with the truth, we experience a slight jolt and have to remind ourselves of the reality.

In the early stages of shock, you may want to repeat certain details about the person or event over and over to anyone who will listen in order to make the reality of the loss sink in.

2. Yearning. When we lose someone or something we love, we feel as though a limb has been amputated. A part of us has been cut off without benefit of anesthesia. The yearning to be whole again, to restore the person or object we've lost is so great that we think about our loss day and night. We cannot brush our teeth, see a flower, or hear music without yearning to have our loss restored. Yearning is an attempt to keep the attachment alive.

◊ EXAMPLE: "Yes, I still yearn for my mother. It's my way of showing my love for her. It's all I have left. If I stop grieving, the attachment will be gone forever. Maybe I'll forget. That would be a betrayal; it would mean I am callous and uncaring, that my love wasn't worth much."

◊ EXAMPLE: "I was paralyzed in a car accident four years ago and have no chance of recovering. Yet I still dream of running and swimming one day. Perhaps if I stopped yearning, then I'd give up and have to accept that I will be crippled forever. But I can't accept that. My yearning is my only connection with myself as I used to be — healthy, whole, strong and independent."

3. Anger. It finally hits us that the loss is real. The loss of control makes us angry that this happened. Why me? We are angry at Fate, at doctors who weren't attentive enough, at the businessmen who caused us to lose our money, at the friends and relatives who didn't come through for us, at our own stupidity and carelessness, at those who failed to show us respect and understanding. We may be angry at the person who died. "Why didn't he provide for me in a will?"

"Why didn't she treat me better?" Anger is an attempt to control something or someone at a time when we tend to feel the most powerless.

◊ EXAMPLE: "Since my divorce, I find myself angry at everyone and everything. I obsess about all the terrible things my wife did, and the stupid advice people gave us which never helped, and the insensitive people who minimize what I've gone through and who think it's easy to go on and find someone else when I'm grieving for my children and hate coming back to a crummy apartment every night."

◊ EXAMPLE: "When I got up after sitting *shivah* for my husband, I went out into the street and couldn't believe that everything was as it was a week ago. I was angry at people. I wanted to scream at them, 'How can you go on living normally? How can you shop and drive your cars and go to school and eat as if nothing happened, while I am all alone and can never be normal again?'"

4. Depression. We feel helpless and despairing and terribly envious of those who have what we don't. Our sense of control, security and wholeness is gone. We are untrusting: if this could happen, what will be next? What can we count on in life? We feel terribly vulnerable and fragile. We realize the extent to which:

Man is like a breath; his days are like a passing shadow.
—TEHILLIM 144:3-4

◊ EXAMPLE: "Since my son died, I find myself at a loss for words, absent-minded, empty and numb. I have no appetite. I got on the bus the other day and forgot to pay. Life seems senseless, unreal and unimportant. I walk around feeling mechanical, unreal. The things I did so easily, like driving the car or even tying my shoes, are suddenly so difficult. Every move requires conscious effort, so that I am exhausted after doing the most trivial chores. I wonder how I'll go on. I look at people with sons who are my son's age and I'm eaten up with pain."

5. Reorganization and acceptance. Slowly we pick up the pieces of our life and redirect our energies. Our old world has been destroyed, but we begin to build again. What we build isn't anything like the old familiar life we were used to. From the ashes, we rebuild

a new life. We re-learn to function and accept life as it is, and we come to express joy and love again.

◊ EXAMPLE: "After my wife died of cancer, I found a support group. Talking about my loss was very helpful, but it only helped when I talked with people who were newly grieving. Others didn't seem to understand. The only time I felt normal was when I was in that group. That was the beginning of my return to life."

◊ EXAMPLE: "For a year after my youngest child died in a car accident I was so immersed in my grief that I neglected my other children. I felt like a total failure — I had failed to protect him. I also felt that God had singled me out for punishment and that I was a failure in His eyes, too. I was sure that if I were a better human being this would not have happened to me. Then one day my daughter said to me, 'Aren't I important, too? Don't I count as much as he did?' That's when I realized that not only had one child died, but that I was destroying the lives of the others. I began to work at accepting God's will, which took constant mental effort. I forced myself to find pleasure in being with my other children, which made them feel loved. That effort is what eventually helped me to function as a normal wife and mother again."

Achieving acceptance

Few people reach true, heartfelt *hashlamah* over a major loss without some inner struggle. Even then, acceptance is not a one time achievement. One has moments of peace and then a lapse into bitterness, envy, anger or depression, especially when one is tired or there is a special occasion. Then he has to struggle all over again to make God's will his will, and to trust in His wisdom and goodness.

There are five major pitfalls to avoid in order to reach the stage of *hashlamah*, which in Hebrew means "to be at peace with."

1. Don't feel bad about feeling bad. Don't add to the pain you're in by being ashamed of your feelings. All our Matriarchs and Patriarchs grieved for their personal losses. Ya'akov grieved for Yosef for twenty-two years. Sara, Rivka, Rachel and Chana grieved over their barrenness. Leah grieved over the fact that she was not loved as Rachel was.

Grief is not an indication of lack of faith. Human beings have a wide range of emotional responses. Some people simply do not have strong responses. Others feel deeply, but do not know how to express their feelings. Many people assume that those who show less feeling are stronger, and conclude, "There must be something wrong with me that I'm still so heartbroken."

The expression of emotions is not a sign of weakness.

◊ EXAMPLE: "Forty-five years ago, I married a wonderful, intelligent, capable man. Now he has Alzheimer's disease. I felt I had to be strong and not let people know how badly I was feeling. I numbed myself to the pain. Then I went to a lecture on grief and began to sob uncontrollably. I was ashamed. After all, my husband wasn't dead. So I asked the speaker if I had the right to mourn. She said it was perfectly appropriate for me to mourn, because the man I had married was no longer here. Tearfully, I thanked her for giving me permission to cry."

◊ EXAMPLE: "After my baby died, my eyes were riveted on every pregnant woman I saw. I felt like a crazy person, enveloped in grief. I had never felt such intense jealousy before. I felt devastated around pregnant women and new mothers. Then at night, over and over I'd dream that I had my baby back in my arms again, that the hospital had made a mistake, or that she simply was in her crib when I went to her room. Waking up to the reality was a shock every morning. I just felt so bad, so very sad, and nothing made it go away for a long time."

◊ EXAMPLE: "After my husband died, one of the cruelest things that happened in the wake of this loss was that most of my friends grew very cold and distant. Suddenly, I was a threat. Maybe having me around made them sad or frightened about the fate of their own husbands. I was lonely like I'd never been before. And because my marriage had not been a happy one, I was mourning doubly — for the husband I had and for the husband I'd never have."

So be honest about your grief. If you try to suppress it, the grief may fester and manifest itself in chronic anger, depression or emotional numbness. Instead, whenever the grief returns, just experience it fully. If possible, share your grief with a friend. Shaming thoughts interfere with the mourning process (e.g., "I shouldn't be feeling like this. I should be coping better.").

Even the most intense grief is like an ocean wave: it rises, peaks, then fades on its own. Don't fight the wave. Feel the feelings. Express the love you feel for the person or the object you are missing. As the intensity fades, it is then that you can think the thoughts which strengthen your *emunah* and *bitachon*.

2. Don't try to second-guess God. Events don't happen in a vacuum. You cannot help but ask "why." The answer which you provide for yourself can mean the difference between prolonged depression and the return to a feeling of confidence and joy. You may think, I must be bad if something bad happened to me. Or, I should have been able to prevent this from happening. It's all my fault. Coming up with specific reasons ("It must be because of that time I..." or "A neighbor gave me an *ayin ha-ra* when...") is just guessing. Everything is a test of our *middoth* and an opportunity to experience greater closeness to God.

3. Don't torture yourself with guilt. Healthy guilt causes you to do *teshuvah* and make constructive changes in your behavior. Unhealthy guilt does nothing but serve as an excuse for self-torture. It provides an illusion of doing something positive when, in actuality you continue to hide from the problem and remain stuck in your old, negative patterns of worry, despair and blame. For example, many parents feel guilty for having been physically or verbally abusive to their children. They remain stuck in anger and depression instead of repairing the relationship in the present by talking with the children openly and honestly and saying: "I admit that I hurt you in the past. I am sorry. I was unaware and unhappy, so I could not create an atmosphere of stability or safety. I cannot undo the past. But I want to create a relationship based on openness and honesty now. I love you. Tell me what I can do to help you feel how much I love you."

In addition, if there was a loss due to carelessness or neglect on your part, perhaps you can do something to make others aware of the need to be more cautious; e.g., get others to wear seat belts, to keep poison out of children's reach, etc.

Finally, realize that nothing happens without God willing it to happen.

If you feel guilty for being jealous of those who have not had similar losses, realize that envy is an expression of grief. You cannot overcome envy unless you acknowledge the pain that you do feel over not having what you want, and then move on to accepting what God has given you. Feel the pain and work on making God's will and your will one. That is the only thing that brings inner peace.

If guilt inspires you to do *teshuvah* for some specific sin which you committed deliberately, then guilt is appropriate. But if guilt makes you feel that you are a bad person, rotten to the core, and unworthy of any connection with man or God, the results will be harmful.

◊ EXAMPLE: "For years I felt that my learning-disabled, hyperactive child was a punishment from God. The result was that I was very rejecting and cruel toward him!"

◊ EXAMPLE: "I'm thirty-four and still unmarried. For years I felt this was because God was punishing me. As a result, my shame was so great that I didn't go out on *shidduchim*."

◊ EXAMPLE: "My husband was very abusive. But I never spoke to anyone about it because I felt that this was a punishment from God. I really thought I was a bad person and deserved to be criticized all the time, and that if I were a better housewife, my husband would be happy. I was so ashamed that I just got more and more depressed."

◊ EXAMPLE: "After I lost a baby to crib death, I was devastated. But I felt that my grief was a sign of self-pity and lack of acceptance of Hashem's will. So, I tried to pretend that I was fine. But I wasn't. I got more and more depressed, especially since I kept telling myself that this happened because I was not worthy of having children. It took a long talk with a *rav* to help me overcome my secret shame and guilt."

4. Give the benefit of the doubt to the many people who will be unwittingly callous and insensitive. You will hear all kinds of pat answers and cliché phrases: "It's not so bad." "You'll have another baby." "It could have been a lot worse." "Time heals."

What a grieving person wants most is to share his pain with someone who can mirror his feelings, who will empathize. However, few people know how to do this. People who have never experienced a major loss or who have a shallow emotional life won't understand what you are feeling. Many people do not want to be reminded of their losses and don't want to see your sad face. Some people are arrogant, implying, "Well, I went on with my life; you also should be able to!" So be selective in sharing your grief.

5. Avoid self-pity. There is a big difference between self-pity and sadness. Self-pity paralyzes you with bitterness and anger. It means you are focusing all your attention on what you lack. All you can think of is how unfair life is and how you would be happy if not for this lack. Self-pity isolates you. You think you're the only one who is suffering so much, the only one who feels so deeply, the only one who will not and cannot go on with his life. On the other hand, sadness is the simple acknowledgement of loss. It does not block your sense of gratefulness for the good that still remains in your life.

The way to avoid self-pity is to be aware of your loss and, at the same time, to find ways to give your life meaning and pleasure despite it. It is important to strive to see life as precious in and of itself. Each day offers us opportunities for new awareness and personal growth. We exist to serve God, not to have our personal desires satisfied. And serving God is most admirable if done despite a broken heart. This alone will bring inner solace, even if a part of us goes on mourning.

What you can do

Since almost every loss involves a loss of self-esteem, you need to elevate yourself at this time, not sink into shame and despair! One action which many people have found helpful is to keep a diary and write letters to your lost loved one. Express your love, your longing and your fears. Share the happy events and the sad ones as well.

Another thing you can do is to maintain a positive attitude by focusing on the gifts. E.g., "This happened so that I will...(1) have greater sensitivity and awareness," (2) relate better to others who have been through this," (3) appreciate the gift of life so much more," (4) develop skills which I never would have developed if this hadn't happened."

Learn to maintain my faith in Hashem's wisdom and mercy even when things seem absurd, unjust and cruel from a human perspective."

It's important to engage in healthy activities to stay functional, even if you must push yourself. But push gently. "A person is molded by his actions" (*Sefer Ha-chinuch*, #16). So keep your actions positive, even if that means simply brushing your teeth, making your bed and getting out of the house for a walk.

When you reenter the world after a major loss, you feel split. Part of you is functioning more or less normally, saying "Fine, *baruch Hashem*," when people ask how you are, smiling politely and pretending to be over the pain. But inside, you feel like you are being torn apart.

In time, you will feel less torn. But don't push the process. You can't force emotional or intellectual growth any more than you can force a plant to grow. But you can encourage growth by providing the proper conditions, such as a non-shaming attitude and self-nourishing activities. Expect the process of "making Hashem's will your will" to be a long struggle. There are no instant cures when it comes to grief.

Dealing with those who try to comfort you

In a study done on bereaved people, it was found that the most helpful thing was to be offered immediate concrete help with funeral arrangements, food, child care, laundry, etc., not philosophical platitudes or pat answers. Therefore, do not be ashamed to tell people what practical help they can offer.

If appropriate, you can also:

1. Teach people to empathize. When dying cancer patients were asked what words they most wanted to hear, the most common response was, "I just want people to agree that it's so hard to go through this. I don't want to play games and pretend that everything is going to be just fine."

Tell people that the best thing to say to you is, "I'm sorry about your loss." Or, "It must be very difficult for you." Let people know you want empathy. Being sad with someone lessens the loneliness a bit.

2. Find someone who will allow you to talk about all the details of the event — doctors, nurses, relatives, procedures, what was done, said and seen at the time. This helps you accept the reality of the loss.

3. Find someone to whom you can talk about how this event will affect your life, marriage, feelings about people, and changes that

will have to be made. For example, a woman who had major surgery was worried about being rejected by her husband. A man whose wife had died felt that no one would ever care about him again.

4. Talk to a professional about your feelings of guilt and inadequacy. Ask if these feelings are appropriate. Many people think of a loss as a punishment, that if they were really good, this wouldn't have happened. A woman who lost a child in an accident said, "It was my fault. God took her away because I'm not a good enough mother."

Talk about your shattered dreams, how different life would be if this hadn't happened. Express any anger you may feel toward the person who is gone. For example, widows often feel angry that their spouses have left them to struggle alone, have failed to make a will or provide financial security, which may be interpreted as having failed to really love them.

5. Express your love for the person (or relationship, job, community, etc.) who is gone. This can also be done in writing.

6. Ask others who have been through the same experience about fulfilling activities which helped them heal.

7. Tell people to respect your need to be silent if you don't feel like talking.

Be tolerant of those who mouth pat answers

People can hurt you inadvertently by making suppressive statements which imply that "it's bad to be sad," or that you can rush through the grieving process. For example:

1. "Time heals." Though true, this statement is rarely helpful because it refers to a future time, while you are immersed in your present grief. When you hear this expression, you may think it means "Time makes you forget." In the midst of grief, you do *not* want to be told that you will soon forget about the person you have just lost! How callous such a statement seems at a time when you are trying to hang on to every memory you can think of in order to keep the person alive.

Furthermore, the expression "time heals" is not always true. Many find that the sense of loss deepens in time.

2. "It's all for the best." This is true, but in the midst of grief, these words are not likely to reflect what you are really feeling at the

time. In the midst of grief, you don't want to be philosophical. At such a time, your pain is augmented by hearing such callous words. If you have a catastrophic illness or an abusive spouse who is destroying the lives of you and your children, it is certainly a difficult struggle to see how this can be good.

3. "Hashem only gives people what they can handle." True, we see all around us people managing to cope with incredibly tragic situations. But there are others who do break down, who don't feel strengthened or ennobled by the experience. In the midst of intense grief, you may not have the confidence that you will be able to go on or feel that you have any reason to do so.

4. "It's a *kapparah*." True, pain in this world cleanses us. But in the midst of grief, the loss often does not seem worth whatever spiritual gains we are getting. Furthermore, we may wonder, "What sin could I possibly have committed to deserve having to see a beloved child or mate die, or be in constant pain, or see everything I have worked for crumble like dust?" Suffering does not automatically purify, sensitize or strengthen us. That happens only after years of work to accept God's will.

5. "Be happy with what you have." Yes, counting one's blessings is one of the things which brings us all joy. But being sad does not automatically imply that we are ungrateful for all that Hashem has done for us.

> ◊ EXAMPLE: "I appreciate my two children. But the very fact that they give me so much joy makes me sad that I cannot have any more. It may seem terribly greedy of me to feel so sad about having only two when so many women have no children at all. But the house feels so empty and I still long for a baby's arms around me."

When one suffers a loss, there is a hole in one's heart which nothing else can fill.

6. "There are worse things." True. No matter what happens to us, we know of many greater tragedies. Does that mean that you have no right to be sad about your particular loss?

7. "It happens to everyone." True, just about everyone loses someone they love. Still, just because it is normal does not make it a routine occurrence for the person who has just gone through it.

Be tolerant of those who think that by simply saying a few words, the pain will magically disappear. They are doing the best they can without the benefit of much insight into people's feelings.

In the case of a miscarriage, you will encounter unhelpful statements such as:

1. "You'll soon be pregnant again." People like to act like prophets. It makes them feel better, though it may not take away the pain you're feeling. At this moment, you do not want to negate or forget your attachment to this particular baby.

2. "It was probably deformed, so you're better off." True, there probably was something wrong. Knowing how difficult the lives of parents of severely handicapped children can be, some women might prefer not to have a deformed child. But there is still grief over lost opportunities and lost dreams.

Head vs. heart

Rav Eliyahu Lopian *z.l.* said, "Man's head and heart are like two different persons. The head knows and understands everything; nevertheless, the heart does what it feels and wants to do" (*Lev Eliyahu*, p. 188). You can say all the right phrases to maintain faith in Hashem's wisdom and goodness. You know intellectually that everything Hashem does is for the best, that pain is an atonement, and that from this experience you will ultimately be wiser and stronger. Your mind tells you that in the *Olam shel Emeth* (the World of Truth — the World to Come) everything will make sense and be seen as totally fair. At some point, when you look back at this event, you will see how it had to be this way. I told myself over and over that I had to work to accept the will of Hashem, that it was for the best.

Why then, with all this intellectual knowledge, does your food taste like dust and your body feel paralyzed and your mind become so disoriented and distracted? If you are telling yourself all the right things, why don't they work? Why is it such a struggle to glue yourself back together and carry on with normal activities? Why the cruel dreams in which you have that which you long for, only to awaken and reexperience over and over again the shock of the loss? Why doesn't the pain stop when you say with complete sincerity, "I accept this totally as Hashem's will"? Because grief is above logic.

When our personal longings and dreams of perfection are in conflict with God's plan, we experience pain. Intellectually, we can say, "It must be this way." But our heart cries, "It's not fair. There's been a mistake. I don't accept this! I don't deserve this!"

In healthy mourning we resolve this conflict. For example, I wanted a large family, yet suffered repeated miscarriages. I was crying, "Babies!" But God was saying, "Books!" I kept arguing, "All I want is another baby. I wouldn't need to write books if I had a baby in my arms." God kept saying, "Books!" God won. Since book writing was one way in which I assuaged my grief, it was obvious what He wanted.

However, this process of finding solace takes time. It takes time to mend. The first few weeks and months are terribly difficult. Then, slowly but surely, the pieces of our lives come together in a new configuration, like blades of grass popping up after a terrible forest fire. It is one of life's miracles that we do go on, and do learn how to laugh and love again. The pain is always there, but it is like a minor theme in the symphony of our lives, instead of the major one.

At some point, we say, "Enough pain. It is time to go back to life and the living." And in so doing, we discover an inner core of strength which gently prods us back to health.

Patience

> Weeping is lodged in one side of my heart, and joy is lodged in the other. — ZOHAR II, 255a; III, 75a

One of the most frequently asked questions is, "Will this pain never end?" You think you have achieved a state of really sincere *hashlamah* (heart-felt acceptance). Then you hear a particular bit of music, eat a certain food, or see an old acquaintance who does not know what you have been through, and suddenly you are overcome with pain again. You light the Sabbath candles or prepare for a holiday and think, "The last time I did this, everything was fine. I was happy and whole. Now there is an empty chair. Will I ever feel pain-free again?"

◊ EXAMPLE: "I've been widowed for three weeks now. I hate the word *widow*. I can't accept it. I hate being alone. I sleep with the light on and sleep only for a short time. I wake up crying and go to sleep crying. Nightmares haunt me. I keep dreaming that my husband is back, that we are together again. Then I wake up and have to get used to the fact that he is gone all over again. It's awful.

Instead of expecting to get rid of the pain, it is more realistic to think of learning to live with it.

Expect setbacks. The milestone days, such as holidays, birthdays or the *yahrtzeit* are especially difficult. People may expect you to be over it. There is nothing wrong with you if the pain never leaves completely.

When you first resume normal activities after a major loss, you feel a bit mechanical and stiff, like trying to walk after an operation. You will learn to function with a level of pain you did not have before, just as you have learned to function with other difficulties.

The best thing to do is to resume normal activities to the best of your ability. I remember going back to the pool where I swim in the mornings and forcing myself to do laps. At first, I could only do ten or twelve. Suddenly, I would start to cry. The grief would overtake me and I could not go on. So I would leave, but give myself an "endorsement" for at least having gone. Gradually I pushed myself back to my usual number of laps.

Faith

Every major loss involves a test of faith. We question how God could allow this to happen. Does He really care? Was this really supposed to happen?

To keep yourself strong, repeat over and over to yourself those phrases from the *siddur* or *Tehillim* which maintain your faith in Hashem's wisdom and mercy. Do this even if you still feel bitter and angry about what you have lost. It does not matter that you feel insincere and hypocritical at first. Eventually, the words will become real.

◊ EXAMPLE: "When my wife was dying, I was sometimes full of tremendous faith in Hashem. Other times, I found it very difficult to *daven*. When this happened, I *daven*ed that I should be able to *daven* with real *emunah* and *bitachon*. There is always something to pray for."

Dedicating the pain

By resolving to make some positive change in our lives, the loss becomes meaningful. Not everyone can make a major dedication in tribute to someone who has died. But we can all make a personal "memorial," such as being more strict about a particular mitzvah, taking on a few extra minutes of prayer or study, or doing more for others who may be suffering. My friend with the brain-damaged baby started an afternoon day care center for other mothers with severely retarded children. A man started teaching Torah to inmates in a local prison in order to help him cope with the grief of losing a child.

When the loss impels us to contribute something to the world, it helps us transcend the grief. It helps greatly for bereaved people, including those with ongoing bereavement — such as those who are childless or who have never married — to find their particular "memorial." Suffering without a sense of greater awareness just stays meaningless.

> ◊ EXAMPLE: "After I lost a child, the only thing that made me feel better was doing *chesed* work. The worse I felt, the more hours I spent doing volunteer work in the hospital."

The butterfly phenomenon

Pain is a powerful force which can bring us to greater depth and understanding of ourselves and others. With prayer, *cheshbon ha-nefesh*, and a decision to make some actual change, pain will bring about a greater sense of connection with God. In the initial stages of grief, we may feel like we are in a cocoon, surrounded by darkness. But when we emerge, we may find that we have been greatly enriched. This is what I call the butterfly phenomenon. Knowing that this will happen is something to hang on to in the midst of that darkness and pain.

The Chafetz Chaim concluded his tearful eulogy over his beloved son by saying, "I try to serve God, but I am only a human being. No matter how much I love God, some of the love in my heart belongs to my children. Now my son is gone...and I will take that love and give it all to God.''

An encounter with death can make us appreciate life more. It can make us more loving and humane. Death reminds us to make the most of every minute and not to waste time on hatred or petty pursuits.

There is a time to laugh and a time to cry. A healthy person is able to experience both sides of the spectrum. Learning how to mourn is just that — a learning process.

We all have shattered dreams, unfulfilled wishes, fears and worries. Don't be afraid to admit that you need some help mending. It may bring closeness to others that you did not have before. Despite the pain, there are always gifts. Malka, mother of a multiply-handicapped child who died just before his second birthday, said: "There are so many gifts which Rafael gave us during his short life. Mostly, he taught me to love for free, without wanting anything back. The gift for my other children was that they learned tremendous sensitivity. They don't laugh at handicapped people. They know how hard life is for them. And for me, I don't think anyone appreciates healthy children like a mother who has had a handicapped child. Instead of complaining about my children, I say, 'Thank You, God, for children who can make a mess and be rowdy. Thank You for giving me healthy, normal problems!'''

> ◊ EXAMPLE: "Soon after we were married, my wife discovered she had a malignant lump, but she seemed so happy, healthy and full of life that I was sure everything would be all right. Then came chemotherapy, frequent hospitalizations, and bleak moods that enveloped her in a cloud of gloom. In the end we learned that we will never have children and that we will always have the worry of a reoccurrence hanging over our heads. We try to look happy for each other's sake, but we are both crying inside. We struggle to love each other and love God and love life even with this pain.

Only one who is able to cry is able to love. May all our losses bring us to a greater level of humility, compassion, love, understanding, and faith.

Be patient with yourself as you learn how to grow from your pain — and with your pain. Very patient.

19 | The Gift of Accepting the Pain

Most people are surprised at the intensity of the pain they experience when a loved one dies or a traumatic loss occurs. They may wait impatiently for the thirty-day period or the year to pass so that they will be "over it." They may consult a therapist in the hope that talking will help them get "over it" faster.

Those with ongoing grief, such as those with spouses or family members who suffer from severe physical or emotional illnesses, may think, Why can't I just accept it and stop feeling bad?

Thus, when people find that the pain lingers month after month without waning appreciably, they are upset. What they do not realize is that the head can comfort the heart, but the heart may refuse to be comforted. The heart has a timetable of its own which must be respected and validated.

Accepting God's will is not an easy or one-time achievement. We may go through many years of struggle before coming to real heart-felt acceptance, or *hashlamah*. With many losses, the goal to strive for is to be able to grieve "purely," i.e., to feel the grief without undue concern and without condemnations of yourself or others.

You are not a failure

If you continue to feel heartbroken after a loss, do not berate yourself for being unspiritual, stupid, weak or overly emotional. Being in emotional pain does not mean that you have failed to successfully pass through the stages of the grief process. We don't pass quickly from grief to serene acceptance in the same smooth manner that we once passed from first grade to second.

We can see with our eyes the struggle of a paralyzed person to walk. But we cannot see the process by which a person struggles to do the smallest thing while his heart is paralyzed by grief. Time and faith help us accept the loss; we must wage an inner struggle to reach *hashlamah*. *Hashlamah* comes from the root "to make peace with," implying that an inner war must first take place. The struggle to accept Hashem's will is not an easy one. If you compare yourself to those who, for one reason or another, accept a particular loss with serenity, you end up not only with the pain of the loss, but with the added pain of feeling that you have flunked at being truly mature or spiritual.

Losses make us wiser and more compassionate. But the ache remains. The sudden flashbacks, the unexpected nightmares, the welling up of tears when we hear certain music or see certain people are reminders that grief has a life of its own which we cannot completely control.

When a limb has been amputated, the patient often suffers from what is called phantom limb pain, excruciating pain in the area where the limb once was. Something similar happens when someone we loved is gone or a dream remains unfulfilled.

◊ EXAMPLE: "My father died three months ago. We were very close and I miss him terribly. Yet I'm upset because I still can't think of him without crying. I can't understand why I'm still hurting so much. The pain just *schleps* on and on. I thought by now I'd have accepted his death and be over the pain. I thought it would disappear on its own. I keep being surprised when it comes back again and again in full force. Doesn't it ever end?"

◊ EXAMPLE: "I was the chief orthopedic surgeon in a Moscow hospital. Since I've come to Israel, the only work I've been able to find is as a janitor. I know that many Russian immigrants are happy just to be here. I wish that were enough to sustain me psychologically, but it's very depressing. I'm affected physically, too, and just don't have the energy I used to have."

◊ EXAMPLE: "I recently talked to a woman who has been married to a very disturbed man for almost forty years. I thought she would give me hope that I would get used to my own situation. Instead, she cried and told me that she'd never given up wanting to be loved, that his criticism still drags her down and that as she got older the loneliness has been more oppressive than ever. She described her marriage as slow murder. Her words made me realize that I must work very hard not to let my spirit die. I can't just have good *middoth*, I have to have spectacular *middoth*!''

As with physical pain, there is a vast degree of variability in the amount of pain people experience over a loss. Some people are naturally more optimistic and resilient. Competing with others and comparing to see who can ''get over it'' the fastest causes additional emotional anguish to those who continue to grieve, as if they are inferior to those who experience less sorrow.

Thinking vs. feeling: different responses to loss

If you are a Thinking type (see *Appreciating People*), you may find it easier to suppress or ignore grief and be surprised that your Feeling spouse or child is still experiencing profound grief months or years later. You may think you are more mature and having greater *emunah*. The difference in responses is due to the fact that Thinking types feel grief, but handle it in a typically cerebral manner. They are able to tell themselves, ''It's all for the best. The show must go on. I will close the door and not think about it, etc.'' These phrases are often enough to provide solace and comfort.

In contrast, the challenge for a Feeling type is not to suppress or eliminate the pain, but to find some way to use the pain as an impetus for growth. Feeling types may be inconsolable for a longer period of time and think there is something wrong with them when the feeling of emptiness, fear or longing doesn't end.

If you are a Feeling type, grief can act as an internal force, pressuring you to turn to Torah, and also to find physical or creative outlets: art, dance, writing, music, community work, etc.

Take the pain and do something useful with it

During the *shivah* for their two-year-old son, who was born severely brain-damaged, Helene and Jack Delowe spoke to me about what their child had given to the world. To keep his muscles from atrophying, he had to be patterned (moved in a rhythmic manner for hours every day). The Delowes organized volunteers from the community to come into their home and perform these special exercises throughout the day.

With tears in her eyes, Helene told me, "You can't imagine what this child did for us and for the entire community. He developed in us a capacity to give that we didn't know we had. He gave to us far more than we gave to him."

Helene lived with an oxygen tank next to her bed because her son, Aaron, would often stop breathing, sometimes as often as twenty times a night. Yet she treasured the opportunity to give.

When the Delowes moved to Israel, they set up the Aaron De-Lowe Center for multiply-handicapped children, in Ra'anana.

At the age of one, the son of Malka and Kalman Samuels had an allergic reaction to a routine immunization which caused him to become deaf and blind. Malka told me, "I wouldn't be the same person if I hadn't had this child. People usually think of what a parent does for a special child, but they forget what the child gives to the parent. The love a person feels for an ordinary child isn't the same. It's a special 'baby love' that goes on and on because they need you. Yossele is an extraordinary child, very intelligent and very special. On his fifteenth birthday, I asked him, 'Do you know what gift Hashem gave me fifteen years ago?' And right away, he smiled and answered, 'Me!'"

Kalman told me, "Without personal experience, one is incapable of truly grasping the agony of dealing with a handicapped child or any other major difficulty. That's just the way life is; there is an enormous abyss between those who have experienced a traumatic event and those who haven't. I feel very strongly that knowledge obligates. Once you have experienced something, there is somehow that question, 'What do I do with it?' We all go through various difficulties. If we believe it's God-given, we must ask how we can utilize it."

Malka and Kalman established the Shalva Center in the Har Nof section of Jerusalem, which provides afternoon care for handicapped children. A neighbor of theirs told me, "You can't imagine how much they give to others. Shalva gives parents a rest from the constant care these children need, and gives them the strength to go on."

One parent whose severely hyperactive child uses the Shalva Center told me, "The truth is that it was only after six months of Shalva that I began to unwind and sense real love toward my child, because I finally had relief from the constant demands. It was only when I was out of the pressure cooker that I could alter my focus. Now I can welcome her with genuine love when she arrives home."

In the beginning, you may think your *mesiruth nefesh* is aiding others, giving of yourself. But eventually, you realize that from giving to others, you gain the most.

Sometimes, what is most helpful is to create.

> ◊ EXAMPLE: "While I sat by my son's hospital bed, I kept my hands busy with embroidery work to keep my mind off the terrifying thoughts which never left me for long. I found that the ability to create something of beauty in the middle of so much fear and sorrow was very comforting. It gave me some sense of control at a time when everything else seemed out of control. It made me feel, I will be able to go on. I will be able to cope and create and give."

Any major loss forces us to confront how ephemeral and transitory our existence is. This awareness of our mortality, in turn, is what compels us to attach to a Power which is greater than ourselves. Making that attachment is part of the healing process. It takes time and great effort to make this bond solid.

You can't rush the process

The process of coming back to the land of the living after a loss takes place is totally individual.

> ◊ EXAMPLE: "After I lost my teenage daughter in an accident, one of the frightening things about the *shivah* period was to see people who had also lost children years ago crying as if the loss had happened yesterday. I was scared to think that perhaps there would be no end to my grief, that I too would have to live with this horrible, constant pain. I had thought that grief is something that passes. Now I know it's not true. You just learn to go on somehow and find ways to keep from drowning in grief. I'm like a person who was suddenly paralyzed and had to learn to walk

again. I will never be the same. For a long time, the feeling of emptiness was so overwhelming that I had difficulty doing the simplest task. I only wanted to be with my daughter. But I am alive and I'm trying to find joy and give to others despite the pain that is always there, just under the surface. It helps to write. I write to her often. And I share my feelings with others who are grieving, which seems to help them and myself as well."

Hashlamah doesn't mean an absence of pain, but rather the point at which you are no longer consumed by it. This process is different for each person. It cannot be rushed. You are not a failure because you are not "over it." There are some losses for which there is no consolation. Pain over these losses is a kind of companion which takes the place of the loss and reminds us of our undying love. This is a pain which many of us can and must learn to live with.

It is a struggle to accept God's will, to make the pain become part of the background instead of the dominant theme in our lives. At times, the ratio of grief to acceptance may be 90:10. At other times it may be reversed. Getting through the rough times is a little like being caught in a giant wave. If you fight it, you'll go under. If you flow with it, you'll survive.

It is important to find sources of pleasure and solace.

◊ EXAMPLE: "By the time I was twenty-five, I felt like my life was over, because my husband was so cold and uncommunicative, while I'm very gregarious and lively. It hurt so deeply that I kept hoping I would die. I'd tell myself, 'Don't make a big deal out of it. Lots of people are unhappily married.' Finally, I went to a therapist who asked me what made me happiest when I was a teenager. I told him that I loved acting. She said, 'So, find a way to put your acting talents to work in a kosher way. She said that there is *kedushah* in acting if it teaches people to become more sensitive to others' feelings. I organized a group of Observant women who enjoy acting, and we set up a *middoth* workshop for children. We make up plays that allow them to feel what it's like to be old, blind, deaf, crippled or the harried mother of many children. They really do become more sensitive. And it gives me something to live for."

◊ EXAMPLE: "After I was widowed, I struggled mightily to accept God's will. I told myself, 'You had a wonderful marriage and healthy children, so don't wallow in pain. Be thankful for all you have. It's God's will.' And I struggled to hammer these thoughts into my mind like a sculptor working on a rock. Then suddenly I'd be consumed with pain when I saw other women whose husbands were still alive. I see my husband in every flower and every cloud. He's with me when I light my Shabbos candles and he sits at the table with us when we eat. I hear his voice in my mind all day long. Finally, I accepted that maybe this is the way it's going to be for me. I can't push it away. I can't fight it. I talk to Hashem a lot, asking Him to help me bear my burden. I give myself orders, like, 'Put your makeup on and go out with a smile, even if it's fake.' It took a lot of courage, but I enrolled in a women's *yeshivah* and also began tutoring girls at an orphanage near my home, which gives me tremendous satisfaction.''

If your sadness doesn't disappear, don't assume that this is due to a lack of *emunah*, for this attitude will distance you from God. Feel the pain, and pursue your goals despite it.

Creating positive memory traces

The American Health Magazine of March 1990 reported that, ''When a memory is formed, neurons undergo structural changes that affect the strength of synaptic connections. Much of what you remember depends on your emotional state — fear, excitement, surprise — at the time.... Trivial events are best forgotten. But if the event is important, your brain modulates its storage through neurotransmitters and hormones associated with specific emotional states. Adrenaline, for example, can indirectly strengthen the connection between neurons in a memory trace.'' This would explain why the emotional responses and memories which are established when we are frightened and hurt can be so resistant to change.

Because these memories are so powerful, you may have a tendency to dwell on painful events. If you do not want to remain stuck in intense pain forever, you must make continuous, conscious effort to put your mental energy into strengthening those thoughts which make you feel loved, capable and trusting. *You* are the one who can strengthen or weaken the connection between the neurons in a memory trace. That is an awesome responsibility — and a great gift.

A major loss forces you to become a kind of juggler; you love, laugh, cry and mourn all at the same time.

Pain doesn't always mean something's wrong

Because physical pain is often a sign of illness, we often think emotional pain means: "There must be something wrong with me." In reality, emotional pain is often a healthy sign of the need to find new sources of fulfillment and love. When we find the right thing to satisfy that need, the pain is more bearable.

◊ EXAMPLE: "I always assumed that the painful memories and effects of my traumatic childhood would fade away and disappear. I went from one psychologist to another, expecting that when I was all talked out, the depressions would disappear and I'd have self-esteem and self-control. But as time went by, I felt more hopeless and isolated. I finally realized that nothing and no one can make up for the love I never got as a child. Even if it's hard for me to believe anyone can ever love me, I can treat others in a loving manner instead of abusing myself as I'd been abused. So I forced myself to go back to school. I earned a degree in teaching exercise to the elderly. Most of them are neglected or have been abandoned by their children. I have a special love for them because I know what it's like to be rejected. I work hard to bring joy into their lives, which brings joy into mine."

◊ EXAMPLE: "When my business went bankrupt, I went into a major depression. I couldn't deal with the loss, not only of money but of self-esteem and a whole way of life. To be begging for a job at my age, in my late forties, to see the people I thought were good friends abandon me, and to be treated in such a humiliating manner by the people who used to respect me — it was one blow after another. I decided to take responsibility for my own happiness. I formed a music group and played my grief away. I feel dead sometimes, but when I'm performing, I'm alive again."

One woman found a unique solution. She calls it, "Make every day an adventure."

◊ EXAMPLE: "I'm going through chemotherapy now and having a terribly hard time, especially since my doctors don't know if it will work. At first, I wanted to just give up and stop eating, just to get it over with. It took a while for me to get my fighting spirit back, and I did it with the help of my youngest daughter, who is four. I noticed how much joy she got from the simplest little things in life, like a flower or a new box of crayons. I decided that this is what I had to do — become a child again without fears for the future or attachments to the past. I would live in the present moment! Every day would be an adventure. As long as I discipline myself to think this way, I cope well. I'm now writing a book to help others who have cancer live each day as fully as possible. Writing this book gives me a strong sense of purpose and brings great joy into my life because it forces me to look for sources of joy every minute!''

No matter how qualified a therapist or how caring a friend may be, the work of acceptance is our own struggle. It takes great effort to create love and joy in the midst of pain.

Of course, no one wants to experience pain. It makes us feel so alone, powerless and insignificant. But if we work at accepting the ultimate rightness of all that God does and find some way to dedicate the pain to a higher purpose, we will not be dragged down into despair and bitterness. We alone must find some way to give meaning to the pain. By dedicating ourselves to serving God, we attach ourselves to the ultimate Power and the pain becomes a gift which lifts us above ourselves.

After a tragic auto accident in which his son suffered permanent injury, Rabbi Aaron Segal, of Jerusalem, wrote the following:

WHEREFORE?

In the silence of contemplation,
My children's tones are heard;
One remote,
One quite clear,
One diffused,
One confused,
Ascending toward my ear.

Woven into Mystic Patterns:
"Wherefore? Wherefore?

Why? Why?"
In the continual cry,
In an abyss of misunderstanding,
And pessimistic pits of forlorn hopes.

Yet...no rainbow, no cloud, no bird, no flora,
Nor any artifact of nature can substitute for the inward joy
Of the Supreme Creator's Beneficence,
When a renewed Divine Majestic solace,
As piercing the depth of another Red Sea Revelation,
In a majestic embrace, unifies my children's voices,
Quite discernible, that prophetic insight of consolation,
And all enigmas resolve to joy,
As with *tallith* I declare the Psalm of Praise.

It is difficult for an ordinary person to realize the effect of his actions on himself spiritually. This effect is often hidden from us. For example, we don't see the immediate spiritual effect of eating kosher food or not speaking *lashon ha-ra*, of giving the benefit of the doubt or appreciating a smile. When we are in pain and make those first halting, unconfident steps toward overcoming despair, we don't know what the results will be. It may take many years before we can look back and see the profound spiritual influence which has resulted from our declaring the Psalm of Praise in the midst of pain.

20 | The Gift of Borderline Anxiety

*Man has an unconscious awareness that he doesn't
exist in an absolute sense; hence he searches, he
struggles to become, even if only through an
illusion. All of life represents his struggle to
achieve real existence. All of creation is ephemeral,
all existence contingent. In reality, we have no
existence of our own at all.*
— FUNDAMENTALS OF FAITH, p. 30

We all experience moments when our perception of ourselves, of others, or of the nature of reality is suddenly altered, either positively or negatively. In a sudden flash of revelation, we say that life and people are not what we thought they were. For example, a sudden loss may make us acutely aware of just how tenuous, helpless, unstable and impermanent we are, with a resulting sense of existential anxiety. A crisis can make us see everything in a new light.

These borderline or transition moments can last from a few seconds to months. They are particularly likely to occur during times of transition or uncertainty, for then the familiar borders which separate reality from fantasy and the reliable from the unreliable can suddenly disappear and we feel confused and disoriented, not knowing where to find some sense of safety and stability.

A friend recounted, "We took our children to visit a wax museum. Coming out of the exhibit, our son, aged five, saw a woman walking by and asked, 'Is that lady real?'"

For this child, the borders between what was real and what was illusion had temporarily become blurred.

Our sense of who we are can also change radically at times:

◊ EXAMPLE: "I thought of myself as a basically decent person until a neighbor smashed into my car and then refused to pay damages. A vicious side of myself emerged which I'd never seen before. I wondered, Is this me?"

◊ EXAMPLE: "I've always thought of myself as a fairly competent, intelligent person. Then I signed up for a computer course and felt like a total idiot when I couldn't catch on to the terminology."

◊ EXAMPLE: "I'd thought of my marriage as a basically good one until my husband made a very critical statement to me. With a kind of devastating flash of insight, I saw that he has no sense of who I am or any appreciation of my essence."

The Holocaust was the ultimate borderline experience. Every standard of justice, sanity and normalcy was overturned, with everyone's sense of self pretty much lost in the wake. On a radio program aired on The Voice of Israel, a man who had been in Auschwitz for three years, spoke of his response when he spotted a Jewish child somewhere on the grounds of the camp. To paraphrase his remarks: "I looked at the child with disbelief," he reported sadly. "I had adopted an Auschwitz reality in which there were no more Jewish children in the world. I thought they had all been killed, my own children included. Suddenly, here was this Jewish child, with *peyoth* and all. I burst into tears. I was profoundly shaken because I was momentarily thrown back into a former reality. It had taken such effort to block out that reality of me as a father, husband and businessman, and to adjust to a different one. It took me weeks to readjust to Auschwitz all over again, even longer than when I had first arrived, because, for some reason, it was more difficult to readopt my identity as a person who did not feel."

Borderline moments, when the foundation of our belief system seems to totter or shatter, are common in everyone's life. We are often like a chess player with a carefully thought out plan of action who is surprised by a sudden move on his opponent's side. Life surprises us with many borderline moments, when we must readjust our beliefs or actions to fit a new reality, and incorporate new insights.

Positive borderline moments

Borderline moments can also be very positive, for they can allow us to experience a dimension beyond our limited, physical existence. For example, we may suddenly think of someone we haven't thought of for a long time and the person "just happens" to call or arrive for a visit. Or, we may experience telepathy, knowing what someone is thinking. We may see, in a flash, something which is going to happen, and then it does. Or, we seem to hear very distinctly from some place beyond ourselves, the answer to a problem. While many people deny that these paranormal experiences exist, they can happen even to those who deny them.

In addition, we may sometimes be blessed with an experience of ecstatic union with God, in which we sense the essential divinity of this world and ourselves. Afterwards, we may have difficulty returning to the confines of our narrow physical existence, with all its petty preoccupations. On the one hand, we come to long for self-transcendence. On the other hand, we fear that this would mean self-annihilation, the loss of individuality and free choice. A narrow perception of reality makes us feel separate from God and man, leading us to feel jealous, anxious and vulnerable. But that painful state of separateness at least provides us with a sense of self, of mattering as individual beings.

Borderline moments remind us of our primal terror of death, our fear of dying and disappearing forever, of all our efforts having been in vain. It is the desire to resolve this existential dilemma, to go beyond the borders of our limited physical existence and yet retain our selfhood, which causes many people to turn to religion and seek the means whereby we can spiritualize our lives.

Borderline moments are common and normal

However, it's the negative borderline moments which produce the most anxiety. It does not take a major event to put one into a borderline state. Any period of transition, unexpected event, or loss of predictability, order and stability can produce anything from mild anxiety to panic as we question: Who am I? Where am I? What am I doing here? Are the values and structures I cling to in order to give me a sense of stability, order and permanency really reliable?

* "Since I lost my job, I've been in a kind of fog. I sometimes wake up not knowing where I am or what day it is. I become easily depressed and overwhelmed. I've lost my anchor and my structure. I must adjust to a whole new reality, physically and emotionally. I've been terribly disillusioned by the heartless people who have tried to take advantage of me, yet heartened by those who have offered their friendship."

* "I found out someone I always trusted and thought of as a close friend had betrayed me in a business deal. The revelation left me wondering if I can ever trust anyone again."

* "I think I've been in a semi-borderline state since we made *aliyah*. I didn't realize I'd feel so helpless and incompetent."

Sound familiar? When you lose predictability, order, structure, identity or control, you may go into a borderline state; you may have difficulty making simple decisions and have feelings of unreality. You may become overwhelmed by the most trivial tasks. You may feel overwhelmed until you readjust and reorient yourself.

Who's more at risk?

Some people are rather obdurate, imperturbable, impermeable and unflappable. Nothing fazes them. They are not easily swayed or influenced by external events or demands, or unsettled by internal fatigue or pain.

Others are at the opposite extreme. They are more excitable and sensitive. These people can cross into a borderline state whenever there is even a minor change in their inner or outer environment. They tend to be more flexible, imaginative and intuitive. Highly creative people are likely to have more borderline experiences.

Intuitive types (see *Appreciating People, Including Yourself*) tend to have more borderline experiences because they naturally feel comfortable with the non-physical dimensions of reality. Even as children, they were concerned with ideas, theories, abstractions. They questioned the meaning and purpose of life in the face of an existence which seems so uncertain, fragile and fleeting. This is in stark contrast to the more sensory types who experience the physical world as the most real and solid realm, and see themselves as an integral part of it.

People with strong borderline tendencies are often emotionally insecure, overreacting to minor changes as if they were catastrophic or presaging danger. If you are this type, you might sometimes feel you are on the verge of mental or physical collapse whenever your familiar routines are disturbed. From an objective point of view, whatever is going on probably isn't all that terrible: you may be lacking sleep, have unexpected guests, be planning a *simchah*, or have a critical relative on your hands. You may feel embarrassed when you see others handling similar situations without all the inner turmoil. Why, then, are you so upset? Why does it feel awful?

It feels awful because, for one reason or another, this particular person or event challenges your sense of worth, your mental or physical stability, or your sense of identity, and causes you to question the validity of the values, structures, ideals and people you count on to make you feel real, competent, safe, loved and sane.

It is important to recognize when you are in a borderline state for many reasons:

1. So that you will not feel abnormal. Everyone has borderline moments. Once you spot them, you can determine whether or not your feeling of danger is rational or irrational, and whether you are exaggerating the discomfort you are in. For example, if you suddenly feel as though you are unreal, unsafe or threatened when faced with certain stressful people or events, instead of becoming paralyzed with anxiety and hostility you can say to yourself, "For some reason which I do not yet understand, this person (or event) puts me in a borderline state. It threatens my sense of stability, my sense of myself as mattering, of having importance and control. I will not panic, but will try to find out what I can do to respond in a way which maintains my sense of dignity. I cannot control people or events, but I can keep my will in tune with God's will, and by doing so, lessen the threat I feel from this external source."

This kind of talking to oneself lessens the sense of temporary insanity which can arise when we are in stressful situations.

2. So that you will not be so afraid of new situations. If you have borderline tendencies, you might become highly anxious when facing unfamiliar situations, even positive ones, such as a trip or a

simchah, because you fear having to endure borderline symptoms (e.g., disorientation, loss of control, etc.). By understanding your fear, you will not take your nervous symptoms so seriously.

3. So that you will accept your inner complexity. The more multi-faceted you are, the more inner turmoil you have to deal with. In an attempt to achieve predictability and stability, you may try to avoid all doubt and avoid expressing your true feelings of vulnerability and anxiety. You may have narrowed your identity to one identifying label, such as "I am an inadequate, depressed person," as if "inadequate, depressed person" describes the entirety of your being.

The truth is that questioning and doubt are necessary for growth. Furthermore, you are a complex combination of many traits. You are sometimes up and sometimes down; sometimes nice and giving and sometimes mean and selfish. To limit yourself to any narrow self-definition for the sake of security and predictability is to deny your Godly essence and your potential for growth.

4. So that you will not be afraid of transition times. The term borderline is helpful because it contains within the solution: readjustment by accommodating new information. If you feel out of control, get your sense of safe borders back by doing some things which require discipline or courage, and tell people precisely what you want and don't want. Doing things which require self-discipline demonstrates that you have the power to bring order into your life no matter how unstable your external circumstances might be.

5. So that you will be more open to positive borderline experiences of union with God and to the reality of the spiritual dimension that also exists in this world.

The most important thing is not to be afraid of this state. Everybody goes into a borderline state at times. Some people are able to ignore them or shrug them off more easily than others. Once you understand this state, you will see how important it is for you to create structure and order, and not to rely on anyone else to do it for you. This is the first stage in being able to have some control over the intensity and duration of a borderline state. Although you cannot directly control the feelings produced by this state, you can control the frightening thoughts and restrain the destructive impulses which may arise with it.

Events which shake us up even more

When a traumatic event occurs, such as an auto accident or serious illness, God forbid, the mental confusion and emotional turmoil may be even more severe. Your usual standards of what's fair vs. unfair, thinkable vs. unthinkable, normal vs. abnormal, acceptable vs. unacceptable are thrown into confusion. Your world turns topsy-turvy. You may think, What can I count on in this world? If my previous beliefs could be so wrong, how can I ever trust my judgment again? What's real and what's normal? Whom can I trust? People can be so shaken up by these moments that they may have heart attacks or act temporarily deranged.

◊ EXAMPLE: "Since my home was burglarized, I've been in a state of shock. I just can't grasp that this has happened to me. It's not just the loss of the material things which was so shattering. What was worse was my loss of faith in this world as a safe place to live in. Yet it forced me to realize that there is no real security in this world. I've become a lot more strict about my religious observance since then, because I want to attach myself to what is permanent."

◊ EXAMPLE: "After being single for many years, I finally married a wonderful, loving man. The only problem is that I keep expecting to be abused, rejected and abandoned as I was during childhood. I know how to be a cold porcupine or an angry witch. But I don't trust feeling secure and loved. This is a whole new world for me. I feel guarded, vulnerable and anxious. Thankfully, my husband is understanding and is willing to help me through the hard times."

◊ EXAMPLE: "Since my wife entered the hospital for open-heart surgery, I seem, on the surface, to be handling things just fine. Mr. Joe Cool. But then, when I have to write, my hand shakes so much that I can hardly read my writing. I get disoriented quickly. Yesterday, I got on a subway train going in the wrong direction. At work, I'm often in another reality. I forget to eat. I can't remember where I've put things. In short, I'm just not myself. And yet, I've been *daven*ing like I've never *daven*ed before."

Many people are easily swayed. They have trouble retaining their own values, opinions and feelings, quickly losing the borders which constitute their own sense of identity.

◊ EXAMPLE: "I'm a very suggestible person and soak up people's feelings like a sponge. If I'm with someone who is depressed, I feel depressed. If I'm with a disturbed person, I feel like I'm the crazy one. If I listen to a person with a certain point of view, I often find myself agreeing with him even if it's the opposite of what I believe in. I even buy something I don't want just to please the salesperson. Now that I understand what's happening, I've become much more assertive and self-protective. I say no more easily and without guilt. I count to ten to give myself a chance to think before I accept someone's opinion or agree to someone's demand that I do or buy what they want."

◊ EXAMPLE: "I just enrolled in a new school. The first few days were very hard because I don't do well with the unfamiliar. I felt like crying a lot and had feelings of unreality. But I kept up my smiling front and I'm feeling more in control as time goes on."

◊ EXAMPLE: "When I heard that some critical relatives were coming, I started to go into my old pattern, cleaning frantically, screaming at the kids not to touch anything, and getting a splitting headache from trying to figure out how to avoid their disapproval. Then I stopped. I remembered what a friend said — that those who love me will love me as I am and those who don't, won't like me no matter how much I clean. Because I lose my borders around critical people, I minimize my contact with them even though some family members accuse me of being mean and selfish for not inviting them more often."

Borderline states are common after the death of a loved one, when it is natural to feel lost, bewildered and fragmented. You wonder, If this person whom I loved so much could be gone in an instant, then how permanent am I or anything I hold dear? What is this reality, only a dream? Or, I still feel like he's here, like I can communicate with him. Am I crazy?

◊ EXAMPLE: "After my husband died, I felt as crazy as a person can be without someone putting him in a mental institution. I had to fake being sane. No one knew that I was walking around feeling that I had died too, and that it was only a shell of a body that people were talking to. I was in a twilight zone, not dead, but not alive either. When people talked to me, I felt as though a thick glass barrier separated us and I was unable to make meaningful contact. The loneliness was excruciating. I couldn't make the smallest decisions. I lost all sense of who I was or what I should be doing. From those ashes of grief, I have developed a new relationship with God, because He was all I could turn to in those hours of despair."

People who live alone and have too little stimulation often go into borderline states.

◊ EXAMPLE: "I live alone and am very introverted, so it's hard for me to reach out to people. I'm also very insecure and am always afraid that people won't like me. When I'm at work, I feel pretty normal, but when weekends or holidays come, I lose touch with what it means to be able to relate. I can't wait to get back to work and feel human again."

◊ EXAMPLE: "I thought retirement would be wonderful. But now I feel so useless and lost. There is nothing to structure my day. Nothing to make me feel needed. I thought something would just turn up on its own, but I now realize I must assertively find something to make my life meaningful again."

We set up our lives like a chessboard, moving the pieces around to maximize our sense of control, success and pleasure. Then something happens and we are shown that we don't have as much control as we thought we did.

Children are often in a borderline state

Children often lose their sense of borders. Parents must often help children define the borders between reality and fantasy: "No, people can't fly." "No, people don't turn into animals if they're bad." "No, thoughts don't make things disappear or appear." "No, there's no such things as ghosts." "No, rocks don't move around at night."

Children are also so impulsive and easily overwhelmed by passion, that they may define what's right and good according to what they want at that moment. Furthermore, their identities are not yet secure. They wonder, "Am I good or bad?" "Am I a little *tzaddik* or a horrible monster?" "Am I smart like the teacher said I was last year, or stupid according to this year's teacher?''

A child can feel that his whole world is collapsing whenever he hears his parents fight, if there is a death in the family, a new baby or if he is constantly hit or criticized.

Children are also confused about their borders because they live in a magical world where there is no clear separation between reality and fantasy. When a child pretends to be a soldier, he isn't just pretending; he is a soldier. When he talks to the trees or flowers, he's sure that they hear and perhaps that they are talking back to him. It takes a while for him to figure out the limits of his powers over people and things. He may imagine that with a thought he can make his dreams — or his nightmares — come true.

Older children (and sometimes parents as well) often take advantage of younger children's gullibility and permeable boundaries by teasing and tormenting them with stories about ghosts and other disembodied entities. Children often imagine themselves to have magical powers which give them control over people and nature — a natural result of their feeling so small and helpless.

> ◊ EXAMPLE: "I overheard my older daughter teasing her five-year-old sister that if she said certain magic words she would turn into a gerbil. The little one looked at her with wide open eyes and said, 'Really?' I told the older child to stop it immediately, that it was cruel to tease people in this way."

> ◊ EXAMPLE: "A relative kept saying to my daughter, 'You're so sweet that I'm going to eat you up.' I had to ask her to stop saying this since the child had nightmares about this actually happening."

Lying to children often puts them in a borderline state, since reality is already a rather fluid concept for them. They become even more confused and mistrusting if others lie. Chronic criticism and abuse often lead to a severe disturbance called the Borderline Personality Disorder.

Confused borders: when others invade ours

Each of us has a sense of personal space that we don't want violated. The amount of space differs with different people and our mood at the time. We may welcome some people, but bristle when others get close. When someone violates our personal space, we are likely to react with hostility, just like countries whose borders have been invaded. We lose trust if we are invaded too often.

◊ EXAMPLE: "A family moved in next door to us. I liked the woman very much and we became very close friends. But she started coming over at all times of the day and night and sent her kids over whenever she felt like it. She borrowed things without bringing them back until I'd nagged and nagged. She would also look at the bills on my desk and ask very personal questions. I established visiting times and tried to explain about boundaries, but she never respected my wishes. I realized that since she has no sense of borders, I would have to be extremely assertive about what she can and cannot do. I had to let the relationship grow distant to keep my sanity."

Pushy, critical and demanding people don't realize that they violate others' borders when they try to force their will on them.

◊ EXAMPLE: "I have a chronic illness. When people find out, some are very insistent that I take their advice about seeing certain doctors or trying certain medications. It was as if I had no sense of me as a separate person, with the right to make my own decisions. I felt like my borders were constantly being invaded. I'd get hostile until I realized that they are just trying to be helpful and that I simply have to be very emphatic about just how far they can go. If people detect any weakness on my part, they jump in and try to take over my life."

If we recognize what is happening, we can sometimes find some polite way to recreate the borders which are more comfortable for us.

Closeness and independence are often in conflict. When someone wants more closeness than you want, your tendency is to pull away, which can make the other person cling even more frantically, and, in turn, cause you to become much more adamant about having your independence. It may be helpful to talk frankly about what you want. Help people realize that closeness isn't achieved by clinging, dictating, guilt-tripping or shaming. Closeness is achieved through a mutual respect for each other's borders, i.e., for each one's independence and individuality.

Some people take advantage of those with fuzzy borders, knowing they can get away with almost anything if they exert enough pressure. Others keep testing or questioning borders because they feel unsafe unless they know precisely what is expected of them.

When you respond angrily to prevent repeated attacks by people who are too demanding or pushy, the invader may be quite bewildered as to why you are so upset.

> ◊ EXAMPLE: "After a rough day at work, I longed for the moment when I could come home and relax in peace and quiet. But when I walked in the door, my wife, starved for attention, wanted to talk. The more I'd try to get some space for myself, the more she'd jabber away, trying to get me to listen. She'd go on and on, totally unaware of my needs. I used to explode to make her leave me alone. But feeling rejected, she'd attack me. I didn't know how to break this pattern until I explained that when I come home from work fatigued, every demand feels like an attack on my borders. If she'd just give me time to recharge my batteries, I'd be more pleasant."

Motherhood

Mothers of young children often go into a borderline state: there is often too much stimulation for the nervous system, too little sleep and a total lack of structure or predictability, combined with endless demands. Life-and-death tensions prevail throughout the day as little ones fall off the furniture or put in their mouths a small object on which they could choke. Even doctors experience burnout when they are on duty too many hours. Yet many mothers live in an emergency room atmosphere day after day, with no relief from the constant demands and decisions. Women who felt stable and confident when they were single often feel unstable and incompetent when they face endless sleepless nights and a variety of conflicting demands at the same time.

> ◊ EXAMPLE: "It's the second week of summer vacation and I'm beginning to lose my marbles. Everyone goes to sleep and wakes up at a different time. Someone or other is always asking me to make a meal. My baby is a poor sleeper. I never know when she'll

awaken or go to sleep, or if I'll be able to sleep or for how long. I've become overly alert and overly sensitive. Anything can set me off. I can't concentrate for long or make trivial decisions. I can't make plans because the older kids don't want to do anything that would be pleasurable for the younger ones. There is no predictability. No structure. Mass confusion. Fights over everything. I don't know who I am — other than a machine that makes food and does chores. Thankfully, I know that as soon as I'm able to establish some kind of schedule, I will perk up and get back to myself again."

◊ EXAMPLE: "My five year old is hyperactive. She's on me all the time, wanting attention and reassurance. She even jumps on top of me whenever she feels like it. She talks to me when I'm in the bathroom. She interrupts my conversations and has a tantrum if I tell her to leave me alone. It's like she has no sense of there being borders between herself and me, as if we're not separate beings. I used to get angry and slap her. But then my doctor defined her as a high need-level child who really needs a lot of physical reassurance. So now I realize that I must hug her a lot, reassure her of my love constantly and pray that she develops her own secure borders instead of relying on me to define them for her."

Fathers also go into borderline states.

◊ EXAMPLE: "As long as I'm in *kollel*, studying in my quiet little corner, I'm okay. But when I get home and see the confusion and commotion and get hit by the high noise level, I blow up. It's like being in a war zone."

On the other hand, motherhood often helps people pull out of their borderline states.

◊ EXAMPLE: "I used to be very unstable and had a very stormy temperament. The external mess around me reflected my internal state of chaos. Thankfully, I found a therapist who would see me only if I would cooperate in becoming more disciplined. For example, I had to get myself and my children to sleep at regular hours. I had to prepare a weekly meal plan and keep the house neat. By role playing in her office, I learned to respond calmly when my children were upset or demanding. No criticism was allowed. Because I was so determined to give my children a more stable childhood than I had had, I overcame my resistance to this and in time my borderline symptoms began to fade."

Some people are in a borderline state most of their waking hours. These people have a disturbance called Borderline Personality Disorder. When the borderline state goes on for any length of time to the point where the person becomes dysfunctional or abusive, it is essential to get help from a therapist who can provide the loving concern and the discipline necessary to help the person feel whole again.

The female connection

Women have more of a tendency to enter borderline states for numerous reasons. For one thing, women are expected to be permeable, more adjustable, more easily influenced and more flexible than men. They are expected to give up their own desires and accommodate the needs of others. When a woman marries, her husband may not only expect her to take on his customs, he may expect her to be his shadow and give up her sense of having a separate identity. In focusing only on pleasing others, she can, indeed, lose all sense of herself and may become severely depressed.

Women, especially highly sensitive types, are the most permeable of all the personality types. They cannot help feeling what others are feeling and empathizing with those in need, to the point where they can lose touch with who they are and begin to see others' needs as their own. When criticized, they are likely to absorb the criticism as Absolute Truth.

> ◊ EXAMPLE: "I always assumed that my parents knew the real me and that whatever they thought about me was true. The result was I'd lose all sense of my own value because they don't value my life style. I'd overreact angrily or go around crying for days after an encounter with them. But once I realized that their vision of me is not Absolute Truth and that I don't have to accept their opinions, I stopped being so super-sensitive to their remarks. In fact, I can carry on a polite, superficial conversation and not lose my borders! That's a real accomplishment for me."

In addition, many women have trouble doing things which come more naturally to men: giving orders, setting firm limits, establishing rules and regulations, demanding obedience, being assertive and living within a hierarchical system. Using these male "power tools" of strictness and assertiveness may threaten a woman's primary needs for approval, harmony and closeness, and petrify her with fears of rejection and abandonment. It is important to realize that setting firm limits and safe boundaries is a form of love which is essential for a healthy home.

> ◊ EXAMPLE: "I used to feel like my children were attacking me all the time until I realized that my own borders were so fuzzy and permeable that they felt as insecure as I did! I wasn't clear about exactly what I wanted from them. I made rules, but was inconsistent and didn't follow through. I gave double messages, saying no when I meant yes, or maybe when I meant no. I was brought up amid a lot of chaos and confusion, so I feel like I'm flying blind, not knowing when to be stern or lenient, what limits to set, what's appropriate or inappropriate. Now that I understand this, I try to think through more clearly what exactly I want *before* I give an order. I'm still not a great disciplinarian and probably won't ever be, but I've become assertive about following through instead of giving up in despair. I also validate my need to get away from the children at times so that I can regain some sense of myself. I go to classes, talk to other mothers who understand me, and keep my life as scheduled as possible. When I feel like I'm about to fall off the cliff, instead of panicking like I used to do, I do some minor thing to give me a sense of having at least partial control over my environment, like folding laundry, making a dentist appointment or taking everyone out to the park."

Dealing with the borderline experience constructively

Borderline experiences can be quite frightening. The mental confusion, disorientation, feelings of unreality and helplessness can lead you to question your sanity, especially if you are not one of those unflappaple, unperturbable, super-confident types. If you enter borderline states quite easily, you need to learn how to stay objective and disciplined. Remember the initials SOC: stability, order and control.

Anything you can do to regain any or all three will help you ride the wave until things calm down again. For example, during this time you can:

1. Retain religious disciplines. Whether it's the morning hand-washing or the evening *Shema*, these are anchors which will give you some sense of order during the emotional storms you may be experiencing. They help you maintain contact with what is eternal in the midst of uncertainty.

2. Make a schedule and stick to it to the best of your ability without being compulsive about it. This is especially true if you have a house full of children, which means unavoidable confusion, disorder and unpredictability. Have specific days and hours when you: cut nails, change linen, write letters, arrange the photo album, clean the stove, wash *tzitzith*, clean out the toy box, etc. The more ordered your life is, the more you will feel in control of something despite the chaos and disorder.

3. Keep regular hours. Go to sleep and awaken at a normal hour (as much as possible). Being out of sync with the rest of humanity increases the likelihood of going into borderline states. Get adequate sleep. Events seem far more awful and overwhelming when you're sleep deprived.

4. Do things which bring joy to your life. Don't wait for "happily ever after." Look for the little things which make life pleasurable, such as flowers and trees and the laughter of children. Bring a gift to someone. Whenever you feel down, think, What could I do right now to bring joy into my life? Take responsibility for your own happiness. Exercise is especially important as it is fun and builds self-esteem because it requires self-discipline. Exercise helps you feel in control of something — your muscles, if nothing else! Exercise gives one a sense of order and sanity.

> ◊ EXAMPLE: "I don't have a happy marriage, so I have to be extra disciplined about doing things that keep me happy or I could get stuck in a depression forever. For example, I started taking music lessons recently. After each lesson, I return in a happy mood, determined not to lose my borders and get sucked in by other people's negative states. Practicing lifts my spirits and makes me feel that I have my own identity, something that is all mine."

5. Do something — anything — which requires self-discipline. Any decision, even the decision to brush your teeth or go to a class is endorsable because it signifies that you're taking charge of your life and taking responsibility for being more orderly, fulfilled, structured and happy instead of waiting for others to take care of you. If you are angry at people for not giving you a sense of value or stability, learn to take responsibility for your needs. Other people can't give you value or stability. Acting in a self-disciplined manner is what builds self-confidence and self-esteem.

6. Distinguish between real danger and mere discomfort. If there is no danger, don't listen to that internal voice which is screaming, "Danger! Emergency!" Ignore the nervous symptoms as much as possible. Keep saying, "This is temporary." Take the secure thought that, "I will get back to myself. I will handle it! I can ride out this storm for a short time more."

7. Befriend only nurturing people. Stay away from invasive, critical people, or be assertive toward them if you can do so without getting hurt.

Helping children with borderline moments

High anxiety-level children can panic when they are in a borderline state. Two mothers did the following:

◊ EXAMPLE: "I've had seven children in ten years, so my ten year old has been through a lot of upheavals. When I came home with the latest baby, she became so anxious that the slightest sound would set her off. She wouldn't even sleep in her own bed. Finally, I tried the following. I bought her a pretty gold ring. After I gave it to her, I told her to close her eyes and remember when we went to the beach, how relaxed she had been. She smiled at the memory. Then I anchored this happy state to the ring by telling her to rub it while remembering to relax. I did this a few more times during the day, each time telling her to remember how happy and relaxed she was at the beach and then to rub her ring. After a few days, she told me, 'I can calm myself down!' She was very proud of herself. Before that, I was her anchor. She needed me to calm her down. Now she can do it on her own."

◊ EXAMPLE: "My eleven year old was very fearful, and the only thing I could think of to help him was to share my own method for staying calm, which is to constantly say 'Whatever happens, it's Hashem's will.' For his sake, I started saying it out loud more often. No matter what happened during the day — a red light, cookies burning, a guest who didn't show up or did show up unexpectedly, a sprained ankle, a toothache — I said, 'This is what Hashem wanted! I accept His will with love.' After a few months of this, Moshe came home from a class trip which he had been very worried about. He told me, 'I'm not a scaredy-cat anymore.' I asked him how that had happened, and he said, 'I just kept telling myself that it's all Hashem's will. If I throw up on the bus, it's His will. If I don't, that's Hashem's will too. If I fall off the cliff we're climbing, it's Hashem's will. If I don't, that's Hashem's will too. If I can't get to sleep in the tent, that's Hashem's will, and if I do, that's Hashem's will. And I just kept saying it over and over and I was okay!'"

What is the gift?

> Then I looked at all the things that I had done and the energy that I had expended in doing them; it was clear that it was all futile and a vexation of the spirit — and there is no real profit under the sun. Then I turned my attention to appraising wisdom...
>
> — KOHELETH 2:11-12

The major gift in a borderline experience is that it shakes us up out of our lethargy and complacency. It provokes us to question our goals and our behavior, to ask ourselves, "Where am I going? What is my purpose here? What can I count on to give me a sense of safety, love, permanency and power? What am I? Who am I? Am I what others think I am? Am I what I think I am? Am I more than this or less?"

King Solomon states, "Man cannot comprehend what God has done...," but concludes, "Thus I perceived that there is nothing better for each of them than to rejoice and do good in his life" (*Koheleth* 3:11-12).

In other words, from all this questioning, bewilderment, grief and frustration, mature awareness is born, the humbling awareness that ultimately, all we need to focus on in this world is our duty to fear God and keep His commandments (*Ibid.*, 12:13). It is this which gives us direction, identity and security.

As long as we experience this world as the source of pleasure and success, we will not gain this awareness. It is the painful losses which make us realize that all our petty jealousies and resentments and our bitterness over not getting all we want in terms of respect, power and stability in this world is all vanity and futility.

Thus, if used properly, borderline moments activate our longing to bind ourselves to the Eternal and to stay within the borders of Torah. In these moments of profound existential questioning, we are given the opportunity to face the truth — that there is no security in people or things, but only in God, the only true Source of power and security. If we believed that we could ever gain firm control of anything outside of our own personal thoughts, speech or actions, these borderline moments show us the folly of such thinking. Torah gives us borders. It alone gives us meaning and identity.

So when one of these moments occurs, we can stop and say, "You are all I can cling to in the midst of this storm. Thank you for reminding me to remember You." In this way, the likelihood of having positive borderline experiences of true union with God is increased.

21 | The Gift of Overcoming Childhood Programming

*God said to Avram, "Leave your country, your
kindred and your father's home..."*

— BERESHITH 12:1

A child growing up in normal circumstances comes to certain conclusions: that life has a purpose, that the world is a basically benevo-
lent place, that people can be trusted and that he has value. Repeated
traumas, including physical and verbal abuse, can produce the opposite assumptions: that life is meaningless, that the world is basically
malevolent, that people are untrustworthy and that he is essentially
unlovable and worthless.

It is not hard to imagine how difficult a person's life can be if he
leads it according to the second set of assumptions, how fearful and
defensive he can be if his faith in himself or life has been shattered
or never established in the first place.

Thus, many people reach adulthood with grave psychological
problems which manifest in destructive behavior: food disorders,
hostile outbursts, depression, paranoia, criticalness, compulsivity
and panic attacks.

How do we heal ourselves? The healing process involves using
the same stressful events that all people experience to build faith in
God, in others and oneself. For example, all people at times feel bad,
sad, lonely, angry, depressed, bored, jealous or resentful. What spells
the difference between a mentally healthy person and a mentally
disturbed person is that when the former feels bad, he picks himself
up and does something positive, while the latter uses his negative

mood state as an excuse to become destructive, such as by wallowing in self-pity or picking a fight with someone.

Those who have suffered repeated traumas in childhood are like people who wear a brace to correct their curvature of the spine. Their deviant psychological "bent" will not be straightened in a day or a year. It will require a lifetime of discipline to keep the unhealthy tendency from going back in the direction in which it originally grew.

Mental health does not mean being free of pain. It is measured by one's capacity to work hard despite discomfort, to find joy in life in the midst of hardship and to love others despite their deficiencies. If you have destructive tendencies, you will have to develop a will of steel and fight diligently for your mental health.

There is no pill, blessing, charm, herb, therapist, rabbi or doctor that can give you maturity, strength of will, depth of understanding, a loving heart or a hard-working nature. It is your work, and yours alone, day after day, to overcome patterns of negativity which have been programmed into your mind and muscles.

Can therapy cure?

If you are unhappy, at some point you will probably turn with hopeful anticipation to a therapist for a cure. You will be sadly disappointed if you believe the following myths:

1. That by talking about traumatic childhood events, the memories and effects of these events will disappear, and then you will be cured and live happily ever after.

2. That if you just find the proper communication techniques, you will get along with everyone and everyone will like you.

3. That if you find the right technique, you can get people to change the behavior that bothers you.

4. That therapists are perfectly "together" people who have the magic key which, if you pay enough money and go long enough, will enable you to breeze through life easily and happily, just as they seem to be doing.

5. That your therapist will "re-parent" you (i.e., s/he will be the all-wise, all-protective, always available parent you never had), so that any damage to your psyche during your formative years will be undone and you will now live securely with a permanent sense of

certainty, confidence and safety.

No mortal can reduce your existential anxiety over your mortality. The truth is that, at best, a therapist can only do the following:

1. Help you identify your errors in thinking which reinforce your negative behaviors in the present. Awareness is just the first step in the process of becoming more positive. Then it's up to you to change your thoughts and move your muscles in a healthy manner, despite the discomforts and disappointments of life.

2. Make suggestions about concrete changes which will help you to think and act in a healthier manner. Whether people like or love you or not when you make these changes is in God's hands, not yours.

3. Help you give up trying to change others. People don't change their behavior unless they have the inner determination to put forth tremendous effort to do so.

4. Offer encouragement as you wage the long battle to change your past programming, and let you know that everyone, including therapists, must engage in this struggle if they want to grow spiritually. The emotional scars remain, but you can lead a normal life if you keep your thoughts and actions positive.

5. Provide a sympathetic listening ear and perhaps a taste of what it's like to be cared about, which is very important for those brought up in dysfunctional homes, who never experienced a nurturing atmosphere.

Talking does not change negative behavior. In fact, prolonged talk therapy causes some people to become even more dysfunctional and infantile, because they become totally absorbed in the analysis of their feelings and dependent on the therapist for their sense of self-worth and security. True, there is great value in gaining understanding and insights about one's past. But there is a point at which rehashing the past actually becomes counterproductive. Happiness will not come through analysis, but only from spiritualizing one's life. One must go beyond one's personal disappointments and put one's heart and soul into Torah, *avodah* and *gemiluth chasadim* (*Avoth* 1:2).

Whatever you have experienced in life was a gift which was necessary in order for you to develop certain sensitivities and awarenesses. Your task is to use your past to enlighten you in the present and to do something useful with the knowledge gained from what you have gone through. This is something which no therapist can do for anyone, just as no one can lift weights and thereby strengthen someone else's muscles.

Signs of a dysfunctional home

In a dysfunctional home, children do not get their basic needs for stability, protection, guidance and affection met. In most cases, this is because the parents were products of dysfunctional families in which incessant criticism or major traumas created an overwhelming sense of fear and mistrust in them. They simply could not give their children what they didn't have.

The most difficult thing about growing up in a dysfunctional family is that abnormal behavior seems normal, inevitable, unavoidable and permissible. For example, if you saw your parents argue constantly, act depressed, throw things, hit or scream when they were angry, you probably promised yourself not to act like that when you grew up. But these acts are likely to be your most automatic response today when a stressful event occurs.

How can you change these patterns? How can you give and receive love if you didn't experience it as a child? How can you stop being so destructive? The first step is to recognize the major signs of a dysfunctional home so that you can start changing these patterns now in your own home.

1. Love is conditional, i.e., you are loved not for who you are but for what you achieve.

2. Children and the inferior-status spouse are constantly shamed and humiliated with ceaseless criticism. No one can live up to the dominant spouse's standards.

3. Children and the inferior-status spouse are not allowed to express their individual opinions or feelings. If they try to do so, they are ridiculed, ignored or punished.

4. At least one member of the family focuses all the energy on him/herself by being constantly angry or depressed. This person blames other family members for his/her destructive behavior.

5. Lack of trust. Promises are not kept.

6. Problems are denied or ignored. Parents deny that they or their children have learning disabilities, emotional problems or marital

problems. They get enraged or depressed about their problems instead of taking action to solve them.

7. Lack of consistent discipline. Discipline is chaotic, unpredictable or meted out with sudden outbursts of hysteria or violent rages. One minute the parent is being indulgent and overprotective, the next minute s/he is furious and abusive or withdrawn, cold or indifferent.

8. There are no firm guidelines, moral standards and obligations to which people are held accountable.

9. There is much chaos, instability, and unpredictability.

10. Minor mistakes are considered catastrophic. There is a lot of hysteria about food, messes, lost keys, etc. Children and the inferior-status spouse live in fear of the dominant spouse's outbursts of rage.

11. Perfection is demanded; anyone who doesn't live up to the dominant parent's standards is considered an absolute failure. Love is promised at some future date, conditional upon success.

12. Everyone lies to or withholds information from everyone else. There is a great deal of secrecy and fear.

13. Parents are afraid to give, as if they must defend themselves against manipulation and exploitation. They may make statements like, "What am I, a taxi service, a maid, a waitress?"

14. Parents are overprotective and over-giving, crippling the development of their children's sense of confidence and competence.

In short, in a dysfunctional home there is an underlying message: don't be honest, don't trust anyone and don't express feelings. This is what you must now work to overcome.

It is not an easy task. Even the greatest musician must practice many hours a day to stay in shape. It's the same with the spiritual exercises which enable us to be mentally healthy.

The results and the tikkun

Now that you know what you have to overcome, the second step is to discipline yourself to change your thoughts and move you muscles in a new way. As you read this list, remember that blaming others for how you act is childish and destructive. No matter what went on in the past, you are responsible for your actions today. Taking responsibility means understanding your symptoms and the particular disciplines which are required to counterbalance these tendencies.

Abandonment fears: You are terrified of being rejected, but think it is inevitable since you are so worthless. You crave closeness but run away from it. You monitor people's words and actions, waiting for the dreaded abandonment to come. You never feel safe. You feel you must prove yourself to win people's love.

The *tikkun*: Develop the will to love others even if you do not feel they love you back, even if you feel unappreciated (unless, of course, you are being abused, in which case you should cut off as quickly as possible). Love for the sake of loving, without thought to the future. If you are forgiving and accepting, reliable and trustworthy, you will gradually experience closeness.

Addictive behavior: You try to numb yourself to loneliness and disappointment by abusing your body with food, alcohol, drugs, cigarettes, etc. You may abuse your spouse in your intimate marital relationship, either by acting coldly indifferent or excessively demanding. You keep hoping that objects will provide the comfort you never get from people. You believe that you deserve pain. Pain makes you feel alive. Self-abuse provides a sense of control.

The *tikkun*: Develop the will to treat yourself in a truly caring manner. Find nourishing activities and people. Think only those thoughts which make you feel strong, sane and loving. Find pleasure in "M & Ms" — performing mitzvoth and improving *middoth*.

Anger: You are irritable and angry much of the time. You react violently to people whom you perceive to be disrespectful or disobedient. You distance yourself from people by constantly picking on them for one thing or another. Then you wonder, "Why don't people respect me more? Why don't people do more for me?" You scream angrily, throw things, threaten and hit. You scream: "Finish your food or I'll hit you." "Clean up your room or I'll punish you." "Do what I want or I'll hurt you."

The *tikkun*: Develop the will to be patient, forgiving and compassionate. Lock your lips and refuse to talk unless you have love in your heart. When you don't get what you want, assume that God doesn't want you to have it. Give the benefit of the doubt. Practice compassion. Go out of your way to do things for others. Force yourself to give positive feedback. Ask others, "What can I do to help you?" Or, "How can I improve our relationship?" Keep a list of the good that others do on the refrigerator. Write positive things down every single day.

Anxiety: You feel anxious much of the time, thinking something disastrous is about to happen that you won't be able to cope with. Your fear of being rejected or failing paralyzes you. You fear that if you relax, you will become apathetic or immoral. You panic easily and are on guard all the time.

The *tikkun*: Develop the will to trust that with God's help, you can handle any pain. Have the courage to do things you fear to do to strengthen your self-confidence. If you have a high-strung nervous system, this will not change greatly. Learn to go on in spite of it.

Approval seeking and people pleasing: You are so obsessed with trying to please or rescue people, especially your family members, that you turn yourself into a doormat and a martyr. You don't discipline your children, then complain that they don't listen to you and are unmanageable. You let your mate order you around, then stew in resentment. You yearn for closeness, but befriend people least able to give it to you. You care for others in ways you don't care for yourself. You feel that your worth comes from others. You are easily intimidated, bullied and exploited.

The *tikkun*: Develop the will to let go of needing others' approval. You are not responsible for others' happiness, sense of security or self-esteem, nor are they responsible for yours. Your worth is determined by God, not man. Your goal: not to let your sense of value be determined by your external image or possessions.

Blame: You blame your parents/spouse/children for your moods and destructive behavior. Or you blame yourself for events and others' behavior over which you have no control.

The *tikkun*: Develop the will to take responsibility for your mental health. Blame is a manifestation of the desire to remain a child and escape adult obligations.

Catastrophization: You get hysterical over trivial mistakes and petty things such as dust, dirt, spilled juice, overcooked noodles or social snubs. You are constantly in a state of crisis. You use words like *awful, shattered, terrible* and *tragic* to describe minor losses and discomforts.

The *tikkun*: Develop the will to discipline your mind so that you distinguish between what is important in life and what is unimportant. Important means an event which is connected to our Godly mission. Everything else is in the realm of triviality.

Communication problems: You show little interest in others or you monopolize conversations and don't listen. You withhold your feelings or talk endlessly about them. You keep trying to get through to people who cannot be gotten through to, refusing to see that they cannot give you the closeness you crave.

The *tikkun*: Develop the will to relate in a healthy manner to nurturing people. Learn skills such as empathy, active listening and calm problem solving. Dissociate yourself from critical, non-nurturing people.

Compulsions and obsessions: You are obsessed with rules, with issues of right and wrong and conforming to schedules. You obsess about food, death, cleanliness, etc. You feel compelled to repeat actions, such as cleaning or checking hundreds of times. You have a set system for doing everything. If you do not do it right every time, you panic and feel compelled to start all over again. You count and recount words, socks, dishes, steps, etc. These rituals give you a pretense of control, while inside you feel chaotic. You drive others crazy with your checking, your systems, your compulsions and your rigid, joyless approach to life.

The *tikkun*: Develop the will to relax and let go of the need to control God and prevent bad things from happening with these magical acts. Medication can greatly help reduce the compulsivity of repetitive thoughts and actions, but you must help by practicing the self-control not to repeat acts and note that no catastrophe occurs as a result of it. Focus on acting like others.

Control issues: You try to force others to give you respect, approval, a sense of superiority, security, or self-worth. You explode angrily if your needs and standards aren't met. You use punitive tactics such as hostile withdrawal or anger to get what you want.

The *tikkun*: Develop the will to focus on your own growth and leave others' growth up to them. Avoid all coercive tactics.

Chronic criticism: You constantly put others down with labels (e.g., brat, pest, jerk, stupid, slob, baby, etc.) and negative programming (e.g., "You ruin whatever you touch." "You'll never amount to anything." "You can't do anything right."). You always feel either one-up or one-down.

The *tikkun*: Develop the will to love. Praise the positive in others. Open your mouth only to say something positive. Welcome the opportunity to do things for others.

Denial: You deny that anything is wrong with you, despite identifying with this checklist. You deny that you have the ability to control yourself. You deny that you are unhappy. You deny the need for self-improvement, insisting that everything would be just fine if only you had a lot of money or could find the right therapist, job or spouse. You deny that family members have serious disturbances.

The *tikkun*: Develop the will to be emotionally honest, and to say, "I'm in pain," instead of hiding from it by getting into any addictive mood (e.g., anxiety, numbness, resentment, guilt, shame, depression) or escaping into addictive behaviors (e.g., overeating, oversleeping, overworking, smoking, alcoholism). As a child, the pain of feeling unimportant, small, helpless, rejected or alone — i.e., of being mortal — was too great to bear. But now you can face that pain without artificial buffers because Torah has connected you to that which is immortal.

Dependency problems: You are either super-independent, priding yourself on the fact that "I don't need anyone for anything," or, you are very needy, feeling, "I can't do anything. I want to remain a child, to be taken care of." You are easily overwhelmed, panicked or sick to escape adult responsibilities. You keep looking for a mommy or daddy figure to nurture you and tell you what to do.

The *tikkun*: Develop the will to be more self-sufficient if you are super-dependent. Have the courage to do whatever you can on your own. Give to others instead of waiting for them to give to you. If you are super-independent, learn to ask people for time, help and concern.

Depression: You feel like a failure and give up easily, going into despair, feeling weak, vulnerable and dependent, helpless to change yourself or gain control of your life. You keep thinking, It's no use. I want to die. I'm no good. Yet you want to stay depressed so that you can escape burdensome adult responsibilities.

The *tikkun*: Develop the will to give and be creative. Depression is 50 percent laziness, of the mind and the muscles. Don't let thoughts flit through your mind randomly; screen them carefully and accept only those that will help you grow. Give your lethargic muscles firm commands to move. Stay functional despite your sadness. With every move you make, say, "I'm grateful." Use Reb Aryeh Levin as a model. His whole life was spent doing *chesed*.

Disorganization and inefficiency: Although you may be very intelligent, you often act like you are stupid. You forget important appointments. You lose important papers. You can't find your glasses, your calculator, your checkbook. If and when you finally start working, you work unsystematically and impulsively, fail to follow through, or become so overwhelmed with the details of simple tasks that you feel as if your circuits have been overloaded and you give up.

The *tikkun*: Develop the will to be orderly. Make schedules, commitments and plans, then stick to them.

Fear of insanity: Although you act normal most or all of the time, you fear that you are really crazy. If you function normally most of the time, then your fear of insanity may stem from a childhood belief that being crazy is what makes you special, unique, deserving of attention and justified in demanding support from others. It has also been an excuse to indulge in destructive behavior.

The *tikkun*: Develop the will for self-control. Be special, unique and outstanding in your good *middoth*. Then you will not need to fear insanity and you will gain attention in a positive manner.

Guilt and shame: You feel guilty and ashamed over just about everything, including being imperfect, being alive, not making everyone happy, and for anything bad that ever happened to you. You know that you should be changing certain destructive habits, but your resolutions don't get translated into action, which makes you feel even more guilty.

The *tikkun*: Develop the will to think rationally. Resolve to feel guilt only for deliberate sins that were in your conscious control. Do *teshuvah* for deliberate sins and then close the door on the past.

Humorlessness: You see life as a tragedy and take everything too seriously. You are afraid to let go and have fun. You think you must always have a strict, serious demeanor. You fear relaxing. Even when you are supposed to be having a good time, you are tense.

The *tikkun*: Develop the will to enjoy life's kosher pleasures. Cultivate a sense of humor. When a stressful event occurs, tell yourself, "If I won't be upset about it ten years from now, I'm not going to get upset about it now." Take minor problems lightly.

Irresponsibility: You procrastinate, don't return things you've borrowed, forget appointments, don't keep promises, arrive late or don't let people know you're not going to show up. You neglect your health, your children, your marriage. You avoid hard work. Being sick gives you an excuse to be irresponsible.

The *tikkun*: Develop the courage to be disciplined. Return things you've borrowed on time. Keep your environment neat. Take care of your health.

Jealousy: You are intensely envious, feeling that others have it better than you, are happier, luckier, richer, more competent. You feel that you got a raw deal in life.

The *tikkun*: Develop the will to trust that God gives you exactly what you need. You can't have anyone else's reality.

Low self-worth: You feel you are essentially weird, defective, inadequate and unlovable. You not only recognize your faults, which is healthy, but you magnify them to the point where you feel helpless to change them. You castigate yourself ceaselessly for not being better. You feel, I'm not worth spending money on. I'm not worth having a vacation, not worth spending money on to get help, not worth having my teeth fixed or saying what my needs are.

At the same time, you think you are better than others in some ways, perhaps more aware and sensitive, and put others down for not being on your level of sensitivity.

The *tikkun*: Develop the will to stop condemning yourself. Get off your judgments and start doing something with your life.

Magical thinking: You think a magic cure exists which will make all your pain go away easily, quickly, effortlessly. You think a phrase, an amulet or a medicine will give you control over people, will make you rich or healthy, etc.

The *tikkun*: Develop the will to put forth the needed effort. Develop the will to take responsibility for your physical, mental and financial well-being. Don't count on magic. Mental health doesn't come easily; start working for it.

Narcissism: You are preoccupied with your own fears, feelings, aches, pains and problems. You demand that people serve you and put you first, no matter what else they have to do. However much others do for you or give you, you are dissatisfied. You complain about your life constantly. You demand that your wishes and demands be met instantly. You can't bear frustration.

The *tikkun*: Develop the will to give to others, to be concerned about others, and to put others first.

Paranoia: You are overly vigilant and suspicious, sure that others are planning to hurt, betray, exploit, dominate or reject you. You are so touchy that a raised eyebrow, a refused invitation or a private phone number is proof that you are being betrayed.

The *tikkun*: Develop the will to trust. Look at the positive in others. Constantly give others the benefit of the doubt by saying, "S/he is doing and loving the best s/he can with the tools s/he has right now," to erase hatred, grudge bearing and vengeance.

Perfectionism: You feel that only perfect people deserve to be respected and loved. You try to be super-neat, super-organized, super-religious to the point of torturing yourself and those around you. No one ever measures up. You think, If I'm not the best, I'm garbage.

The *tikkun*: Develop the will to accept your limitations as an act of humility. Let go of your unrealistic demands whenever you start to feel anxious and angry. Every person needs *tikkun* or the person wouldn't be alive.

Religious abuse: You use religion in an abusive manner, denying yourself even permissible pleasures. You are grim, overly serious and self-punishing. You are terrorized by religion and terrorize others with your perfectionism and threats of punishment. You cannot imagine a God Who is kind, forgiving and compassionate. You constantly feel, "I must be doing something wrong" and instill this fear in those around you.

The *tikkun*: Develop the will to serve God with joy. "Scrupulously avoid any act deemed strange by everyone else [in the Torah world] (Chazon Ish, *Igroth*, I:20). Motivate yourself and others with love, not hatred, resentment or terror. This is especially true with young children. Terrorizing young children into praying or saying *berachoth* creates a negative feeling toward God.

Somatization: You are a hypochondriac, suffering from vague, chronic aches and pains which keep you from functioning and which are resistant to all the remedies prescribed by the numerous doctors you have consulted.

The *tikkun*: Develop the will to be healthy. Eat healthy foods. Follow a regular exercise program. Don't expect to be pain-free. Expect to live with discomfort. Divert your attention from yourself and learn to function despite the pain.

Trust issues: You don't trust that anyone will ever really be there for you. You are paranoid, always thinking that others are plotting to harm you. You don't trust your judgment. You are afraid to make decisions, sure that you will make mistakes.

The *tikkun*: Find a reliable Torah authority who can guide you. Make a firm decision to love others even if they do not meet your expectations. Do not reject people unless they are abusive. If you become a trustworthy friend, you will eventually see others as trustworthy. If you have paranoid tendencies, focus on giving the benefit of the doubt. If people do hurt you, tell yourself that they are acting from their own pain and fears.

Victimization: You feel like a helpless victim of your own bad habits as well as others' abusive treatment of you.

The *tikkun*: Develop the will to be assertive, to protect yourself from abuse and to treat yourself in a caring manner.

Healing the wounds from a dysfunctional childhood

If you have any of the above symptoms, have hope! These were survival skills which you adopted as a child to minimize the pain of abuse and rejection. But you can learn new skills. You may not completely overcome the effects of an abusive childhood, but you can learn to use your experiences for growth. You will have setbacks, flashbacks and nightmares which remind you that the past is still part of the present. During stressful times, old fears and negative habits may come back in full force. However, once you are on the path of spiritual health, you can use these setbacks and flashbacks as reminders to work harder on your *middoth*! See yourself as a survivor who has had the strength to go on despite much pain.

If you had a perfect childhood, you probably would not have the humility, sensitivity and understanding which you now possess. Your childhood was precisely what God wanted you to have. There were no mistakes. It was not a fluke that you were born into your family, or that you have your particular nervous system or predispositions. Keep asking yourself, "What were the gifts I took from those childhood experiences?" You have an inner wisdom which will respond if you are patient. Know that you will appreciate the light only because you have known darkness.

The important thing to remember is that you have to watch yourself for your entire life, or you will fall back into your old, destructive patterns.

Reframing the past: making it meaningful

When you think of your childhood, do not allow yourself to be left with a feeling of victimization and self-pity. Instead, when you think about a particular experience, see what you learned from it. See yourself not as a victim, but as a survivor, a strong person who can survive anything. Thank God for giving you the strength to come this far. In addition, make a resolution about the future. For example,

1. Memory: "I remember coming home from school and no one being there. I don't remember anyone listening or caring much about me. My parents treated me like a pesky fly. They were always screaming, 'You're driving me crazy. Go away!' I felt so unwanted. From this, I learned how important it is to be there for others, to not be indifferent to others. I learned how important it is to let people know that they are important to me."

Resolution: "I will be available for my children and for others who need me to the best of my ability. I will take the time to listen and be empathic. I will let my children know they're important to me. I will not abandon others. I will not abandon God."

2. Memory: "My father had terrible mood swings. He was either depressed or violent. He fought all the time with my mother. Sometimes he was nice, but most of the time he was wrapped up in his own world. From this I learned how important emotional modesty is, i.e., not to vent my feelings wherever or whenever I want, but to restrain myself and only reveal what is necessary and appropriate. Verbal restraint has brought me a tremendous sense of self-respect because this is the most difficult discipline for a compulsive talker and a highly emotional person like myself."

Resolution: "I will not let my moods control me. I will be as stable as possible and work on self-control. If I'm depressed or angry, I will work on myself instead of exposing others to my negativity. I will work out my marital differences in private and not criticize my spouse in front of our children."

3. Memory: "I was hit a lot. It was terrifying — all the screaming and violence at home. I learned from that how vulnerable children are and how important it is to have self-control."

Resolution: "Just because I was beaten doesn't mean I have to continue beating myself up with criticism. I will control myself around my children, settle my differences with my spouse in private, and do everything possible to create a happy home atmosphere."

4. Memory: "I remember bringing my report card home and being screamed at me for not getting all A's. I learned from that to let people know that what counts in life is people, not their accomplishments."

Resolution: "I will focus on loving people as they are, accepting them as they are, and not offering conditional love anchored on achievements only. I refuse to rely on anyone for my sense of value, only on God."

5. Memory: "I was physically abused as a child and lived with terrible feelings of shame and guilt my whole life. I finally went to a *rav* and asked him how to do *teshuvah* for what happened. He told me, 'You need to do *teshuvah*, but not the kind you think. Your *teshuvah* is to be good to yourself, to respect yourself and to be happy with your life.' From this I learned that God doesn't want us to constantly torture ourselves in order to win favor in His eyes. He wanted me to learn that the body can be damaged, but it is my task to keep my spirit free and pure."

Resolution: "To think well of myself. To focus on my own and others' *tzelem Elokim*, which is all that really counts."

6. Memory: "I suffered from so much rejection, both at home and at school. But this eventually taught me not to care what others think of me. Being so unhappy with my life, I turned to Orthodox Judaism for help. If I'd have been happy, I probably wouldn't have searched for anything else or had the courage to turn my back on my secular life."

Resolution: "Knowing how painful it is to be rejected, I will not reject others. I will not reject God, but will make Him a part of my life by talking about Torah and *middoth* throughout the day."

A helpful exercise

In the space provided at the back of this book, recall as many painful events from your childhood as you can remember. Then write down what you learned from them and also your resolution not to act the same way in the future.

> ◊ EXAMPLE: "When I was younger, I got a lot of attention by being tragic and dramatic. But as I got older, I found that no one wanted to hear me always complaining and agonizing over everything. For years, I was angry at family members, neighbors and religious leaders who didn't give me the attention and consideration I felt I deserved because of my fragile emotional state. It took me a long time to realize that I was the one who was alienating people with my gloomy attitude. I finally made two rules for myself. First, 'Don't agonize over anything you can't change.' Second, 'Be for others what you want them to be for you.' From that day on, my life began to change. Slowly but surely I stopped acting like a whiny child and became more productive and cheerful."

If you work on yourself, you will eventually come to see the gift in the pains from your past, because in overcoming your negative behavior patterns you come to achieve true self-respect and experience the deepest joy. God, in His great wisdom, wanted you to have an awareness of pain and evil, of rejection and abuse, so that you would know precisely what you need to overcome now. And it is in fighting for change that you will feel closer to Him, the source of strength Who gives you the ability to keep moving forward.

PART V

Children

22 | The Gift of Solutionizing with Children

When a child has a tantrum, most parents get caught up in a storm of negativity. To stay out of that negative force field, you must do something which seems totally unnatural and strange, i.e., tell yourself, "I see this as a gift which gives me the opportunity to demonstrate Torah ideals in a difficult situation."

If you have a very moody child or one who has frequent tantrums, this is an opportunity to give that child the gift of how to focus on solutions. Use the word *solutions* about 100 times a day and demonstrate solutionizing in your own life.

For example, when you are thirsty, say out loud in front of the child, "I'm so thirsty. Let's see. What's the solution? I know, I'll get something to drink!" Or, "I'm so bored. Hmm...what's a solution? I know, let's all go out for a walk." "I am SO ANGRY! What's the solution? I know. Let's have a family conference!" Or, "I'd better give you the benefit of the doubt so I calm down!"

Then, the next time a child, even a very young one, says, "I'm thirsty," don't jump right in and say, "Go get a drink." Instead, say, "What's your solution?" This trains him to realize that he has the resources to find solutions within himself. Finding those solutions is what builds self-confidence.

As children get older and face major stresses, continue to focus on the gift of becoming a problem solver instead of a complainer. For example, your child has a fight with someone, hates getting up in the morning, has trouble with school or homework, etc., first empathize, and then say, "Let's look for a solution." This attitude helps them (1) remember that you do care and take their pain seriously, and (2) focus on goals, not the pain. Even if it turns out that there is no

342

solution except to live with the problem, you have shown him how comforting it is to communicate honestly with you, which is also a gift.

Sometimes, you have to model solution-oriented behavior first.

◊ EXAMPLE: "When it's bath time, my three older children either don't want to take baths or else they all want to take their baths first. I used to get so angry. Now I tell them, 'I have a solution.' On a bathroom shelf, I have three little pieces of paper on which are written 1, 2 and 3. I let them choose. Whoever gets '1,' takes the bath first. I use the word *solutions* all day long. A few days ago, there was an argument about who was going to play a computer game first. I watched with joy as my oldest son tore a piece of paper into three, wrote numbers on each piece and then held them out in his hand for his younger brothers to choose, just like I do."

The following is an example of this kind of training.

◊ EXAMPLE: "I was in my last month of pregnancy and desperate for rest. I sent my six year old to the park next door to watch her four-year-old sister, Faigi. When she came back two hours later, she told me. 'When Faigi knocked over her canteen and all her apple juice spilled, I told her that I knew she was very disappointed and sad (note how she first validated her little sister's feelings!), but I told her not to worry, that we'd find a solution. I told her that the first solution was to dry her off. The second solution was to go home and get more juice. But if Mommy is sleeping, I told her, then we'd have to find a different solution because we can't wake her up. The next solution would be to ask a neighbor for some juice.'"

This was a six year old talking!

◊ EXAMPLE: "The night before my daughter was scheduled to open a little summer camp for children in the neighborhood, the girl who was going to work with her called to say that she was sick. My daughter looked crestfallen. I asked her what she was going to do, and she replied, 'I'm not quite sure yet. All I know is that I'm going to stay calm by focusing on solutions.'"

◊ EXAMPLE: "I used to have a terrible time getting my children to help. Now, when one says, 'Later,' or, 'But it's not my turn,' I simply say, 'I have a solution. Put the timer on any number. When it rings, take the garbage out (or, do your homework, etc.).'"

Always have your goal in mind, i.e., to get across to your children that when someone is unhappy or has a destructive impulse, the best thing to do is focus on solutions.

Although it is best to start around the age of two or three, you can start at any age. Just be aware that it often takes a few years before this concept becomes deeply ingrained in their consciousness, especially with temperamental children.

This is especially important when you are dealing with teenagers and have many more serious conflicts. If they are insolent, say, "I know you're in pain, but disrespect is forbidden by the Torah. So tell me what's bothering you. Maybe we can come up with a solution."

When the only solution is compassion

Obviously, this doesn't always work. Children face many losses and disappointments for which there are no immediate solutions — except perhaps to share the pain with you. But that, too, is a solution because it brings you closer, even if it doesn't take the problem or the pain away.

> ◊ EXAMPLE: "My daughter is a bit on the chubby side and there is one girl in particular in her class who torments her. It was awful until she began to focus on solutions. She remembered how we reacted to some very abusive neighbors before we moved here, and how we had to pretend that they were trees or rocks and go on with our lives. She said that each time she sees this girl, she looks at it as an opportunity to practice this kind of detachment, and also to pity this girl for being so insensitive and mean."

Another solution is to look at the list of Rav Salanter's Thirteen *Middoth* and to pick out the one they think is most appropriate to work on at this time. Or, they can pick a few traits from the Forty-Eight Ways to Acquire Torah (*Avoth* 6:6).

The important idea to get across is that God brings painful people and events into our lives in order to give us opportunities to grow in *middoth* and understanding.

◊ EXAMPLE: "I have a learning-disabled twelve year old who has a lot of difficulty keeping up with the children in his class. I was taking a walk with him after our Shabbath meal a few days ago when he revealed that he had gotten only a 7 out of 100 on a test. Not only that, but the teacher had left his class records open and everyone saw his mark and laughed at him. I empathized with him about how painful this must have been. I told him that when I think of what he has to go through in school, I sometimes feel like crying. I told him that I'm proud of him for having the courage to go to school each day. It made him feel so good that I was sharing his pain and was proud of him. Then I told him that the pain of an insult atones for our sins [*Madregoth Ha-adam*: *nekudath ha-emeth*, ch. 9]. I told him that the pain is like a scrubber, cleaning him off. He laughed and said, 'Boy, do I feel clean!' It's a way of reminding him that we can always find some spark of Godly joy even in the most painful situations."

Don't assume that children have solutions

Many books on child rearing say very authoritatively, "Do not interfere when children fight. Let them work it out themselves." Let's face it, "working it out" usually means that the oldest or strongest bullies the others. Children don't usually have civilized solutions to problems. Unless we give them some training in polite problem solving, they will not solve their problems politely, humanely or fairly.

Children throw tantrums and use force because they don't know any other way to feel powerful and get what they want. Hitting or punishing them may stop the behavior in the short run, but it does not teach them how to solve problems in the future. And it reinforces in their minds the notion that you are the source of control, rather than helping them realize that they have to develop the self-control and decision-making abilities which will make tantrums unnecessary! Furthermore, you are demonstrating that violence is the way to solve problems. Force is sometimes necessary, but it should be only one of many tools which we teach children.

◊ EXAMPLE: "I have four rambunctious and aggressive boys. If I let them work things out themselves, they could seriously injure each other! I used to either throw my hands up in despair or get violent. But now, when they get wild, I get them to think of solutions. Little by little, they're getting the idea that I will not allow them to get out of control. And they're coming up with their own solutions, like taking turns, putting on the timer, going into in separate rooms or finding alternate sources of fun other than tormenting each other."

◊ EXAMPLE: "Being poor means we're constantly having to find solutions. The children have learned to share a lot, including food and space and possessions. They have learned to budget and think of ways to earn a little pocket money here and there. The girls have to sew their own clothes. When they express envy of richer children, I remind them that there's a solution for envy, i.e., making a list of all we're thankful to Hashem for!"

Focus on the learning experience

If a problem has no concrete solution, focus on the learning experience.

◊ EXAMPLE: "When my daughter burned the cookies, I asked her, 'What did you learn?' And she said, 'To put the timer on and not to rely on my memory.'"

◊ EXAMPLE: "When my son flunked his test, I asked him what learning experience he had gained. He said, 'To go to my tutor instead of looking for excuses not to go.'"

◊ EXAMPLE: "When my husband blew up at my daughter, I went to her room and asked her what the learning experience was. She said, 'I have to watch my mouth!'"

◊ EXAMPLE: "We have very nasty neighbors who have caused us a great deal of misery. The parents yell at my children, stare at them with evil looks and call them names. Their children are no different. They've punctured the tires on my children's bicycles, have spit at my children and done other terrible things. Since we cannot move away, we're trying to use this experience for our growth. They know that I have called the police and the youth authority. A social worker is investigating. In the meantime, my children have learned to say, 'Even if other people have bad *middoth*, we don't have to respond with bad *middoth*.' They can say, 'We're *bnei Melech,* no matter what anyone else thinks we are!' They've learned about wearing the mask of detachment and even having compassion for people like this. It's a difficult situation, but we're trying to use it as a learning experience.''

Solutionizing results in greater self-respect

The ability to make decisions, solve problems and do things one fears to do is what gives people a sense of inner mastery, self-confidence, and self-esteem. This leads to a reduction in their level of rage and anxiety. Your child does not like being out of control. It scares him. He feels better about himself when he's in control. Helping him to learn how to do this is one of the most important gifts that you can give your child.

23 | The Gift of Teaching Children How to Avoid Returning a Hurt with a Hurt

Most children, when they are upset or in pain, think it is perfectly legitimate to hurt whomever they think has caused their pain. Thus, for example, when a mother asks, "Why did you hit your brother/sister?" they are likely to respond:

"She was humming."

"He burped."

"She wouldn't clean up her side of the room."

"He opened my drawer without permission."

"I didn't like the way she looked at me."

In the child's mind, the excuse, "He was bothering me," somehow legitimizes cruelty and revenge. It is the parents' responsibility to teach children how to express their feelings politely when they are in pain. Otherwise, they will grow up to be adults who behave destructively when things don't go their way.

One way to instill the concept of not returning a hurt with a hurt in children's minds is to use stressful events to teach them how to communicate their needs respectfully. When the child is upset (but not overwhelmed), take his hand and say in a very low, soft voice, "Hold my hand, look into my eyes, and tell me exactly what you want."

If you start early enough — and children as young as two years old will respond to this simple approach — you will be giving them the gift of being able to express dissatisfaction without having to sulk or explode angrily. You can also teach your children to share their feelings with each other using this method.

◊ EXAMPLE: "I was making toast for the kids. All I had left was whole wheat bread. So, I toasted a slice and put it on my nine-year-old's plate. He looked at me angrily and yelled, 'You know I hate whole wheat bread! Why did you give me it to me?' My usual reaction would be to slap him or yell at him that's he's an insolent, spoiled brat. But I've been learning that it's up to me to model good manners. So, I pulled up a chair and, holding his hand said, 'Hold my hand, look into my eyes, and tell me kindly exactly what you want and don't want.' He calmed down immediately, and with an embarrassed smile (which told me that he had done *teshuvah* and felt sorry for losing control), said calmly, 'I don't want whole wheat bread. I want white bread.' I calmly told him I'd get some from the store later, but that we had none in the house, so he'd have to eat what was available. Instead of running away from the table and being uspset for hours, he ate his toast and went off to *cheder*. In the afternoon, I held my son's hand, looked into his eyes, and told him that whole wheat bread is a lot healthier, and that he might get fewer stomachaches if he ate it. He really listened and said he'd try!"

Obviously, we cannot always give our children what they want, but at least we can empathize with them and, by so doing, let them know that we take their feelings seriously.

◊ EXAMPLE: "We didn't have money to put the kids in camp or travel during summer vacation. One day, my eleven year old was going nuts from having nothing to do. He started whining, 'We never go anywhere! Everyone else is going to exciting places and I'm stuck here with nothing to do.' I know that he's happiest in a structured environment. I am too! I wanted to help him get some structure in his life, but I knew that it had to come from him or he'd reject my suggestions. I held his hand and empathized. 'I'm *really* sorry you're bored. I'm sorry we don't have the money to go away. Now, let's figure out what we're going to do with the next two weeks.' That calmed him down and then we sat and brainstormed until we came up with some ideas. I can't give him the exciting vacation he wants, but I can help him figure out alternatives."

Of course, no solution works all the time. No matter how constructive we try to be, the reality is that children are going to fight with each other, make messes and be disrespectful at times. Furthermore, not all problems have solutions: some children are going to be bossy and aggressive, others high-strung and insecure, others slow and passive. While there is much parents can do to encourage good *middoth*, there are stages and personality traits that we simply have to put up with.

Staying in control: humor and positiveness keep you calm

Of course, if you're hysterically angry, you won't be able to put this tactic into practice. This is because your usual response is more deeply programmed into your brain, e.g.:

"The messier the house, the crazier I get!"

"The more they fight, the more I hit!"

"The more demanding they are, the more I give up in utter despair!"

This kind of mental programming makes it impossible to stay in control. So, if you're having problems staying in control, it is extremely helpful to program yourself ahead of time by repeating certain paradoxical statements in a very soothing tone of voice to yourself, such as:

"The more the kids fight, the calmer and more solution-oriented I will become."

"The messier the house is, the calmer and more patient I will be."

"The more upset they are, the more empathic and reassuring I will become."

"The more tired I am, the more I will trust in God to help me through the day, seeing it all as a gift."

"The more demanding they are, the more I will think of my infinite Godly value."

"The more the baby cries, the more I will be aware of my inner strengths."

Try this exercise: before going to sleep at night, imagine some irritating situation and say the soothing words to yourself as you fall asleep. You will almost certainly find yourself staying calm as you deal with the next day's problems.

The "love bank"

Think of every endorsement, hug or calm solution-oriented interaction as similar to a bank deposit. If you make a lot of such deposits, you'll have a good-sized balance. Then, when you occasionally make a withdrawal (i.e., scream or smack), it won't ruin the relationship.

> ◊ EXAMPLE: "My oldest son had a fit when he couldn't find an ironed shirt. He was really carrying on about how everything in the house is such a *balagan*. Ordinarily, my response would be, 'The more demands they make, the more out of control I feel.' I could feel myself starting to get hysterical, so I repeated to myself, 'The more out of control I feel, the more softly I will talk.' So I said in a very low, but firm voice, 'You are not allowed to talk to me in an angry tone of voice. Just look in my eyes and tell me precisely what you want, and say it respectfully.' He said that he wanted to have clean, ironed shirts at all times. I told him, 'I agree. That would be nice. But since the baby came, I'm exhausted and things are disorganized. So we have to find a solution without making anyone feel bad.' He said he was sorry and, surprise of surprises, told me he wanted to learn how to iron his own shirts! I'm glad I didn't scream and make a withdrawal from the 'love bank' because my relationship with this child hasn't been so great. Thankfully, it's improving as I stay in control of my voice."

> ◊ EXAMPLE: "My nine year old desperately wanted a new bike. I was getting upset from his constant nagging. It used to be that I'd think, The more he nags, the more I hate him! Instead, I thought, The more upset he is, the more empathy he needs. I held his hand, looked him in the eye and said, 'I know how much you want a bike. I feel bad that you don't have a new one, but we don't have the money right now. I'll write it down on your Wish List.' Before, when I attacked him angrily and told him he was selfish and a pest, he only got angrier. When I empathized with him about not having a bicycle, he realized that I cared about his feelings and stopped nagging me. So, even in a situation where I couldn't give him what he wanted, it was an opportunity to make a deposit in the 'love bank.'"

Like any new skill, you will probably feel awkward using it at first until you have practiced it over and over and over again. Practice is the only way to establish new neural patterns in your brain. And, with children, you have plenty of opportunities to practice a non-shaming method of communication.

> ◊ EXAMPLE: "I asked my teenage son if he had called the dentist to make an appointment, as I'd asked him to do, and he replied angrily, 'Get off my back!' I was so hurt that my first impulse was to slap him across the face. Thankfully, I controlled myself and instead I said,'The Torah forbids you to talk to me that way. Tell me what you want.' He refused to answer. So I realized that I'd better supply the words for him, since he's not used to expressing his needs politely. I said, 'Do you want me to leave this matter up to you?' He nodded. I said, 'So tell me in words that you want this to be your responsibility.' He grudgingly said, 'Mom, I want to handle this by myself.' I praised him for saying the words calmly, without anger. Then I asked, 'And what if you haven't made the appointment by the end of the week? Can I remind you? Tell me what you want.' He said, 'Please leave a note by my bed at the end of the week.' 'Beautiful,' I told him. 'This is how we should be communicating with each other.' Since then our relationship has improved greatly, and I'm beginning to get the hang of this technique."

You may be so used to hitting, screaming or withdrawing from an uncooperative child that you'll think, This isn't me. I can't do it! So, as always, be patient with yourself. Start with very minor events. You will find that once you have demonstrated this non-inflammatory response to their emotional upsets, your entire household will be calmer, and your relationship with your husband will improve, as you both get used to using this technique.

Remember, since the time they are born, children are used to getting what they want by screaming. It's not an easy habit to give up, just as it isn't easy for us to give up our own scream response! So don't expect instant miracles. It's best to start young to teach them to overcome this tendency to use force to get what they want, but if your children are older, you can still teach them how to communicate in a respectful manner.

> ◊ EXAMPLE: "We made a lot of mistakes with our two oldest children, especially by hitting them a lot. Now these are our most difficult ones, and they are still very angry with us and each

other. I see a big difference with the younger children. This morning, I heard my six-year-old son say to his five-year-old brother, 'I love you, but when you whine like that it's hard to be with you.' I was flabbergasted! That was all the proof I needed to know that what I was trying to teach about mutual respect was getting through to them.''

Of course, no method works for every problem. The important thing is to focus on solutions, not condemnations. Trying to solve problems while condemning yourself or your children is like trying to swim with concrete shoes on! Instead, make some deposits in the only bank over which we have some control!

Why does this method work?

The "hold my hand" method works because it involves the following elements:

1. Touch: Touching the child lovingly lets him know that you care. That reassurance takes the edge off his anger. Even the most secure child has moments when he feels insecure and doubts whether we really love them. This is even more true if the child is naturally anxious or has a volatile emotional nature due to Poor Sensory Integration (see Chapter 13 of *Raising Children to Care*). Touch also calms *you* down.

2. Reassurance: When children feel hurt, they often adopt a paranoid position, assuming we are deliberately causing them pain, deliberately not buying or giving them what they want. And the reason they come up with for this refusal? We must not love them! When the child in the first example got whole wheat bread, he assumed that since his mother knows he hates it, she must have done it because she doesn't really love him! That's just the way many kids think. They are basically insecure. They don't know how to give the benefit of the doubt. They don't know how deep our love is. By touching the child and looking in his eyes, the mother reestablished for him that she cares. Reassurance also reminds *you* not to be paranoid and think that they are out to hurt you deliberately. It reminds you that children often feel helpless and fearful and cover these feelings with anger.

3. Regret: When a child is angry, he's lost control. If you lose

control and get angry back, he is so focused on his own hurt feelings which are aroused by your anger that he forgets what he did to arouse your anger! But when he looks into your eyes, he realizes that he did something wrong. That makes it more difficult for him to continue hurting you. Unless you have done severe damage to your relationship in the past with verbal or physical abuse, your loving eye contact will usually cause him to do *teshuvah* without you having to say a word of reproach. When he looks in your eyes, he will see the love and hurt of a caring parent, which makes him feel bad for having hurt you. In contrast, if you are angry, he looks at you and sees hate, and that makes him want to defend himself against you by being even angrier! Eye contact also reminds *you* of your love for him. It helps defuse your anger if you don't take his anger personally.

4. Logic: By asking the child to state what he wants, he is forced to think logically in order to formulate his needs. This automatically calms him down by reducing his emotionalism. It also reminds *you* to stay logical.

5. Concern: By asking him to tell you what he wants, you let him know that you take his feelings seriously. One of the most painful aspects of childhood is that adults often do not do this. They ignore, invalidate or ridicule children's pains, not realizing that life is as painful and disappointing to a child and as difficult for him to bear at times as it is for us. It is important for them to learn to share their feelings, but in a respectful manner. Even if you cannot give him what he wants, there is satisfaction in knowing that his opinion is important enough to you for you to want to listen. If you consistently show concern for his needs, he will lend importance to yours.

With this powerful formula, a parent is teaching the child the fundamentals of good communication, which will last him for the rest of his life:

1. To let him know you care by touching him,

2. To reassure him that you have done nothing to hurt him on purpose,

3. To let him know that his angry response is unacceptable by getting him to state his message without anger,

4. To teach him how to express angry feelings without hurting others, and

5. To let him know that you care enough to listen and to take his

feelings seriously.

Try this method with adults as well. People report great success using this technique with their spouses and other relatives.

> ◊ EXAMPLE: "After spending a day using this 'hold my hand' tactic and having great success, I reached that hectic bedtime hour and I started to feel overwhelmed. I screamed at my husband, 'Don't you see I need help? How can you be so selfish and insensitive!' He came over and said softly, 'Look into my eyes and tell me respectfully exactly what you want.' I immediately felt bad that I had lost control and said I was sorry. Then I calmly told him to bathe one child and help another with his homework for fifteen minutes. I'm so used to getting hysterical in order to get him to listen to me, that it's hard to remember that I have other alternatives. Slowly but surely, I'm learning to re-program my mind and muscles."

Parents don't have to be brilliant, talented or creative to be good parents. They just have to get their messages across in a caring manner. The "hold my hand" technique is one of the best ways to do so. Every stressful situation is thus an opportunity to model self-discipline. And seeing parents model self-discipline is one of the most important gifts you can give a child.

24 | The Gift of the Hyperactive Child

One of the most difficult challenges a parent can face is having a hyperactive child in the house. The parents feel shame, guilt, anger and fear and must face the anger of neighbors and teachers as well as store owners, clerks and complete strangers.

> ◊ EXAMPLE: "By the end of Shabbos I'd had it! Ben didn't stop jabbering, touching, moving, pinching, pushing, giggling, grabbing, jumping, provoking and arguing with me about everything for twelve hours straight! Whenever he saw his younger sister, he would stick his foot out to trip her or in other ways make her life miserable. Then she would start howling and I'd have to deal with her. He'd provoke the older ones until they hit him, and then he'd start howling. I put him in his room a zillion times, but he ran out and I had to keep chasing him back in again. I couldn't go to the bathroom or turn my back to prepare a meal without fearing that he would do something destructive. I tried to be nice to him, but it was like he was in another world. I couldn't reach him. I tried to find things for him to do, but he was so bored! I read to him, but he squirmed so much that I stopped. I tried to stay calm, but when he sat on the baby, all my pent up frustration exploded. I lost control. I hit him so hard that I hurt my hand. I called him every name I could think of and told him he was stupid and that I wished he were dead. Afterwards, I felt so miserable. I know he needs love, but how can I love a child who is so obnoxious and defiant? I'm allergic to him — I just see him and get hostile. What will be with him? Where will he fit in in the Torah world? How will he ever feel good about himself? Will he abuse others?"

Like approximately 10 percent of all children (80 percent of them boys) Ben suffers from hyperactivity, a disorder characterized by impulsivity, distractability, restlessness, lack of organization and irritability. Ben also has another problem which is often associated with hyperactivity, called Attention Deficit Disorder (ADD). ADD compounds the problem by making it difficult to concentrate on external stimuli or remember anything his parents or teachers tell him. When the house is quiet and he can find a corner to himself, Ben can sit and play happily with construction tools for an hour. But construction is an internally motivated task, requiring no interaction with the external world. Unfortunately, in a small home with an ever-increasing number of siblings, Ben can rarely find a quiet corner!

When bored, especially during unstructured time periods such as Shabbath and holidays, Ben becomes provocative, chaotic and violent. In school, the effort of having to concentrate on external cues makes him irritable and anxious, and he comes home charged with hostility. He seems to be in a world of his own, and resists his mother's attempts to hug and caress him. When told to do something, he is quickly distracted by whatever happens to catch his attention at the moment and he completely forgets about his mission.

Hostility breaks their spirit and makes them more defiant

When faced with a child like this, most parents think that they are at fault for not being strict enough, and that the solution is simple: hit and scream more. However, this makes the hyperactive child even more hostile and defiant, which, in turn, makes the parents angrier and more determined to "break" him. By the time these children are ten or eleven, they may be suicidal, running away from home, stealing or engaging in other destructive acts.

By the age of six or seven, most such children have received so much abuse in the form of slaps, punishments and negative labels, that their sense of self-worth is around zero. At school, these are the children most likely to be hit by teachers. Their constant demands for attention, their unpredictable outbursts and provocations, and their irrational paranoia and hostility hardly make for a happy family or school life!

Left untreated, the odds are that this child will grow up into an impulsive adult who has difficulty following through on anything he starts, who has a violent temper which may manifest in outbursts of physical and verbal rage, who feels picked on and victimized by everyone around him, and leads a life characterized by self-loathing, underachievement and failure. Approximately 40 percent will be involved in criminal activity.

These are often the "hated kids," the ones parents give up on. As one mother said about such a child:

> ◊ EXAMPLE: "I love him and hate him at the same time. In my heart, I've given up on having a relationship with him. He's too difficult. I never feel like I can reach him. He's ruined my self-esteem. I used to be calm and happy. Now I'm hitting and screaming all the time, which makes me hate myself. And he's ruined my marriage because my husband constantly accuses me of not being strict enough and is constantly angry about my inability to control him or keep everything together. It's ruined my relationship with my other children, because I'm so nervous all the time. My nerves are shot. It's like being in a war zone, never knowing when the next bomb will drop."

A family problem

Hyperactivity has a strong hereditary tendency. About 25 percent of hyperactive children have hyperactive parents. The father of Ben (the child in the first example) was also hyperactive as a child. Now he is a hot-tempered, impulsive, hyper-critical and high-strung adult. When he is irritated, he lashes out, hitting, yelling and generally terrifying everyone in the vicinity. Ben is learning from him that violence is the path to peace.

Ben's mother is high-strung and suffers from anxiety. The fact that she tends to crumble under pressure and has difficulty getting organized indicates a problem. Nervous and unconfident, her negative feelings about herself are exacerbated by her inability to control her children's destructive behavior and by her husband's incessant criticism.

The atmosphere is ripe for child and wife abuse.

Hyperactive children are often hit by parents and teachers alike. They spend countless hours standing mutely in classroom corners, moodily walking the school corridors or glumly warming the bench in the principal's office. They have tantrums when they don't get their way, laugh at inappropriate times and are often rejected by peers for being weird, overly loud and uncooperative.

Hyperactive boys usually hide their feelings of inferiority by developing a tough, insensitive exterior. Untreated, they usually become explosive and abusive. Girls, on the other hand, often become hyper-sensitive, self-abusive and depressed.

It's not just lack of willpower, it is a physiological defect

Handicaps which can be seen, like blindness or paralysis, are easier to accept because no one can deny that they exist and they are no one's fault. But hyperactivity is subtle and does not manifest itself consistently. Parents will often say, "The kid's just wild. He's just stubborn and lazy. He can play quietly by himself for hours when he's in the right mood, so there can't be anything really wrong." Or, the father may blame his wife, saying, "It's all her fault. She's not tough enough." This attitude can ruin the marriage as well as the mother's relationship with the child.

Thus, hyperactivity may seem like an imaginary ailment with no real basis in reality. But it certainly is real. And it can make a child's life — and an adult's life — torture.

Years ago, experts believed that hyperactivity was something children grew out of. But that opinion is changing. Drs. Gabrielle Weiss and Lily Hechtman, of the Montreal Children's Hospital, found that more than half those diagnosed as hyperactive children are still struggling with the problem as adults.

Most experts also assumed that hyperactive children were the products of poor parenting. But recent research, using PET scans, has found that hyperactive adults have damage in two regions of the brain which are used when paying attention and sitting still! Brain activity in the pre-motor cortex and the superior pre-frontal regions was significantly lower than in normal people, as measured by rates of glucose metabolism, the brain's source of energy (source: Alan J. Zametkin, M.D., *The New England Journal of Medicine*, November 1990).

Brain damage can also occur during birth, when even momentary oxygen deprivation or other traumas can harm those areas of the brain that control concentration and coordination.

Hyperactive adults can achieve a suprisingly high level of success if they live in loving environments, and if they are taught to control and direct their high-level, restless energy. As adults, hyperactive people do best in careers which do not demand sitting still for long periods of time, but instead allow for short interpersonal interactions and the constructive release of their physical impulses (e.g., medical technician, salesman, reporter, chef, etc.). However, most hyperactive adults grow up convinced that they are hopeless failures. Constant rejection convinces them that they cannot love or be loved, hence the high possibility for abuse.

What's wrong?

Another source of problems is in the Reticular Activating System (RAS), which is like an internal strainer in the back of the brain. In the hyperactive child, the RAS does not function properly. Either it lets in too much stimuli (e.g., sights, sounds, thoughts and sensations), flooding the brain and making the person feel overwhelmed and unable to focus on the task at hand, or, the RAS shuts down and allows too little stimulation to enter the brain, making the child feel painfully bored and desperate for stimulation, which he obtains by picking a fight, fidgeting in his chair or touching things in a mindless, random manner. When the RAS is not functioning properly, the child feels threatened and withdraws into a dream-like state or explodes angrily in an attempt to lessen his feeling of being threatened.

> ◊ EXAMPLE: "I've been ultra-sensitive since I was a child. I get overstimulated so easily. Noise, commotion, demands, people talking loudly — it all drives me crazy, especially when I haven't gotten enough sleep. I explode before I even know what I'm doing! When I'm interacting with one child or one demand at a time, I'm fine. But when I have to deal with a lot of children or numerous demands, I feel like I'm under attack."

For hyperactive adults, relationships are usually marked by mistrust and frequent explosions. If they do not understand their problem, they remain at the mercy of their impulses. With their low frustration tolerance, they can't wait in line at the bank or wait for dinner to be ready or take time to get a child to cooperate peacefully without getting aggravated or enraged. They feel chaotic, frantic and disorganized, and usually blame those around them for their nervousness. They may be fine in a structured situation, such as at work, but at home, with all the unpredictable tensions and emotional demands, they are left feeling more chaotic and paranoid.

Those with hyperactivity know something is wrong with them, but they don't know what. Psychologists rarely diagnose the problem for what it is, and suggest that the person is depressed or high-strung. A neurologist can diagnose this condition. Once diagnosed, a person can be put on a diet which is rich in calcium and other essential vitamins and minerals and eliminate junk food (especially caffeine, sugar and food coloring). He can learn relaxation techniques that utilize the breath to calm his nerves. And he can be especially determined to calm his thoughts with "Torah tools," such as giving people the benefit of the doubt to avoid anger and paranoia and focusing on the good in himself, his life and people.

Medication can help

For many years, I opposed giving medication to hyperactive children, partly because of the danger of negative side-effects from the amphetamines and the negative self-image which can be attached to taking them (e.g., "I must be sick/crazy if I have to take pills!"). I counseled parents to use chiropractic, homeopathy, sugar-free diets, acupuncture, dance and physical therapy — anything but medication! But all too often, the years passed and these children fell further and further behind in school, causing their self-image to deteriorate. Their social skills failed to develop, because other children don't want to associate with children who are so impulsive, volatile and untrustworthy. In other words, the psychological side-effects of *not* taking medication (if it is truly necessary) can be far more devastating.

In contrast, I have seen incredible improvement with the use of

Ritalin. If the child is suffering from true hyperactivity, this medication will elicit positive changes within a few days. Teachers will report that the child is more cooperative and attentive. Parents see that the child is less antsy and nervous. The child himself will report that he feels more relaxed and will ask — even beg — for his pill. Given a choice between a low-dosage pill, with its possible negative side effects, and spending one's formative years thinking of oneself as a dummy and a weirdo, most children and parents should consider trying medication for a week or two, on a trial basis, to see if it has an effect.

However, medication cannot undo the negative effects of having a family in which there has been a great deal of physical and verbal abuse. Medication will not get parents to sit down each night with the child and give him a soothing massage for five minutes before he goes to sleep. Medication will not automatically create a home atmosphere which is calm, soothing, structured and protective, or make the parents more self-disciplined. Medication will not overcome the addiction to criticism or violence, or give the person the will to use the disciplines necessary to overcome paranoia. Overcoming these addictions takes hard work.

Don't get mad; get disciplined

Hyperactivity is a very real disorder and it must be taken seriously. Pretending that it doesn't exist or that it will disappear by itself is irresponsible. The following are some suggestions that will help:

* Get medical confirmation: A neurologist can determine whether or not one suffers from hyperactivity. With a diagnosis in your hands, you'll know it's not all in your imagination. You can stop blaming and guilt-tripping.

* Check for allergies: Most hyperactive children have allergies, particularly to milk, sugar, wheat and food coloring.

* Have a supervised exercise program: Studies have shown that when a person engages in coordinated physical activity, brain activity becomes more coordinated! (See *Sensory Integration and Your Child*.) Daily school breaks, with children running wild, do not provide such movement. Children need organized activities involving coordinated, right-left movement to calm the brain. Swimming

is an excellent coordinating activity.

One reason why hyperactive people are so aggressive is that they tend to be paranoid, viewing people as threatening and deliberately trying to hurt them. They also view their own inner environment as threatening and chaotic. Research has shown that self-defense classes help hyperactive children feel less hostile and more confident about their ability to deal with external threat. As a result, they no longer perceive others as hostile. While many people might imagine that such classes would make people more aggressive, the truth is that they actually reduce aggression, increase self-esteem and improve interpersonal relationships.

* Get counseling: Family therapy with a specially trained therapist who understands hyperactivity can help you learn how to build a nurturing environment which is loving yet disciplined. One of the goals of counseling is to learn not to blame others for one's own unhappiness and destructive behavior, but rather to focus on positive solutions which will create a stable atmosphere of consistent trust and love, which helps everyone to calm down.

Unfortunately, parents, especially fathers, are often resistant to getting help, because they fear the social stigma and the implication that they can't handle something. They will often say, "Nothing's wrong with me and nothing's wrong with any of my kids! They just need a good whipping and everything will be fine. If something's wrong, I can deal with it myself. I don't need anybody."

In such situations, mothers will simply have to take the initiative and get the help they need. If the mother refuses to take the responsibility, the school should do so.

* Take responsiblity for your behavior: Take responsibility for your own *middoth*. Yes, it is especially difficult to be civilized if you are hyperactive or have a hyperactive family member. However, if you or someone close to you has this disorder, it means it is a Divine gift meant for your benefit. It will force you to work on your *middoth*. If you explode, so will your children. "It's either discipline or death."

◊ EXAMPLE: "I've learned that if I fall apart, everyone else does, too. The home atmosphere revolves around me. It's an incredible responsibility, especially for someone like me who always welcomed any excuse to explode, binge or get depressed. Now I *have* to keep everything together and myself under control. I have no choice. If I have an outburst or give up insisting on everyone having good manners, making beds, helping with the housework, etc., it turns into a madhouse again. As long as I stay calm, everyone calms down pretty quickly."

* Join (or create) a support group: Living with hyperactivity isn't easy. No matter how much you do to lessen the severity of the symptoms, no matter how much medication or therapy you might have, you (and/or a family member) do have a handicap which will never disappear. You need people you can talk to who won't put you down — because they're going through the same thing! They know how heroic you must be just to cope on a daily basis.

* Be realistic: If you or any of your children are hyperactive, you do have a handicap. This must be faced and taken into consideration when making decisions. Unfortunately, it often takes years to face that there really is a problem. After all, no one wants to think of himself or a family member as handicapped. See a *rav* if you have a hyperactive husband or child, because of the likelihood of abuse. Ask the *rav* what you can do to lessen tension in the home and create an atmosphere of love and joy, which is necessary for emotional health.

* Become super-structured: Parents and teachers must use behavior modification and positive reinforcement to keep the atmosphere safe for the hyperactive child. The more structure, the greater the feeling of safety. Have set times to awaken, eat and play. Have rules about almost everything: brushing teeth, cleaning up, where to put things, what behaviors are and are not allowed, etc. However, this must be done without compulsive rigidity or the devastating physical and verbal abuse which goes on in most families. The mother in the opening example, for instance, realized that she could not expect to spend Shabbath at home with all her children and remain calm. She had to make arrangements ahead of time for her hyperactive son to have at least a half-hour with a tutor and at least one hour with a baby sitter. The other children also had to make plans to be out of the house part of the day.

* Become super-disciplined: Adults must model self-control if they want their children to do so. If one parent is screaming and hitting a great deal, the children will automatically mimic that behavior. Self-discipline is the key to self-respect. So, if you are

hyperactive, focus on disciplining yourself. If your child has a problem as well, you'll have to be super-disciplined.

* Get help at home: If you are disorganized, see if your budget permits the hiring of a maid. It is also helpful for the mother to consult with a woman who is an expert in home management in order to learn organizational skills. Finding a place for everything and making sure that things are put in their place is a lifelong struggle for hyperactive people, but organization is necessary for a safe, tranquil atmosphere. Take the extra time to help your children be organized as well. Each should have his own shelves and drawers. Make set times each week to go through the drawers and organize them. Don't expect it to come naturally. You'll have to put forth the extra effort on a continual basis.

* Focus on solutions, not condemnations: Condemning oneself for having this handicap is as futile as condemning oneself for being nearsighted or diabetic. Our task is to take responsibility for being self-disciplined and create a safe, nurturing, loving, positive atmosphere despite the inner tension and turmoil.

* Learn relaxation skills: Deep breathing and calming visualizations can be very helpful. Use the PEP (Positive Experiential Programming) exercise mentioned in *EMETT* to prepare yourself ahead of time for what you know will be tense situations. Whenever you lose control, replay the scene in your mind and, this time, work out some constructive solution.

> ◊ EXAMPLE: "My husband is a very hot-tempered, hyperactive type. Since, like many men, he won't go to anyone for help, my *rav* has been helping me figure out solutions. The main thing he told me to do is to endorse him when he gets angry by saying, 'I know you're angry, but I'm glad that you're not getting as enraged as you used to.' He told me to say the words even if I didn't think it was true, and that this would make him feel that he was making progress, which would help him gain control. At first, I thought I couldn't do it, but then I used the PEP (Positive Experiential Programming technique mentioned in *EMETT*). I imagined him getting angry and imagined myself reacting calmly. This preparatory work paid off. Yesterday, he lashed into me for being late, and instead of screaming back, I responded as I had programmed myself, and said firmly but calmly, 'I didn't

do this on purpose to hurt you. I'm very sorry. I will really try not to do it again. And I want to thank you for not being as angry as you were the last time I was late. Thank you for controlling yourself.'"

◊ EXAMPLE: "I use the PEP a lot with my kids because it teaches them to get control of their aggressive impulses and not fall apart when things don't go their way. I have them imagine difficult situations and then imagine themselves responding in a Torah manner, without hatred or vengefulness, either forgiving, giving the benefit of the doubt or being assertive without being hostile. It has helped us all greatly. We're all in better control now."

* Plan fun times: The added stress of a hyperactive nervous system means that life is more difficult. Therefore, make sure you schedule enjoyable activities into your life. Exercise is essential. Family picnics and outings can offset the tense atmosphere at home. Going out alone with friends can restore your own peace of mind.

* Forgive: Forgive the hyperactive person. Keep telling yourself, "S/he's doing/loving the best s/he can with the tools she has right now." Forgive yourself. You're trying to function under extremely difficult circumstances.

* Rebuke with love in your heart: When you need to rebuke a child or spouse, do it with love in your heart. If you can't, be quiet.

◊ EXAMPLE: "When my five-year- old son wrote on my best table-cloth with a permanent black marker, I wanted to throttle him. But I thought, How will it help if I beat him up? What is my goal? My goal is to teach him self-discipline. I can't teach him to control himself by being out of control. But then I thought of asking him if he wanted to pay for the damage by doing extra jobs around the house. He agreed. I had passed a test! Until the next time..."

* Be flexible: At school and at home, adults need to adjust the routine to accommodate this disorder. For example, hyperactive children cannot be expected to sit for a long school day. They simply go berserk from the effort of having to sit still. They must have organized (not *hefker*, wild recess) physical activities and opportunities to create with their hands, for this is extremely calming and also builds their self-esteem.

* See it as a gift: Love means acceptance of God's will. Love brings joy. One way you can bring more joy into your life is to be thankful that you or your family member has this handicap. It was given to you for your *tikkun*, so that you would be forced to practice unconditional love, patience, acceptance, cheerfulness and determination. There's nothing like a hyperactive child to force you to perfect your *middoth*.

Despite therapy and personal growth, hyperactive people remain high-strung, nervous and super-sensitive to some degree. Inevitably, there will be moments when everything falls apart, when you (the hyperactive person) just can't manage to stay in control, when your impulses overwhelm you, when the lack of sleep, the noise and the commotion leave you feeling helpless and hopeless. When this happens, don't despair. Continue to work on yourself so that you are less reactive, but realize that your basic sensitivity won't change drastically. So accept yourself and the people around you. Model self-discipline. That's what *middoth* work is all about. But don't fool yourself into thinking that there is any magic cure or formula to make you or the people around you different.

It takes tremendous effort, on an ongoing basis, to keep the atmosphere calm and structured. You won't always achieve that goal. When you make a mistake, learn from it and move on. This is one gift which forces you, in a very obvious way, to constantly grow in understanding, patience, sensitivity and self-control.

25 | The Gift of Giving the Benefit of the Doubt

A newspaper clipping quoted someone by the name of Martin Mull who said, "Having a family is like having a bowling alley installed in your brain." I don't know who Martin Mull is, but I like his sense of humor — and you certainly need one when raising children, along with tons of patience, courage, self-discipline, objectivity, wisdom and love. The problem is, we tend to lose it all whenever we get angry. To give the benefit of the doubt is the first — and sometimes the only — step needed to control our destructive anger when we are hurt.

A Jew has a Torah obligation to judge every person favorably (*Pirkei Avoth* 1:6), unless the person is a publicly acknowledged evildoer. To judge favorably means to tell yourself, "This person did not hurt me deliberately. He is really doing the best he can with the tools he has at this moment." Since few children fall into the category of publicly acknowledged evildoers, they provide us with continual opportunities to practice this important mitzvah.

A parent can read hundreds of books on child rearing and fail to put any of the suggestions into practice if he has the wrong attitude. A destructive attitude is: My children are my enemy. They're demanding little manipulative tyrants who constantly hurt me intentionally. See what that little brat just did? He purposely spilled it (or lost it, jumped on it, hit it). They deliberately deprive me of sleep, deliberately disrupt my peace and quiet, drain me of all my money, and deliberately act uncivilized in order to destroy my joy and sanity. So I must constantly be on the defensive to keep them from manipulating, exploiting and taking advantage of me. I must not give an inch or they'll take a mile. I must not give one ounce of affection or attention more than they absolutely need, otherwise they'll manipulate me even more.

A more constructive attitude is: When my kids hurt me, they are not doing it deliberately. They are doing the best they can with the tools they have at this particular moment. They're in pain, or bored, scared, insecure, lacking in self-control, unwise, impulsive, hungry, tired, coming down with something — and that's why they behave the way they do. It's my job to teach them good character traits: to help them develop patience, self-control and respect for others. And the only way I can do that is to model these traits myself.

Don't think you're doing people any great favor when you give the benefit of the doubt. You're doing it for yourself, for *your* mental health, as you will see.

Throw out the word davka!

The number one way to keep yourself calm is to stop using the word — or even thinking the thought, *davka!* If you would throw this word out of your mind, you would immediately reduce 99 percent of your anger. What would be left would be justifiable indignation over deliberate sins or pain over unavoidable difficulties that have no solution. In addition, you would find yourself with a clear head, and able to be creative and rational in solving the problems that can be solved.

But taking away the *davka!* is not easy. After all, you just told the kids two seconds ago not to jump on the couch and there they are, jumping on the couch! You told them to finish everything on their plates, and they've hardly touched the food you put so much effort into preparing. You told them not to tease each other, call names, kick, pinch or poke each other, and then you turn your back for one second...You told them not to make noise because Abba's sleeping, and they're banging pots and pans on the floor. You just told them that it drives you crazy when they get into fights over absolutely idiotic matters and there they are, at it again. Come on now, let's face it, isn't it *davka?* Why take away the *davka!* when it is obvious that they're doing these things deliberately?

Why take away the *davka?* Because it is a word which enrages. It keeps you from thinking clearly. You take away the *davka!*, not for them but for yourself, because it's the only way to preserve your relationship with your children.

Until the age of six or seven, most children haven't developed the ability to control their impulses. Most of what they do is not with pre-planned malice, but the result of impulsive, spontaneous passion.

Without the davka! you respond compassionately and constructively

When a child fails to cooperate, if you think it's deliberate, you'll feel enraged. And when you're enraged, you'll overreact and do or say something which will ruin the relationship and probably destroy the child's spirit. A lot of adults still go around thinking that they're unlovable, selfish, lazy, incompetent idiots because that's what they heard from their enraged parents.If you don't want the next generation to grow up with the same problems, then even if you are 100 percent sure that they're doing something to defy you or hurt you, still take away the *davka*!

◊ EXAMPLE: "I was hospitalized for two weeks because of problems with my pregnancy. When I came back home, my fourteen month old was very hostile, even biting me at times. Feeling hurt, I hit her really hard. I felt, She's a bad girl! What she's doing is bad, therefore I must hit her to educate her. But my EMETT leader told me, 'Take away the judgment from the child. The child isn't bad. She is in pain. She's scared that you're going to go away again. Perhaps she even had some unconscious feeling that you were rejecting her. She's not doing this deliberately to hurt you; she simply has no other way of expressing her terror. She needs reassurance that you still love her. She is also trying to defend herself against getting close to you and then having to go through the pain of being abandoned again. If you think *davka!*, you lose control, and instead of reassuring the child, you make her even more insecure, which makes her even angrier.' I never thought of anger as a way of hiding pain. But as soon as I saw the truth in what she was saying, I calmed down, and as I did, so did the child."

◊ EXAMPLE: "My fourteen-year-old son was having a lot of problems in school. I kept thinking, *Davka!*, this kid just wants to make trouble to get attention. I was very hostile toward him and he withdrew. His marks only fell even further. It wasn't until toward the end of the year that I found out from another mother that his teacher was really abusive. I could have kicked myself for not taking him more seriously."

Change your attitude and calm down

When you train yourself to give your child the benefit of the doubt immediately and automatically, you will be able to respond to him more sanely. You will be able to say no firmly and without hostility, take swift, assertive action when necessary or calmly explain your feelings to the child whenever appropriate. You will be able to discipline the child fairly, without excessive harshness or callous indifference to his needs and feelings.

Children experience adult anxiety as rejection, and respond by increasing the very behavior which the adults are anxious about!

◊ EXAMPLE: "My three-year-old son started hitting people who came to visit. I was very upset and my husband and mother-in-law were aghast. They demanded that I slap him every time he slapped someone. The more upset I got, the more he did it. I started putting him in his room and locking the door, but he would wreck the room and scream. When I would take him out, he would be even more defiant. A counselor helped me to change my attitude. She advised me to think, He is not doing this deliberately to hurt anyone. He probably gets a lot of pleasure out of feeling powerful enough to be able to get the adults around him so upset. As soon as I stopped thinking *davka!*, I calmed down. Being calm helped me think more creatively. Whenever he hit someone, I gave him a stick and told him to hit a toy drum. I got an egg timer and said, 'Hit the drum until the sand goes down.' For a few days, he gave me a few half-hearted smacks, testing to see my reaction. I just gave him the drum in a very neutral manner. And I told my husband and in-laws to stop giving him the pleasure of their horrified faces. He hasn't hit anyone since."

◊ EXAMPLE: "Before leaving home, I asked my twelve year old to clean up the kitchen. When I came back, it was even messier than before. At first, I thought, Boy, when I catch her, I'm really going to give it to her! Then I remembered to drop the *davka!* Mentally,

I gave her the benefit of the doubt and assumed that she didn't forget on purpose. Maybe something had distracted her. The minute I dropped the *davka*!, I calmed down. She had left a note saying she had gone to a friend's house. It turned out that she had gone to help this girl study for a final exam they were having the next day. The girl had been ill and had missed a good deal of the material. When she came home, she said she was sorry she hadn't done the dishes and went into the kitchen to do them. I told her that I had given her the benefit of the doubt and that had kept me calm. If I had attacked her in my usual furious way, there would have been in a major blow-up and she probably would have stormed out of the room. Then I would have punished her and she would have been even more defiant. Instead, I modeled for her the mitzvah of giving the benefit of the doubt. In fact yesterday, when I realized that I had forgotten to buy a school book she had asked me to get for her, she said, 'That's okay, Mom, I gave you the benefit of the doubt.'"

◊ EXAMPLE: "My twelve year old would drive her thirteen-year-old brother crazy with teasing and name calling, and then he'd hit her back. I'd get all enraged and sometimes slap my daughter. Finally, I dropped the *davka!* That's when I got smart. I told her that every time one called the other a name, the victim would get a quarter. Well, that was the end of the name calling!"

Scream something useful

When you feel enraged and want to scream, at least scream something useful! For example, scream, "I am telling myself that you did not do this on purpose to enrage me! I am assuming that you forgot the rules!" "I'm sure you're doing the best you can with the tools you have right now, but that's not good enough. So I'm going to give you some new tools!" You might also stand there fuming and say, "I want you to know that I am controlling my own harmful impulses right now! I could hit and scream right now, but I'm not. I am showing you what self-control is, even though it is very difficult for me right now. And I expect the same from you!"

Such phrases remind you to stay in control and help your children to do the same. When you can control yourself, you can think more creatively and clearly.

It's okay to "lie"

When you start off a sentence with "I know you didn't mean to hurt me," you might not be sincere at first. You might actually be filled with doubts. You must have the humility to realize that you really do not know what is in the head or the heart of your child. Assume that he is:

(1) Coming down with an illness.

(2) Tired.

(3) Hungry.

(4) In pain.

(5) Bored and restless. Boredom is physically painful for many children. They begin to feel extremely uncomfortable and act impulsively.

(6) Suffering from hyperactivity or ADD.

Any of these situations make it harder to control oneself. Children who have ADD or hyperactivity have enormous difficulty controlling their impulses. Even if they want to be good, their impulses seem to have a life of their own. They also tend to be paranoid, assuming that others are deliberately hurting them! They desperately need to have calming activities which provide organized (not random!) stimulation to the brain, reassurance, safe limits and structure. What they don't need is more chaos and confusion in their minds, or confirmation of their belief that they are unwanted and unloved.

You can add your own mitigating circumstances to explain your child's behavior, in order to calm yourself down. *Remember, the goal is not to become overly merciful, passive or withdrawn, but to be able to act with love in your heart so that you can help your child become more responsible, considerate and self-disciplined.*

Yes, it may be true that the child did something in a deliberate attempt to hurt you! Children certainly can be vindictive. But when you judge favorably, you bring love back into the picture. You let the child know that you care. Instead of attacking you, as he will if you get angry, he is likely to feel ashamed for having betrayed your trust and is less likely to repeat the behavior. Giving the benefit of the doubt may be a lie at first, but you both win in the end. It's a deposit in the "love bank."

An added bonus

When you take away the *davka!* with your children, you will find that the entire atmosphere in the home improves, including your relationship with your spouse and everyone else you encounter.

> ◊ EXAMPLE: "It was one of those late Friday nights and we were all exhausted and starving. When I served dinner, my husband made a negative comment about one of the dishes. I was about to attack him for his lack of manners and pettiness, when I said, 'I'm giving you the benefit of the doubt and assuming that you did not do this to hurt me deliberately. I'm sure you were just tired.' The next day, I did something very innocently which he took offense at, but he smiled and said, 'I'm assuming you did not do this deliberately.' I find that our children are also giving us the benefit of the doubt!"

> ◊ EXAMPLE: "My life has changed since I've been diligently practicing giving my children the benefit of the doubt. I'm calmer when I drive, when I'm at work, when I'm with relatives and when I have to deal with clerks. All my life I've walked around with a chip on my shoulder, sure that other people were deliberately being inconsiderate and incompetent. Now I tell myself, 'They're really doing the best they can with the tools they have at this time.' Let me tell you, you can deal a lot better with reality when you're accepting it than when you're fighting it."

> ◊ EXAMPLE: "I got stuck in traffic and was late picking up my son. I felt terrible and was sure he would be furious. But when I got there, he said, 'Don't worry, Mom, I kept telling myself to give you the benefit of the doubt.' I was glowing inwardly to see that my hard work had paid off!"

If only we could experience the *kedushah* which comes into the world when we give the benefit of the doubt, we would certainly perform this mitzvah far more often. Furthermore the way we act toward others is the way God acts toward us (*Sotah* 1:4). When we *dan le'chaf zechuth* (*Avoth* 1:6), we will be able to stay calm when irritated. It is helpful to remind ourselves to think, Thank you for giving me the opportunity to give you the benefit of the doubt and, in so doing, to overcome my worst impulses and grow spiritually. What a wonderful gift!

PART VI

Assertiveness

26 | The Gift of Overcoming Compulsive Approval Seeking

*It is related that one of the pietists asked another,
"Do you possess equanimity?" "In what respect?"
asked the latter. The former replied, "Are praise
and blame the same to you?" "No," the latter
answered. "Then you have not reached (the right
standard)." Persevere therefore, and you may
possibly attain this, the highest degree of the pious,
the most desirable of moral qualities.*
— DUTIES OF THE HEART, vol. II, p. 45

We all grow up wanting others' approval, at least to some extent, and expecting that our sense of happiness, self-respect, security, importance and worth will come from others. This erroneous belief leads some people to use others to make themselves feel superior and powerful. These people are nasty, bad-tempered bullies and tyrants. Others become overly accommodating, fearful people-pleasers. If you fall into the latter category, you are the kind of person who:

Is so easily intimidated or worried about hurting people that you let them step all over you.

Lies a lot to avoid confrontations and to make people like you.

Freezes in fear around people in positions of authority or power, even if there is no real threat to you.

Is shattered by the merest hint of disapproval.

Feels constantly taken advantage of, exploited, ridiculed, gyped, conned and rejected by just about everyone.

Never knows when to be strict and when to be flexible.

Would rather forget about abuse than confront it.

Are so good-hearted that you submit to outrageous demands from family members in order to avoid being rejected.

Still hopes you'll get a certain person to love you even after five, ten or twenty years of ill treatment.

If you are a compulsive people-pleaser and approval seeker, you need to work on the *middah* of *gevurah*, which includes the courage to be honest, to stand up for your rights and to hold fast to your principles in the face of external pressure or internal fears. You must learn not to think of yourself as humble, when, in reality, you are being cowardly and lazy.

You need to do this for three main reasons:

(1) For your own self-respect. If you are a compulsive people-pleaser, you will do just about anything to make people like you, including lying to impress them and allowing yourself to be abused. The result is that you are probably depressed and feel like a *shmatteh*, a nothing and a nobody. You probably think about death as a relief from the pain of living.

You don't realize that you're a "fancy liar," and that you lie to impress people so that they will value you more or in order to avoid facing rejection. For example, you may exaggerate the details in retelling a story, flatter people you don't like, and buy things you don't want or need in order to please others, and tell people "Oh, it's nothing" when they've hurt you, instead of telling them how badly you feel. You excuse yourself by saying that you are being nice, that you don't want to rock the boat, that you must tell white lies in order not to hurt people's feelings, or in order to save your marriage, your job or your relationships. This is sometimes true. But you lie even when it is not necessary, because you value approval more than you do truth. As a result, people don't trust you and don't know where they stand with you. Nor do you trust yourself or know where you stand, either.

(2) For the sake of your relationships. If you don't tell people when you are hurt, your relationship with them will either get cold and die, or you will explode angrily in a moment of weakness. If you let people abuse you, their abuse will increase as time goes on and you will transgress by harboring hatred, vengeance and grudge bearing in your heart (*Vayikra* 19:17). So, doing what is best for

yourself really is what will ultimately be best for your marrriage or other close relationships!

> ◊ EXAMPLE: "A relative used to drop in and sit in my kitchen telling me what to do: how to cut my carrots, what to put in my soup, how to organize the drawers, etc. I'm sure she meant well, but she was still undermining my whole sense of competency. I took it from her in silence, proud of my self-discipline. But I eventually came to despise her. One day, she made an innocent suggestion and I exploded at her with all my suppressed rage after many years of resenting her. I thought I was humble. In reality, I was cowardly. There's so much pain on both sides that now I feel I can't break down the wall of hostility between us."

(3) For the sake of the world. There is a great deal of violence, exploitation and cruelty in the world — even in hospitals, schools, places of work and the home. If you don't fight it, you encourage it.

If you are an unassertive person, it will be difficult for you to stand up for yourself. You feel too fragile, vulnerable and frightened. But you can learn to oppose abuse when doing so will not cause you grave harm. There is no mitzvah in becoming someone's doormat and allowing yourself to be abused.

Co-dependency

Co-dependency is defined as the compulsion to change, rescue, protect or care for another in order to win his love and approval to the point where one person takes upon himself excessive responsibility for the other's welfare, and denies his own needs and feelings in the process. Co-dependents lose touch with their own feelings, often complaining, "I don't know what I feel or what I want. I just know that I'm dependent on my husband for my sense of identity and security. Therefore, I automatically do whatever he wants in blind submission." They do not really feel worthy of being loved, and usually choose partners who are incapable of loving them to any degree. Co-dependents often suffer from a variety of problems, especially eating disorders, depression and severe anxiety.

Because they see themselves as being so nice and helpful, co-dependents often overlook the fact that they are being abused. Because they need others to provide them with a sense of self-importance and worth, they constantly monitor everyone's behavior, anxiously measuring the amount of approval and attention they are receiving. They become desperate and distraught if they feel unloved, or not loved to the degree they want. They look at every person they meet and think, *If you treat me as if I have no value, then, indeed, I am truly worthless.*

Co-dependent people are almost always in pain over the failure of others to love them enough, and feel anxious and insecure. They are also worried about being abandoned by those they turn to. Afraid of being labeled as selfish, lazy or unspiritual, they bend over backwards to please and prove themselves worthy, but always feel "I'm never doing enough."

> ◊ EXAMPLE: "As a young married woman, I desperately felt I needed meaningful emotional relationships and intellectual stimulation. But my mother-in-law insisted that I should stay home, cook fancy meals and scrub everything spotless. As a result of my giving in to what she wanted, I got very depressed. It took years to get up the courage to be myself. I now teach part-time, and my mental and physical health have improved greatly since I've started doing things that nourish my *neshamah*."

> ◊ EXAMPLE: "For three years I studied in a very cold, impersonal *yeshivah*, which was totally wrong for the kind of person I am. But because it had such a prestigious name, I didn't want to lose status by leaving. I was afraid my parents would be crushed and look down on me. The result was that my love for learning diminished and I fell into a deep depression. It was only after recognizing my deepest needs that I found the courage to change to a warmer atmosphere, where I am now much happier. It's true that my parents were upset. My father even refused to talk to me for a while. But I stuck to my guns and when he saw that my love of Torah was stronger than ever, he realized that I had done the best thing."

Object constancy

The main source of co-dependency is lack of object constancy. This term refers to a developmental stage which takes place between the ages of two and three, when a child develops an inner sense of trust in the world. However, if there is no consistently loving mother figure, or substitute caretaker in a child's life (e.g., the mother is hysterical, sick, depressed, sick, bad-tempered, etc.), he never feels secure. He can never relax with people because he is sure he is going to be met with cold indifference or rejection whenever he reaches out. Even if people are nice, he is sure they will abandon him eventually. He is quickly shattered and enraged because his memories of abandonment are reawakened by the most minor rebuffs.

> ◊ EXAMPLE: "It was *erev chag* and I was overwhelmed. At one point, my husband innocently asked, 'Why didn't you take my suit to the cleaners?' Well, I fell apart. I was crushed. I felt like a totally incompetent idiot, totally rejected, a total failure. I am so insecure that I just can't believe that he loves me and doesn't mean to hurt me when he makes these statements. I come from a very rejecting background, so I never developed the object constancy that would make me feel secure about a man's ability to love me. I have to keep reminding myself that he does love me and that he can just tell me these innocent statements are not indications of rejection."

Why can't you be honest?

Unfortunately, the term *assertive* is often confused with being pushy, aggressive and impolite. In reality, healthy assertiveness means expressing honesty with love. Why is honesty so difficult? The main reason is fear.

(1) Fear of being condemned. You fear: What if the person thinks I'm stupid, pushy, petty, crazy, cruel, unkind, unspiritual, selfish, incompetent, lazy, materialistic, immature? That would be horrible because I'd be rejected and unloved; I am then of no value.

> ◊ EXAMPLE: "My husband, a rabbi, has an open-door policy for visitors. His students come at eleven or twelve o'clock at night to talk to me about their problems. I'm so exhausted from it that I'm short-tempered with the children and I'm sick a lot. But it would be awful for my husband to think I'm selfish, or for his students to think I'm mean. So I never say no. Better that I should be in pain than that they should think ill of me.

◊ EXAMPLE: "I'm afraid to tell my wife that she hurts me with her comments because I'm afraid that she'll think I'm weak. So I either remain silent or explode."

◊ EXAMPLE: "I'm not the type of person who can sit and learn all day. I want to go into business and learn part-time. But I'm afraid my wife and everyone else will lose respect for me. I'm miserable. Each day is torture. But I couldn't bear the public shame if I were to stop learning full-time."

◊ EXAMPLE: "I did a major editing job for an acquaintance. Then, when I asked for a very reasonable fee, he said that he assumed I'd do this for him as a favor. I couldn't bear for him to think I was petty and materialistic, so I said, 'Oh, it's okay,' even though I need the money desperately."

◊ EXAMPLE: "I'm afraid to ask my doctor about a certain health problem for fear he'll think I'm a hypochondriac."

(2) Fear of people's vengeful anger. You don't speak up because you fear: What if this person tries to hurt me back, talks behind my back or refuses to have anything to do with me? That would be horrible! This fear is probably true if the person really is a mean, vicious and punitive type. If you might lose your job as a result of speaking up, you will have to decide whether to accept the abuse in silence or leave. You must carefully consider whether the emotional damage is too severe to warrant staying in a job or a relationship. In most cases, however, the fear that you will be hurt and that you are helpless to defend yourself is not justified, and is linked to excessively severe punishments in early childhood.

◊ EXAMPLE: "I want to tell my father to stop criticizing my husband. But I'm afraid that if I speak up, he'll stop sending us money. So it's a choice between which situation is worse."

◊ EXAMPLE: "I want to confront the principal of my son's school concerning the amount of hitting that the teachers do, but I'm afraid they'll take it out on my son. I must be willing to switch schools if necessary after I take this step."

(3) Fear of seeing the truth. You fear: If I find out how the other person really feels, that will be horrible. I won't be able to stand it. I can't face how alone I am, how insignificant I am to this person.

◊ EXAMPLE: "I know we need to see a marriage counselor. But I'm afraid to have all our secrets out in the open. I'm afraid that I'll see how really bad the situation is."

◊ EXAMPLE: "I know something is wrong with my son. He doesn't do well in school and is very moody and hostile. But I'm afraid to take him for testing. What if he really has a learning disability? People will look down on us. It will be hard to marry him off. Better not to find out."

(4) Fear of being invalidated, ridiculed or stonewalled:

◊ EXAMPLE: "When the repairman asked for an outrageous sum just for coming to look at the refrigerator which he then said he couldn't fix, I just paid him. I knew it was useless to even try to get through to him! I knew he'd just yell at me and I can't stand that."

◊ EXAMPLE: "I wanted to tell my husband to stop being so critical, but I knew he'd just laugh and tell me that I'm overly emotional, overly sensitive and stupid."

(5) Fear of hurting others' feelings. Because co-dependents feel so vulnerable and afraid of rejection, they assume others feel the same. They say, "If I speak honestly, I'll destroy the other person!"

◊ EXAMPLE: "A neighbor came to the door and asked for a contribution to a cause I don't believe in. But I gave so I wouldn't hurt her feelings. Then I lied to my husband about how much I gave, so he wouldn't be angry at me."

◊ EXAMPLE: "My sister wants to spend her summer vacation with my husband and me. That means having her here for seven weeks in our tiny two-room apartment with our two small children. How can I say no and insult her? Maybe she'll never speak to me again."

◊ EXAMPLE: "A relative calls me all the time and speaks *lashon ha-ra* about her husband. I want to tell her to stop, but I'm afraid of hurting her."

6. Fear of becoming cold and cruel.

◊ EXAMPLE: "I come from an abusive home. When I got married I decided that I would do anything to please in order not to hurt anyone like I was hurt. I didn't realize this would be a problem until I became a mother. I couldn't discipline my children because each time I tried to be strict, I felt like I was just like my parents, who either hit me or treated me like some burdensome pest.''

Some of these fears are legitimate. People do sometimes lose jobs and relationships by being honest, or invite insult and attack by standing up for themselves. However, co-dependent, unassertive people have an exaggerated fear of the harm their words might cause. They take too much responsibility for other people's happiness, and too little for their own.

The witch-wimp trap

Unassertive people alternate between two extremes: the explosive release phase (witch) and the self-suppressive control phase (wimp). When unassertive people are in their self-suppressive control phase, they show a deceptively nice, calm exterior. But beneath that surface is deep hurt and a feeling of being helpless to do anything about it. However, the more suppressive they are, the more compelling the release phase becomes and the more violent it is when it finally comes. If they don't express this violence outwardly, they turn their anger inward and get depressed or indulge in self-abusive behavior, such as overeating or chronic fatigue. (The concept of these two alternate phases is described in *Facing Shame*, by Merle Fossum and Marilyn Mason.)

Any compulsion is a sign of deep-rooted fears. By understanding your fears, you can become less abusive to yourself as well as to others.

The female connection

Unassertive co-dependent types see themselves as vulnerable and incompetent, and see others as powerful and competent. Women are more prone to feel this way than men, for the concept of femininity has traditionally been associated with being compliant, passive, stupid, indecisive, weak, sensitive, subordinate, obedient, hidden, vulnerable, emotional and in need of protection. Thus, being assertive is especially difficult for women who fear that they'll be rejected for being pushy, mean and masculine. If they want to be treated with respect, they must learn to bear the pain of not having everyone's approval. Otherwise, they will never be able to teach those around them to be considerate of their feelings.

> ◊ EXAMPLE: "I've been very weak since my operation and I can't do much. But my husband says that I'm just being lazy and that I should be back on my feet by now, inviting guests and taking care of the house no matter how I feel. Even though I know I haven't recuperated, I keep thinking that he's right, that his needs come first and that I can't trust my feelings."

Women are also more people-oriented than men, meaning that closeness is their most essential need. Many women are willing, for the sake of that closeness, to allow themselves to be violated, manipulated, and even abused rather than be left alone. However, if the abuse is not stopped early in the marriage, it will escalate and she will end up terrorized and alone anyway, either literally or figuratively.

> ◊ EXAMPLE: "I've loaned money numerous times to a relative who, despite my kindness, treats me in a very nasty manner and never returns the loans. I didn't want to alienate her by saying no when she kept asking for money. I was afraid that if she cut me out of her life, I would feel grief-stricken as she is very important to me. Somehow I got the courage to be honest. I told her that on my limited pension, I could not give her more money. As expected, she accused me of being selfish and stingy. She never called again. It was very painful, but I handled it. In fact, I realized that all along, I was deluding myself into believing that she cared about me. When that illusion died I was surprised to find that I felt a freedom and dignity I hadn't felt before."

People who are dependent on others financially are naturally terrified to be honest about their feelings if, by doing so, they might jeopardize their financial security. Many women are trapped in this situation.

Finally, women are also taught that because men's egos are so fragile, they must act stupid, weak and inferior in order to make men feel smarter, stronger and more capable. This attitude of "I'll feel bad to make you feel good" has a devastating effect on women's self-esteem and their ability to cope with life.

Giving is not the same as giving in

> The greatest service of God lies in the purification of motive.
> — STRIVE FOR TRUTH! vol. I, p. 99

Unassertive people often confuse giving with giving in. These two behaviors may look the same from the outside, but the difference in motivation is essential. Giving is motivated by love for others; giving in is motivated by fear of them. Giving is other-oriented. Giving in provides an illusion of self-protection, but often ends up encouraging abuse.

Giving is the most Divine of all human traits. We must often overrule our initial feeling of resentment when people ask us for something, and do the *chesed* anyway if we know that our resentment is rooted in selfishness or laziness. We know we've done the right thing if, afterwards, we feel pleasure at having done an act of *chesed*. It's the opposite when we give in to something. Afterwards, we feel victimized, defeated, used and humiliated.

It is not always easy to know when to give and when not to:

◊ EXAMPLE: "I hate going to my in-laws for the holidays. However, my husband asked me to please go, once a year, for his sake. I was in a dilemma until I asked myself two questions: What would be best for our marriage? And is there any danger? I had to admit that there was no danger, only discomfort, and that it would be best to go. I decided to do the *chesed* for him, not from fear but love. He was so grateful. I don't feel I gave in. I gave."

◊ EXAMPLE: "My husband got a very good job offer in another state. However, I felt that there would be a real danger to our spiritual health if we moved to a place with so few *frum* families. He isn't as strong about religion as I am, so I felt I had to refuse. Even though he was very upset at first, I kept saying that I would rather be poor than have our children exposed to non-*frum* values."

Giving in, on the other hand, arises from fear, not love.

◊ EXAMPLE: "I didn't mind driving my teenage son to school if he woke up late on occasion. But it got so that he dawdled around until he 'suddenly' realized he had to be in school in a few minutes and then demanded that I take him. I was afraid to say no for fear that he would get enraged and be moody. One night, I put my foot down and told him that I would not take him to school anymore. I was afraid that he would explode, but I had in mind my goal of helping him to be more responsible. I finally realized that by indulging him, he was turning into a tyrant. Would he also expect his future wife to jump when he snapped his fingers and bully her if she didn't? That thought gave me the courage to be firm. I was motivated by love for him, not hatred. He left for school late the next day, but I told him I would not take him. The day after, he was on time."

When giving in is done out of fear of being rejected, both sides suffer. The receiver is corrupted by his power to manipulate others, and the giver is corrupted by his powerlessness and feelings of resentment. Giving in out of fear of disapproval is no different than giving in to blackmail. Emotional blackmailers are people who threaten others with loss of love unless they get what they want. In fact, their so-called love and friendship are phony and worthless. It is impossible to have a healthy relationship with emotional blackmailers because such people have no love to give.

When you stand up for yourself in a Torah manner, then those who love you will love you even more. Those who reject you because you are standing up for your right to be treated with respect never loved you in the first place! So you haven't lost anything.

If you are undecided as to whether or not to be assertive, test your motivation by asking yourself: Am I being assertive out of anger, hatred, a desire for vengeance or a desire for honor or power? Or am I being assertive out of true love for Torah, myself and the people around me? When you have healthy goals in mind, you will have little trouble being assertive when necessary.

Assertiveness: honesty rooted in love

Assertiveness is very different from hateful aggression. Assertiveness should always be motivated by love — for God, others and yourself. When you're being assertive, you're protecting yourself and your principles. It is a way of saying "I count. I have value." You are not out for vain ego victories; you are simply maintaining your essential dignity as a human being. You are protecting your *tzelem Elokim* when you fight for worthwhile ideals, values and goals.

In contrast, aggressive people fight because they need to feel dominant and superior. They gain a sense of self-importance by controlling, crushing and humiliating the people around them. They are destructive rather than constructive.

If people accuse you of being aggressive when you are merely standing up for your right to be treated with respect, that is their way of causing you to feel one-down so that they can continue to control you. Keep your emotional distance from these types, if not your physical distance as well.

So, the first step in becoming an assertive person is to become aware of your goals and your right to protect your physical and mental health. If you have love in your heart, you will act correctly.

Goal: To show love for others.

> ◊ EXAMPLE: "I was constantly yelling and hitting my kids for every little thing. For jumping on the couch, making messes, leaving their things around, walking on my newly washed floor, bad manners, not finishing their food, etc. I hated myself and them, too! I thought I was being a good disciplinarian, but I was simply out of control. Finally, I made a firm decision to either talk politely or to keep my mouth shut! I have a long way to go, but little by little I'm getting control of myself."

Goal: To protect your mental health.

> ◊ EXAMPLE: "I had three extremely aggressive, obnoxiously insolent children in my classroom who were driving me crazy and ruining things for the rest of the class. I kept telling the principal that they needed private tutoring, but he said there was no budget. I was ready to quit teaching, which I love, until I finally had the courage to tell him, 'It's either the kids or me.' Well, he found two grandmothers who were able to come in and tutor them on a volunteer basis, and things quieted down considerably. I now realize that setting firm limits is a sign of love. When I do the things I fear to do, I feel more self-respecting."

Goal: To protect the rights of others.

> ◊ EXAMPLE: "The contractor who put in our new kitchen took three times as long as he promised, charged five times as much as his original quote, and did such shoddy work that the entire job had to be redone. I didn't want to go through the emotional and financial distress of a court case, but I felt I had to do so in order to protect others from him."

Goal: To show love for the principles of Torah.

> ◊ EXAMPLE: "When my niece came to Israel for a two-week visit, she was dressed in immodest clothes. At first, I was afraid to tell her that I wanted her to dress more modestly because I thought she might never come back or that she'd think I was a religious fanatic, and be turned off forever to Orthodox Judaism. But for the sake of Torah, I knew I had to have the courage to tell her that in the Torah world, we emphasize what is eternal, which is the *neshamah*, and not the body, and that this is why we dress modestly. I then asked her if she'd like one of my daughter's skirts. I told myself that the outcome would be up to Hashem; if she disliked me, that was His will, and if she respected me more, that would be His will, too. I guess my explanation helped, because she agreed to wear a skirt and even showed interest in learning about Jewish law."

Goal: To show love of self.

> ◊ EXAMPLE: "We had violent neighbors who were extremely nasty to my husband and me, and who were cruel to my children. They also beat their own children mercilessly. For a while, I tried to just be nice and block them out of my mind. But they were so damaging that I finally realized that action was necessary. We had to move for the sake of our mental and physical health. Before leaving, I also made sure to call in the proper authorities to deal with the child abuse."

Goal: To create a joyful home atmosphere.

> ◊ EXAMPLE: "I have a weak back and am also rather disorganized. I wanted a maid once a week, but I was afraid my husband and neighbors would think I'm lazy, spoiled and incompetent. So I continued doing everything myself, even though my back always hurt and I was abrupt with the kids. Finally, I got my priorities

straight: a joyful atmosphere is more important than pretending I'm Superwoman, which I'm not."

Goal: To have a healthy marriage.

◊ EXAMPLE: "For years I didn't go for marital counseling because I was too ashamed to admit I needed help. To me, a person who goes to a therapist is crazy, stupid and weak. Finally, I realized I was preoccupied with my pride and my public image, while my marriage was going down the drain."

Goal: to have healthy relationships.

◊ EXAMPLE: "My husband made a major purchase without consulting me. I was terribly hurt. It took me days to work my anger down and get up the courage to ask him in a respectful manner why he hadn't consulted me beforehand. Thankfully, we were able to work things out and he apologized. If I hadn't spoken up, I think I would have been burning with resentment for a long time."

Goal: To protect oneself or others from abuse.

◊ EXAMPLE: "I'd often walk out of stores and offices feeling gypped, but powerless to do anything about it except grumble to myself. I hate feeling that someone's taken advantage of me. But if I focus on the next guy who walks in and might be abused, that gives me the courage to speak up and demand proper service. I now threaten to call the Better Business Bureau or go to court if I feel a situation can be corrected."

◊ EXAMPLE: "My daughter's teacher was very critical, constantly putting the girls down and making them miserable. I finally got up the courage to speak to her about her methods and the importance of a teacher loving her students. At first, she was very resistant, but I remained positive. I gave her books on the technique of positive reinforcement and even bought special stars and stickers for her to hand out as prizes. As the year went on, she really improved."

If your motivation is love, you are bound to be successful. Even if you don't get what you want, you can be proud of trying and secure in the knowledge that God must not have wanted you to get that particular demand satisfied. Effort is up to us; success is in God's hands. If your actions are "for the sake of heaven" (*Avoth* 2:17), you will have the courage to be honest.

When to fight? When to go with the flow?

It is often very difficult to know when and how much you should push for change and when you should just forgive and let go. In almost any situation, you can usually find someone who says, "Forget it. Let go. Make peace." And someone else who tells you, "Get tough!" If you have difficulty knowing when to fight and when to let go, use the "health and safety" test. Fight when there is a threat, either physical or spiritual, to yourself or to others.

> ◊ EXAMPLE: "I didn't take my son for testing for several years, even though I was sure that he had some kind of learning disability. My husband kept saying nothing was wrong, and I was too fearful of contradicting him. As a result, this child is twelve years old now, and can barely read. I kept silent because I thought my goal was *shalom bayith*. But I sacrificed my child, who needed help. I finally put my child first. I saw that when I was really determined to do what was right, my husband did not oppose me."

> ◊ EXAMPLE: "I was determined to make a modest wedding and not take out huge loans which would have put us in great debt and caused tremendous emotional strain. I bore the discomfort of certain relatives' disapproval to stand up for a principle. I hope we'll serve as a model for others who don't want to spend ridiculous sums for these celebrations."

> ◊ EXAMPLE: "My wife was always critical of me and I of her. I knew that I would have to either speak up or lose the marriage. So one day, I firmly said, 'Criticism is *traif.* Either we focus on the positive in each other or we will destroy each other.' It took two years to fully wean ourselves away from this evil habit of fault-finding but we did it. And the result is that we now have a more peaceful atmosphere in our home and feel truly loving toward each other."

When you are motivated by Torah values, you will have the courage to speak up when necessary and the self-discipline to be silent when asserting yourself would do no good.

27 | The Gift of Facing Disapproval with Dignity

My God, guard my tongue from evil and my lips from speaking deceitfully. Let my soul be silent to those who curse me; let my soul be as dust to all.
— AMIDAH

No matter how much we try to be kindhearted, gracious and accommodating, someone, somewhere, will find fault with us and let us know, in words or by gestures, that our way of thinking, dressing, behaving and living is not to their liking. And no matter how much we try to have love in our hearts for others, there will be people who will so annoy, betray or hurt us that it will be difficult to be "as dust" and avoid responding with hatred, resentment or vengeance. Nothing shows our nobility of spirit, or our lack of it, as does our response to disapproval.

Disapproval is painful for three reasons. First, it causes us to question our worth and to feel defective and isolated. Second, it makes us want to hurt the other person back. Third, it makes us feel rejected and isolated, especially if the one doing the disapproving is someone whose love and respect we want. In response to disapproval, we may want to act in a way which says, "Oh, no, I'm not the defective, worthless one. You are!" Or we may try frantically to get that person's approval, losing our dignity and identity in the process.

The fear of disapproval goes back to childhood, when we were shamed by others and experienced how easily people could devalue us, shattering our spirits in an instant. We saw how wonderful we felt when we were praised.

The result of these experiences is that we came to believe our value was determined by people's eyes and words, and that we had the power to determine their worth as well. We felt we were at the mercy of people's judgments; people gave us worth or made us feel worthless. We, too, thought we made people big or made them small. If subject to chronic rejection, we may have made ourselves feel even smaller, hoping, If they see how vulnerable and helpless I am, perhaps they won't hurt me any more.

Breaking these habits is not easy. Spiritual maturity means having an internalized awareness of our Godly essence which is independent of other people's judgments. We don't give value and we don't take it away; God does. We delude ourselves into thinking that we make people big or small. In fact, only God does. Until we reach this level of awareness, anyone, at any time, can come along and make us feel stupid, bad, humiliated, alone and insignificant with a gesture or a word. It's not the disapproval which hurts so much, but the implication that we are somehow very defective and unworthy of love and respect, from God or man. And that feeling, in turn, is the source of mankind's most destructive behavior.

We cannot deal positively with disapproval until we no longer feel essentially unworthy and no longer want to make others feel that way. Being able to be "as dust" and, at the same time, feel worthwhile requires a strong attachment to God. This is why disapproval is such a difficult, yet essential, test. It provides us with a tremendous opportunity for spiritual growth, because only a sense of our Godly essence will help us retain our dignity in the face of insult and indignity.

Insulters and insultees

Insensitive, aggressive people feel no remorse or anxiety over the fact that they scowl, grimace, scream, insult and in other ways put people down, because they have a desperate need to make themselves feel big by making others feel small. More emotionally sensitive types tend to agree with the fault finders of the world and torture themselves with self-criticism. These two types have a mutual attraction to each other and often marry, to the dismay of both. If you are the victim, you probably identify with the following example.

◊ EXAMPLE: "I often feel that I'm made out of glass, not only because it is so hard for me to hide how I feel from others, but also it seems that I lack some sort of protective shell that most people are born with. Insults shoot straight into my heart and into my spirit. If someone gives me a mean look, it feels like an actual physical assault. Even if I only hear someone else being insulted, it hurts me deeply. I don't know how to bear people's crass insensitivity."

If you are this type, you can overcome the feeling of victimization as well as the anger which often accompanies insult. This requires four steps.

(1) Stop putting yourself down. You are probably being criticized to the extent that you torment yourself with criticism. Recognize that your Godly essence is not something anyone can take away. When you stop feeling that you deserve to be abused for not being perfect, fault finders will eventually stop criticizing you or will find some other victim.

(2) Have compassion. Focus on the spiritual growth you make by not returning a hurt with a hurt or by taking action in a constructive manner.

(3) Remove yourself to a higher level. See yourself mentally moving upward when someone attacks you verbally, so that the words pass right by without your ego being in the way to stop it. The Book of *Mishlei* speaks of a number of types of people from whom we should distance ourselves: e.g., the *peti*, the *letz*, the *evil*, the *chasar lev*, the *kesil* and the *rasha*. We must not be blind to their actions or pretend that they do not exist. Instead, we are told, "Answer not a fool according to his folly, lest you also become like him" (*Mishlei* 26:4). Do not try to get their love, approval, respect, appreciation or understanding, or you will end up feeling like a total failure because it is unlikely you will get them to change their attitude and you will come to see yourself from their viewpoint.

(4) Stop your own condemnations. As much as you feel victimized, you probably silently condemn people all the time for being insensitive, low level and rude. Notice people's behavior, but with an attitude of compassion and forgiveness. When you stop sending out negative messages, there is a good chance that they will stop coming back to you.

Motivate from love

Responding constructively demands that you be motivated by love, not fear. If you are motivated by fear and hate, you will:

Hurt others back in order to give yourself an illusion of having power and control over them.

Be enraged, venting emotions impulsively and recklessly to give yourself an illusion that you are doing something.

Argue for the sake of arguing, to feel self-important and superior by making others feel unimportant and inferior.

Being motivated by love will help you:

Fight injustice and evil effectively, constructively.

Protect your own or others' mental or physical health in a digni-fied manner.

Express your God-given talents and fulfill your emotional and spiritual needs in a Torah fashion, no matter what others think.

Be "as dust" and accept with love what cannot be changed.

◊ EXAMPLE: "I didn't want to make a speech at the parent-teachers conference about the plight of the teachers who are not paid on time. I'm a shy and anxious person. But I overcame my timidity by focusing on my goal of correcting an injustice which was being done to the teachers. That gave me the courage to speak up."

◊ EXAMPLE: "I was cared for by a very nasty-tempered doctor following an operation. When I returned home, I just wanted to forget the whole experience. Plus, I was afraid that if I made a fuss and ever had to be in that hospital again, that doctor might harm me in some way. But a friend said that I was obligated to save others from being hurt by this man. She was right. I couldn't live with myself knowing that he was causing pain to other patients. I wrote a letter and kept calling the hospital director until he assured me that he would take action."

◊ EXAMPLE: "Our upstairs neighbors make a lot of noise at all times of the night and day. I wrote the father notes. No response. I tried to talk to him. He slammed the door in my face. Never before have I felt like punching someone, but when I see this man, this is how I feel. He doesn't care about anyone but himself. I can stew in resentment, I can move to a different apartment, or I can accept that God has put this person into my life to see if I can overcome my hostile impulses and remain civilized in the face of such crassness. What I have in my heart is my choice."

◊ EXAMPLE: "We live on a very limited budget and I was hoping to use the little money we had in our savings account to send the children to camp. Then my husband withdrew it to buy an expensive set of books. My first response was to get hysterical and scream angrily. Then I thought about my goal: Do I want to hurt him or get the kids to camp? If I attacked him, he would turn stubborn. I had to approach him without hostility. That meant doing some work on myself to give him the benefit of the doubt and give up trying to control him with anger. So I simply told him, 'I know that you realize how much the kids need to go to camp. Please help me find a solution.' He didn't answer right away, and I again had to surrender my desire to control through hostility. But later on, he came back and said he would try to find some way to earn extra money. If I had yelled, he would have felt rejected and we would be fighting with each other instead of solving the problem."

When we have the right goals in mind, we don't always get our way, but at least we preserve our self-respect.

Know your rights

If you want to have healthy relationships, then there must be *mutual* respect for each others rights. Many people, especially women, do not think of themselves as having rights. But they do!

* The right to be loved and respected.
* The right to express your feelings and be taken seriously.
* The right to be with people and be involved in activities which nourish you emotionally, intellectually and spiritually.
* The right to privacy and boundaries.
* The right to feel secure in your own home.
* The right to protect yourself and your family members from verbal and physical abuse.
* The right to make mistakes and not feel that you are a horrible sinner or that you've committed major crimes.

Abusive people will not respect your rights. You will have to fight for them.

Two responses to disapproval: stoic acceptance or active protest

You may suffer whether you speak up or remain silent. You have to make the choice of which discomfort you want to bear.

◊ EXAMPLE: "My son told me that the son of a neighbor was bullying the younger children on the school bus. I was afraid to do anything and I was trembling before I called the boy's mother. If I spoke up, I could risk the lifelong enmity of a neighbor. If I didn't, then not only my son, but a lot of other little children would be hurt. In my EMETT class I learned that doing the things I fear to do is the way to develop self-confidence. It is also the only way to stop violence. So I decided to risk this woman's wrath to protect my son and the other children, even if I suffer for it."

◊ EXAMPLE: "My wife always tends to be late. If I go by myself to social events or appointments, she gets angry. If I wait around, I feel irresponsible and hurt the people waiting for me to come. I finally decided that if I needed to get someplace on time, I would say in a calm, noncondemnatory voice, 'I am leaving at such and such a time. If you are not ready, I'll go by myself.' She was angry the first few times I did this, but I remained calm and noncondemnmatory. Now she accepts that this is the best solution to the problem. I could never have done this years ago, when I was so paralyzed by fear of her disapproval."

◊ EXAMPLE: "I was about to leave a bar mitzvah because the music was so loud that I was physically pained by it. I couldn't even talk to anyone over the noise. If I stayed, I'd have to bear the pain. If I left, I would upset the hostess. I finally decided to tell her, if only to overcome my tendency to hide my feelings. I was surprised when she agreed with me. So together we told the band leader to lower the volume. Everyone I spoke with afterward said that they, too, hated loud bands but didn't speak up for fear of hurting someone's feelings. They chose to suffer in silence."

◊ EXAMPLE: "I hired a maid who worked slowly and inefficiently. I had to decide whether to keep her and be frustrated or fire her and bear the pain of her anger and the pain of having to hurt someone."

◊ EXAMPLE: "I can stay quiet and not remind my boss again about the overtime he owes me, in which case I will lose money, or I can request *din Torah* and risk being fired."

◊ EXAMPLE: "I can hire a lawyer and fight this injustice, with all the aggravation that it will cause, or I can let go and lose my rightful share of my inheritance, but have peace."

When you are in a "whatever you choose, you lose" situation, do what is best for your mental and physical health.

Reframing disapproval

Reframing refers to the process by which you learn to give a positive meaning to an event which you previously viewed in a negative light. This entire book is an attempt to teach you to reframe painful events so that instead of feeling bitter and discouraged, you feel ennobled and uplifted.

There are two possible responses to insult: stoic silence or assertive defense of your right to be treated with dignity. Whichever path you choose, it is essential to do some inner spiritual work so that you don't end up feeling like a resentful, passive victim or act in a hostile manner which you will regret later.

Reframe the event by focusing on the spiritual rewards:

"If I pass over my feelings (let go and don't hold a grudge) my sins will be passed over (*Rosh Hashanah* 17a). So I bless this person for doing me this great favor."

"Disapproval is humbling. When I'm treated like dirt, it reminds me that I really am nothing. Only my Godly soul has lasting significance."

"I am like a gigantic jigsaw puzzle. This person condemns me because he sees only one tiny part. Only God has the whole picture."

"When my hot-tempered boss gets that frightening look on his face, I use the opportunity to practice compassion. He's like a frightened little boy, making himself feel big by making everyone feel small. He must be very lonely and insecure."

"Before I respond to this relative, I focus on the tremendous

Divine reward I get from giving the benefit of the doubt and dropping the *davka*! I am convinced that she is really loving the best she can with the tools she has. She simply has very few tools. After I've purified my heart in this manner, then I'm ready to talk."

"I endorse myself for the mitzvah of not speaking up when I know that what I have to say will not be accepted" (*Mishlei* 9:8, *Yevamoth* 65b).

"Let this be a *kapparah* for any pain I caused anyone else."

"I imagine that the angels are dancing and cheering me on for not speaking in a hostile manner" (*Shabbath* 88b).

"I thank God for giving me the opportunity to overcome my compulsion to get through to everyone and have everyone's approval."

◊ EXAMPLE: "I had written a number of checks for the amount my ex-husband was supposed to deposit in my account. When the checks bounced, I realized that he had never deposited the money. I was burning with fury until I called my EMETT leader. She said that my hatred tied me to him emotionally. I could get rid of it by imagining my ex-husband going up in a rocket ship, and my resentment going up with him. She said, 'Since in this case there is nothing you can do to force your husband to give you the money, let go and let God handle it. Keep putting him in the rocket.' That calmed me down. I let go of wanting to force life to be my way. I accepted God's will and began to think of other ways to cover those checks. My job is to remain distant by dropping my condemnations."

◊ EXAMPLE: "As a child, I was very unpopular and felt like the class *nebbechel*. Since then, I've worked hard to become a competent wife and mother. Yesterday I was out shopping. My kids weren't looking the greatest and two of them were tearing around the store, when I suddenly bumped into an old schoolmate, one of the popular ones. She was beautifully dressed and her children were so well behaved. Instantly, all the intense pain of my childhood came flooding back. I felt like a total failure and was in the dumps until I called a friend and asked her to help me reframe the situation. When she asked me what the gift was, the words came out that the rejection and loneliness in my childhood was God's way of making me a sensitive person. I might have been an arrogant snob otherwise. The pain of others' disapproval reminds me not to look down on anyone, but to love people non-judgmentally and have compassion for myself. As soon as I saw the gift, my mood lifted."

Tactics for confronting disapproval

If you think that speaking up might help, the following techniques may be effective.

1. Have a non-condemnatory tone of voice.

Normal, decent people will care about your feelings and try to accommodate you. Bad-tempered, insulting people not only will not care about your feelings, they will become even nastier if you speak up. If speaking assertively is futile or dangerous, you may have to seek legal help, get police protection or try another third party.

Most people grow up thinking that you must respond to anger with anger. Unless there is real danger, stay calm. To do this, you can avoid thinking thoughts such as: If he sees me as a failure, then I am a failure. Or, if he doesn't respect me, it means I don't deserve respect. Or, I can't stand not being loved. Or, I'm going to show him that he's a big nothing!

People, places and things don't give you value. You have infinite Godly worth no matter what others think of you. Getting angry or depressed won't make people love you, and will only push them further away. You won't get angry or depressed if you don't tie your sense of self-esteem to others' judgments.

> ◊ EXAMPLE: "When my son tasted something I made, he said he didn't like it. At first, I was furious. When I thought about why, I realized that I connect food with love — i.e., if he doesn't love my food, he doesn't love me! Well, I quickly threw that belief into my mental garbage bin and responded in a calm voice. I told him, 'If you don't like what I've made, tell me in a respectful voice that you would like something different.'"

To assume the right tone of voice, imagine that a guest walked into your home with non-kosher food. How would you tell the person that you do not allow this food in your home? Think of the firm, no-nonsense voice you would use. That's the voice you want to cultivate, even if you have to pretend to be calm and confident.

◊ EXAMPLE: "A day after I came home from the hospital with a new baby, my twelve-year-old daughter said she was angry because I hadn't made her a Purim costume. I wanted to scream at her, 'You selfish brat! You have no consideration for other people! Don't you see how exhausted I am?' Instead, I got control of myself and replied in a calm voice, with love in my heart, 'I'm really sorry. I know how disappointed you are, but I have to save my strength just to get through the day. I hope that next year, I'll be able to make you something special.'"

◊ EXAMPLE: "My husband had a growth on his face which worried me. He got angry every time I told him to go to the doctor. Finally, I made an appointment for him and said in a calm voice, with love in my heart, 'Here is the day and the time. Do you want me to go with you or do you want to go alone?' He made a face, but I didn't back down. And he kept his appointment."

Remember KIS: Keep it simple! This is especially important if you're the type of person who gets more dramatic the more you talk. Use short sentences and focus on your goal.

2. Use one or two words.

Avoid hostility by saying only one or two words about what you want: "Hang jacket." "Bath time." "The dishes." "Your voice." "*Lashon ha-ra*," or "*Chafetz Chaim*." Keep repeating the word if necessary. The less you say, the more likely people are to cooperate. Therefore, if necessary, make simple, short informational statements without accusations or condemnations:

"Coats go on hooks."

"You'll have fewer cavities if you brush your teeth."

"Your bike may get stolen if it's left out."

"It's not polite to say that you don't like my food when guests are present."

"When you get up from the table, your dish gets up, too."

"I want to hear you. Say it over politely this time."

3. Avoid temperamental lingo and name calling.

In responding to disapproval, don't use words like *killing, horrendous, catastrophic, shattered*, etc., in describing how you feel, because these words will make you feel even more vulnerable and helpless. For the same reason, don't say "You're driving me crazy" or "You'll be the death of me," unless the person is so abusive that this is likely to be true. Avoid calling people names like *jerk, fool, creep,* etc., because they keep you from doing your spiritual work, which is to focus on the good in things and to take constructive action.

4. Ask questions.

Asking questions is useful when people are upset with you, because it forces them to be rational rather than emotional. For example, you can find out if the person has any emotional sensitivity by asking, "Can you imagine how that remark made me feel?" If the person gives you a blank stare or denies that he hurt you, the person may have a very low level of sensitivity, and trying to get the person to understand you by talking about your feelings is probably useless. Instead, try to awaken some sensitivity by getting them to think. You might ask:

"I may have hurt you in the past. Does that mean you have the right to keep on hurting me in the present?"

"What do you hope to accomplish with that remark?"

"Do you want to know why I'm so upset about our relationship?"

"What would I have to do to deserve your respect?"

5. State rules.

If you live with a fault finder, you cannot point out what he's doing directly because he will deny it and get angry. However, if you repeat certain phrases to your children whenever the person is within earshot, it may have some effect. Even if not, it will certainly elevate the atmosphere for the rest of the family members.

"Children are not allowed to talk angrily to parents. What you have to say is important to me, so please restate what you want in a respectful voice. Talking respectfully when you are hurt is a sign of maturity."

"The Torah forbids us to say anything which would hurt another person's feelings, including name calling (*Vayikra* 25:17). I hear the angels singing whenever I restrain myself. You can, too!"

6. Elevate the atmosphere.

Three nonconstructive responses to disapproval are: anger, guilt and perfectionism. All three will drag your spirits down and make you even more hostile and anxious. Instead:

* Have a book of *Tehillim* in your hands whenever the critical person is around. He may restrain himself if he sees you repeating these holy words. If someone does speak to you disrespectfully, the words will lift your spirits and help you deal with the pain.

* Keep a stock of Torah cassettes on hand, especially cassettes having to do with *shemirath ha-lashon*. If you are working diligently on keeping your own speech pure, others usually will, too.

7. Don't feel guilty for who you are.

Since it is impossible to get everyone to like you, prepare in advance for disapproval with a PEP so that you can say something humorous about yourself or be firmly assertive without being hostile:

* "I appreciate hearing your opinion." (You really can appreciate it if you see it as an opportunity not to return a hurt with a hurt!)

* "I'm sorry that I can't have your relative for the holidays. It is painful for me to be around her. She undermines my self-esteem. I may be hypersensitive, but that's something I cannot control. I need to be in a loving, supportive atmosphere. The children don't need the emotional trauma which is involved in a long visit. An hour or two with her is enough for me."

* "I love to learn. I know you think I should spend my time preparing elaborate meals or making fancy clothes, but my interests are more spiritual than material, so you will just have to accept me as I am. The children are well fed, the house is tidy and we are all happy. So these complaints are unwarranted."

8. Validate the person's pain or dispute the accusation.

Most criticism comes down to five basic accusations: you are either mentally unbalanced, unloving, stupid, unspiritual or incompetent. If the accusation is true, admit the other person has a point and reassure him that you will work on the problem. If the accusation is wrong, challenge it:

* "I agree. It's hard to live with someone who has such trouble making decisions and getting organized. I am working on myself. However, remember that the total picture is positive. I'm not totally incompetent. I am an excellent teacher."

* "I am sorry I made the mistake. I was careless. You have a right to be upset. I will try to be more careful next time."

* "I may seem like a needy, demanding person. But a marriage

is like a plant; if it doesn't get watered, it will die. I'm only asking for a few minutes sharing time in the evening."

* "I do have trouble controling myself. I am trying not to scream. However, I need your cooperation. When you are upset with me, please do not criticize me in front of the children. They won't ever respect me if you continue."

* "Wanting your help before Shabbos doesn't make me a selfish or incompetent person. Here is a list of jobs that need to be done, like sweeping, vacuuming, bathing kids, shopping, putting candles in place, folding laundry, making a salad. Which one do you want?"

* "I am not unspiritual and materialistic for wanting to move to a larger apartment. This place is simply too small for all of us. I will try to do the negotiating myself and keep you out of it as much as possible, so that you can go on with your learning."

* "You may think that I am a crazy religious fanatic. Before I became Observant, I used to think the same about religious people. But now that I am living this way, I value the Torah's principles and moral standards. Therefore, please do not ridicule my views, especially in front of the children, or I will not be able to bring them to visit."

* "True, I am hypersensitive. That doesn't make me crazy, just protective. I still don't want to be criticized."

* "I do tend to overreact. I am more insecure than the average person. This means that I go to the doctor if I need reassurance because my imagination goes wild when I'm in pain. Also, I probably do need to ask how you feel about me because I worry more about being rejected. That's just the way I am. The more I accept myself as I am, the more I can accept you as you are."

> ◊ EXAMPLE: "Before I had EMETT tools, I was a very hostile mother and did a lot of screaming and hitting. Yesterday, as I was reading to one of my younger children, my oldest daughter started yelling at me that I was spoiling him rotten. At first, I went into my old pattern of seeing her anger as a threat and I wanted to slap her. Thanks to EMETT, I realized that beneath anger is pain. To calm myself down, I focused on my goal: to teach her how to express herself in a mature way. So I said, 'You are right. When you were little, I made a lot of mistakes. I didn't give you the kind of loving attention that I am giving your little

brother. I'm learning to be a more loving person. I'm sorry I was not more loving to you. We both have a lot of healing to do.' She started crying, which surprised me because she has never shared any emotion with me before other than anger. I hugged her and we both vowed that in the future we would share our feelings with love, not anger."

9. Find something in common to defuse anger.

To overcome your own tendency to attack, point out something you have in common with the person.

◊ EXAMPLE: "My daughter's teacher called to say that she hadn't done her term project. I was furious, thinking about how irresponsible and lazy my daughter was. Thankfully, I worked my temper down before she came home by keeping my goal in mind: to teach her to be more responsible. I told her that I, too, have a problem with procrastination, and that I understand how difficult it is to face up to obligations that we don't want any part of. She admitted that I was right, and asked me to teach her how to overcome her own resistance. We set up a schedule of work to be completed for her project, and she promised to report back to me each day. If I'd have gotten angry, she would only have been hostile in return and nothing would have been accomplished."

◊ EXAMPLE: "I saw a neighbor slapping and screaming at her three-year-old boy because his *kippah* had fallen off. I was thinking to myself what a cruel, insensitive, stupid mother she was. I was afraid she would tell me off if I tried to stop her, but I couldn't let her go on. I defused her anger and my own by saying, 'I also have a tendency to hit when I'm upset. It's hard for me to control myself, but I've found that once I start hitting, it's hard to stop. I know that you are a very devoted mother and I'm sure you're just tired.' I could see her lips trembling. Then she said that she had been told that hitting was necessary in order to educate children. I told her that I would teach her non-violent tactics to gain their cooperation and she agreed to visit me. I took a risk by talking to her, but it was worth it!"

10. Use the broken record technique.

The broken record technique keeps you from getting worked up or feeling intimidated by people's anger, because it forces you to focus on a specific goal. Keep repeating over and over precisely what you want in a neutral tone of voice. Keep it simple! Use as few words as possible. Focus on one goal.

To a child: "Leave the room now. Right now. Yes. Leave now. I do not talk to people when they are disrespectful."

To a clerk: "I want a refund right now. No, not credit. A cash refund. I want cash. Now. The product is defective. I want a cash refund right now."

To an interfering relative: "I do not want to get involved. I do not want to hear *lashon ha-ra*. Please talk directly to the person. For the sake of our friendship, let's change the subject. I really do not want to talk about it."

To a compulsive talker: "I have to get off the phone now. Yes, I know you want to say one more thing, but I have to go. I am hanging up the phone. I care about you. Bye."

To a visitor who keeps dropping in at the wrong time over and over again: "I cannot have visitors between 5 and 7 o'clock. I must feed the children and put them to bed. I'll see you to the door. I know it seems rigid of me, but this is the way I am."

To a child: "Take ten things off the table now. I know you are tired. Ten things. Right. Whichever ten you want."

To a tease: "I don't like being teased. I know you think these words are harmless, but your remarks are rude, crude and infantile."

To a spouse: "You must stop criticizing me. I realize that it hurts you to hold your anger in, but I will not tolerate being criticized anymore. I am not a dart board. No more put downs. Well, if you get depressed or get an ulcer from holding it in, I'm sorry. No more put-downs if you want this relationship to survive."

You can also have children "broken record" themselves, especially if they forget what you told them to do three seconds after you told them to do it. Tell the child, "You need to find that library book. Keep saying the word 'book' until you find it." Or, "Keep saying 'teeth' until your teeth are brushed."

11. Give I-messages.

When someone is upset with you, give an I-message about how you feel. Do this only if it's someone who cares about your feelings. For example:

"I'm uncomfortable with your decision. I respect your right to your opinion and I expect you to respect my right to mine."

"I'm trying to develop confidence in myself, and your advice implies that I'm doing a lousy job. I know that you don't mean to undermine me, but I'd like to be able to make my own mistakes and figure things out for myself. That's how people gain confidence."

"It's true, I do nag you about smoking. But that's because I'm worried about your health as well as my own. Frankly, I'm scared. At the very least, do not smoke in the house or in my presence."

"I have a policy of not speaking to people when they say things with anger. So, please say the same thing to me respectfully."

12. State psychological principles briefly and unemotionally.

Just as there are laws of physics, there are psychological principles. For example:

"When you feel like criticizing me, just remember that whatever behavior you mention, you strengthen. Because you keep telling me I'm incompetent, I feel more nervous when you're around and do stupid things that I don't normally do."

"When you endorse a person for a good act he does today, he will have a desire to do more tomorrow."

"When religion is forced on children with hostility, they fail to internalize the duties of the heart."

"Excessive fear destroys love and turns to hatred. Is that what you want to happen in our marriage?"

"People get depressed when they have spent years being submissive and compliant against their will."

13. Focus on solutions.

Be solution-oriented, not emotion-centered:

"Throwing accusations at each other won't help. Let's take this to a third party. Do you want a therapist, a lawyer or a *rav*?"

"I'm sorry dinner isn't ready. The baby is sick and needed to be held all day. Getting angry won't take care of your hunger. Let's consider your choices."

"I know you're having a hard time. But you don't have to rant and rave. Just tell me what you want in a respectful voice."

◊ EXAMPLE: "There are three *agunoth* [married women whose husbands refuse to give them a religious divorce] in our neighborhood. The neighborhood women would get together and complain bitterly, but we felt totally helpless. Finally, we decided to take action. We set up a committee to help these women financially, and also went to the members of the congregation where these three men pray to ask that they be shunned and rebuked. Within a month, one of the men agreed to give his wife a *get*."

14. Fogging.

Fogging is a technique which can get people off your back. Instead of giving a clear no answer, you give a foggy answer such as: We'll see about it./Let me sleep on it./I can't decide right now./You have a point. It may appear that you are not being assertive. But you may need to fog to get someone to stop interfering in your life.

15. Refuse to feel guilty for non-transgressions.

Don't feel guilty about other people's anger unless you have deliberately transgressed and done something to hurt them. If you tend to be guilt-ridden much of the time, you are probably in the habit of feeling guilty even when you've done nothing wrong and of taking excessive responsibility for other people's behavior.

> ◊ EXAMPLE: "After my operation, so many people came to visit that I was exhausted and in terrible pain. At first, I felt I couldn't insult people by asking them to leave. Then I realized that if I speak with love in my heart and they feel insulted, that is not my responsibility."

> ◊ EXAMPLE: "A friend called at least once a day to tell me how depressed she was. Often, I would leave my family and rush over to her house and listen to her complain. Finally I realized that, by letting her go on and on for hours, I was only making things worse. Plus, I was getting depressed just being around her. The last time she called, I listened and sympathized briefly. Then I suggested that we study *chassidus* together as an antidote to depression. I also told her she had to get involved in some *chesed* project before I would come over again. At first, she was very angry and didn't call for a few days. Then she called to say that she was ready to study with me and that she also had become involved in a community project, Once I stopped trying to rescue her, she began to take responsibility for her life."

Women, in particular, tend to feel, If someone is upset with me, I must be guilty. I must try harder. I must be failing in some way. So they give even more. The truth is that happiness is a by-product of giving, not taking. If you give 100 percent, the other person will never learn to make himself happy.

16. Ignore your nervous symptoms and irrational fears.

If you suffered from repeated rejection as a child, the memory of those times still affects you. Whenever someone scowls, ridicules or criticizes you, you may become frozen with terror, feeling helpless and small. These are called reminder symptoms. When this happens, you tend to relate to others as you did as a child, forgetting that you have adult strengths and choices now. Remind yourself, "I am an adult now. Disapproval is distressing, but not dangerous. I can handle this."

You must also ignore your nervous symptoms. Your legs may shake, your stomach may get queasy and you may have heart palpitations. Ignore them as passing nuisances. These are automatic responses based on past threatening experiences. Remind yourself, "I feel endangered, but there is no actual threat." Feel the fear, but act assertively anyway. You will be surprised to see that you don't die from the discomfort!

> ◊ EXAMPLE: "I had difficulty being strict with my step-children because I was afraid of their hostility. My EMETT leader asked me, 'What do you fear will happen if you don't jump when they make a demand?' All I could think of is that I would have to bear the pain of sometimes feeling lonely, rejected and unloved, which was how I felt as a child. I desperately needed them to love me. But my leader said that in the end, these children would be unhappy if I never taught them to give or be sensitive to my feelings. That gave me the courage to make some demands, and to ignore their whining and pouting. I was surprised to discover that they respected me more when I set firm limits. And without respect, there is no love."

If disapproval brings back reminder symptoms of childhood, when rejection *was* experienced as catastrophic, keep telling yourself, "It was awful then, but it is bearable now." Objectively rate your discomfort on a scale of zero to ten. How bad is it, in comparison to a real tragedy? Be honest. Usually, this will help you see the disapproval as a temporary discomfort.

◊ EXAMPLE: "I wanted to see a marriage counselor, but my husband said that only crazy people go for therapy. My *rav* said to go for help, but I kept thinking that I wouldn't be able to stand my husband telling me I'm crazy and walking around angrily and snapping at me. I also worried that he wouldn't be able to take the stress of so much hatred. But I really had nothing to lose. I had to ignore my fears and do it anyway. I became much calmer with the children and was able to deal more assertively with my husband's abusive behavior. If I hadn't been willing to bear the discomfort of those first few months, I think my sanity would have been destroyed."

◊ EXAMPLE: "I enjoy helping people because doing *chesed* makes me happy. However, I've discovered that there is a *chutzpah* line which some people cross very readily. They will practically take over your life if you don't set firm limits. No matter how much you do, it is never enough and they are always angry when you stop giving. When I begin to feel overwhelmed and resentful, I know I have to say no for the sake of my mental health."

17. Identify the person's hidden agenda.

When people are angry, it is helpful to realize that they are really afraid. They fear that you will reject or abandon them, that you or they will suffer mental or physical collapse, or they fear the loss of power and status in the family or community. Try to reassure the person.

Fear of poverty: "Are you worried that I will spend my money recklessly? Let me show you my bank book and savings account. I've made many wise decisions. You can be happy with how I am handling my life. I'm very responsible."

Fear of losing love: "Just because I'm going to a *shiur* doesn't mean I don't love you. I do love you. You matter very much to me." Or, "The fact that I don't eat in your home doesn't mean I don't love and respect you. I do love you very much. However, keeping strictly kosher is extremely important to me."

Fear of loss of control and prestige: "Perhaps you think the children won't cooperate unless you scream and threaten. Perhaps you think they'll think you're weak and wishy-washy if you don't. Actually, you'll have more control and be more highly thought of if you don't rant and rave. Children will respect you more if you're in control of yourself."

18. See "no" as the opening bid in a negotiation.

Some people automatically oppose every request because this is the only way they have of feeling powerful. Instead of being crushed by their initial rejection, think of some way to allow them to feel that they are the ones in power.

> ◊ EXAMPLE: "When I asked the *gabbai* of the synagogue if he would let me use one of the basement rooms for a weekly class, he said 'Absolutely not! I don't want to be responsible for the mess people make.' At first, I was crushed and began to walk away, angrily condemning him for being so stingy and mean. Then I remembered to think of his no as merely the opening bid in a negotiation. I sympathized with all the work he has to do, then promised that we'd be responsible for keeping the place spotless. If not, he could refuse us in the future. When I told him that I'm sure he wants to see the spread of Torah, he softened and agreed to let me have the room. I was sorry for condemning him. He's really a good person."

> ◊ EXAMPLE: "When I asked my husband to turn up the thermostat, he said it was a waste of money! My body was frozen but I was burning with rage until I remembered that if I want something, I have to negotiate calmly, as if it's a business deal, or I end up with nothing. I calmly stated that I needed heat for only two hours. I asked him to calculate the cost to see how much it would amount to. Next thing I knew, he told me to turn it on. I wish he weren't so stingy, but since he is, I have to accept this reality instead of attacking furiously or withdrawing in resentment."

Of course, some no's are absolute and some people get more hardened and furious if you push.

19. Ask: "What if?" and "So what?"

Take your fears to their worse possible consequences. Then ask yourself, "So what?" Are you sure that you will lose your job, your marriage or an important relationship if you speak up?

> ◊ EXAMPLE: "My son's teacher was hitting the students a lot. And because my son is a fidgety type, he was often the one who got smacked. I was afraid to confront the principal because I feared he would tell me I'm a pampering, overindulgent mother who

doesn't realize that hitting children is necessary to teach them to fear God. But my son was having asthma attacks and nightmares. He hated school. Before I approached the principal, I suffered from a lot of physical symptoms, but I said, So what if he thinks badly of me? If I'm a responsible mother, I have to fight abuse."

Facing abuse: tactfully, diplomatically, forcefully

It is poverty of spirit and patient endurance of injuries which might have been averted but were endured because the sufferer was ignorant of the right methods of averting them. This sort of humility is found among foolish and ignorant people...whose mentality is too weak to understand the soul and its capacities. This is humility, so called by conventional usage but in reality it is spiritual poverty and blindness, brought about by stupidity that...prevents it seeing what will secure its well-being...
— DUTIES OF THE HEART, vol. II, p. 75

It is essential to fight abuse whenever possible. You may not be able to stand up to a tyrannical boss or every abusive person you meet publicly, but you must certainly stand up to abusive people in your family in order to preserve your sanity.

Critical people crave control. They feel powerful when they intimidate others by scowling, grimacing impatiently, smiling condescendingly or having an angry outburst. Seeing you cower in fear feeds their lust for power. They will get more and more abusive unless you stop them with a combination of flexibility, diplomacy, force and even threats.

First, however, you must stop thinking that you don't deserve respect because you are defective. Abusive people will abuse you as long as you feel you deserve it. And it will get worse if you do not stop it. The only thing wrong with you is thinking that there's something terribly wrong with you. Perfectionism is a form of emotional abuse, whether it is done by you to yourself or by others. If you feel inferior, you will allow yourself to be abused.

The only way to deal effectively with abusive people is to give up wanting their love or approval. When you no longer want anything from the person, you will feel liberated. They may be able to hurt you physically, but your spirit will be free.

If you are from an abusive background, you may not realize you are being abused, because abusive people insist that what they are doing is perfectly normal and justified. They may even try to justify abuse by twisting quotations from Torah to support their sadistic behavior. Anyone who forces you to do something you find disgusting or painful, or who makes you feel worthless and inadequate, is abusive and is transgressing *halachah.*

Do not think you can please a fault finder. History has shown that the more you give in attempting to appease tyrants, the more they want. Do things that bring you joy and fulfillment or you will fall into despair. You fear their anger? They'll be angry anyway.

When you detach emotionally, people who are used to manipulating you with anger will get even angrier that you are no longer reacting with your usual terrified, people-pleasing behavior. They need you to cower because this gives them a false sense of importance and significance. If you act indifferent, you deprive them of their primary source of ego inflation. Until they find some new source, they will stomp around angrily for a while, but they will eventually leave you alone if you persist in being indifferent.

The biggest mistake you can make is to try to change an abusive person into a warm, sensitive, understanding, unconditionally loving human being. This hope is a false belief which those from abusive backgrounds often carry into adulthood. They hope for sudden miracles and try to get love from people who do not know how to love, in an attempt to fulfill their childhood wish.

Once you make a firm decision that you will not tolerate abuse any longer, you will find ways to stop it. The following tactics may minimize abuse:

(1) If the person keeps harping on an issue, say "I refuse to discuss this subject." Or, "I refuse to discuss this unless a *rav* or a therapist is present."

(2) If the person is your husband and he attacks you or threatens to attack, call the police. Abusive people only respect a show of power. Make group therapy for battering men a condition for parole. The threat of prison may be the only thing that stops the abuse from escalating. So you are doing him, as well as yourself, a favor by making a police report.

(3) When the person gets enraged, say, "I'm leaving the room so

that I don't respond with hostility." Or, "I will talk to you when you can speak respectfully."

(4) If the person makes paranoid statements, accusing you of engaging in immoral behavior or deliberately causing them harm, say, "This is a figment of your imagination. It has no basis in fact. I had absolutely no intention to hurt."

(5) If there is any physical abuse of children, including "innocent" acts such as pinching or slapping, call your local child abuse center to find out what to do.

(6) If the abusive person threatens you with divorce, call his/her bluff and agree. Abusive people keep abusing until they find that their victims will no longer stand for it.

(7) Sing words of *Tehillim*. It helps you accept God's will and resist the temptation to scream back.

Liberation from an abusive person comes when you no longer want anything from that person — not respect, approval, understanding, appreciation or even love. As long you tie your sense of meaning and value to the person, s/he will be able to hold you hostage. When you stop wanting, you will be free. This process will take time. Be patient. In the meantime, demand a minimum level of good manners.

The lust for control can masquerade as concern

If "love covers all faults" (*Mishlei* 10:12), then the opposite is also true: those who cannot love delight in pointing out your deficiencies. They think they simply are making innocent suggestions, and that they are being helpful. In truth, excessive advice is abusive because it is humiliating and undermines your self-confidence.

Some people have a such a strong need to control that they automatically take an oppositional position to anything you say or do. They are often referred to as mismatchers. For example, if you say how much you paid for an item, the mismatcher will say he could have gotten it cheaper or gotten a better quality for the same price. If you state an opionion, they'll say, "You're wrong." If you say that you liked an event, he'll say he went to the same event and it was awful. If you say "It's cold," he'll say "It's hot." If you want to take a walk, he'll find a reason for you not to go out. If you say, "I'll wash the floor," he'll say, "It's not needed." If you say that you're planning a project, he'll say, "It'll never work out." It doesn't matter whether you're talking about a recipe or a politician, whatever you say will provoke an argument!

Because critical people are concerned with maintaining their positive self-image, they indulge in massive denial, insisting that, "I don't criticize." Or, "I'm only doing this out of love." They are so lacking in self-awareness, they can make the most painful statements (e.g., "This place looks like a garbage dump." "You're slow, stupid and nothing but a *kvetch*.") and then insist that,

"I did not hurt your feelings when I made that statement."

"I had no intention of hurting your feelings."

"If your feelings got hurt, there's something wrong with you." People who say, "I could love you if only you were tidier, smarter, thinner, etc." will never be satisfied. People who fear emotional intimacy will *always* find excuses to criticize. Something will *always* be wrong.

If you tell fault finders that you are hurt by their critical statements, they will attack you back and accuse you of being the critical one for having criticized them for being critical!

If you generally feel frustrated, incompetent, stupid and fearful around a certain person, it's probably because that person is extremely critical and unaccepting. If you have to walk on eggshells and bend over backwards to keep someone calm or get the person's approval, then what you are getting from them isn't love or concern, but abuse. It may be the best the person can give, but it is a poor substitute for the real thing.

Those who can love, love you as you are. Real love isn't dependent on you being anything other than what you are. Those who make love conditional won't like you no matter how much you do for them. You can prove this by noting that despite all your efforts, they give you the feeling that you haven't done enough and can never measure up. If they do, at times, act lovingly, their "love" vanishes the minute you make a mistake or fail them in any way.

There is no way to win the love of someone who wants to control you. Love is the opposite of control. The more submissive and fearful you are, the greater will be their contempt for you.

If you were brought up in an abusive home, you may think that abuse is a sign of caring. Even if you realize that you are being abused, you may be afraid to speak up for fear of being rejected and abandoned. Sadly, most bullies learn to control themselves only if you are the one who turns cold and rejects them.

Humor can be very effective with critical people

Humor is a powerful tool with fault finders. It shows them that you are not crushed by their comments and that you don't take the person so seriously. This deprives them of a sense of power. Using humor on bullies is effective because it makes them less powerful in your own mind and shows them that you do not take their illusion of superiority seriously. Humor reduces tension because the parties involved don't take themselves so seriously. Try the following in a humorous tone of voice:

"Have you checked the *hechsher* on what just came out of your mouth?"

"Boy, am I glad that my value is determined by God, not you. If my worth were dependent on you, I'd be lost."

"Sorry, the complaint department is closed right now."

"Sorry, my appointment book for criticism is filled until 1998. I do have an opening on January 14 of that year if you like."

"Thank you for giving me the opportunity to remind myself that I am a being of infinite value — at least in God's eyes."

"The Torah says that the pain of an insult wipes away our sins. So, thank you. I feel cleaner already!"

◊ EXAMPLE: "My husband had a habit of always walking in the front door and making a critical remark. So I purchased a surgical mask and put it on when he came home. This surprised him, and when he asked why, I said that this was because his criticism was poisoning us."

◊ EXAMPLE: "Before my mother-in-law would visit, my husband would make me scrub and polish the entire house. I'd race around frantically, scream at the kids and be a nervous wreck. But no matter how hard I tried, she still criticized. Finally, I decided that I would clean to the extent that was good for *my* self-esteem, so I would be proud of my home, and not out of fear of her disapproval. For the sake of my mental health, I keep our visits

PSS - polite, superficial and short, and don't take responsibility for this poor woman's pain."

Practice non-defensive replies

The less emotionalism you display when responding to a critical remark, the better. Practice non-defensive responses to disapproval ahead of time by imagining how you would respond if someone made the following statements to you:

"Why weren't you more successful?" Your response:_____
"That was a stupid purchase." Your response:_____
"Why are you so hysterical?" Your response:_____
"You're so needy!" Your response:_____

◊ EXAMPLE: "I was having a conversation with a relative who kept mismatching me. So I told him, 'Wow, it's really challenging to be mismatched like this.' He looked startled and asked what I meant. I explained that he always took the opposite position from the one I took. He, of course, mismatched by saying, 'That's not true.' So I said, 'See, you just did it! It's really interesting to see this behavior which I've just learned about.' My sincere appreciation for this learning experience kept me from being angry with him. In fact, I felt sorry for him because he has no friends and is a very unhappy person."

◊ Example: "My daughter and I were baking for the holidays and she kept criticizing everything I said or did. At first, I was furious and resorted to silent condemnations. But then I began to feel sorry for her. She doesn't get along with anyone and can't understand why. I decided that every time she disapproved of me, I would hug her and say, 'I really love you.' Within the hour, she had stopped making negative comments."

The gifts which disapproval offers you

The desire to make others feel small is so ingrained within us that it takes a very strong will to overcome it. We must engage in this struggle if we hope to grow spiritually. The Maharal states that the feeling of smallness or the attempt to make others feel inferior, is the source of all sin (*Netivoth Olam*, vol. 2, see chapter on *ka'as*).

If we decide to stand up assertively to fault finders, we have the opportunity to strengthen our *middoth* of courage, honesty, perseverence and determination. If we decide on stoic silence, we can work on emotional detachment, patience and acceptance of all that is beyond our control.

It is no mistake that disapproval makes us feel "as dust." The more we feel our nothingness, the more we can experience God's greatness — if we don't give in to the temptation to make others feel like dust in return.

Disapproval is a gift if it forces us to focus on "duties of the heart," such as not bearing a grudge, not being vengeful, giving the benefit of the doubt, and having forgiveness and compassion for others as well as ourselves. Then we emerge as winners, not losers.

Appendix
The EMETT Example:
Turning Darkness into Light

Every day we face a multitude of stressful events from within our own bodies, hearts and minds as well as from people, places and things in our external environment. Finding the Godly gift in the midst of these events is not an easy task. Whether the event is a minor inconvenience or a major trauma, we have only two choices: (1) to sink into temper, becoming bitter, enraged or despairing, or (2) to discover how we can use the event for our spiritual growth.

The EMETT definition of temper is "an inappropriate, unconstructive response to an event." Temper causes us to feel isolated from people and distant from God. The goal of the four-step EMETT example is to restore our emotional equilibrium and ability to think rationally by:

(1) Strengthening our attachment to God.

(2) Gaining greater understanding of and compassion toward ourselves and others.

(3) Improving our *middoth*.

(4) Coping with the legitimate pain of the event in a dignified manner.

If you are a beginner in this method, it is suggested that you use the EMETT process first with very minor stresses, such as a slight headache, a small financial loss, a minor dispute or a mild disappointment (e.g., a traffic jam, a snippy clerk, a delayed meal, a minor headache, an unexpected bill). It is best to have someone read to you the verbal commands in each step. However, it is also effective to write out the answers by yourself on paper.

Step one: the event

Briefly describe, in three to five minutes, the painful event, giving essential details such as time, place and people involved. (If you are sharing this with another person, avoid *lashon ha-ra* by disguising the person's identity or referring to him/her as *ploni*.)

Step two: the temperamental working-up process

In Step Two you become aware of how you create anxiety, depression or anger, and why you want to maintain these negative emotional states. (The following lists are not comprehensive. You can certainly supply your own additions as needed.)

A. NEGATIVE MENTAL RESPONSE

1. What were your insecure thoughts? State what you feared losing or already lost. (E.g., loss of love, approval, respect, status, prestige, self-esteem, closeness, pleasure, control, fulfillment, trust in yourself or others.)

Did you draw catastrophic conclusions, such as mental or physical collapse, divorce, death, death of your spirit, etc.?

2. What were your condemnations of yourself? (E.g., mediocre, phony, weak, stupid, abnormal, selfish, pushy, cruel, unspiritual, boring, insensitive, uncreative, immature, lazy, inept, rigid, wimpy, greedy, overly emotional, overly sensitive, crazy, bratty, irresponsible, shallow, petty, *kvetchy*, a total failure.)

3. State your unfulfilled demands. What did/do you want that you did not get or are not getting? (E.g., love, control, respect, closeness, success, perfection, reliability, comfort, competence, trust, sanity, fairness, health, maturity, pampering, financial security, understanding, fulfillment, tranquility, confidence, a different personality, unconditional love and acceptance from everyone and for everyone, for life to go smoothly, etc.)

B. HARMFUL IMPULSES

State your harmful impulses, even if you did not give in to them. (Only after you become aware of your automatic reaction to stressful events can you learn to change it.)

Active: to criticize, scream, swear, complain, reply with hostility, hit, defend myself, lie, overeat, bend over backwards to please, give unwanted advice, nag, splurge, indulge, overextend myself for others, run away, throw things, punish angrily, try to get through to someone who does not want to be gotten through to, threaten suicide or homicide, etc.

Passive: to "process" (obsess), give up, give in, not stand up for myself, oversleep, not set firm limits, agree, procrastinate, wallow in self-pity, stew in silent condemnations against myself or others, deny the problem/take it too seriously, under function, allow my imagination to catch fire and review all my pains and failures.

(Note: Thoughts and impulses are under our control. The next two — emotions and physical sensations — are not. The first two determine the degree of distress in the next two.)

C. UPSETTING EMOTIONS

FEARFUL TEMPER

abandoned	invisible
afraid	isolated
alone	jealous
ashamed	manipulated
attacked	misunderstood
bitter	neglected
cheated	numb/deadened
conflicted	overwhelmed
desperate/panicky	patronized
disappointed	punished unfairly
discouraged	rejected
disillusioned	sad
exploited	stifled
feelings of unreality	stupid
frustrated	threatened
guilt-ridden	unappreciated
helpless	unloved
hopeless	unwanted
humiliated	violated
hurt	worn out/drained
incompetent/inadequate	worthless

ANGRY TEMPER

angry	hostile
aggravated	hypercritical
annoyed	impatient
cold/frozen	outraged
condemning	punitive
disgusted	resentful
contemptuous	sarcastic
explosive	vengeful
hateful	

D. UPSETTING PHYSICAL SENSATIONS

Did you have dry mouth, air hunger, heart palpitations, rapid breathing, head pressure, stomach distress, teeth clenching, general restlessness and tension, nervous fatigue, insomnia, nausea, tremors, twitches, etc.? (You may not realize you are in temper until your physical sensations alert you to this fact.)

E. DEFINE THE GOAL OF YOUR NEGATIVE RESPONSE

Say the first thing that comes to your mind, even if it seems silly. "I *must* stay angry (or hopeless, jealous, depressed, distant and cold, guilt ridden, moody, punishing of myself and others, dishonest, anxious, passive, people pleasing, etc.) because it is the only way I can _____.

(Possible answers might be: get love, protection, approval, respect, attention, a feeling of self-worth, a sense of identity, freedom, control over myself/others, keep my sanity, motivate myself/others to improve, escape from unwanted obligations, stay dependent, feel that I have significance and importance, keep from being hurt, get others to take me seriously.)

F. REALITY TESTING

Ask yourself, "Is this negative mood really helping me reach my goal?"

(Although your goal may be positive, negative mood states are ultimately ineffective and destructive. Getting mad, bad, sad, sick or crazy helped you cope with pain and control people when you were a child. However, maintaining these states now is what keeps you from growing spiritually. Step Three will help you to discover a more mature approach to solving problems and will help you cope with unavoidable pain by reminding you to accept God's will with love.)

Step three: spiritual disciplines — turning darkness into light

In this step, you learn how to overcome your negative response by focusing on the changes you can make in thought and behavior, or the mitzvoth to be performed and the *middoth* ("M & Ms") to be strengthened because of this painful event. In Step Two, you feel separate from people, distant from God and unworthy. In Step Three, you move toward *teshuvah*, reconnecting with God, man and your Godly essence. Step Three may not eliminate your pain, but it will help you calm down, take assertive action, or bear your pain with dignity.

A. MENTAL DISCIPLINES.

Start with, "Suddenly, I realized I had choices such as..." (During the actual event, repeat the pertinent phrases even if they feel phony. In time, they will penetrate. Keep repeating until calm.)

1. I choose to solutionize, not emotionalize. I will either fix it or ignore it. I will do what is useful, not stew in temper.

2. I will do the difficult and take a risk. Doing the things I fear to do builds self-confidence.

3. I choose to protect myself and maintain my boundaries with love, not hostility.

4. I choose to wear the mask of love, sanity, detachment, confidence, etc. An insincere gesture (pretense) of love and hope is better than a sincere gesture of hate and despair. Insincere efforts generate sincere feelings.

5. I choose humor. Joy deflects negativity.

6. I choose to accept God's will. It's not a mistake; this is my *hashgachah pratith*. I will it to be this way since God gave me this for my growth. It is a *tikkun*, a *kapparah*.

7. I choose to focus on my priorities: *ratzon Hashem, shalom bayith*, self-esteem, mental health.

8. I choose to see this as a triviality in comparison to my spiritual goals. I calm down by taking away the thought of danger or *davka*!

9. I choose to focus on the *nisayon*. (To figure this out, ask yourself: What have I learned about my strengths and weaknesses? Why did my *neshamah* beg for this?)

10. I choose to see myself/the situation/the other person as average, within the normal (95%) range. I am not weird, exceptional or hopelessly defective. I am part of humanity.

11. I choose to give the benefit of the doubt. ("He is doing the best he can with the tools he has right now.") I choose compassion. I drop the *davka*! for the sake of my mental health.

12. I choose peace, not power. I'll let God run the world.

13. I choose emotional detachment. ("Oh..., this is an interesting challenge.") I look at the event from a "mental helicopter" in order to achieve calm objectivity.

14. I avoid the judgment of right and wrong unless there is a *halachic* violation.

15. I *can* bear the discomfort. This is distressing, but not dangerous. Comfort is a want, not a need. I can respond in a civilized manner even if I am in pain and others are uncivilized.

16. I choose the total view: My relationship with this other person is basically positive. Most of the time I feel good. (Note: If the total view is negative or danger is involved, get professional help.)

17. I choose to take the pain in part acts; I can cope with one minute (one step, one dish) at a time.

18. I choose not to compete or compare to my disadvantage. I am unique. Perfectionism is a form of emotional abuse.

19. I choose to cultivate the spirit of gratefulness. Gratitude is the foundation of faith.

20. I choose humility, to know that I don't know. I don't know the ultimate reason for this event, don't know the future outcome of it, don't know what is going on in others' hearts or minds.

21. I choose to see this as temporary. I can let the pain rise and fall and fade away.

22. I choose realism over romanticism. I will raise or lower my standards for myself and others as needed. (E.g, romanticism is expecting everyone to always get along, expecting oneself to always know what to do and be smiling and confident, etc.)

23. I choose to drop my condemnations against God, man and myself. My goal: unconditional love for God, man and myself.

24. Feelings (fears) are not always facts. (E.g., I may feel rejected or endangered or fear that I am on the verge of a nervous breakdown, which may not be true. I will check out the facts.)

25. I choose to forgive myself and others for our initial response.

26. I surrender everything beyond my control to God, including other people's *middoth*. I can control only my own thoughts and deeds. I let go of everything not in my control. (I put it in a hot air balloon and send it off, including my entire Step Two.)

B. CHANGE IN BEHAVIOR.

What Positive Muscular Acts (PMAs) did/can you do to help you cope? (E.g., prayed, studied Torah, apologized, asked a *rav*, called the police, hired a lawyer, kept silent, relaxed, allowed myself to grieve, confronted the person assertively, stopped seeking approval, shared feelings, made an insincere gesture, took a risk, set firm limits, consulted an expert, practiced REACH*, did a PEP**, etc.

"Our thoughts are shaped by our actions" (*Sefer Ha-chinuch* #16). Every act of self-discipline builds self-respect.

Step four: endorse yourself

A. What would you have done before you had EMETT skills? What negative habits did you break or insights did you gain? (The mere recognition of the need to change is endorsable. Endorse yourself for every effort. Effort is up to you; success is up to God.)

B. What illusions about life and people did you give up?

1. Erroneous beliefs: I don't deserve love or respect unless I'm perfect. I'm inferior/superior. To get what I want I must get mad, bad, sad, sick or crazy. I cannot control my impulses. I can change others. I can be all things to all people. Disapproval is disastrous. My rights

---

*REACH is a communication tactic which stands for R: Reflect the other person's feeling; E: Encourage him to talk more; A: Accept without judgment whatever he feels; C: Help him consider new choices in thought or behavior; H: Honor the person for sharing. (See *Raising Children to Care*, pp.120-123, for a fuller explanation.)

**PEP stands for Positive Experiential Programming. This technique is described on pp. 197-99 of *EMETT*.

and feelings aren't important. People and things can give me a lasting sense of value, security and happiness. Anger is power. I'm hopeless. I'm a total failure.

2. Erroneous demands: I must have complete perfection, love, attention, recognition, control.

3. Exceptionality: I must be outstanding and unique, not average.

4. Exaggeration of discomfort: It's awful and dangerous (when, in actuality, there is no real threat).

5. Extrapolating gloomily into the future: It can only get worse.

6. Excessive responsibility for others' behavior and *middoth*: It's my job to make everyone happy and make them improve.

7. Evading responsibility: The problem will disappear if I don't do anything about it.

8. Eclipsing the good (the Godliness) in myself, others and life: I have nothing to be grateful for.

(Many of these "Eight Es" are present whenever you are in temper. By identifying your cognitive errors, the temper fades.)

C. What *middoth* did you strengthen as a result of this event?

acceptance	humility
assertiveness	logic
cheerfulness	love
compassion	modesty
courage	orderliness
decisiveness	patience
detachment	positivity
determination	resourcefulness
emunah and *bitachon*	respect for self and others
flexibility	self-control
forgiveness	self-sacrifice
gratitude	silence
honesty	

Affirmations that maintain love between:

1. You and God: "I will it to be this way since God willed it to be this way."

2. You and others; "I bless you for giving me the opportunity to

perfect my *middoth*."

3. You and your *neshamah*: "I am a being of infinite worth. My value comes from God, not man."

In a group setting, each example takes between 15 and 20 minutes. To save time, the leader asks the example giver to choose a few items in each list. The leader should not offer advice or probe beyond what the example giver is willing to reveal, as this prevents others from developing trust and independence.

Glossary

The following glossary provides a partial explanation of some of the Hebrew and Yiddish (Y.) words and phrases used in this book. The spellings and explanations reflect the way the specific word is used herein. Often, there are alternate spellings and meanings for the words.

AGUNAH: a woman whose husband has left her and disappeared or refuses to give her a divorce, as a result of which she cannot remarry.

AHAVATH CHINAM: lit., baseless love; love which one gives to another even when the person does not seem to be deserving of it.

ALIYAH: lit., going up; a spiritual elevation.

AVODAH: lit., work; spiritual effort.

AYIN HA-RA: lit., the evil eye; a curse.

B'SIMCHAH TAMID: always joyous.

BA'AL TESHUVAH: a penitent; a formerly non-observant Jew who returns to Torah observance.

BALABUSTA: (Y.) an efficient housewife.

BALAGAN: (colloq.) a chaotic situation; a mess.

BEN MELECH: a child of the King (God).

BERACHAH (-CHOTH): blessing(s).

BITACHON: trust in God.

BITTUL TORAH: the misuse of one's time in non-Torah pursuits.

CHALILAH: "God forbid!"

CHEDER: (Y., colloq.) a religious primary school for boys.

CHESED: lovingkindness.

CHESHBON HA-NEFESH: moral stocktaking; introspection.

CHINUCH: education; Jewish education.

CHIZUK: lit., strengthening; encouragement.

DAVEN: (Y.) pray.

DAN LE'CHAF ZECHUTH: to judge others in a favorable light; to give others the benefit of the doubt.

DAVKA: only so; intentionally; just to spite.

DIN TORAH: lit., Torah law; a dispute judged by a Rabbinical court.

EMUNAH: faith in God.

EREV CHAG: the day, or period of time, preceding a holiday.

FRUM: (Y.) religiously observant.

GABBAI: a treasurer or a beadle of a synagogue.

GEMILUTH CHASADIM: lovingkindness; benevolence.

GEVURAH: lit., strength; self-restraint.

GET: a bill of divorce according to Torah law.

GEZERAH: a Divine decree.

GIBBOR: a courageous, strong person; a hero.

GILGUL: an incarnation.

GOLEM: a mindless, robot-like person who has no will or ambition.

HASHGACHAH PRATITH: Divine Providence.

HASHKAFAH: attitude; outlook.

HASHLAMAH: heartfelt acceptance (of God's will).

KA'AS: anger.

KAPPARAH: atonement.

KAVANAH: intention.

KAVOD: respect.

KIDDUSH HASHEM: the sanctification of God.

KIPPAH: a skullcap.

KOLLEL: a *yeshivah* for married men.

LASHON HA-RA: slander; malicious gossip.

L'SHEM SHAMAYIM: for the sake of Heaven.

MASHAL: a parable; an example.

MESIRUTH NEFESH: self-sacrifice.

MIDBAR: a desert.

MIDDOTH: good character traits.

MITZRAYIM: Egypt.

MODEH ANI: "I thank," the opening words of the prayer recited upon arising.

MUSSAR: ethical or moral instruction.

NESHAMAH: the soul.

NISAYON: lit., a trial; a spiritual challenge.

OLAM HA-BA: the World to Come.

PARNASSAH: livelihood.

RASHA: an evil person.

RATZON HASHEM: the will of God.

ROSH YESHIVAH: the dean of a *yeshivah*.

SEFER: a book; a holy book.

SIMCHAH: joy.

SHEMA: the first word of the fundamental prayer which proclaims the unity of God.

SHALOM BAYITH: domestic harmony.

SHACHARITH: the morning prayer service.

SHEMIRATH HA-LASHON: lit., guarding one's tongue; keeping one's words pure.

SHIDDUCH: marital match; a prospective marital partner.

SHIUR(IM): lecture(s) or study group(s) on some aspect of Torah.

SHIVAH: lit., seven; the seven-day of period of mourning.

SIDDUR: a prayer book.

SHMATTEH: (Y.) a rag.

TALMID CHACHAM: a Torah scholar; a learned man.

TALLITH: a prayer shawl.

TEFILLIN SHEL YAD: the phylacteries worn on the arm and hand.

TEFILLIN SHEL ROSH: the phylacteries worn on the head.

TEHILLIM: psalms; the Book of Psalms.

TESHUVAH: lit., return; repentance; regretting and rectifying one's past behavior.

TIKKUN: lit., repair; self-improvement.

TZEDAKAH: lit., righteousness, charity.

TZELEM ELOKIM: lit., the image of God; one's Divine essence.

TZITZITH: the four-cornered fringed garment worn by Jewish males.

YETZER HA-RA: the evil inclination.

YETZIATH MITZRAYIM: the Exodus from Egypt.

ZEMIROTH: songs of praise sung at mealtimes on the Sabbath and Festivals.

Bibliography

ENGLISH (JEWISH TRADITION)

Adahan, Miriam. *EMETT*. Feldheim Publishers, Jerusalem–New York, 1987.
    Raising Children to Care. Feldheim Publishers, in conjunction with Gefen Publishing House, Jerusalem–New York, 1987.
    Appreciating People. Feldheim Publishers, in conjunction with Gefen Publishing House, Jerusalem–New York, 1989.
    Living with Difficult People. Feldheim Publishers, in conjunction with Gefen Publishing House, Jerusalem–New York, 1991.

Rabbi Bachya Ibn Paquda. *Duties of the Heart*, Feldheim Publishers, Jerusalem–New York, 1962.

Dessler, Rabbi Eliyahu. *Strive for Truth! Part One.* Feldheim Publishers, Jerusalem–New York, 1978.

Feldman, Rabbi Aharon. *The River, the Kettle and the Bird*. Feldheim Publishers, Jerusalem, 1987.

Freidman, Rabbi Manis. *Doesn't Anyone Blush Anymore?* Harper, San Francisco, 1989.

Finkelman, Rabbi Shimon. *The Chazon Ish*. Art Scroll Publications, New York, 1989.

The Jewish Press. October 30, 1987.

Kitov, Rabbi Eliyahu. *The Book of Our Heritage*. Feldheim Publishers, Jerusalem–New York, 1968.

Lopian, Rabbi Eliyahu. *Lev Eliyahu*. Translated by Rabbi B.D. Kelin, published by Rabbi Kalman Pinski, Jerusalem, 1975.

Luzzatto, Rabbi Moshe Chaim. *Path of the Just*. Translated by Shraga Silverstein. Feldheim Publishers, Jerusalem–New York, 1966.

Maimonides, Moshe. *Guide for the Perplexed*. Dover Publications, New York, 1956.

Oratz, Rabbi Ephraim. *And Nothing but the Truth*. Judaica Press, New York, 1990.